THE WORLD BANK AND THE COLD WAR IN LATIN AMERICA

The Argentine Challenge

CLAUDIA KEDAR

STANFORD UNIVERSITY PRESS
Stanford, California

Stanford University Press
Stanford, California

Library of Congress Cataloging-in-Publication Data

Names: Kedar, Claudia, 1968– author.
Title: The World Bank and the Cold War in Latin America : the Argentine challenge / Claudia Kedar.
Description: Stanford, California : Stanford University Press, 2025. | Includes bibliographical references and index.
Identifiers: LCCN 2025025731 (print) | LCCN 2025025732 (ebook) | ISBN 9781503645080 (cloth) | ISBN 9781503645097 (ebook)
Subjects: LCSH: World Bank—Argentina—History—20th century. | Cold War—Economic aspects—Latin America. | Argentina—Economic policy. | Argentina—Politics and government—20th century. | United States—Foreign relations—Argentina. | Argentina—Foreign relations—United States.
Classification: LCC HG3881.5.W57 K43 2025 (print) | LCC HG3881.5.W57 (ebook)
LC record available at https://lccn.loc.gov/2025025731
LC ebook record available at https://lccn.loc.gov/2025025732

Cover design: Daniel Benneworth-Gray
Cover art: NASA
Typeset by Newgen in 10/15 Source Serif Pro Regular

The authorized representative in the EU for product safety and compliance is: Mare Nostrum Group B.V. | Mauritskade 21D | 1091 GC Amsterdam | The Netherlands | Email address: gpsr@mare-nostrum.co.uk | KVK chamber of commerce number: 96249943

Printed and bound by CPI Group (UK) Ltd, Croydon, CR0 4YY

WITH LOVE TO
MY PARTNER, ALEXANDRE (SANDY) KEDAR
AND OUR CHILDREN, MICHAL AND YOAV KEDAR

AND TO THE MEMORY OF MY PARENTS
FRIDA KAÑEVSKY AND LEÓN ANÍBAL NIEMETZ

Contents

Abbreviations and Acronyms

ACINDAR	*Industria Argentina de Aceros, S.A.* (Argentina's Steel Industry)
AFPC	American & Foreign Power Company
AyE	*Agua y Energía* (Water and Energy—a utility company)
BANADE	*Banco Nacional de Desarrollo* (National Bank of Development)
BCRA	*Banco Central República Argentina* (Central Bank of Argentina's Republic)
CEPAL/ECLAC	Comisión Económica para América Latina (Economic Commission for Latin America and the Caribbean)
CFF	IMF's Compensatory Financial Facility
CGT	*Confederación General del Trabajo* (General Confederation of Labor)
CIAP	Inter-American Committee of the Alliance for Progress
CONADE	*Consejo Nacional de Desarrollo* (National Council of Development)
DGI	*Dirección General Impositiva* (General Tax Administration)
EB	World Bank's Executive Board
EDs	Executive Directors of the WB's Executive Board

EFEA	*Empresa Ferrocarriles del Estado Argentino* (State Railways Company, Argentina)
Eximbank	Export-Import Bank of the United States
FED	Federal Reserve
GATT	General Agreement on Tariffs and Trade
IDB	Inter-American Development Bank
IBRD	International Bank for Reconstruction and Development (WBG)
IDA	International Development Association (WBG)
ICSID	International Centre for Settlement of Investment Disputes (WBG)
IFC	International Finance Corporation (WBG)
IFIs	International Financial Institutions
IMF	International Monetary Fund
IMF-WHD	IMF's Western Hemisphere Department
IMFA	IMF Archives
IPC	International Petroleum Corporation
LAFTA	Latin American Free Trade Area
LIO	Liberal International Order
MDBs	Multilateral Development Banks
NDP	National Development Plan
NIEO	New International Economic Order
NSD	National Security Doctrine
OAS	Organization of American States
SBA	IMF's Stand-By Arrangement
SEGBA	*Servicios Eléctricos del Gran Buenos Aires* (Electric Services of Greater Buenos Aires)
UCR	*Unión Cívica Radical* (Civic Radical Union)
UIA	*Unión Industrial Argentina* (Argentina's Industrialist Association)
UNCTAD	United Nations Conference on Trade and Development
US-DLF	US Development Loan Fund
USAID	United States Agency for International Development WB World Bank

WB-CPD	Country Programs Department of the WB
WB-WHD	WB's Western Hemisphere Department
WBG	World Bank Group
WBGA	World Bank Group Archives
YPF	*Yacimientos Petrolíferos Fiscales* (Fiscal Oil Fields)

Tables and Figures

Tables

Figures

Acknowledgments

I am grateful to many people for their support and advice throughout the years I spent researching, planning, dreaming, and writing this book about the World Bank—one of the most central and powerful players in the global economy. I have been fortunate to engage in enriching dialogue with Rory Miller and Raúl García Heras, both renowned scholars of Latin America's economic history and its intricate connections to the centers of financial power. Thank you to my colleague and dear friend Arie Kacowicz for reading parts of the manuscript and helping me outline the puzzle of the World Bank's relations with Argentina and the United States. I am grateful to Yoram Z. Haftel for our conversations on how scholars of International Relations analyze international organizations like the IMF and the World Bank. Arie and Yoram have certainly helped trace the analytical framework of my work. I am particularly grateful to my colleague and friend Moshe Sluhovsky for his support and advice all along the way. Although the topic of this book is far from Moshe's research interests, he meticulously read several sections of the manuscript and provided me with insightful questions and recommendations. I would like to thank Sarah Babb, David M. K. Sheinin, and Vanni Pettinà for their illuminating comments when I began planning to write a book on the World Bank and Latin America. I am also deeply grateful to my colleagues at the Hebrew University—Elisheva Baumgarten, Liat

Kozma, and Louise Bethlehem—for reading, providing feedback, and helping me shape the final version of the book prospectus.

I am grateful to Carlo Edoardo Altamura and Sebastián Alvarez, with whom I have organized and participated in several conferences and panels. I had the privilege of presenting papers at these events, many of which, in one way or another, found their way into the following pages. I am grateful to the participants of the *Colloquium on the Latin American Debt Crisis of 1982*, held at the University of Oxford in 2019, for their constructive comments on my presentation about the World Bank's role in attempting to resolve Argentina's debt crisis—a crisis that the Bank itself had helped create. Likewise, I thank the participants of the *Democracy and Finance Conference* at the Geneva Graduate Institute in 2023 for their questions and feedback on my working paper about the World Bank's stance towards a variety of democratic regimes in Argentina and beyond. I am particularly grateful to the members of the Center for the Study of Business, Economics, and Development (CEED) at the Faculty of Economics, Universidad de Buenos Aires, and to Raúl García Heras for inviting me to discuss my work with such an extraordinary group of experts on Argentina's political and economic history. I would like to express my gratitude to my friends and colleagues Atalia (Tuli) Shragai, Aya Elyada, and Ruth Fine for their encouragement throughout the many years of writing this book.

Many people and institutions provided me with vital support while I worked on this manuscript. This book would not have been possible without their work and dedication. I extend my deepest thanks to the incredible archivists of the World Bank, especially (but not only!) Bertha W. Wilson and Shiri Alon, who assisted me in identifying the most relevant files for my research on Argentina and Chile. They also conducted a meticulous declassification process for hundreds, or even thousands, of revealing documents that form the core of this book. The World Bank Archives are, with no doubt, a very precious treasure for historians. Thanks also to the staff of the IMF Archives, the Archives of the Banco Central de la República Argentina, and the Instituto Gino Germani at the Universidad de Buenos Aires. I owe a special debt of gratitude to Sara Tropper, who did an outstanding job editing the manuscript.

My sincere thanks also go to Marc Sherman, the great indexer, and to my former and current students—Shai Efrat, Cecilia Lazzaro Blasbalg, and Tamar Shafran—for their research assistance, as well as to my students at the Hebrew University in both my undergraduate and graduate seminars on the Cold War in Latin America. This research was generously supported by an Individual Research Grant from the Israel Science Foundation (Grant No. 631/19).

I cannot express enough gratitude to the editorial team at Stanford University Press, especially to editor-in-chief Kate Wahl, my editor Genevieve Aoki, and her editorial assistant Natalie Rovero. Their professionalism, enthusiasm, and patience reassured me that my book was, and is, in the best possible hands. I also appreciate the anonymous reviewers provided by the press for their thoughtful insights and suggestions, which helped me clarify several issues and arguments in this book.

I would like to express my special thanks to family and friends outside of academic circles. I am grateful to my father, León Aníbal Niemetz, for his interest and encouragement in this and other projects. I deeply regret that my mother, Frida Elena Kañevsky, passed away too soon and that I missed the opportunity to share this book with her—and, of course, much more than this book. I also want to thank my entire family in Argentina for their support in different ways and at different times. I am highly indebted to my in-laws, Ruthie and Paul Kedar, for their support and their unlimited intellectual curiosity. When I started writing this book, I asked Paul to wait until I finished it. Unfortunately, it took me too long. I am grateful to Jonathan Yovel, Dondon, Tamar, and Daniko for providing me with critical help at the last stages of writing the manuscript.

Finally, I want to express how fortunate I am to have Sandy (Alexandre Kedar)—my partner, best friend, and greatest academic adviser—by my side. No matter how chaotic or tragic the world around us becomes, Sandy always stands firm and strong for me and with me. Thank you to our children, Michal and Yoav Kedar, for their love and friendship. Writing a book is a lonely journey, but I was never truly alone.

INTRODUCTION

THE WORLD BANK (WB, BANK) grew out of a need for international economic cooperation in the aftermath of World War II. Today it is one of the most influential financial organizations in the world, directing the global development agenda and providing financial and technical assistance for thousands of projects in developing countries in Asia, Africa, Latin America, and Eastern Europe.

Established at the Bretton Woods Conference in July 1944, along with the International Monetary Fund (IMF, Fund), the WB soon emerged as a central pillar of the Liberal International Order (LIO) that the United States promoted in the postwar period. Since its establishment, the Bank expanded from a single unit—the International Bank for Reconstruction and Development (IBRD)—to a powerful group of five institutions called the World Bank Group.[1] During the early Cold War, the WB shifted from a bank that granted reconstruction loans to Western European countries to a development bank that extended loans to co-finance projects in middle-income and low-income countries outside of Europe, beginning with Chile in 1948. Over time, the Bank evolved into a powerful institution that supported development projects but also advocated for sweeping structural reforms, as it did intensely in Latin America following the debt crisis of the early 1980s. This period also saw the WB backing the transition of former Soviet states from socialism to capitalism, marking a substantial expansion in its operations and impact during the final stages of the Cold War and the early post-Cold War era.

From an initial membership of forty-five Western states (including all Latin American republics except Argentina), the WB has evolved into an almost universal institution with 189 member-states today (compared to 193 in the United Nations). Predominantly designed and funded by the US government, invariably headed by a US citizen, and symbolically located within walking distance of the White House, the WB remained anchored exclusively within the Western bloc throughout the Cold War (1945–1989), a period that coincided with the Bank's first fifty years of existence. During the Cold War, the WB exerted considerable influence by promoting economic and trade liberalization, as well as capitalist models of progress and development among its borrowing member-states. It thus not only contained the spread of socialism and communism, but also alleviated pressures on the US administration to provide direct assistance to Latin America in exchange for often controversial policy reforms.

Despite its influence, the Bank's emergence and workings during this critical period in the history of the twentieth century remain largely uncharted territory. Given that the Cold War was fundamentally a clash between two competing economic systems and ideologies, each bolstered by a different superpower, and that the Soviet Union ultimately collapsed due to economic weaknesses, it is surprising that historians have thus far overlooked the Bank as a noteworthy actor in this conflict. Tracing the evolution of the development ideas, policies, and lending practices of the WB since its establishment until 1989, this book opens a new space to rethink the international political economy of the Cold War.

The multilateral composition of the WB and the fact that in order to remain active it must establish collaboration with its member-states implies that the WB's role cannot be fully understood in isolation. Based on the premise that the Bank's lending operations are just the tip of the iceberg, decoding the Bank's black box requires delving into the negotiations and decision-making processes driving both its lending and non-lending decisions. This book, which uncovers extensive, previously unexamined WB records, conducts a detailed case study as a first step in understanding the workings of the Bank. It provides a comprehensive exploration of the WB's pivotal role in the Cold War in Latin America, specifically in its interactions with Argentina—one of Latin America's largest economies, a leading political player in the region, and a heavy borrower from the WB. The following chapters investigate the often-counterintuitive responses of the WB to six major economic and political challenges posed, in chronological order, by Argentina: populism, *developmentalism*, economic nationalism, authoritarianism, human rights violations, and the Lost Decade of the 1980s. By analyzing how and why the WB's responses to these challenges ranged from full alignment with US Cold War interests to apparent neutrality and even subtle dissent and semi-autonomy, the book unveils a complex interplay of factors including the WB's own bureaucratic goals, its symbiotic, albeit surprisingly ambiguous relationship with the United States, and Argentina's pro-active efforts to make the Bank serve its national interests. The book examines the WB both as an individual actor in the Cold War and as a dynamic arena where inter-bloc rivalries unfolded. It assesses the impact that the WB had on the economic, political, and ideological dimensions of the Cold War and traces the reciprocal process in which the dynamics of the Cold War in Latin America influenced and reshaped the Bank itself.

THE WORLD BANK AS A COLD WAR ACTOR

Though Cold War studies focus predominantly on states, the global, regional, and national arenas where that conflict took place were filled by a variety of actors. These actors include international organizations, multinational corporations, revolutionary movements, political parties, and other entities whose impact has remained surprisingly understudied. This book seeks to fill part of the historiographical vacuum by focusing on the WB, a Cold War actor different from all others—not the superpowers nor their satellites or allied states but a multilateral development bank whose policies, manifold operations, and inner workings shed new light on this multidimensional conflict.

Currently, there are only two historical overviews of the WB, both co-published with the Bank: Devesh Kapur, John Lewis, and Richard Webb, eds., *The World Bank: Its First Half Century* (1997); and Edward Mason and Robert Asher, *The World Bank since Bretton Woods* (1973). Other than an article that I published on the WB's relations with Pinochet's dictatorial regime in Chile, there is no scholarly work that examines the WB as a distinct actor in the Cold War.[2] Some important contributions have been made, such as Eric Helleiner's innovative work on the role that Latin American representatives played in the Bretton Woods conference[3]; Michele Alacevich's detailed book on the WB's shift from reconstruction to development with Colombia as a case study[4]; and Patrick Sharma's illuminating book on the WB during Robert McNamara's presidency (1968–1981)[5]. Notwithstanding these pioneering works, it is astonishing that there is no book devoted to the WB's early intervention in Latin America, except the work by Raúl García Heras which focuses more on the impact of WB and IMF policies towards Argentina than on the inner workings of the Bank or its role as a Cold War actor.[6] Scholarship on the WB's relations with specific countries in Africa and Asia shows similar lacunae. As in the case of Latin America, most of the publications, produced by economists and political scientists, focus on the post-Cold War era.

The lack of academic literature on the WB is even more striking given the growing interest in the history of development, the WB's prime mandate, within the Latin American context. Significant studies—including Sara Lorenzini's work on development during the Cold War, primarily in Europe;[7] Christy Thornton's *Revolution in Development* on the case of Mexico;[8] the edited volume by Agustin E. Ferraro and Miguel A. Centeno on the rise and fall of the development state in Latin America and Spain;[9] Amy Offner's book on the development project in Colombia;[10] and Sarah Foss's pioneering bottom-up analysis of development in Guatemala[11]—are certainly relevant for this book. However, none of these studies dedicate more than a few pages to the WB. The same applies to the recent wave of scholarship on the Cold War in Latin America, including seminal publications by Odd Arne Westad, Christopher Darnton, Tanya Harmer, Vanni Pettina, William Schmidli, Hal Brands, Gilbert Joseph, and Daniela

Spencer.[12] By introducing the WB as a proactive and influential player in the Cold War, this book is the first to put the political economy of the Cold War in the region at the center of attention.

In dialogue with these revealing bodies of historiography, the chapters that follow demonstrate that the WB's trajectory has been deeply intertwined with the Cold War. The study builds on a unique corpus of records from archives in Argentina (including the Central Bank and the Ministry of Foreign Relations), the United States (including the National Archives and the IMF archives), and Britain. Most significantly, this is the first work to make extensive use of hundreds of files from the WB archives, most of which were declassified and accessed through my direct initiative over the years. Documents from the WB archives include internal memoranda, mission reports, sector studies, correspondence between members of the WB staff and between them and key figures in Argentina, and transcripts of Executive Board discussions regarding loan proposals to Argentina.

The WB was, as mentioned, created in tandem with the IMF as part of a US initiative to establish permanent international institutions that would prevent another Great Depression in the postwar era and, consequently, another world war. US President Franklin D. Roosevelt, the main promoter of the Bretton Woods system, believed that US collaboration with the Soviets would continue after the war. This belief was reinforced by the participation of a large Soviet delegation, as well as representatives from Czechoslovakia, Poland, and Yugoslavia, at the Bretton Woods conference. In December 1945, however, Joseph Stalin chose not to ratify the Bretton Woods agreements, making it clear that wartime alliances would not transform into peacetime partnerships. Thus, institutions conceived as bridges between the capitalist and communist worlds ultimately emerged as purely Western institutions.

The forty-five founding members of the WB and the IMF (membership in both institutions was required) were exclusively Allied countries, including all Latin American republics apart from Argentina. Argentina, along with all other wartime neutrals and the Axis powers, was not invited to participate in the 1944 conference or to join the nascent institutions.

The Bank's membership underwent frequent changes in the early Cold War. For example, Poland, which joined the Bretton Woods institutions at their inception, withdrew its membership in 1949 (effective 1950), when negotiations for a WB coal loan were halted due to strong US opposition. Likewise, Cuba, another original member of both institutions, rescinded membership in 1964, prompting concern among WB management that other Latin American nations might follow Fidel Castro's lead.[13] Other nations joined, however, during the Cold War and after. Italy became a member in 1947, followed by West Germany and Japan in 1952. The US administration lifted its veto against Argentina in 1956, allowing it to join the Bretton Woods institutions. During the decolonization process of the 1960s and 1970s, there was a wave of entries into the IMF and WB by newly independent African and Asian states. For example, the Democratic Republic of Congo and Algeria joined in 1963, Singapore in 1966, and Bangladesh in 1972. By 1969, the IMF and the WB had 115 members—forty-four of them were from Africa. Romania joined in 1972, the Republic of China in 1980, and Hungary in 1982. Poland rejoined in 1986. As the case of Argentina shows, however, membership alone was never enough to secure access to WB's development assistance.

What were the expectations of the United States in creating the World Bank? The United States emerged from the war in a superior position vis-à-vis the European powers and Japan. It represented nearly half of the world's economic production and a third of its total exports, possessed a victorious and dominant military, showed leadership in advanced technologies, and owned vast surpluses of oil and food. According to John Ikenberry, the notable power asymmetries, the total defeat of its enemies, and the disintegration of the old international order left the United States in an unprecedented position to shape world politics. Among weaker states, this power raised fears of domination but, paradoxically, also of abandonment. Seeking to establish a stable hegemonic order and determined to create the conditions under which postwar European states would remain capitalist and democratic, the United States orchestrated a Washington-centered international order, known as the Liberal International Order (LIO). It was built around economic openness, political liberalism, and multilateralism. In order to gain the consent of weaker Western states, the United States set limits on the exercise of its own power, embodying what Ikenberry refers to as a "reluctant hegemonic power,"[14] or what Daniel Deudney and Ikenberry call a "penetrated hegemony," in which subordinate states had (at least in theory) a say in US decision-making processes.[15] The multilateral institutions that the US government founded towards the end of World War II and the early Cold War—including the United Nations founded in 1945, The North Atlantic Treaty Organization (NATO) established in 1949, the General Agreement on Tariffs and Trade (GATT) established in 1947, and certainly the WB and the IMF—reflected and promoted LIO principles among their members.[16] The multilateral character of these institutions echoed an effort on the part of US officials to infuse the postwar system with a sense of legitimacy and reciprocal consent rather than coercion. This approach allowed the United States to pursue its own interests while reducing resistance from weaker member-states.[17] The WB, notwithstanding sporadic bursts of criticism from Third World nations, largely met these expectations set by the United States. Multilateralism made a difference.

Focusing on what I identify as the triangular dynamics between the WB, Argentina, and the United States, this book offers a new prism to the recent scholarly debates on how the LIO shaped Latin America and vice versa—a fascinating discussion advanced by scholars such as Eric Helleiner, Tom Long, Juan Pablo Scarfi, Carsten-Andreas Schulz, and Christy Thornton.[18] Although it is not my intention here to engage with the theoretical debate on the LIO, the book aspires to contribute to a better understanding of the actual workings, promises, and limitations of the LIO from two main perspectives. The first is that of Latin America, particularly Argentina—a country that at critical junctures during the Cold War aimed to mobilize regional support for reforming the rules of international finance. The second perspective concerns the WB, a powerful organization often seen as emblematic of the LIO and as a strategic tool in the hands of the "reluctant" hegemon. The book unveils important and hitherto overlooked cracks among the Washington-based institutions that are perceived as the engines of the postwar liberal order and provides a more nuanced understanding of this period. While the WB advocated for capitalism (be it in a monetarist or neoliberal form), it avoided (openly) aligning with the political principles of the LIO. In other words, although the WB saw itself as an agent of capitalism, it refused to officially incorporate the promotion of political liberalism, democracy, and human rights into its mandate and official operational criteria.

The WB began operating in June 1946, with an initial authorized capital of $12 billion comprised of unequal contributions from all its member-states. The initial goal of the US administration, and consequently of the WB, was to promote European recovery.[19] Thus, its first clients were countries such as France, the Netherlands, Denmark, and Luxembourg, to which it granted reconstruction loans. This approach shifted in March 1948, when the Truman administration launched the European Recovery Program, or Marshall Plan, as a key component of its early Cold War strategy. The plan, which funneled some $13 billion into Western Europe, rendered the WB and IMF activities in the region redundant. European signatories of the Marshall Plan were banned from using WB and IMF funds. Deprived of their original clientele, both institutions turned their attention away from Europe. Latin America, then constituting almost half of the WB membership, emerged as their main priority. For their part, the Latin American nations looked to the WB with great hope, expecting that it would provide them the funds needed to achieve long-wished-for economic development and independence. In March 1948, the same month that the Marshall Plan was put in place, the WB provided Chile with two loans that were the Bank's first development loans. In very little time, the Latin American states became the WB's primary borrowers. Brazil and Mexico, for example, received their first WB loans in January 1949, with Colombia following in August 1949, Uruguay in August 1950, and Peru in January 1952. It was only a decade later, however, in 1961, that Argentina received its first WB loan.

In order to reach a better understanding of the workings of the WB during the Cold War and of its intra-organizational tensions, it is important to take a close look at its dual structure. On one hand, the Bank is a multilateral organization, which, through a complex scheme of differential voting power, is dominated by its strongest member-state and the only member with *de facto* veto power—the United States.[20] The Executive Board (EB) represents this multilateral and political facet of the WB. Traditionally composed of twenty-four directors (twenty-five today) that unequally represent individual countries or groups of countries, the EB is responsible for conducting the day-to-day business of the Bank and is in charge of policy issues and loan approvals. On the other hand, the WB is also a large bureaucracy of highly qualified and allegedly neutral experts who (unlike executive directors) are meant to avoid political considerations while dealing with member-states. The WB's Articles of Agreement, approved in 1944, defined the scope of the Bank's political neutrality. Article III, Section 5 (Use of Loans), Point 5 established that "The Bank shall make arrangements to ensure that the proceeds of any loan are used only for the purposes for which the loan was granted, with due attention to considerations of economy and efficiency and without regard to political or other non-economic influences or considerations." Likewise, Article IV, Section 10 (Political Activity Prohibited) stipulated that "The Bank and its officers shall not interfere in the political affairs of any member; nor shall they be influenced in their decisions by the political character of the member or members concerned. Only economic considerations shall be relevant to their decisions, and these considerations shall be weighed impartially [. . .]." Stressing this same idea, Article 5, Section 5 added that "The President, officers and staff of the Bank, in the discharge of their offices, owe their duty entirely to the Bank and to no other authority."

The politicized EB and the WB's professional staff did not always share the same goals. It was in those cases where members of the Board, in particular the US representative, and the WB staff disagreed that the WB's capacity to act autonomously was seriously tested. To be sure, the WB's organizational structure and its carefully designed differential voting system practically impeded it from becoming an autonomous agent. Hence, in most cases, it ended up, whether reluctantly or not, aligning with US Cold War goals. Over time, as revealed in the analysis of the WB-Argentina-US triangle, the US administration developed ways to encourage the Bank to align with its Cold War interests. Examples include augmenting US financial contributions to the Bank when it granted loans to US allies, or threatening to deny positive US votes on loan proposals in the EB to anti-US regimes. The Bank, for its part, employed various strategies to resist US pressures. These included citing technical justifications to maintain engagement with countries that had expropriated US assets without providing compensation or to lend to regimes that supported Cuba.

The Bank's semi-autonomy continues to be affected by the fact that only part of the Bank's resources come from quotas paid by its members and that the US remains its main financial source. Accordingly, non-alignment with US interests could be costly to the Bank. To raise the bulk of its capital, the Bank depends on voluntary contributions by its wealthiest members (during the Cold War, mainly the United States) and on selling bonds in capital markets (at the time, primarily Wall Street). Throughout the Cold War, the WB failed to develop major non-US bases of financial support, and Washington remained critical to the Bank. By "Washington," I mean the US President, the State Department, the Treasury, Congress (which attaches conditions to contributions to the Bank), and also private US companies and US-based rating credit agencies that since 1959 have granted the Bank its triple-A ranking.

The capacity of the Bank to act with some degree of autonomy is important for understanding the particular role that the WB played in the Cold War in Latin America. For the Bank, to act autonomously meant being able to avoid succumbing to US pressures. The degree of the Bank's autonomy significantly influenced its authority, ultimately shaping its capacity to induce Latin American borrowers such as Argentina to adhere to its policy recommendations. A rich literature from the field of International Relations asks whether international institutions should be treated as actors in their own right rather than as epiphenomenal (the realist position), as arenas within which states interact (the classic neoliberal position), or as social contexts that shape state interests (the constructivist position). As the case of Argentina indicates, these positions are complementary. Although this book is historical in its essence, goals, and methods, it is informed by insights from two major theoretical traditions: constructivism and principal-agent (PA) theory. Constructivist approaches center on the bureaucratic apparatus of international organizations. They explain how factors such as staffing procedures and professional training lead bureaucrats to develop their own preferences.[21] A central constructivist claim is that international organizations can become autonomous sites of authority because their bureaucracies possess legitimate authority and control over expertise, as in the case of the WB staff. In contrast, PA approaches, state-centric in their essence, highlight that states may, acting as principals, delegate a conditional grant of authority to an international organization (the agent), empowering it to act on their behalf.[22] While these scholarly approaches help us identify the conditions under which the WB could operate independently of its strongest principal, scholars define the term "autonomy" in various ways. In this book, autonomy is understood as concrete outcomes—actions or interactions (such as negotiations and lending) and inactions or non-interactions (such as non-lending or a halt in bilateral meetings)—that principals, particularly the United States, did not intend.[23] Another stream of social science scholarship, closer to the historical approach of this book, seeks to explain the WB's lending patterns in those cases where the WB supported US allies, and those cases where it did not. Research points to the more political aspects of WB lending, including lending to members of the United Nations (UN) Security Council or WB backing of close US allies.[24] Particularly relevant for this book are the seminal works of Sarah Babb, Catherine Weaver, Ngaire Woods, and Kim Moloney, to name just a few.[25] As my research examines historical periods preceding much of the work done by these social scientists, there are significant differences in the political factors influencing decision-making during the Cold War compared to the post-Cold War era. While the borrowers' proximity to the United States has consistently impacted WB lending decisions, during the Cold War, this proximity was primarily evident not in UN votes but in Argentina's stance towards Cuba, legislation regarding the status of foreign capital and labor unions, ties with the Soviet bloc, and participation in anti-US initiatives like the Non-Aligned Movement and the New International Economic Order.

ARGENTINA AND THE COLD WAR

Having established a broad framework for approaching the study of the WB's role in the Cold War, we must ask, why Argentina? One of the largest economies in Latin America, Argentina presents a puzzling case study. Although Argentina first joined the WB in 1956 (ten years later than all other countries in the region), over the years it became one of its largest borrowers (receiving 244 WB loans to date). In addition, throughout the Cold War period, Argentina experienced significant instability and was ruled by a series of democratic and dictatorial regimes that differed in duration, strength, and economic policy. While all of these regimes conducted negotiations with the WB, only four—two democracies and two dictatorships—out of ten reached accords with it. This situation provides fertile ground for assessing the extent to which WB lending was influenced by political factors and offers insights into the motivations that drove the various regimes to engage with the WB. Lastly, Argentina's relationship with the United States, the WB's dominant member-state, has long been characterized by tension and ambivalence, adding further significance to the multidirectional dynamics that evolved between it, the WB, and the United States.

This book asks what the WB's development policy and operations in Argentina can tell us about the role it played in the Cold War in this country and the broader Latin American context. This question is of considerable significance for three interrelated reasons. First, Latin American countries constituted the largest group at the Bretton Woods conference as well as during the WB's formative period. Second, during the Cold War, both superpowers—the United States and the Soviet Union—used development aid as a tool to build alliances, exercise power, and disseminate their distinctive vision of modernity throughout the world. Like the rest of Latin America, Argentina had sought to close the gap between itself and the industrialized and developed nations since obtaining independence in the nineteenth century. It regarded the new approach to development inherent in the creation of a multilateral development bank as a golden opportunity to intensify its levels of foreign assistance. Under these circumstances, Argentina construed the WB as a legitimate source of aid, free from the adverse political connotations of bilateral aid. Third, the question addresses a persistent quandary concerning the precise manifestations of the Cold War in Latin America, whose exact definitional features and periodization are still a matter of scholarly debate.

Table 1 below lists the regimes that governed Argentina during the Cold War and the early post-Cold War period, indicating the number of loans and the amounts that the WB granted to each of them:

Table 1: World Bank Loans per Regime, 1946–1999.

President	Term in Power	Amount (in million US dollars)	Number of Loans
*Gral. Edelmiro Farrell**	Feb. 1944–June 1946	0	0
Juan D. Perón	June 1946–June 1952	0	0
Juan D. Perón	June 1952–Sep. 1955	0	0
*The Liberating Revolution**	Sept. 1955–May 1958	0	0
Arturo Frondizi	May 1958–March 1962	143.5	2
*José María Guido**	March 1962–Oct. 1963	0	0
Arturo Illia	Oct. 1963–June 1966	0	0
*The Argentine Revolution**	June 1966–May 1973	388.8	7
Héctor Cámpora	May 1973–July 1973	0	0
Raúl Lastiri	July 1973–Sept. 1973	0	0
Juan D. Perón	Oct. 1973–July 1974	0	0
Isabel Perón	July 1974–March 1976	0	0
*The National Reorganization Process**	March 1976–Dec. 1983	1386	14
Raúl Alfonsín	Dec. 1983–July 1989	3184.16	18
Carlos Saúl Menem	July 1989–Dec. 1999	12704.95	66

**Military Regime*

Source: Data from World Bank Group Site, Projects by Country, Argentina (https://projects.worldbank.org/en/projects-operations/projects-summary?countrycode_exact=AR&title=Argentina)

MAIN ARGUMENTS AND BOOK STRUCTURE

The book advances four main arguments. The first is that the WB's lending activities during the Cold War period in Argentina were inconsistent, with relatively long breaks in lending and two unusual interruptions in the disbursements of already approved loans. The book identifies the underlying reasons behind the WB's fluctuating and semi-autonomous positions and attributes them to the interplay of several major factors. These include the WB's autonomist aspirations and bureaucratic interests, especially its need to remain active and to secure its own existence; the WB's relationship with the United States, its main donor, strongest principal, and the only member-state with a *de facto* veto power on its dominant EB; and the ability of countries like Argentina to induce the WB to provide them with development aid regardless of their political situation or their stance in critical Cold War issues such as Cuba.

The second argument has to do with the impact of the Cold War on the WB and the imprint that the WB left in the region during the Cold War. The WB, through its steadfast promotion of a capitalist development paradigm rooted in Washington's vision of modernity, contributed to shaping the Cold War in Latin America, especially following the Cuban Revolution, when the lines dividing development diplomacy and Cold War diplomacy blurred. Concurrently, the Bank itself underwent a process of adjustment and adaptation to the evolving dynamics of the Cold War in the region, which led to the creation of specialized departments in the WB, the design of new lending instruments, and the evolution of conditional lending.

The third argument is that contrary to widespread assumptions, the WB did not exhibit a specific preference to collaborate with dictatorial regimes. It remained largely indifferent to the type of regime in power, as long as the regime proved stable enough to enact the Bank's policy recommendations and fulfill its debt obligations. Likewise, the WB showed little concern about sensitive Cold War issues like human rights violations in the 1970s, even while the Carter administration passed legislation vetoing WB lending to regimes that violated human rights. Finally, the book claims that far from being a passive Cold War actor and a powerless aid recipient, Argentina, with its changing governments, whether democratic or dictatorial, actively developed its own policies and strategies to make the WB serve its interests, albeit with mixed results.

The book is divided into six chapters that are both thematically and chronologically organized. Each chapter focuses on a different challenge that Argentina posed to the WB and examines the efforts made by the Bank to navigate between contradictory pressures coming from the changing governments in Argentina, the US administration, and its own staff. The book opens with the exclusion of Argentina from the Bretton Woods conference.

Chapter 1 examines the WB's stance on the so-called "First Peronism" (1946–1955), often seen as the prototype of classic populism in Latin America. Juan Perón's administration promoted economic measures that were at odds with WB's policy recommendations as well as with US liberal capitalism. Key areas of controversy included state interventionism, central planning, distributive measures, nationalizations, the alliance with dominant labor unions, and a confrontational stance towards foreign investments. The chapter shows how, although the WB was unable to overcome the US veto against Argentina's membership in it while Perón remained in power, the Bank invested remarkable efforts in fostering connections with his administration. Attesting to the early clues of its bureaucratic drive to set up an autonomous agenda, WB representatives engaged in confidential meetings with key Argentine officials. Autonomist aspirations aside, the WB was ultimately unable to secure Argentina's membership. Following Argentina's acceptance into the WB in 1956, the US administration pressed the WB to extend loans to its new Cold War ally—the anti-Peronist administration of José M. Guido (1955–1958). However, the WB, displaying further indications of its autonomous aspirations, repeatedly postponed lending to a pro-US administration.

Chapter 2 and Chapter 3 focus on two stages of the turbulent 1960s. In the early 1960s, the triumph of the Cuban Revolution prompted the US administration to intensify the use of development aid as a means of preventing another Cuba. The US development strategy, in particular Kennedy's launching of the Alliance for Progress in May 1961, generated high expectations in the region. This was certainly true in the case of

Argentina's President Arturo Frondizi (1958–1962), a keen advocate of *developmentalism* (Chapter 2).[26] While the growing emphasis on development in both the United States and Argentina could have freed the WB from the need to navigate among conflicting pressures, the Bank soon encountered a new dilemma. It prized the liberal components of Frondizi's economic policy but criticized him for the slow pace of the reforms, and for the apparent mismanagement of public enterprises. Ultimately, the Bank's decision to launch lending to Argentina in June 1961 was driven neither by Frondizi's *developmentalism* nor by the alignment of the WB with US Cold War policy. Rather, it emerged from WB concern that the Kennedy administration was interfering in its main area of operation—development.

Chapter 3 focuses on the WB's relations with President Arturo Illia (1963–1966) and underlines his independentist economic nationalism. At a time when the United States was unable to distinguish between Latin America's nationalism and Castro's socialism, Illia's cancellation of contracts with powerful US oil companies in November 1963 sparked tension with the US administration. Illia expected the WB to remain impartial in the face of his confrontational stance towards the US administration, the oil companies, and the IMF. The United States, for its part, pressured the WB to withhold funds from Argentina until compensation disputes between Argentina and the oil companies were resolved. For the WB, the resolution of compensation disputes has always been an inviolable condition for lending. However, since a variety of regimes in countries such as Brazil, Chile, and Peru expropriated foreign assets during the 1960s, the WB feared that the adoption of a rigid position towards Argentina would harm its activity in the region. Evidence reveals that even while the WB's stance on compensations coincided with basic precepts of US foreign policy, the WB strove to avoid portraying itself as an arm of US Cold War interests. The WB thus conducted negotiations with Illia's administration as though the problem of compensation, a sensitive Cold War issue, did not exist.

Chapter 4 centers on the authoritarian regimes that were established in the region from the mid-1960s onwards. The military regime that replaced Illia, the self-proclaimed "Argentine Revolution" (1966–1973), seemed to possess all the necessary requisites for cultivating a fruitful partnership with the WB. Inspired by the US-promoted National Security Doctrine, the regime was staunchly anti-Peronist, anti-Communist, and pro-market. Furthermore, it aimed to enhance the managerial and planning capabilities of the state's apparatus in order to align them with WB requirements. Like WB President Robert McNamara (1968–1981), the military regime saw national security and economic development, as well as poverty and communism, as two sides of a single, integrated process. In July 1967, the WB resumed lending to Argentina after a five-year halt. However, the Bank suspended operations again in 1971. Examining the WB's relations with the Argentine Revolution and with the Peronist administration that followed (1973–1976), this chapter seeks to overturn the widespread notion that the Bank preferred military over democratic regimes. Although the WB approved seven loans to the dictatorship but refrained from providing any new loans to the Peronist government, it imposed a stricter approach towards the pro-market dictatorship than towards the more socially oriented Peronism. The picture is counterintuitive: the higher the ideological affinity between the WB and the regime in power, whether democratic or dictatorial, the more stringent the conditions set forth by the Bank became.

Chapter 5 addresses the challenges that the "Process of National Reorganization" (1976–1983), the most brutal dictatorship in Argentina's history, posed to the WB. It covers a period during which the US-WB relationship deteriorated significantly. While Cold War interests led the Nixon and Ford administrations to back the military coups that deposed populist and reformist governments in Latin America, the WB confronted a dilemma: should it avoid lending to brutal dictatorships or, alternatively, use its political neutrality as a pretext to ignore the systematic violation of human rights and lend to neoliberal dictators like Jorge R. Videla and Augusto Pinochet? Ultimately, the WB used its self-imposed principle of political neutrality as a wildcard that allowed it both to lend and not to lend, at different times and under various pretexts, to Argentina and other dictatorships.

Chapter 6 opens with the so-called Lost Decade of Latin America in the 1980s, when Argentina, Brazil, Chile, Mexico, and other countries were unable to serve their foreign debt, including debts owed to the WB. It examines the new strategies developed by the WB towards debtor nations like Argentina, which, under the presidency of Raúl Alfonsín (1983–1989), had returned to democracy. The WB was again confronted with a serious dilemma: how to help countries like Argentina solve their structural problems without losing their fragile democracies. I argue that by establishing Structural Adjustment Lending in 1979 and by "selling" non-project loans to heavily indebted countries, the WB found a way to turn potential loss into a windfall of lending activities and influence. The chapter advances the notion that the debt crisis that emerged in the region in 1982, viewed as a crisis inherent to the capitalist system, represented the pinnacle of several decades of WB-supported economic liberalization. Instead of prompting Latin American leaders to question the purported advantages of capitalism, they implemented adjustment plans rooted in an even more extreme form of capitalism—neoliberalism. Consequently, it is proposed here that the debt crisis in Latin America both stemmed from and signaled the triumph of Western capitalism and the culmination of the economic Cold War in most of the region.[27]

Chapter 6 concludes with a brief mention of the administration of Carlos Saúl Menem, who took office in 1989, coinciding with the end of the global Cold War. At the time, the WB filled a vital role in assisting former members of the Eastern bloc to make the transition from socialism to capitalism. The Bank drew on its substantial experience, acquired through financial and technical assistance to countries such as Argentina and its promotion of economic liberalization in Latin America, to pursue its liberalizing mission globally. In the meantime, Argentina embarked on a profound neoliberalization of its economy, which secured Menem a place of honor at the WB and IMF. However, the harsh social consequences of Menem's reforms, particularly the massive privatizations and de-regulation, resulted in widespread disenchantment with neoliberalism. In 1999, when Menem completed his second term, Argentina turned to left-wing populism, thereby putting into motion a pendulum movement between neoliberal and anti-neoliberal leaders that has continued until today.

1 THE WORLD BANK AND CLASSIC POPULISM

ARGENTINA JOINED THE BRETTON WOODS institutions in September 1956, a decade later than all other Latin American countries, and only after a military coup ousted the populist president, Juan D. Perón, in September 1955. Despite the willingness of the subsequent military junta to access needed development funds, the WB consistently declined to engage with it in loan negotiations. Focusing on the period from 1945, when Perón became the most dominant figure in Argentina's politics, to 1958, when the military regime that replaced him relinquished power to elected President Arturo Frondizi, this chapter examines the first challenge that the WB confronted in Argentina—populism.

Though each of the six major challenges analyzed in this book arose under unique circumstances and presented distinct political and economic characteristics, the populist challenge was exceptional also in terms of the unfolding of the Cold War in Latin America. It was the only challenge that the Bank faced before the Cuban Revolution of 1959, and before the US intensified its efforts to utilize WB development assistance to advance its Cold War agenda in Argentina and the region as a whole. By examining the WB's workings in Argentina from the early postwar period until 1958, this chapter offers a new perspective for evaluating the Cold War's impact on the development landscape in Latin America in the years preceding the emergence of a Soviet satellite in the US backyard. In doing so, it allows us to examine the early attempts by the WB staff to adapt its working procedures and lending instruments to the problems affecting Latin American countries like Argentina and to find its own voice at a time when US-WB relations were particularly close.

During the period studied here, which coincided with the WB's formative years, the United States had an unparalleled influence both *on* and *within* the Bank. This influence stemmed from the fact that the WB management and staff were predominantly recruited from the US government and Wall Street, as well as from the Bank's historically low number of member-states. Moreover, since the Bretton Woods institutions were the first international organizations to set aside the principle of "one country, one vote" in favor of a complex scheme of differential voting power, the United States secured a dominant position in both the WB and the IMF. The translation and formalization of international inequality into a system of unequal voting power constituted a central pillar of the multilateralism inherent to the Washington-centered Liberal International Order. In practice, the United States's power extended far beyond its original 30 percent share of votes in the Bank's powerful EB, which was, in any case, twice that of the second-strongest member-state—the UK—holding less than 15 percent of the total votes. This influence was significantly greater than that of Brazil, the strongest Latin American member of the Bank at the time, which held a mere 1.7 percent of the votes.[1] To this should be added that the closest US partners, including the UK and France, were themselves in need of WB assistance to recover from wartime destruction. These singular circumstances had a major impact on the workings of what I call the WB-Argentina-US triangular dynamics. During Perón's tenure (1946–1955), the United States barred Argentina from membership in the IMF and consequently in the WB, as the WB's Articles of Agreement stipulate that only members of the Fund are allowed to join the Bank. This chapter shows that although it was incapable of overturning the US veto, the WB strove to create ties with the Perón administration. These endeavors attested to the Bank's first attempts to act autonomously at a time when its membership was confined to nations within the Western bloc.

According to principal-agent theory,[2] for the nascent Bank, functioning as an independent agent would have meant being able to pursue preferences distinct from its strongest principal—the United States. Autonomy would have also implied that the Bank's bureaucracy advanced its own organizational interests, or even exerted influence on the policies of the states that governed it.[3] Yet, given the dominance of the United States, the WB's interactions with the Perón administration were more of a statement of the Bank's ambitions for the years to come than a realistic course of action.

With regards to populism itself, a major question raised here is the extent to which the country's exclusion from the Bretton Woods conference of July 1944, its prolonged struggle to join the Bretton Woods institutions, and its difficulties in procuring WB loans were rooted in the populist character of the Perón regime. It is important to note that, at the time under discussion, the United States had not forgiven Argentina for its neutrality during World War II. Moreover, in the view of the United States, Perón, who had been a central member of Argentina's military regime during the war years, was among the main promoters of the neutrality that the country maintained until March 1945. The situation worsened in the early postwar period when Perón became president, as many steps that he promoted were at odds with US principles of economic liberalism and liberal democracy. Stances such as economic nationalism and *statism*,[4] the confrontational attitude towards foreign capital and investment, the close alliance with the country's powerful labor unions, the attacks on the press, and the adoption of a Third Position of non-alignment with either the capitalist or the communist bloc were core elements of the "classic populism" prevalent in Latin America during the 1940s and 1950s. For the United States, Perón's populism was particularly problematic. The administration insisted that "Perón's nominally impartial [foreign] policy has been predominantly anti-US rather than anti-Soviet in targets and tactics,"[5] a criticism that did not apply to other populist leaders who had aligned themselves with Washington. The fact that, while denying Peronist Argentina membership, the WB provided generous assistance to Brazil, Chile, and Ecuador, which were also under populist regimes, reinforces the claim that the real problem lay in Perón-US relations rather than in populism *per se*.[6] Undoubtedly, Perón himself played a part in prolonging Argentina's longstanding exclusion from the new institutions. While he strove to join the WB, he did so on his own terms. Hence, he tried to convince the Bank to change the rules of the game and exempt Argentina from the requirement to join the IMF. Additionally, he asked the WB to extend loans to specific government agencies (e.g., the electricity company) rather than to the central government. These requests were aimed at safeguarding Perón's image as a nationalist and anti-imperialist.

Studying the dynamics of the WB-Argentina-US triangular relations in its early stages, this chapter advances three main and interrelated arguments. First, from its inception, the WB had to navigate between the interests of the United States, its most powerful member state, and the needs of its borrowing member states, as its own survival depended on both donors and clients. The second argument is that the WB shared the negative stance that the United States took towards Peronism, even as it tried to conceal this alignment. Not only did the WB inherit its ideological DNA from its primary creator, the US government, but during its formative years, as previously noted, its staff consisted primarily of US citizens, many of whom were former government officials who brought with them ideological biases as well as the organizational culture they had internalized while working within the US establishment. As shown in the next chapter, it was only following the military coup of September 1955 that the WB felt free to openly criticize the Perón regime. The third argument is that for Latin American countries such as Argentina, joining the Bretton Woods institutions implied an alignment with the United States and a commitment to adhere to the demands of the Western bloc, an alignment often at odds with their own ideological position and *independentist* foreign policy. Ultimately, the need for development funds led many populist leaders in Latin America to view loans from a multilateral institution like the WB (in which they themselves were unequal and peripheral members) as less politically risky than loans provided directly by the US government. However, the privileged position of the United States within the WB often clashed with this positive perception.

In order to advance these arguments, the chapter is divided into three parts. The first delineates Latin America's populism, and specifically Peronism, as well as the main policies and concerns of the WB during its first decade. The second part reconstructs Argentina's early and rather rocky relations with the WB. It starts with the Roosevelt administration's decision that Argentina would not be invited to the Bretton Woods conference, and then moves through the twists and turns of Perón's fruitless efforts to join both the IMF and the WB, ending with his overthrow in 1955. The third part of the chapter deals with the immediate post-Peronist years. It begins with the rescinding of the United States's longstanding veto against Argentina and the acceptance of the country into both Bretton Woods institutions in August 1956. It then goes on to cover the period from the launching of formal WB-Argentina interactions until May 1958, when the *developmentalist* Arturo Frondizi became president of Argentina.

PART 1: CLASHING INTERESTS

Latin America's "Classic Populism": Peronism as an Obstacle

Populism (from the Latin *populus* or "people") is a highly contested and, arguably, increasingly overused concept.[7] Scholars employ diverse approaches to define and examine it. Some concentrate on the study of populist leaders, while others delve into the analysis of their supporters, discourse, and/or policies. In this book, populism is defined as a context-dependent political strategy devised to allow a leader to be elected and remain in power.[8] It appeals to a perception of "the people" as pure and moral, against that of the corrupt "elite" or "the establishment." By the "people," a populist leader refers solely to his/her supporters, and most of his/her actions are aimed at benefiting them, thereby securing their sustained political backing and votes. The classic populism of 1940s and 1950s Latin America, of which the first Peronist regime (1946–1955) is often considered exemplary, had a number of common characteristics. Leaders such as Perón, Brazil's Getúlio Vargas (1934–1945, 1951–1954), and Chile's Carlos Ibáñez (1952–1958) shared a charismatic and *clientelist* political style, a Third Position in international affairs, and a nationalist, centralist, and *statist* economic approach. In addition, classic populism, and particularly Peronism, was economically expansionary, stressing income redistribution in favor of blue-collar workers (Perón's main base of support). It tended to underestimate the significance of inflationary trends, fiscal deficits, and balance of payments problems, particularly when these issues posed a threat to the continued execution of social welfare programs, subsidies, nationalization of public utilities, and similar initiatives. Naturally, not all populist leaders advocated for identical policies or experienced the same turbulent relationship with the US government as Perón did. Furthermore, not all Latin American countries shared Argentina's belief at the time that they could compete with the United States over the hegemonic position in the Americas.

Until the mid-1950s, the WB took a positive, albeit inconsistent, approach to lending in Latin American countries. As noted above, at the same time that the United States banned the entry of Peronist Argentina into the Bretton Woods institutions, it supported the granting of WB development assistance to other Latin American countries with populist regimes. The lack of evenhandedness in loan approvals, even to more US-friendly populist leaders than Perón, may have stemmed not solely from occasional disagreements with their populist policies. After all, in the immediate postwar years, the Bank and the Fund saw themselves primarily as *facilitators* of policy change. In other words, the work premise in the WB was that granting loans was the most efficient tool available to encourage those governments to adopt "better" policies (and not the other way around). Hence, it is probable that the relatively low level of lending to those populist governments was not primarily due to populism itself but rather resulted from the fact that, up until 1948, the Bank had not prioritized either development or Latin America. Suddenly, it had to react and improvise, but its wheels were somewhat slow to grind. In effect, the Bank was undergoing a learning process in transitioning from dealing with postwar European countries to engaging with developing Latin American nations and adapting its working procedures to the context of development rather than reconstruction of already advanced economies. Ultimately, Brazil, during Vargas's last term in office (1951–1954), received seven WB loans for projects related to the railways, highways, hydroelectric energy, electric power, and urban transportation. In Ecuador, President José María Velasco Ibarra (who between 1934 and 1972 served as president five times) secured two WB loans, the first for a highway project and the second for a power project. In Uruguay, Luis Batlle Berres (president from 1947 to 1951) signed the country's first loan agreements with the WB in 1950 for a power and telephone project. In Chile, the Ibáñez administration obtained four Bank loans for a pulp and paper project, for the expansion of the electric company Endesa, and for a coal project. Ibáñez's case is indicative of the actions required to unfreeze WB lending to Latin American nations that embraced populism. Jon Kofas has argued that an economic crisis compelled Ibáñez to implement stringent anti-inflationary measures and austerity plans recommended by the US administration, the IMF, and the WB, which secured him assistance from the Bretton Woods institutions. These policies included the enactment of laws that curtailed the influence of powerful labor unions (a step Perón refused to take) and the abandonment of plans to nationalize Chile's copper sector.[9] Simply put, unlike Perón, Ibáñez was ready to offer concessions in exchange for WB loans, even though these concessions were unpopular among his supporters.

Beyond these important factors that had been at play while the WB defined its stance towards Latin America's populism, the study of its intricate relations with Argentina has revealed that the Bank has always been more interested in approving loan requests than in rejecting them. This tendency can be explained simply: the WB is, above all, a bank, and, in that capacity, it must "sell" loans. Hence, with only forty-five founding member-states, almost half of them from Latin America, the WB refused to give up on an important potential client like Argentina. In conducting back-channel meetings with Perón and members of his ruling guard, the Bank developed a better understanding of one of the largest economies in the region and laid the groundwork for commencing operations at the earliest feasible moment.

The World Bank: A Nascent Western Institution

The WB, as detailed in the book's Introduction, began operating in June 1946. During its first two years of activity, the WB, aligning with US Cold War policy, focused exclusively on postwar reconstruction loans to Western Europe. This changed in March 1948, when the Truman administration (1945–1953) launched the Marshall Plan, directing roughly $13 billion to Western Europe and effectively sidelining the WB and IMF. Under the plan's terms, participating countries were disqualified from receiving further WB and IMF funds, leading both institutions to redirect their efforts towards Latin America—a region with vast development needs. In March 1948, the WB granted its first development loans to Chile, followed by loans to Brazil, Mexico, and Colombia in 1949, Uruguay in 1950, and Peru in 1952. As analyzed in Chapter 2, it was only in 1961, when the Cuban Revolution prompted the US administration to blur the lines between Cold War diplomacy and development diplomacy, that Argentina received its first WB loan.

During the period addressed here, the WB endeavored to define its role, policy, and working procedures, as well as expand its workforce. In its first decade, the Bank had three presidents in succession, all US citizens (like all WB presidents since then): Eugene Meyer, John McCloy, and Eugene Black. Although the Bank was designed by New Dealers and Keynesians, during its formative years, most of its presidents and senior staff were lawyers, bankers, and economists close to Wall Street and the Republican Party.[10] The composition of the WB management and personnel reflected and reinforced the notable influence that the United States held over this institution, possibly even more so than over the IMF, where the Managing Director has always been European-born.

Eugene Meyer (a former economist at the Federal Reserve) was appointed by US President Harry Truman to preside over the WB in June 1946. Meyer resigned his post six months later, mainly due to disagreements with the WB EB over the division of labor and power between the Bank's president and the executive directors (EDs), and over the role and influence of the United States and the UK in the organization.[11] John McCloy, an investment lawyer from New York who had been a senior US government official, assumed the WB presidency in March 1947. McCloy worked closely with his vice president, Robert Garner, and with the US ED Eugene Black, formerly a vice president at Chase National Bank.[12] Under McCloy, the Bank issued its first bond on the New York Stock Exchange in July 1947, defined its basic policies and operational procedures, made its first reconstruction loan (to France, totaling $250 million) and development loan (to Chile, totaling just $13.5 million), filled out its management team, and enlarged its staff to four hundred employees. McCloy strove to avoid the over-politicization of the WB's decision-making process by keeping its management autonomous. He settled the conflict regarding the balance of power between the Bank's bureaucratic apparatus and its EB (the body composed of representatives of all member-states). The executive directors would be responsible for policy and lending decisions, but policy recommendations would come from the Bank's management.[13] It is against this background that WB's confidential interactions with the Perón administration could be interpreted as fertile ground to test the autonomy of the Bank's professional apparatus.

McCloy resolved, if only in principle, the tension regarding criteria for WB lending. During McCloy's tenure, the WB determined that it was a "financially sound lending institution" whose lending criteria were to be based strictly on economic factors acceptable to Wall Street. This would presumably strengthen the Bank's creditworthiness and raise its bonds' sale rate, thus augmenting its lending resources.[14] Nevertheless, political considerations in the Cold War environment proved hard to neutralize. For instance, following a request from Poland in 1947, McCloy opened negotiations with the government in Warsaw for a coal loan. At the time, Poland was led by a coalition government with communist leanings. As Martin Rosen, a Bank staffer involved in these negotiations, recalled, in 1948, when the US government notified the Bank that it would veto any loan proposal to Poland, McCloy stopped negotiations. Poland, a founding member of the WB, complained that the Bank favored Western over Eastern countries and became the first nation to voluntarily renounce membership in both Bretton Woods institutions.[15] Like the decision to bar Peronist Argentina from membership in the IMF and the WB, the decision to abandon negotiations with Poland was the direct result of US Cold War interests and a US veto. To be sure, the Bank was unable to act autonomously.

In June 1949, Black, who, as was already mentioned, had been serving as the US representative at the Bank's EB, replaced McCloy as WB president, a position he held until January 1963. With the establishment of the International Finance Corporation (the WB's agency focusing only on the private sector) in 1956, and the International Development Association (working with low-income countries) in 1961, and their association with the original International Bank for Reconstruction and Development (IBRD), the Bank became the World Bank Group (WBG). In 1952, Black introduced important reforms to the Bank, establishing a functional division between specialized departments and setting up three regional departments in charge of the preparation, management, and evaluation of loans: Asia and the Middle East; Europe, Africa, and Australasia; and the Western Hemisphere, which essentially focused on Latin America.[16] Under Black, the volume of lending to mid-income member-states increased significantly, which earned the WB a Triple-A credit rating. This creditworthiness further improved when Black announced that the Bank would not grant loans to countries that were in default on past loans—which was the case with many Latin American countries.[17] Black also stressed the need for carefully prepared national development plans and expected governments to establish investment priorities before he would allow the WB to proceed with loan applications.[18] As we shall see, the WB's planning requirements posed a serious obstacle to lending to Argentina.

PART 2: WB-ARGENTINA-US RELATIONS DURING THE PERONIST ERA, 1944–1955

The WB was officially established on December 27, 1945, following the ratification of the Articles of Agreement by a majority of countries involved in the Bretton Woods conference. Joseph Stalin's decision to abstain from joining the WB and the IMF resulted in both institutions being shaped as Western and capitalist rather than as global and heterogenous in their ideological approach. When the WB officially commenced operations on June 25, 1946, Argentina, under Peronist rule since June 4 of that year, was the sole Latin American nation that had not yet become a member. This situation persisted until September 1956, a year after the overthrow of Perón's government by a military coup. This fact, along with the perception of Perón as distinctly populist, has contributed to the rise of the axiomatic but erroneous premise that the relationship between Argentina, the WB, and the IMF began to develop only after Perón's ouster.[19] The few historical studies that examine Argentina's relations with the Bretton Woods institutions begin their story, without exception, in the post-Perón era.[20] One of the commonly accepted explanations for Argentina's delayed membership is that it was Perón who, on populist grounds, refused to join.[21] It is also claimed that the presumed decision to stay out of the WB and IMF was due to ideological considerations on his part, with Perón accusing "the Bretton Woods institutions of being tools of US imperialism."[22]

Newly declassified documents, however, show that Argentina's failure to join the Bank and the Fund was not driven by any opposition on the part of Perón, but rather by the US veto against Peronist Argentina. Argentina was excluded from participating in the Bretton Woods conference and becoming a founding member of both institutions because the Roosevelt administration was determined to make the country pay a price for its neutrality during World War II. As early as April 1943, US Secretary of the Treasury Henry Morgenthau Jr., backed by Secretary of State Cordell Hull, had informed the Embassy in Buenos Aires that they would ban the participation of Argentina, as well as all other neutrals, in the Bretton Woods conference.[23] Therefore, in May 1944, when the Roosevelt administration sent its invitations to the Allied countries, Argentina, the only nation in the Americas to remain neutral until late March 1945, was not included.[24]

Argentina's first efforts to join the Bretton Woods institutions were made by *de facto* President General Edelmiro Farrell (February 1944–June 1946), in whose regime Perón played a highly influential role, first as secretary of labor, and then as minister of war and vice president. Farrell had no chance of success. At the same time that representatives of the Allied countries were deliberating the creation of a new international economic order, the State Department was denying diplomatic recognition to his government.[25] Bilateral relations improved only in April 1945, following Argentina's declaration of war on the Axis powers. However, this modest step, so late in the war, was not enough to change the attitude towards Argentina as unwelcome at Bretton Woods.

On January 23, 1946, Carlos Macchi and Rómulo Zabala from Argentina's Embassy in Washington met Harry Dexter White, a senior official of the US Treasury Department who had been deeply involved in the planning of the Bretton Woods institutions, and Raymond Mikesell, White's former adviser.[26] At this meeting, the parties discussed the steps that Argentina needed to take in order to be accepted into the IMF and the WB. White suggested that Argentina present a formal request for membership in March 1946, when the first meeting of the Joint Board of Governors of the IMF and WB was to be held.[27] A few days later, Farrell issued a decree stating "that although our country is not a signer of the Bretton Woods agreements [. . .] the President of the Argentine nation, in agreement with the Council of Ministers [. . .] declares its agreement with the conclusions of the Monetary and Financial Conference of the United Nations that took place in Bretton Woods in July 1944 [. . .]." The decree further stipulated that Argentina was prepared to take the actions necessary for its incorporation into the IMF and WB.[28] So committed to this step was Farrell that in April 1946, Argentina's embassy in Washington contacted the State Department to ask about the technical procedures to join both institutions.[29] It should be noted, however, that the aforementioned decree met with fierce political opposition in Argentina on nationalistic grounds, particularly from *Unión Cívica Radical* (UCR) leader Arturo Frondizi, who, ironically, was the first president that signed loan accords with the Fund and the Bank. As a result, Perón, already in power, ultimately refrained from submitting the decree to Argentina's congress for approval.[30]

Confidential and Semi-Official WB-Argentina Interactions

When Perón entered office on June 4, 1946, he inherited a prolonged crisis with Washington, which rendered Argentina's membership in the WB highly improbable. Perón himself had contributed to this bilateral crisis. As mentioned, officials in the Truman administration identified him as a promoter of Argentina's wartime neutrality and as pro-fascist.[31] Once he was in power, the situation worsened. Perón's autarkic nationalism and economic interventionism, his alliance with the militant labor unions, his ambitions for power on the national and regional levels, and his commitment to a Third Position in international affairs were all causes for concern in Washington. As the Cold War unfolded, many of those populist policies were perceived as tinged by Communism.[32] In June 1946, in an attempt to reduce bilateral tensions, the State Department appointed George Messersmith as the new US ambassador to Argentina, replacing Spruille Braden, who had been involved in a controversial campaign to prevent Perón's election.[33] In July 1947, President Truman and Secretary Marshall replaced Messersmith with the more pragmatic James Bruce.

But Perón had more than an image problem to overcome. There were also such pressing issues as the collapse of the commercial triangle involving Argentina, Great Britain, and the United States. The many bilateral agreements that Perón signed failed to resolve the scarcity of dollars and capital goods that Argentina suffered after a period of apparent abundance.[34] In addition, the accords Perón reached with countries with irreconcilable ideological differences (such as England, Franco's Spain, other Latin American nations, the Soviet Union, and other states of the Communist bloc) constituted the practical application of the principles of Perón's Third Position, which so irritated the government of the United States. Perón, confronted by a growing scarcity of raw materials that hampered his industrialization plans and threatened the policies that had benefited the working class, began to search for new sources of financing.[35]

The increasing economic difficulties led Perón to conclude that his ideal of economic independence could tolerate a certain degree of pragmatism, which included joining the IMF and the WB. Notably, the public rhetoric of the first Peronist government averted all negative references to the IMF and WB, perhaps in order to avoid putting negotiations with the Bretton Woods institutions in jeopardy. The earliest criticism by Perón that I discovered so far dates from 1967 and appears in a personal letter he wrote to one of his supporters from exile.[36] The first adverse reference to the IMF (but not to the Bank) that Perón made public dates from 1968 and was expressed in one of his propagandistic books.[37] In other words, Perón began to criticize the Bretton Woods twins not in real time but after almost fifteen years of exile, based on the bitter experience of the loan agreements between the IMF and the governments of Arturo Frondizi (1958–1962) and Juan Carlos Onganía (1966–1970). It should also be noted that Perón wrote these lines in the years when the IMF and WB played a dominant role in the Third World, at a time when the conditions attached to their loans provoked protests, especially among the debtor nations.[38]

Seeking in vain to evade the US veto, Perón's team contacted the Bretton Woods institutions directly. On August 27, 1947, Juan Mercau, secretary and economic adviser at Argentina's embassy in Washington, met WB and IMF representatives at the office of Irving Friedman, a high-ranking IMF official (who, in the early 1960s, moved to the WB, where he served as chief economist).[39] The parties refrained from adopting a definitive stance on Argentina's possible membership, although Mercau did inquire about Argentina's quota and exchange rate regulations.[40] With regard to exchange rates, there was a considerable gap between what was set forth in the Bretton Woods Articles of Agreement and Argentina's policy. At the time, Argentina implemented a system of multiple exchange rates that was incompatible with the IMF's par value system. However, this was, in itself, not a real obstacle to Argentina's membership. In 1946, thirteen of the forty members of the IMF, including twelve Latin American countries, still used a multiple exchange rate system, without endangering their membership.[41] The same applied to bilateral systems of trade and payments, which were also at odds with the multilateral system set forth in the Bretton Woods agreements. Here, too, Argentina was not exceptional.[42]

Nevertheless, while meeting with Mercau, the WB representatives adopted a reserved approach. Rather than directly addressing the US opposition to Argentina's membership, they alluded to the requirement that membership in the IMF was a formal prerequisite for WB membership.[43] It was at this point that Mercau acknowledged that Argentina's government had already contacted the Bank's president. He stressed that Perón was especially interested in the WB and not in the IMF, which reflected an attitude common in Latin America.[44] The meeting ended inconclusively. In the meantime, Perón's administration showed its first signs of abandonment of centralist approaches that were at odds with US economic policy. In September 1947, Perón announced that a new phase of his economic plan, based on a gradual reduction of state control of the economy and more freedom of action for private enterprise, was on the horizon.[45]

The efforts of the Peronist administration to establish constructive ties with the WB took a significant turn in May 1948. During a working tour encompassing seven Latin American member-states, including Brazil and Chile, countries where loan negotiations were anticipated to commence shortly, WB President McCloy visited Buenos Aires. During this visit, he engaged in a confidential meeting with Perón's government officials, the details of which have remained undisclosed.[46] The timing of this visit was significant as it attested to the Bank's efforts to act autonomously, or, in other words, not merely as the US expected. It occurred shortly after the board of governors of the IMF-WB approved, in January 1948, a resolution stipulating that the European member-states of the Bretton Woods institutions would be ineligible for loans from the Bank and Fund as long as they participated in the Marshall Plan.[47] This resolution, as was already mentioned, compelled the Bank to actively search for new clients. Under these circumstances and when the Bank's own existence seemed to be at risk, it is likely that McCloy wanted to convey the message that the Bank's doors were open to an important potential client like Argentina. While we do not know whether Perón intended to enlist McCloy as an intermediary between Argentina and the US administration or aimed to evaluate the extent to which the Bank could operate independently of the US government, it is certain that he did not try to conceal his interest in entering the Bank. Thus, McCloy's visit to Buenos Aires constituted a visible indication of the first clash of interests between the US administration and the WB concerning Argentina. It also underscored that even in its formative years, the WB was eager to take distinct, albeit modest, actions that ran counter to US Cold

War policy. Nevertheless, shortly after McCloy's visit, in what appears to have been an attempt to assess what the US response would be, Argentina's Foreign Ministry contacted US Ambassador Bruce and asked him to transmit a concise message to McCloy: "Argentina particularly wants to know about what would be her probable quota in the Fund and subscription in the Bank and what would be the cost."[48] The fact that this message was communicated via US government channels, when Perón already had direct ties to McCloy, seems to indicate that the intended recipient actually was the US administration. McCloy's response was immediate, which supports the impression that he and Perón had agreed upon this move. If such was the case, this episode also shows how the WB tried to conciliate between Argentina's expectations, US policy, and its own organizational interests.

The move partially succeeded. The WB staff requested that the IMF review its calculations regarding Argentina's quota, which the Fund immediately did.[49] Even more significant, in November 1948, Camille Gutt, the IMF's managing director, following in McCloy's footsteps, departed for a six-week tour of Brazil, Chile, Colombia, Ecuador, Peru, Mexico, Uruguay, and also Argentina.[50] However, from Buenos Aires, Gutt sent an urgent message to the IMF executive board (which, like in the case of the WB, was strongly influenced by the US executive director) denying rumors that he had proposed to Central Bank President Miguel Miranda that Argentina join the Bretton Woods institutions.[51] Upon returning to Washington, Gutt insisted that he had not had any expectations regarding his meeting with Perón. The Argentines, for their part, were also prompt in refuting any intentions of joining the IMF.[52] Gutt's public denials were probably intended to avoid sparking tensions with the US administration. Nevertheless, it is evident that at least some officials within the Bank and Fund were interested in Argentina's membership and were ready to challenge the balance of power among all parties to the WB-Argentina-US triangle.

Denials notwithstanding, efforts continued to be made to find common ground with Perón's administration. The meetings in Buenos Aires led to additional debates between the IMF and the WB, especially with regard to Argentina's future quota in both institutions.[53]

Argentina's road to membership in the Fund and Bank was obstructed, however, as the US administration continued to apply economic sanctions until 1950.[54] The sanctions gave rise to heated debates within the US government, which was divided between those who insisted on taking a hard line with a leader like Perón, who did not align himself with Washington, and those who warned that such a policy was counterproductive.[55] The US administration was aware of at least some of the meetings between the WB and Argentina and tacitly approved them as long as they led neither to Argentina's membership nor to open conflict with Perón. Edward Miller, assistant secretary of state for Latin American affairs, expressed the nuance of this policy, instructing US representatives in Argentina that "it is even more important than ever for us to play our cards carefully in the near future and avoid any sign of weakness or eagerness. You have been doing a masterful job at this while at the same time not giving Perón any offense."[56] In the meantime, Perón also had reason to keep his interactions with the WB and IMF discreet. Joining the Bretton Woods institutions would not only endanger his anti-imperialist image but also introduce potential conflicts within his government and among his supporters due to the anticipated shifts in economic policies.[57]

Negotiations with Argentina were cut short soon after Gutt's visit in 1948, and talks would not resume again until 1954. During this period, the global Cold War accelerated significantly, with the triumph of Mao Zedong in October 1949, the detonation of the first Soviet atomic bomb in 1949, the signing of a treaty of mutual assistance between China and the Soviet Union in February 1950, the start of the Korean War in June 1950, and the US-supported military coup in Guatemala in June 1954. The Bank also underwent important changes between 1948 and 1954. In addition to the previously mentioned organizational reforms, the WB's list of member-states expanded with significant additions that, for geopolitical reasons, were central to US Cold War interests in Europe and Asia. Most relevant to our analysis was the entry of countries that, like Argentina, were neutral during World War II: Turkey joined the Bank and Fund in 1947, Sweden in 1951, and Afghanistan in July 1955. A number of Axis countries, as well as countries which had been Axis-associated during the war, also entered the Bretton Woods institutions long before Argentina. Italy became a member in 1947, Japan and Germany in 1952, and Finland in 1948.

Archival records do not reveal any specific reasons for the break in negotiations simultaneous with the launch of the Marshall Plan in Europe. It is possible that, at this point, the WB opted to focus on lending to Latin American nations that were already members than on tentative negotiations with a country still subject to US veto. Another possible and complementary explanation for this break relates to the fact that from 1950 onwards, especially following Perón's re-election in November 1951, supporters of a hard line towards Argentina appear to have had the ascendancy in the US State Department. The Department's assumption was that worsening economic conditions in Argentina would ultimately force Perón to turn to Washington for assistance and to further liberalize the economy. Argentina's strategic importance in the Cold War was no less than that of other latecomers to the WB. The main problem, from a US perspective, was Perón himself. Perón, however, took significant steps that demonstrated to the US administration, as well as to the Bank and Fund, that he would not wait passively and indefinitely. Between 1951 and 1953, Argentina reestablished ties with Britain, signed its first commercial agreement with the Soviets, and promoted, together with other Latin American countries, the creation of a regional bloc aimed at maintaining the price of raw materials in international markets.[58] Perón also reached accords with other populist presidents in the region, many of which clashed with US Cold War interests as they further empowered organized labor and offered a regional alternative to the increasing reliance on trade with the United States.

The US administration, in the meantime, used the break in Argentina-Bretton Woods contacts to redouble its efforts to persuade Perón to liberalize the national economy and align more fully with the Western bloc. Gradually, the United States also began to unfreeze lending to Argentina. For instance, in February 1950, following a visit by Edward Miller,[59] the Export-Import Bank (Eximbank), the official export credit agency of the United States federal government, granted Argentina a

$125 million loan[60] with an additional loan in early 1955.[61] As Miller indicated, Eximbank's loans constituted "an opportunity to influence the Argentine government towards sounder business practices including the adoption of further measures to eliminate government control of commercial and financial operations and artificial trade barriers in general."[62] As time passed, the US administration continued to reevaluate its stance towards Argentina. In June 1953, Milton Eisenhower, the president's youngest brother, embarked on a goodwill trip to South America. Argentina was added to the official itinerary at the last minute.[63] Prior to Eisenhower's departure, Burke Knapp, director of WB Latin American operations, sent him a letter tracing a discouraging picture of Peronist Argentina. He maintained, without attempting to hide his own opinion, that "Argentina's aloofness towards the Fund and the Bank may be interpreted as a reflection of the *Peronista* policy of political and economic 'independence.'" He justified his appraisal by mentioning "General Perón's oft-repeated statement that he would under no circumstance accept a 'foreign loan.'"[64] Knapp certainly knew that these negative comments on Perón's economic nationalism did not fall on deaf ears.

Nevertheless, the State Department's Office of South American Affairs was satisfied with the results of Eisenhower's trip. Perón gradually abandoned his anti-US position and continued to implement pro-market reforms. In February 1952, Perón announced the implementation of what was essentially a stabilization plan,[65] and in 1953, he inaugurated his Second Five-Year Plan. The plan implied a transition to a phase centered on efficiency and productivity, the implementation of which required new investments. The WB followed Perón's changing policy closely, especially after the approval by Argentina's Congress of Law 14,222 of August 1953 that regulated and welcomed foreign investment in the country.[66] In February 1954, a WB memorandum emphasized that the Peronist government was increasingly positive towards the private sector, which was good news for the Bank.[67] In light of this gradual shift in policy, the US government supported granting additional financial assistance to Argentina. In 1954, Eximbank granted a $2.52 million loan guarantee to the Baldwin-Lima-Hamilton Corporation in connection with the sale of fifty locomotives to the state-owned railways enterprise

Ferrocarriles Argentinos and approved a $12.3 million loan guarantee to the McKee Company for the sale of a blast furnace to the country.[68]

In early 1954, encouraged by renewed US lending in the form of Eximbank loans, Perón decided to attempt once again to secure membership in the Bretton Woods institutions. To this end, he invited the new WB president, Eugene Black, to Buenos Aires. Black arrived on March 15, 1954, as part of a larger trip to Latin America. This time, the local press followed Black's visit with great interest. "*El Economista*" stated that "the only obstacle for Argentina's membership in the [WB] [was] the much-criticized provision of its Charter requiring, as a prior condition, membership in the IMF."[69] According to Knapp, Black's delegation received "an unusually warm reception from the moment of [their] arrival at the airport until [their] departure three days later."[70] The WB delegation first held "a long interview with Perón and his leading ministers" and then met with Minister of Economy Gómez Morales. They later met officers of the Foreign Ministry, participated in a dinner hosted by Minister Gómez Morales, and enjoyed "an all-day outing arranged by the Minister of Finance and President of the Central Bank, Dr. Miguel Revestido, who was in constant attendance upon Mr. Black during his stay in Buenos Aires."[71] The meeting with Perón was "very cordial." Knapp considered the Argentines to be "very coy about approaching the question of Argentina's membership in the Bank," but their "interest in the Bank and in Argentina's eventual membership became evident." The mission believed that the Argentines were impressed by Black's assertion that WB loans should not be placed in the category of foreign loans, as Perón publicly opposed foreign loans. The Argentines explained that it would be politically "a great deal easier" if WB loans were made not to the Argentine government *per se* but rather to other entities with a guarantee of the Central Bank. The WB delegation avoided responding to this "somewhat hypothetical question except to say that [they] would be glad to study it very carefully when and if the occasion arose." Knapp concluded that it was "abundantly clear that the real concern of the Argentines lay with the fact that in order to join the Bank they also had to join the Fund."[72]

These meetings, which ended with Argentina's promise to do "everything necessary" to join the WB and IMF,[73] and to improve relations with the US government, leave no doubt that Perón was determined to end Argentina's exclusion from both institutions. Doing everything certainly included adapting to the new trends in international finance and trade that were being promoted by the US administration and the financial institutions it created while, in parallel, signing new agreements with US investors and companies interested in expanding their operations in Argentina. Some notorious cases, such as Perón's controversial contract with the Standard Oil Company of California and the new agreement with Eximbank, were supported by the US government,[74] which began to show signs of rapprochement with Perón's Argentina. More than once, Perón sought help from Assistant Secretary of State for Inter-American Affairs Henry Holland in negotiations with US firms. The agreement with Standard Oil was signed on April 25, and the Argentine government issued a decree approving it on May 6, 1955. Meanwhile, negotiations were underway to settle the 1951 expropriation of the American & Foreign Power Company's (AFPC) utility properties in Argentina by the Peronist administration.[75] Argentina's Ambassador, Hipólito Paz, joined Perón's efforts and requested Holland's assistance in negotiations with those firms as well as with the Eximbank.[76] As the US National Intelligence Services stated: "Argentine anti-US propaganda has virtually ceased. The 'Third Position' line has virtually disappeared, restrictions have been lifted on US press services and publications, and more favorable conditions are being created for US-owned business interests."[77] On May 19, two days after Black left Buenos Aires, Ambassador Paz informed Assistant Secretary Holland that he would soon present an official request for membership in the WB and IMF. Holland, in turn, confirmed his willingness to assist in any way possible.[78] Holland was convinced that Perón had aligned with US capitalism, as was reflected in a report he sent to the State Department in December 1954 describing a long conversation he had held with Perón. According to Holland, echoing Cold War dichotomist views, there were two schools of economic thought in Latin America: one socialist, the other capitalist. He believed the socialist school advocated greater government intervention in the economy and the displacement of private enterprise. According to Holland, Perón recognized that when he assumed the presidency, Argentina had long undergone "a process of Marxist indoctrination." Consequently, during his first years in office, he took "a strongly Marxist point of view to capture the support of masses who were predisposed in that direction." However, Holland's report continued, Perón now felt that the masses would support him because he was now "openly anti-Communist and pro-free market."[79] Holland's conciliatory efforts are hard to evaluate as the Peronist chapter of modern Argentina ended abruptly.

On September 16, 1955, Perón was overthrown by the self-identified "Liberating Revolution." While the US administration was quick to recognize the new government of General Eduardo Lonardi,[80] the coup d'état interrupted the negotiations that had been ongoing for almost a decade between the Perón government, the WB, and the IMF. Despite the fact that the new military government was an enthusiastic Cold War ally of the United States, Washington-based institutions were hesitant to establish close collaboration with a temporary regime.

PART 3: POPULISM AND ITS AFTERMATH. DOING BUSINESS WITH DICTATORS?

With Perón's removal from power, a new type of challenge to the WB emerged in Argentina. Although many in Washington had viewed Peronism as authoritarian, the 1955 coup prompted the WB to consider the desirability of dealing with a "real" dictatorship. WB records from this period do not contain any debate on the dictatorial and illegitimate origin of this regime, indicating the effort made by the Bank to adhere to its self-imposed principle of political neutrality. Yet, as detailed below, the WB staff was deeply concerned about the interim nature of this specific military government. The US administration did not share this concern. Seeking to reward the new authorities for putting an end to Peronism, as well as for their pro-US stance and liberal economic plans, the US administration not only approved Argentina's entry into the Bretton Woods institutions but also wanted to see their first loans approved. In effect, the US State Department found new partners in presidents General Eduardo Lonardi (September–November 1955) and General Pedro Eugenio Aramburu (November 1955–May 1958), who it considered to have "a friendly disposition towards US and a democratic orientation."[81]

In ideological terms, the new regime had, at least in theory, an ample basis of understanding with the WB. The leaders of the Liberating Revolution aspired to de-Peronize Argentina and pave the way to a "democracy without Perón."[82] They were determined to abolish Perón's Third Position and adopt an unequivocal pro-US stance in the Cold War. In the economic realm, the new regime was determined to put an end to state interventionism and nationalism and establish solid ties with foreign companies and investors.[83] It was in this context that President Aramburu presented the talks with the Bretton Woods institutions as a new beginning. So, what drove the WB staff to refuse lending to a partner so seemingly ideal, certainly as compared with the deposed Peronist administration? The answer lies in the trees and not in the forest. As detailed below, the hoped-for economic and administrative reforms were slower to come and much less significant than the WB expected. In addition to the WB's doubts regarding the regime's ability to de-Peronize Argentina, its staff was also reluctant to work with a temporary administration that lacked the political clout to address all political and economic challenges.

Two major problems, which became a recurrent cause of friction in the WB-Argentina-US triangular dynamics throughout the Cold War, served as a pretext for the Bank to adopt a cautious stance towards the military regime. The first problem was the payment of compensation to expropriated US companies, in this specific instance, to subsidiary enterprises of the AFPC that, as was already mentioned, had been nationalized by several municipal and provincial authorities during Perón's term.[84] The second difficulty was the provisional character of the regime. It is not that during (or after) the Cold War period the WB had any particular preference for democracies or dictatorships. Rather, its concern revolved around the consequences of Argentina's political instability on the country's economy. As Robert Garner, WB vice president at the time, explained later about non-lending to Latin American countries like Bolivia and the Dominican Republic in the 1950s, the WB had always been reluctant to work with countries that lacked the governmental "stability [needed] to justify loan operations."[85] Not only did political instability often lead to economic instability, but unstable regimes typically had a limited capacity to make the sacrifices necessary to repay a country's debt.

Despite, or perhaps because of, the WB's reservations, the Liberating Revolution made various efforts to turn the Bank into a partner in its anti-Peronist crusade. First, the military strove to consolidate an economic plan significantly different from the one advanced by Perón. With this goal in mind, President Lonardi invited Argentine economist Raúl Prebisch, head of the Economic Commission for Latin America and the Caribbean (ECLAC or CEPAL), to return to Argentina as his special economic advisor.[86] Prebisch, who a decade before had been removed by Perón from his posts at the Central Bank and the University of Buenos Aires, was identified with the conservative policies of former President General José Uriburu (1930–1932) and with the interests of the local oligarchy of the agricultural-exporter sector.[87] In the international sphere, Prebisch's years at CEPAL had increased his prestige, thereby lending Argentina's economic team a professional aura in accordance with the new standards that the WB and the IMF promoted in international finance. The military regime understood that acceptance into the Bretton Woods institutions depended on putting negotiations in the hands of what Jeffrey Chwieroth terms "sympathetic interlocutors." According to Chwieroth, these are local economists who share similar professional training and work experience with their counterparts at the centers of international finance, as well as a common understanding about the appropriate policies to implement.[88] Prebisch and his team were indeed sympathetic interlocutors of the WB, IMF, and US administration.

Blaming Perón for the economic ills of Argentina, Prebisch set forth his new strategy in three documents: the Preliminary Report on the Economic Situation, Sound Money or Run-Away Inflation, and the Plan for Economic Rehabilitation. Although informally known as the Prebisch Plan, it was in fact the combined effort of economists from Argentina, CEPAL,[89] the IMF,[90] and the US administration.[91] The program focused on problems in the balance of payments and inflation, but also on areas that were at the core of the WB lending portfolio, such as transportation, energy, labor productivity, and agriculture.[92] Prebisch, who did not disappoint either the Argentine government or Washington-based institutions, recommended Argentina's entry into the Bretton Woods institutions. Negotiations with the WB and IMF, which were interrupted around the last military coup, soon resumed. In mid-January 1956, Burke Knapp (WB) and Jorge del Canto (a Chilean economist who worked in the IMF Research Department until 1957 when he became the director of the IMF Western Hemisphere Department [IMF-WHD]) began to discuss Prebisch's plans.[93]

On March 7, 1956, Prebisch met Knapp in Washington to make sure that the WB would support Argentina's official request for membership.[94] Prebisch conveyed that the Minister of Finance, Julio Alizón García, had plans to travel to Washington for meetings with US government officials. He stressed that the minister's agenda included possible visits to the IMF and WB headquarters to discuss Argentina's potential membership and to seek the WB's view "on the possible scale of external financing that would be reasonable for Argentina to expect" from the WB, the Eximbank, and the US government. When Prebisch asked whether a borrowing program of $1.2 billion over four years would be deemed reasonable, Knapp responded that he had no knowledge of whether such a substantial borrowing amount could be justified.[95] In a further attempt to obtain the Bank's backing, Prebisch expressed his interest in sending a draft of the final report from his mission to Argentina for comments. He mentioned that the State Department and the Eximbank had already agreed to review it. However, Knapp did not provide a clear response to this request either.[96] Following this meeting, and despite his unenthusiastic responses to Prebisch, Knapp told Black that he "very definitely fe[lt] that [the WB] should take advantage of [Prebisch's] offer [. . .]."[97] He pointed out that Prebisch's stand on monetary and exchange policy was in line with WB precepts. The same held true for Prebisch's emphasis on agricultural development and the imperative to solve budgetary deficits stemming from inefficient state enterprises such as the railway.[98]

In the meantime, aware that membership was impossible without US approval, President Aramburu gave instructions for two parallel missions to Washington. One, headed by Roberto Verrier, deputy finance minister, was sent to carry out negotiations with the US government. The other, led by Alizón García, was tasked with exploring "the question of Bank-Fund membership."[99] In addition, in mid-April 1956, Aramburu issued a decree stipulating that the ministries of finance and foreign affairs should initiate the necessary actions in order to ensure that Argentina would be admitted into both institutions.[100] As contacts with the WB continued, expectations in Buenos Aires and Washington rose. Undoubtedly, Argentina's entry into the Bretton Woods institutions, and particularly the WB, would open up new investment opportunities for US firms and banks. As in the early 1950s, US businesses reached out to the WB to see whether Argentina's membership could contribute to the expansion of their operations in the country. For instance, Henry Kaiser expressed interest to Knapp in investing in Argentina, not only in connection with the Kaiser automobile plant but also regarding large engineering projects, providing that the WB would co-finance them.[101] Other US businessmen, however, asked the Bank to condition Argentina's membership on the settlement of conflicts with firms that Perón had expropriated.[102] Among others, Alfred Benjamin, president of the Anglo-American Trading Corporation of New York, wrote to Black protesting any future loan to Argentina.[103] Transmitting Cold War concerns, Benjamin argued that there was no difference between the Soviet Union and Argentina, which he saw as "two dictatorial regimes" that violated the laws of the United States and of their own countries.[104]

On May 15, 1956, Argentina finally applied for membership in the Bretton Woods institutions. On June 4, 1956, Andrew Overby, assistant secretary of the US Treasury and US ED to the Bank, called Knapp to ask about the status of Argentina's application and potential lending.[105] Knapp responded that "the Bank would not be prepared to finance petroleum development, or to finance power development except within the framework of fair treatment for the private companies operating in the country."[106] He stressed that the WB did not have even a preliminary conclusion regarding Argentina's creditworthiness (a key criterion for lending), but that the external borrowing of about $1.25 billion suggested by Prebisch was "entirely excessive." Knapp, in turn, asked where the United States stood vis-à-vis Argentina and commented that the Bank feared the US government would grant Argentina emergency rehabilitation assistance, which would leave no further room for WB operations.[107] Knapp's apparent lack of information regarding the US position can be interpreted in several ways. The simplest explanation is that there were ongoing discussions within the US administration between hardliners and moderates about the best stance to take towards Argentina. Consequently, Knapp may have found it challenging to assess the US vote. Alternatively, Knapp may have feared the US government, willing to support its anti-Peronist and anti-Communist ally, would grant Argentina direct loans, thereby reducing room for WB activity.

On June 29, 1956, twelve years after the Bretton Woods conference, the US government rescinded its veto and instructed its EDs at the WB and IMF to support Argentina's membership.[108] Under these promising circumstances, Coll Benegas and Krieger Vasena, representing Argentina's government, met Garner, Knapp, and Orvis Schmidt (a former US Treasury official who served as WB director of loan operations to Latin America from 1951 to 1956 and head of the WB-WHD from 1956 to 1961).[109] Later, however, in a meeting with the Argentines, Black and Knapp "made it perfectly clear that Argentina could not count on any quick credits from the World Bank to finance emergency purchases of capital equipment."[110] Black stressed that the Bank would operate according "to a much slower timetable" than Argentina expected. First, the Bank would send a mission to review Argentina's creditworthiness, and only then would it examine projects "which might take a considerable additional period of time."[111] Conveying a sense of urgency, Coll Benegas said that New York bankers and investors had told him that "their assistance would come much more easily if it were joined with loans from the World Bank."[112] Here we see the growing centrality of the WB not only as a provider of financial assistance needed to co-fund costly development projects, but also as an imprimatur of its borrowers' creditworthiness.

On August 9, 1956, after long years of exclusion and only after Peronism was outlawed and Perón was in exile, Argentina was approved as a WB and IMF member.[113] On August 31, 1956, Aramburu passed Law 15.970 approving Argentina's entry into the Bretton Woods institutions and the payment of a $150 million quota to each institution (similar to Brazil's quota).[114] Argentina was now a full member of the Washington-based LIO. Membership in the WB was, however, to bring with it new challenges.

The Long Road to WB Loans, 1956–1958

With Argentina officially a member of the WB and IMF, key institutions in Washington began to evaluate the feasibility of commencing lending activities. The interactions between the WB, the IMF, Eximbank, and the US administration during this period were marked by ambivalence. On one hand, there was significant competition in Washington over influence in Argentina; on the other, the various financial institutions attempted to roll over to the others the risks associated with lending to the country. The main risk was that Argentina's high levels of indebtedness would severely limit its capability to repay its debts.

In mid-August 1956, Samuel Waugh, the president of Eximbank, informed Knapp that they were considering a $50 million credit to Argentina to cover purchases of railway equipment to transport agricultural output. When Knapp asked whether consideration had been given to allocating additional funds for industrial and agricultural equipment, Waugh responded that, from the point of view of Eximbank, the WB was best suited to deal with the Argentine problem, primarily because Argentina's dollar payment capacity was so limited.[115] Partially because of the WB's reluctance to launch lending to Argentina, in September 1956, Eximbank approved a $100 million loan to support the country's economic recovery.[116] This loan, provided by a US government agency rather than by a multilateral institution, reflects the US administration's commitment to assisting its Cold War ally in Argentina and ensuring that the Bank's slow actions did not undermine its endeavors. And yet, although the WB was keen to expand its activities in Latin America, its staff was divided over which approach to take in Argentina. This case illustrates a moment when the Bank's staff did not fully align with US expectations and when its bureaucratic apparatus resisted allowing its strongest member-state to dictate its pace. In August 1956, Lincoln

Sandelin of the WB Loan Office informed Schmidt that he was "strongly opposed to the Bank either offering or accepting an invitation to send a mission to Argentina either late this year or early in 1957."[117] He cautioned that sending a mission might give the Argentines the false impression that a loan would be granted in the near future. Sandelin aimed to prevent such a scenario, not only due to concerns regarding the Argentine perception but also because several borrowing member-states had criticized Bank missions for their failure to produce tangible outcomes. The Bank's reputation was in jeopardy.

While contemplating the timing of a first loan, Sandelin weighed both political and technical factors. He argued that "it [was] improbable that the Bank would make a loan to the present provisional government because of its doubtful constitutionality" and because "there [were] grave questions about this government's ability to continue in power for very long."[118] According to Sandelin, even if the Bank were to dispatch its first mission to Argentina in October–December 1956, it would be unlikely for a loan agreement to be finalized before mid to late 1958. Even under the most ideal circumstances, standard operating procedures required the dispatch of at least three more missions, the preparation and endorsement of mission reports, and the invitation of Argentine representatives for negotiations in Washington. "One can imagine the ill effects on Argentine opinion towards the Bank of a succession of missions without tangible benefits," he warned. Moreover, Sandelin said, it would be a mistake to assume that a new constitutional government would wish to proceed with loans already under negotiation with a provisional administration. Hence, if the Argentines were to request a mission, they "should be left in no doubt that no loan could reasonably be made before mid-1958."[119] In short, the end of populism was not enough. At least some WB staff required a stable administration in Argentina, whether democratic or dictatorial, as a condition for lending.

Knapp followed Sandelin's recommendations. In October, he sent Coll Benegas a letter in which he postponed the Bank's first mission to Argentina, offering a number of pretexts for doing so. The first had to do with Eximbank's ongoing mission to Argentina.[120] The WB, Knapp explained, wished to wait until the last Eximbank staff member had left the country in mid-November. The second and even less convincing reason offered was that the Bank was encountering "some unforeseen difficulties in getting a mission properly organized to visit [Argentina] in the very near future," not only because the staff was "very heavily burdened during the coming weeks" but also because the WB wanted to choose the mission's members very carefully "to assure that [it] ha[d] the best available talent to appraise [Argentina's] economic position and prospects, and to study the various aspects of [their] development program."[121] Thus, Knapp concluded, the WB would send the mission after January 1, 1957. In his somewhat surprising response to Knapp, Benegas wrote that the Minister of the Treasury, Eugenio Blanco, had approached Black to suggest that since the Eximbank mission would leave Argentina only around mid-November, it would be preferable to postpone the WB mission until February 1957.[122] Perhaps Benegas wished to create the impression that Argentina was not in a hurry to receive WB lending, even though this was not the actual situation. Alternatively, Benegas sensed the reluctance of the WB to start operations in the country and preferred to keep this information from becoming public knowledge. There is no doubt that, even in this early stage of the Bank's life, its loans were already regarded as a seal of approval both financially and politically. Likewise, the act of withholding loans on the Bank's part was seen as a symbol of disapproval, be it economic, political, or both. In this case, the main problem was the regime's transitory nature, which meant that the Bank had no assurances that the subsequent administration, democratic or not, would honor its commitments. Neither a pro-US stance nor ideological alignment on economic matters was sufficient to secure WB loans.

The first WB mission arrived in Buenos Aires after midnight on March 1, 1957. Despite the late hour, they were greeted at the airport by a large delegation of government officials, photographers, and reporters. The next morning, Sandelin was interviewed at the popular *Radio Splendid*. Next, the mission was hosted by the Minister of Foreign Relations and Coll Benegas, first at the Central Bank and then at the latter's summer home for afternoon tea. All these efforts, particularly the creation of a high-ranking committee to liaise with the mission on behalf of the Argentines, were clear indications of the heightened expectations that the WB mission sparked in and beyond government circles. While the Argentines strove to achieve concrete results (loans), the Bank's mission showed no enthusiasm about the possibility of launching lending operations.[123] Even the fact that in April 1957, the IMF lent Argentina $75 million did not cause the WB to seriously consider lending to the country. Actually, IMF lending convinced the Bank that "Argentina will not resign from the Fund and Bank even if the Bank [would not] lend [to it]."[124] The mission ended without the results wished for by Argentina.

A meeting at the Bank headquarters on June 13, 1957, sheds additional light on the efforts made by the Bank to act autonomously and secure a prominent role in Argentina's development scene. In this meeting, William Beaulac, US ambassador to Argentina, and Viron P. Vaky, head of the Argentine desk at the State Department, met with Black, Knapp, and Schmidt. Black outlined the challenges that the Bank faced in dealing with Argentina and emphasized that their initial report on the country would not be completed until late July.[125] Beaulac particularly wished to inform Black of his position regarding potential assistance to *Compañía Argentina de Electricidad* (CADE) and to the AFPC. Neither the WB nor the Eximbank, stated Beaulac, should lend to CADE until AFPC's compensation problem had been satisfactorily dealt with.[126] The ambassador noted that governmental decisions in Argentina were conditioned on unanimous approval by the regime's cabinet—an approval that rarely emerged. In short, the US administration wanted the interests of US firms operating in Argentina protected before it would give its go-ahead to Bank lending to the country. Black responded that he was reluctant to create the impression that the Bank was unwilling to assist Argentina.[127]

In early August 1957, the WB Loan Committee discussed the report of the mission to Argentina some four months earlier. According to the report, Argentina's "whole economy suffer[ed] from about 20 years of neglect and [was run] down."[128] The neglect, the report stressed, was particularly conspicuous in the public services. Industrial capacity was underutilized, largely due to power shortages in Buenos Aires, and agricultural products were collecting in inland areas because the railway was unable to transport them. The report, like many others, blamed the deposed Peronist regime for leaving the country stripped of foreign exchange.[129] It also referred to two loans provided by the Eximbank to cover urgent needs: $60 million for a steel mill and $100 million for railways and transport equipment. However, because Argentina had a deficit in its dollar account and a surplus in transactions with Europe, the Eximbank, as in 1956, was keen to see the WB begin to approve loans to Argentina. In any event, the report concluded that Argentina's long-term economic prospect was "decidedly good." Hence, the mission encountered no economic impediments in securing an initial WB loan of $100 million.[130]

The report was not without political considerations. In line with opinions previously expressed by Ambassador Beaulac, the WB Loan Committee considered Argentina's current government to be "so provisional that it dare[d] not play any cards that will not be obvious political trumps."[131] The committee also referred to still unsolved conflicts with the electrical power companies CADE and Italo-Argentina. In terms of potential projects, the committee agreed that Argentina's most acute need was for pipelines to conduct oil to Buenos Aires. However, "the Bank [was] sticking to its policy of not financing oil ventures and [was] hoping—rather unhopefully—that a private company might take up this project." At the end of the day, the railway emerged as almost the only area with a chance of eligibility for WB funding. The committee, though, estimated that it would take ten years until the state-owned railway could start operating in the black, declaring that it would take time to reduce "the surplus of 40,000 in the labor force"—a surplus which, so the WB claimed, was the result of Perón's clientelist strategies. The committee concluded that the WB could not start lending before July 1958.[132] Dissatisfied with the mission's report, Aramburu's team, hoping that the US administration would push the Bank to take a more flexible attitude towards Argentina, contacted the head of the US delegation in Buenos Aires to complain. The State Department duly conveyed to Knapp Argentina's "severe disappointment." Knapp, apparently determined to not let the US administration interfere, responded that the report was "not open for negotiation."[133] In other words, the WB's professionalism was neither in question nor negotiable, at least for Knapp.

In the meantime, Knapp, heading a mission to Argentina, met Krieger Vasena, Coll Benegas, and the Minister of Industry, Julio César Cueto Rúa. Knapp also met, "on a strictly personal basis," with Allende Posse, head of the Government Electricity Authority—an outspoken critic of the deposed Peronist regime and a staunch supporter of private enterprise. In addition, Knapp's agenda included meetings with high-ranking officials of the Central Bank, the British Embassy, and representatives of local private banks and businesses. While discussing the mission's report with the ministers, he emphasized the new prerequisites for WB lending and underlined the Bank's concern over disputes with foreign private power companies.[134] Knapp recognized that Argentina's ministers were "understandably upset" about the WB's decision not to make loans to the present provisional government. Krieger Vasena and Coll Benegas, who had so much in common with WB economists, complained that "it was a great blow to them personally since they had been responsible for Argentina's joining the Bank, and that [the WB's] attitude would necessarily provoke reconsideration of Argentina's membership."[135] It is worth mentioning that Argentina's withdrawal of funds from the IMF in April 1957 rendered moot a possible Argentine withdrawal from Bank membership. Nonetheless, it seems that the Argentines were attempting to exert pressure on the WB by threatening to withhold their membership from the recently established IFC (as membership in the original IBRD does not imply that countries should also join the IFC).[136]

Before leaving Argentina, Knapp met with President Aramburu. Not a word, however, was said about potential WB lending. As Knapp reported, "the nearest the President came to the subject was to comment on the fact that Argentina needed foreign help just at [that] time in order to convince the people that a sound economic policy paid off and that they should not turn to leftist demagogues in the forthcoming elections." Aware of the conditions set forth by the WB and seeking to demonstrate that they shared the same economic ideas, Aramburu declared that, unlike the ousted Peronist regime, he opposed government interference in private enterprises. He also expressed a strong desire to negotiate a resolution for the Buenos Aires electrical power problem that would ultimately maintain power provision in private hands. Knapp concluded that the WB was wise in pursuing a cautious policy vis-à-vis Argentina.[137] As will be explained in the next chapter, the WB took this policy seriously. Although Aramburu's provisional government was replaced in May 1958 by a democratically elected administration, it was only in 1961 that the Bank granted its first loan to Argentina.

CONCLUSIONS

Between 1946 and 1955, when Peronist Argentina was essentially banned from the WB and IMF, and from 1956 to 1958, when the military regime that had ousted Perón attempted, unsuccessfully, to access long-awaited development funds, the Bank shifted its main focus from Europe to Latin America, and from postwar reconstruction to economic development. In the process, it underwent several reorganizations of its administrative structure and objectives, aiming to maximize its influence and role in a bipolar landscape that contrasted starkly with the global vision of its principal architects. Although the Bretton Woods institutions were designed to serve as multilateral—and therefore non-coercive—arms of US foreign policy, the WB, driven by its own organizational interests, soon began seeking opportunities for autonomous action. Within this context, the Bank tried to turn its complex relations with Argentina into a platform to extend its operational space beyond the limits set for it by the United States—the leading power of the Western bloc, the indisputable hegemon in the Americas, and the WB's strongest member-state. As this chapter has shown, the Bank's room for maneuvering at the time was minimal. Nevertheless, it developed ways to signal to the US administration that it was not ready to serve as a mere executer of its Cold War policy. During the critical period analyzed here, the Bank did so twice. First, it conducted a secret affair with the Peronist administration even while the US saw Perón accountable for Argentina's wartime neutrality as well as for its alleged pro-Communist Third Position during the early Cold War. Second, it elaborated pretexts to postpone the launching of strategically significant development lending to the Liberating Revolution—the new US Cold War ally in South America. The fact that the WB knew that both the populist administration of Perón and the economically liberal military dictatorship were interested in its financial and technical development assistance emboldened it to find its own path among the often-clashing interests and concerns of all parties to the WB-Argentina-US triangle. At the end of the day, however, aside from its obstinate delay in lending to the military regime despite US pressure, the WB proved incapable of acting against US expectations. As WB President Black acknowledged: "The power of the [US] governments is not in getting the Bank to make loans; the power of the governments is to prevent the Bank from making loans. It's a veto power."[138]

Central in this chapter was the extent to which the populism promoted by Perón was the main justification behind Argentina's longstanding exclusion from the WB and the IMF. The answer, as argued here, is that Peronism, and not populism *per se,* was the major obstacle in Argentina's road first to WB membership and then to development assistance. While it is true that the WB was critical of Peronism, as its staff openly admitted following Perón's deposal, it seems that if the United States had lifted its veto earlier, the WB might have been willing to assist Argentina and exert pressure on Perón's team to reform its economic policies in exchange for loans. After all, this was the WB's main strategy in other borrowing member-states. In simple terms, although the Bank opposed the interventionist and centralist aspects of Latin America's populism, as well as its policy on wages and prices, its objective was to assist those countries in liberalizing their economy by attaching policy conditions to its loans. In effect, during its first years of activity, the WB did not impose *ex-ante* (pre-conditions) for lending, as it started to do in the late 1950s, but only *post-ante* conditions (to be implemented following the signing of a loan accord). Yet Brazil and other populist states were more pragmatic than Argentina in the sense that they nurtured ties with Washington by, for example, granting better treatment to US corporations installed in their territory and by avoiding conflicts with the US administration. It was for this reason that they received several WB loans.

From August 1956, with Argentina now a member of the Bretton Woods institutions, the interim military government sought to distance itself from the deposed Peronist regime and obtain financial support.

The IMF and the WB, however, had ideas of their own. In 1957, the IMF freed up limited funds to the Argentine military. For its part, the WB made every effort to postpone the launching of lending to Argentina until the political and economic conditions in the country improved. To the US administration, the postponement signaled the Bank's attempts to operate at its own discretion.

The limited availability of primary sources regarding the negotiations between the parties during what I refer to as the pre-historic period of the WB-Argentina-US triangular relationship has left us with an incomplete and fragmented understanding of the situation. Argentina's actions during World War II and the early Cold War era stemmed considerably from its aspiration to safeguard its political and economic sovereignty while finding a beneficial insertion in the international arena. It remains an open question—and one beyond the scope of this study—whether Argentina's decision to remain neutral during the war and to adopt a Third Position afterwards were the best options available in striving towards these goals. On the one hand, it can be argued that Argentina indeed demonstrated its autonomy by not bowing to US pressure. On the other hand, the enduring exclusion from the Bretton Woods institutions was not to Argentina's benefit. The country therefore found itself actively seeking to join the organizations from which it was excluded and taking upon itself the capitalist precepts promoted by the US administration and the institutions it had created.

As we shall see in the next chapter, it took three years of intense negotiation with the *developmentalist* administration of President Arturo Frondizi before the WB agreed to launch financial activities in Argentina. This hard-won collaboration was to prove decidedly short-lived.

2 THE WORLD BANK AND *DEVELOPMENTALISM*

THE WB GRANTED ITS FIRST loan to Argentina in June 1961, five years after the country was finally accepted as a member of the Bretton Woods institutions and a full twelve years after the Bank began operations in Latin America. At the time, Argentina was under the democratic governance of President Arturo Frondizi, who held office from May 1958 until March 1962, when he was ousted by the military. Frondizi, leader of the *Unión Cívica Radical* (UCR), was known for advocating wide-ranging development plans, commonly referred to as Latin America's *developmentalism* (Spanish: *Desarrollismo*). This economic theory, as elaborated below, posits that the world economy is divided into central industrial powers and peripheral agricultural nations. Frondizi aimed to transition Argentina out of its peripheral status, and he and the *developmentalists* who worked with him strove to access the WB's financial assistance towards this end. What, though, finally brought the WB to launch lending to Argentina precisely in 1961? To what extent could the long-awaited WB loans to Argentina be attributed to Frondizi's *developmentalism* or, alternatively, to the steep escalation of the Cold War in Latin America? Recently disclosed files from the WB archives reveal that while Frondizi's determination to place foreign capital at the center of his development strategy was crucial to his fruitful relationship with the Bank, the unfolding Cold War in Latin America also significantly influenced the timing of lending.

The triumph of the Cuban rebels in January 1959, the subsequent establishment of diplomatic and economic relations between Cuba and the Soviet Union, and Fidel Castro's public embrace of socialism in May 1961 brought the Cold War in the Western Hemisphere to an unprecedented intensity. Latin American governments were divided over the position they should take, both individually and collectively through the Organization of American States (OAS), when responding to major events in Cuba, such as the Bay of Pigs invasion in April 1961 and the Missile Crisis in October 1962.[1] Under these circumstances, powerful actors in Washington began to blur the lines between Cold War diplomacy and what can be described as "development diplomacy," by which I specifically refer to the use of development aid as leverage to promote policy change and/or specific actions or non-actions. Of course, foreign aid had hardly been detached from political considerations before that. The shift pertained primarily to the more explicit politicization of development aid. From 1959 onwards, highly sought-after development loans were granted by the Bank and other Washington-based institutions to certain regimes in exchange for their adoption of policies that aligned with US Cold War interests, in particular, regarding revolutionary Cuba, the Eastern bloc, democracy, foreign investments, and legislation against allegedly communist labor unions. In the economic arena, these policies reflected the attempts of the United States and the Bretton Woods institutions to encourage the continuous liberalization of finance and trade, the cessation of economic interventionism, and the adoption of a Western model of development grounded in principles of efficiency, productivity, and self-help. As this chapter demonstrates, the undeniable ideological affinity between the WB and the United States on economic matters did not necessarily imply that the immediate interests of the two always coincided. As seen in the cases of Frondizi and the *de facto* regime that replaced him, the volume and pace of WB lending neither fully aligned with nor directly clashed with President John F. Kennedy's Cold War priorities in the region. Despite its organizational expansion, the WB remained a semi-autonomous institution, reluctant—perhaps even fearful—of provoking an open and risky conflict with its most powerful principal and major donor—the United States.

During the years covered in this chapter, 1958–1963, the WB embarked on a process of reorganization to confront the challenges of the escalating Cold War in Latin America, the Bank's main epicenter of operations at the time. These adaptations, in turn, were aimed at enhancing the effectiveness of WB loans as instruments for promoting a capitalist approach to problems affecting Third World nations. Additionally, they sought to counter the apparently more successful strategies of communist regimes—Cuba among them—for tackling social issues such as high illiteracy and disease rates, and for accelerating the transition from a traditional to an industrial economy, with the Soviet Union as the primary model. In September 1960, the WB founded the International Development Association (IDA) to provide development assistance to low-income and non-creditworthy countries that otherwise could not qualify for Bank lending.[2] The launch of IDA lending allowed the WB and the United States to provide multilateral aid to countries deemed vulnerable to communist infiltration due to high levels of poverty and inequality. Additionally, in an effort to target specific populations within low- and middle-income countries considered particularly susceptible to communist influence, the WB diversified its lending activities to include new sectors such as education, health, and agriculture. Thus, under the presidency of Eugene Black (1949–1962), the WB began to play a more self-conscious role in the Cold War in the region. This role was twofold: it strove to eradicate problems that were considered fertile ground for the growth of communism and to inculcate, instead, capitalist policies and practices. As Black explained in a speech in October 1961:

> "That there is a connection between the need for economic growth [the WB's basic definition of development] and the Cold War is, of course, true: to the extent that the peoples of the less developed areas are better housed, better fed, better clothed—to the extent that they can see some prospect of improving their low standards of living—their loyalty to their own institutions will be strengthened and they will be less susceptible to the insidious sales pitch of communism."[3]

With the WB facing harsh criticism for what Argentina and other Latin American countries called the unjust allocation of development resources, the launch of the Alliance for Progress (hereafter Alliance) by US President John F. Kennedy in mid-1961 provided additional weight in the Bank's decision to start lending to Argentina. Conceived as a soft (i.e., non-military) strategy to contain the advancement of communism in the region, the Alliance offered economic aid to countries that met certain political conditions, including the support of democracy and the promotion of self-help measures and planning—which echoed Black's efforts to make developing nations "development minded." What becomes apparent is that, from the WB's perspective, the Alliance posed a challenge to its potential ascendency in Latin America's development realm. The fact that a middle-income nation like Argentina was not expected to receive funding from the Alliance created an opportunity for the WB to step in and fill the development vacuum in the country—a vacuum that the Bank itself had helped to create. Additionally, the WB was trailing behind its counterpart, the IMF, which was already deeply involved in Argentina. In December 1958, the IMF had granted Frondizi's administration a first loan, signing three additional accords every December until the coup of 1962.[4]

This chapter explores both the difficulties and the opportunities that Argentina's *developmentalism* presented to the WB. It examines the events from Frondizi's election until early 1963, with the end of the short-lived, interim *de facto* regime that deposed him. Although there has been a revival of academic interest in the so-called Development Decade of the 1960s,[5] we know little about the relations that evolved between the WB and *developmentalist* leaders such as Frondizi. The chapter aims to show that even though Argentina was a latecomer to the Bretton Woods institutions, Frondizi positioned himself at the forefront of the fight to make the WB serve Latin America's urgent development needs. He exerted pressure on the WB, claiming that it "had provided credits to the entire world [. . .] except to Argentina."[6] He also warned that, if needed, Argentina could turn to alternative sources of financing beyond the Western bloc. Voicing a common Latin American criticism—that the region had received barely one-quarter of the $3.82 billion in WB loans granted between 1948 and 1958—Frondizi portrayed Argentina's difficulties in securing financing from the Bank as symptomatic of a broader regional problem.[7] Uncovering the hitherto unknown interactions between Frondizi's administration and Black's WB, and their hitherto understudied interplay with US Cold War interests, this chapter seeks to demonstrate that Frondizi's *developmentalism,* which combined elements of economic liberalism with state interventionism, provided ample justification for WB lending. Nevertheless, *developmentalism* alone cannot explain the launch of WB lending to Argentina in 1961. Several other factors also played a decisive role in the Bank's decision-making process. Some were linked to the Cuban Revolution and the US determination to prevent another Cuba in the region, while others stemmed from the WB's bureaucratic needs. As explained below, these two categories were deeply intertwined and mutually reinforcing.

To better understand the multifaceted incentives and constraints that shaped the WB's relations with Argentina at a time when development was a dominant buzzword in the international sphere, this chapter chronologically follows the tortuous negotiations between the parties to the WB-Argentina-US triangle. It concludes with a brief discussion of the events that took place in the aftermath of the regime change in 1962. As we shall see, ideological affinity on economic matters was a necessary but not sufficient condition to secure WB loans.

PART 1: CLASHING INTERESTS

The World Bank: Development Diplomacy and the Cold War in Latin America

By 1959, when Cuba crossed the lines between the capitalist and the communist blocs, developing nations in Latin America—and, to a lesser extent, the US administration—claimed that the WB had failed to fulfill its mission. Between 1949 and 1959, the WB's annual commitments averaged $307 million, far short of the $15 billion vaguely suggested by the US delegation at the Bretton Woods conference. By 1961, this figure had increased to hardly $700 million annually. Another critique of the WB was that approximately one-third of its total loan funds made their way to countries with a relatively high per-capita income, such as

Australia, Japan, and South Africa.[8] Such criticism, alongside the risk of losing member-states due to Cold War divisions—as seen with Poland's withdrawal in 1949—pushed the Bank to rethink its lending strategy. Criticism from its borrowing member-states required the Bank to demonstrate that despite being a Western institution visibly influenced by and dependent on the United States, it was not ready to serve as an instrument of US foreign policy. The analysis of the triangular dynamics between the Bank, Argentina, and the United States reveals that, while both the Kennedy administration and the WB saw Frondizi as a leader worthy of support, the Bank's decision to launch lending to Argentina in 1961 was not necessarily rooted in this shared perception. Rather, it was largely driven by a growing sense of competition—rather than collaboration—with the Kennedy administration over influence in Latin America's development field. To be sure, the WB's actions aligned fully with US expectations, even if its rationale and rhetoric partially differed.

The escalation of the Cold War in Latin America, coupled with the WB's determination to expand its operations, prompted Black to initiate organizational reforms aimed at enabling the Bank to more effectively address the new challenges. These challenges also sharpened the Bank's awareness of the need to establish a more precise definition of development, in terms of both its guiding principles and their practical implementation. True to its DNA, the WB's understanding of development was deeply embedded in US notions of progress and modernization. Like US policymakers, the WB considered economic growth and stability in the context of a free-market economy to be crucial conditions for development. The assumption was that *economic growth*, understood as an increase in real national income and output, would ultimately lead to *economic development*, meaning an improvement in living standards. The educational sector, closely linked to social mobility, serves as a vivid example of how the Cold War impelled the WB to reevaluate its goals and lending activities. Until the Cuban Revolution, the WB only provided funding for the construction of new schools and the procurement of educational equipment. However, in response to the successful mass literacy campaign carried out by Castro in 1961–1962, which showed that socialist nations could redistribute nationalized wealth for the benefit of all, the Bank started endorsing educational initiatives that would highlight the advantages of capitalism.[9] In addition, in the early 1960s, the Bank entered into new arenas that were critical for Latin American development, such as agriculture and water supply.

To WB President Black, economic growth held broader significance beyond the confines of pure economics. Black believed that what stood in the way of faster growth in the underdeveloped world was "not just a lack of capital *per se*, of savings *per se*, of education *per se*, of entrepreneurship *per se*, and so forth."[10] Rather, he considered underdeveloped countries to be suffering from a dearth of entrepreneurs and professionals experienced in the management of public and private businesses, insufficient infrastructures whose lack further restricted the effective application of capital, and disease and illiteracy that negatively affected productivity. Hence, raising the standard of living in poor countries required creating the right conditions and skills to use capital effectively. When a country asks the Bank for loans, Black claimed, "the important thing [for the WB] is to encourage the habit of weighing benefits and costs. When that habit becomes ingrained, society is already most of the way to becoming development-minded."[11] In order to illuminate the choices of the Bank's borrowers and make them development-minded, Black supported the involvement of both WB experts and US private consultants in national development planning.[12] For the Bank, being development-minded meant basically one thing: disseminating a US vision of liberal capitalism among developing nations.

WB lending in the 1960s had two main goals. The first was to stimulate integral economic progress beyond particular projects. The second was to help create conditions that would encourage greater private initiative, which the WB, like the US administration, considered vital. To reach these goals, the WB requested that its borrowers "rationalize"[13] and privatize state-owned enterprises and services. A further request, which became a recurrent theme in the WB's negotiations with Frondizi's team, was that utility enterprises generate a substantial part of their budgets through "adequate" tariffs rather than relying on subsidies.[14] In a speech delivered in April 1959, in which he portrayed Frondizi as a leader who understood the right way to solve structural problems,

Black stressed that "it is dangerous for a developing country to be sentimental or politically expedient about things like railroads and power plants; [. . .] policies based on these attitudes only create intolerable drain on savings which are the lifeblood of every country's future prosperity."[15] As historical sources unveil, tariffs on public utilities, a sensitive social issue, soon became a major problem in negotiations between the WB, Argentina, and other Latin American countries.

Developmentalism in Latin America and Argentina: The Best WB Partner in Town?

In the 1950s and 1960s, Latin American *developmentalism* was widely seen as a framework for addressing the problem of underdevelopment. In Argentina, it reached its peak during Frondizi's term. As a concept, *developmentalism* is commonly associated with CEPAL and with economists like Raúl Prebisch (who served as CEPAL's executive secretary from 1950 to 1963), Victor Urquidi, and Alberto Hirschman.[16] The term *"developmentalism"* was often used in Argentina to refer to the model promoted by the *Frondizistas* of the Intransigent Radical Civic Union (a faction within the UCR) who, while in power, strove to distance themselves from both CEPAL and Prebisch.[17] As part of these efforts, Frondizi appointed Rogelio Frigerio as Minister of Economy.[18]

According to *developmentalism,* the constant deterioration of the terms of trade in agricultural and mining produce was the main cause of underdevelopment in peripheral countries that were producers and exporters of primary products. Frondizi and Frigerio maintained that these unfavorable terms of exchange led to two major bottlenecks in Argentina's economy: one related to the balance of payments and inflation, and the other to Argentina's productive capacity. With regard to the first bottleneck, they claimed that while the budget deficit caused by a negative balance of payments could be resolved by applying artificial or monetary mechanisms, using these mechanisms inevitably led to new inflationary cycles. Attempting to solve these problems, they sought to advance significant changes to Argentina's economic structure, the second bottleneck. In Frondizi's view, the lack of an advanced industrial sector and modern agricultural production condemned Argentina to underdevelopment.

Moreover, this led to the deviation of the available labor force from productive to non-productive activities, one result of which was the creation of an oversized and inefficient state bureaucracy. To combat these problems, Argentina's *developmentalists* called for a transformation of the national productive structure. This transformation, they argued, required a clear state policy and guidance, the establishment of close ties with foreign capital, and the modernization of the state apparatus.[19] These ideas dovetailed with central pre-conditions for WB and IMF lending.

To better understand the challenge posed by *developmentalism,* it is important to note that Frondizi's economic policy echoed a debate over the causes of inflation currently taking place between Latin American *developmentalists* and the IMF. *Developmentalists* advanced a "structural approach" that identified inequalities in the terms of trade between countries at the center and those at the periphery of the world economy as a key cause of inflation. However, based on monetarist ideas then prevalent in Washington, the WB and the IMF saw inflation as the result of excessive monetary expansion and fiscal and exchange mismanagement.[20] For them, inflation was induced by policy distortions in areas such as wages, tariffs, and prices and was incompatible with development. Hence, turning a deaf ear to Latin America's theories and requests, the WB determined that middle-income countries coping with problems in their balance of payments were not creditworthy, and therefore unqualified for WB financial assistance. The Bank thus fueled what historian Margarita Fajardo terms Latin America's "development paradox"—a vicious cycle of loans not forthcoming due to the prevailing inflation and the imbalance of international payments, coupled with persistent inflation because foreign loans were not forthcoming.[21] It is therefore unsurprising that *developmentalist* leaders like Frondizi pressed the WB to reform their lending criteria.

The interactions between representatives of Frondizi's government and the WB reveal that even though both sides held common ground on critical matters such as state reform, planning, foreign investments, and the private sector, their discussions remained technical in nature. As WB records show, *developmentalist* thinking was never seriously discussed. It seems that while the WB attempted to accommodate itself to the evolving Cold War conditions in Latin America, it was not necessarily open to considering development theories formulated within the region. But the WB alone was not responsible for the absence of meaningful discussions regarding *developmentalism*. Frondizi's *developmentalist*-minded team did not remain in office for long. From mid-1959 onwards, the reins of Argentina's economy were removed from the hands of fervent *developmentalists* such as Frigerio and given to sympathetic interlocutors of the Bank, including liberal economists such as Álvaro Alsogaray, Roberto Alemann, and Guillermo Walter Klein.[22]

At the end of the day, WB lending to Frondizi's government and to other *developmentalist* administrations, such as those in Brazil and Chile, experienced ups and downs. For example, during the term of President Juscelino Kubitschek (1956–1961), sometimes called the "Brazilian Frondizi," Brazil received only three WB loans, a significant slowdown compared to previous years.[23] The situation worsened during the presidencies of Jânio Quadros (January–August 1961), Ranieri Mazzilli (August–September 1961), and João 'Jango' Goulart (September 1961–April 1964), all of whom continued to implement certain components of Kubitschek's *developmentalist* program and none of whom received any new WB loans.[24] Other *developmentalist* administrations fared better.[25] These include the Chilean government of Eduardo Frei Montalva (1964–1970), a Christian Democrat who received seven WB loans. Other *developmentalists* received even more generous support. Among others, one can mention Colombia's presidents Alberto Lleras Camargo (1958–1962), Guillermo León Valencia (1962–1966), and Carlos Lleras Restrepo (1966–1970), who received nine, seven, and twenty WB loans, respectively. WB lending to Colombia was also accompanied by substantial US assistance, as Colombia was at that point the poster child for President Kennedy's Latin American policy.[26]

The US and the Alliance for Progress: Development Aid and the Fight Against Communism in Latin America

The US administration, like the Soviet Union, sought to gain influence in the Third World by serving as models and promoters of development.[27] As historian Sara Lorenzini claims, President Kennedy took development more seriously than his predecessors. Kennedy believed that poverty and social and political chaos represented a threat to US security, and that democracy would evolve hand in hand with economic growth.[28] In his view, the success of this process would require Washington's guidance as well as its financial, technical, and technological assistance. As such, he appointed modernization theorist Walt W. Rostow, author of the influential book *The Stages of Economic Growth: A Non-Communist Manifesto* (1961), as an adviser and special assistant Secretary of State in charge of US policy in South Asia. Other proponents of this approach also held key positions, such as Lincoln Gordon, the US ambassador to Brazil. In March 1961, Rostow recommended to Kennedy that he portray the government's foreign aid plans as part of an "Economic Development Decade."[29] Rostow predicted that "through a massive transfusion of foreign aid" it would be possible for countries such as Argentina, Brazil, Colombia, and Venezuela, as well as India, the Philippines, Taiwan, Turkey, Greece, and others, to attain self-sustaining growth for over 80 percent of their underdeveloped populations within a decade.[30]

Determined to avoid another Cuba in the Americas, in March 1961, President Kennedy called for the creation of an Alliance for Progress. He presented this call as "a vast cooperative effort" intended to satisfy the Latin American peoples' basic needs for homes, work and land, health, and schools—which were considered critical to contain the advance of communism. Notably, the Alliance, with its progressive rhetoric highlighting economic growth, structural change, and democratization, was not merely a response to the radicalization of Cuba's revolutionary regime.[31] Rather, it was part of a broader effort to keep countries in the region aligned with Washington by responding to longstanding Latin American demands for US financial assistance, particularly after the launch of the Marshall Plan. This also explains why the US Senate approved the establishment of the Inter-American Development Bank (IDB) only in 1959, a move that countries such as Argentina, Brazil, and Chile had been advocating since 1954, when the Inter-American Conference of Ministers of Economy convened in Brazil.

The Alliance was formally announced in August 1961 at the Inter-American Conference in Uruguay, when the United States and all the Latin American nations except Cuba, represented by Che Guevara, signed the Charter of Punta del Este. The charter's main goal was "to accelerate the economic and social development of the participating countries of Latin America, so that they achieve maximum levels of well-being, with equal opportunities for all, in democratic societies [. . .]."[32] It stressed the need to achieve a sustained growth of per capita income of not less than 2.5 percent per year.[33] The Alliance was intended to accomplish its goals through grants, loans, and technical cooperation, primarily provided by the US administration and private sector.[34] The Alliance's management was housed within the United States Agency for International Development (USAID), which was created by the Foreign Assistance Act of November 1961 to unite all US foreign aid agencies (except the Eximbank and Food for Peace) under a single umbrella and oversee all US foreign aid programs.[35] Significantly, the WB received not a single mention in the Charter of Punta del Este, and the IMF got little more billing.[36]

The Kennedy administration's decision to enact a program that overlapped with the WB's mandate while excluding the Bank from its planning and execution was driven not only by Kennedy's determination to set the terms—similar to the United States's approach in Europe with the Marshall Plan—but also by the intent to pressure the Bank into increasing its lending to the region to prevent the emergence of another Cuba. The US disappointment with WB's sparse activity in Latin America did not evaporate with the launch of the Alliance. A report from a US economic mission that visited Argentina, Brazil, Chile, and Bolivia in July 1962 expressed sharp criticism of the Bank's limited activity in those countries. According to the report, the "WB [was] viewed [in Latin America] as such a rigorous taskmaster in its insistence on comprehensive financial and monetary disciplines accompanying its projects assistance that the governments concerned [were] not enthusiastic about seeking extensive [WB] assistance or sanguine that they can qualify."[37] To conclude, while the launching of the Alliance raised concerns at the WB regarding potential competition for influence in Argentina, these concerns proved groundless. Aside from a modest housing loan signed in September 1963, the United States offered no further assistance to

Argentina within the framework of the Alliance. As the next sections indicate, while the WB, seeking not to be relegated to the sidelines in Latin America, finally began lending to Argentina, it soon found new pretexts to stop doing so.

PART 2: THE WB AND PRESIDENT ARTURO FRONDIZI: BETWEEN IDEAS AND PRAGMATISM

Frondizi was sworn in as president on May 1, 1958. Immediately, his pragmatic stance towards Castro's Cuba came under local fire. His situation was not auspicious in the international sphere either, and many in the State Department suggested taking steps to secure his full alignment with the Capitalist bloc.[38] For instance, Viron P. Vaky (Office of South American Affairs at the State Department) recommended "to demonstrate warmth and sincerity"; otherwise, he warned, Frondizi would turn to the Soviets.[39] Vacky's worries were baseless. The Soviets had no illusions regarding Argentina's Cold War alignment, particularly when Frondizi, albeit for a brief period, outlawed the activities of Argentina's Communist Party. In fact, under Frondizi, Argentine-Soviet relations remained, for the most part, tense.[40]

Frondizi inherited an economy in crisis. Inflation was at 32 percent, productivity was low, exports were stagnant, the 1958 deficit stood at $300 million, and Argentina's total external indebtedness reached $1 billion. As part of his strategy to solve the crisis, Frondizi announced that he would seek to attract foreign investments. He also stressed that although the state would be responsible for coordinating economic activity to promote efficiency and industrialization, it would do so in partnership with private enterprise.[41] Aware that turning to foreign capital was controversial in Argentina, Frondizi and Frigerio explained that Argentina had to take advantage of all available resources, national or foreign. In his argumentation, Frondizi distinguished between "bad foreign capital," which was exploitative and slanted towards export-oriented enterprises, and "good foreign capital," which, he claimed, could finance the industrial infrastructure needed to achieve growth and development. Frondizi took recourse in this argument to justify a number of divisive decisions he made in late 1958, including the signing of the first and highly conditional Stand-By Arrangement (SBA) with the IMF, the authorization of contracts with transnational petroleum corporations (see Chapter 3), and opening negotiations to solve ongoing disputes with US foreign-owned companies that had been partially expropriated by Perón, in particular the powerful AFPC.[42] In light of this shift in economic policy, the US administration promptly announced the extension of new loans to Argentina, including $125 million from the Eximbank, $25 million from the US Development Loan Fund (US-DLF), and the purchase of *pesos* for dollars up to $50 million. In addition, US and Canadian private banks announced a loan of $54 million to meet Argentina's foreign exchange shortage.[43] Frondizi's openness towards foreign capital and investors, the improvement of relations with the US government and US-owned corporations working in Argentina, and the close collaboration with the IMF facilitated more serious negotiations with the WB.

Official contacts between WB staff and Frondizi's team began before his inauguration. On April 24, 1958, Jorge del Canto, head of the IMF's Western Hemisphere Department (IMF-WHD), and Orvis Schmidt, a former US Treasury economist who joined the WB in 1947 and headed the WB's Western Hemisphere Department (WB-WHD) between 1956 and 1964, held informal meetings with Luis Peralta Ramos and Alejandro Orfila.[44] These dealings were more than a mere courtesy, as, at the same time, the WB was engaged in internal debates regarding the possibility of lending to the country. Discussions among Bank staff concerned Frondizi's economic policy, including contentious issues such as tariffs, the role of the state and the public sector in Argentina's economy, the rehabilitation and privatization of utility companies, the requirement to provide equal treatment to foreign and domestic capital, and the settlement of disputes with US companies.[45] Bilateral disagreements over these matters were certainly not new.[46] All Washington-based institutions agreed that the settlement of disputes with expropriated US companies abroad constituted an inviolable requisite for foreign assistance. This shared view was reflected in a series of meetings between representatives of the WB, the US State Department, and even the AFPC. The power company and the State Department, exemplifying one of the ways in which the US administration expected the Bank to serve its interests, urged the WB to act as an intermediary in dealings with Argentina.[47]

After Frondizi took office, the WB's interactions with Argentina continued, but not smoothly. In July 1958, Alejandro Orfila, Argentina's ambassador to Washington, met with Black and Burke Knapp (WB vice president of operations, 1956–1972). Discussions focused on Frondizi's invitation to Black to visit Argentina and on the WB's stand regarding potential operations in the country.[48] Black considered such a visit premature. He preferred to put off negotiations until Argentina settled disputes regarding expropriated US companies and adopted a favorable policy towards foreign investors—two steps that Frondizi planned to take in any case. Furthermore, Black and Knapp initially rejected the principal sectors at the heart of Frondizi's development plans, for which his government sought financial assistance: electrical power, petroleum, and railroads. This rejection reflected the Bank's insistence on increasing the role of the private sector, particularly foreign companies, in those crucial areas. Although Frondizi was resolved to promote privatizations and foreign investments, Black and Knapp wanted to see first whether he was indeed able to leave behind the interventionism and economic nationalism of the Peronist years. Black also referred to Argentina's heavy foreign debt as an obstacle in the way of WB lending. Ambassador Orfila left the meeting empty-handed.[49]

Argentina did not give up. Emilio Donato del Carril, Frondizi's Minister of Economy until June 1959, headed two missions to the Bank. The first, in late October 1958, amounted to a fruitless meeting with Orvis Schmidt (head of the WB-WHD). The second mission arrived on December 23, 1958. This time, Del Carril met with Knapp, Schmidt, and Simon Aldewereld (WB director of technical operations).[50] Del Carril, seeking to open up discussions on loans, stated that "he would now like the Bank to indicate what it would be prepared to do in Argentina."[51] Knapp responded that the WB would first need to see how a soon-to-be-announced stabilization program would work and how much external borrowing Argentina would require in order to service its foreign debt. In justifying his response, Knapp explained that because the Bank relied on borrowing in the private market, creditworthiness was crucial. He added that a lasting solution to the problems of the expropriated assets of the electric companies ANSEC and CADE would remove an important obstacle to WB lending.[52] Again, Del Carril was left with nothing to show for his efforts.

In late December 1958, while the WB was still raising difficulties, the IMF approved the first SBA with Argentina, worth $75 million, to support Frondizi's stabilization plan. Signaling a transformation in Argentine economic policy, the plan listed measures directed at solving chronic problems, including a reduction of public-sector deficits. The government committed itself to a 15 percent reduction in the number of public employees by the end of 1959—saving $2 billion by delaying the completion of public construction projects already underway and postponing new projects—and drastic reductions in the operating deficits of autonomous agencies.[53] The conditions stipulated in the SBA, and therefore also in Frondizi's stabilization plan, and the WB's *ex-ante* conditions for lending showed significant similarities as both institutions strove to push their borrowers to liberalize their economies. These conditions included the focus both on imposing new tariffs (including a substantial raise in electricity rates, a 200 percent increase in the price of petroleum, and the cancellation of subsidies to consumers and producers) and on increasing the railways' economic efficiency.[54] With the IMF already deeply involved in efforts to stabilize the national economy, the State Department began to evaluate "the possible desirability" of encouraging the WB to start operations in Argentina.[55] Simply put, the State Department expected that the WB would join its endeavors to assist Frondizi in liberalizing Argentina's economy, thereby securing the country's alignment with the Western bloc.

Frondizi understandably believed that the US administration was the key to accessing WB funds. In January 1959, just days after the Cuban revolutionaries reached Havana, Frondizi traveled to the United States to meet with President Eisenhower, Secretary Dulles, and other high-ranking officials.[56] He also addressed the US Congress, presenting himself as a Western Cold War warrior. Poverty and economic backwardness, he declared, threatened hemispheric security because they provided fertile ground for the spread of communism.[57] Moreover, communist infiltration would remain an imminent danger as long as the region's underdevelopment was not remedied—an idea Frondizi also articulated in discussions with Latin American presidents regarding the position to be adopted towards Cuba.[58] Frondizi's words were music to the ears of Kennedy's advisers.

In Washington, Frondizi met with WB President Black.[59] Black opened by congratulating Frondizi "on the wisdom and courage" he showed in confronting "some of Argentina's most fundamental problems," particularly economic stabilization, disputes with private power companies, and the new agreements his administration had signed with foreign oil companies, many of which were US firms.[60] Frondizi inquired about the WB's readiness to support Argentina's energy sector against the backdrop of repeated electrical power shortages that hampered the establishment of new industries. Black answered that he intended to dispatch a mission to help Argentina lay the groundwork for a comprehensive power program. Avoiding entering into a discussion on Frondizi's *developmentalist* philosophy, Black stressed that the WB would make a loan only if it was convinced that it would be repaid, and only if the project was well planned.[61] Then Black asked whether Argentina had decided to join the IFC, the Bank's agency focusing on the private sector, as Black was keen to consolidate this entity's status in Latin America. Frondizi answered positively and joined in 1959. Following this meeting, Frondizi met President Eisenhower, Secretary Dulles, Assistant Secretary Rubottom, and Ambassador Beaulac. Frondizi told them that "he would appreciate any help from the United States Government in seeing that the [World] Bank acted quickly in the case of Argentina." Eisenhower did not respond to this request.[62]

In the meantime, Argentina's government underwent a series of personnel changes that exposed Frondizi's political fragility and represented an initial turn away from *developmentalism* towards a more orthodox economic approach. Among the most significant was the appointment of Álvaro Alsogaray as Minister of Economy in June 1959. The first meeting between Alsogaray and the WB management, held in October 1959, exemplified this policy change. Alsogaray was accompanied by other liberal economists: his adviser González Solar, Secretary of Finance Eustaquio Méndez Delfino, Roberto Alemann, the financial counselor of the Argentine embassy, and Carlos Brignone, Argentina's ED to the WB.[63] After stating that the IMF-supported stabilization plan launched in 1958 was succeeding, Alsogaray maintained that his new policy would rely on private enterprise and reduce government intervention.[64] Then, he asked for assistance in carrying out a transport study, which the WB immediately approved.[65] Known as the *Plan de Transporte de Largo Alcance para Argentina,* or simply the "Larkin Report," the study was carried out from 1959 to 1962 under the direction of retired US Lieutenant General Thomas B. Larkin, who was working for the WB as an expert in logistics and transportation. Officially presented in Argentina in February 1962, the study listed numerous railway lines that Larkin suggested be closed because they were not economically viable.[66] It also emphasized that low tariffs, along with the decreasing use of trains to transport goods, produced mounting deficits and caused the overuse of deteriorated infrastructures and equipment.[67] The Larkin study served to heighten the WB's obsession with Argentina's railway system, which, under state control since nationalization by Perón in March 1948, was managed by the state-owned company *Empresa Ferrocarriles del Estado Argentino* (EFEA). The Bank identified the EFEA's financial losses as a chronic aggravator of Argentina's budget deficit and, consequently, as an impediment to lending to the country.

Despite the economic difficulties, the entry of sympathetic interlocutors to Argentina's centers of economic power facilitated negotiations. On February 25, 1960, the same day that President Eisenhower arrived in Argentina for a three-day visit, the liberal businessman and lawyer Guillermo Walter Klein (Secretary of the Treasury), Eusebio Campos (Vice President of the Central Bank), Ambassador Alemann, and Argentina's ED to the Bank, Brignone, met with Black and Knapp at the WB offices.[68] Klein opened by affirming that he hoped that the WB would assist Argentina. Attesting to his close connections with private banks, Black commented that he had already talked with Baring Bros (London) and Morgan Stanley (NY) regarding Argentina's external debt. Closing the meeting, Black expressed hope that the WB would soon be able to assist Argentina.[69] This polite send-off had no teeth; a final settlement with AFPC was still pending.

The Bank's Struggle for Supremacy in Argentina: The First Loan

In June 1960, the long-awaited launch of WB lending to Argentina emerged, for the first time, as a real option. Early that month, the WB Loan Committee approved an initial lending program to the country. With a budget ranging from $50 to $75 million over a twelve-month period, this program served as the starting point for discussions about individual loans directed at two sectors deemed crucial by both President Frondizi and the WB: energy and transport.[70] Based on the Larkin report, the parties agreed to proceed first with the transport sector.

In June 1961, Black sent to the EDs his report and recommendations on a proposed $48.5 million loan for the reconstruction and improvement of some 2,600 km of Argentina's main highways, and for the maintenance equipment and parts needed for the project.[71] Argentina, Black emphasized, had requested that the WB finance part of a ten-year highway program, with another part to be financed by the Eximbank and the US-DLF. The WB-Argentina-US triangular dynamics were in full swing. Black considered the loan easily justifiable, as inadequate means of transportation hindered Argentina's economic growth. The project was to be administered by the *Dirección Nacional de Vialidad*, an autonomous government agency, and would be executed by contractors chosen through a competitive international bidding process, thereby evidencing the change in Argentina's policy, which was moving towards decentralization and opening up to foreign capital.[72]

On June 29, 1961, the WB EB discussed the loan proposal. The WB's explanations during this meeting illustrate the "change of mentality" that the institution was advocating for in Argentina. It also underscores why the Bank identified Frondizi as a partner in its economic Cold War efforts in the region. Knapp, who presided over the meeting, blamed the interventionism and *statism* of the deposed Peronist regime for Argentina's economic problems. Until 1945, he stated, Argentina had been the most advanced country in South America, but "when the Perón regime was overthrown [in 1955], the Argentine economy was in a state of stagnation."[73] Following Perón's deposal, Mervyn Weiner (WB Economic Division) added, "the dismantling of the apparatus of controlled trade and prices [. . .] produced changes in price levels and price relationships which were sharp, and difficult for many [social] groups." Yet, he argued, the most difficult part of the adjustment had already passed, and the benefits of stabilization were soon to be reaped. He emphasized that Frondizi's presidency had led to a significant rise in private investments and a restructuring of a portion of the foreign debt.[74] While discussing the specificities of the highway project, WB staff explained that the proposed loan was similar to a reconstruction loan because it was aimed at the restoration of roads that had been neglected by the Peronist administration. The situation of the transport infrastructure, so members of the WB-WHD argued, was worse than in the case of Europe's postwar reconstruction, because Argentina, unlike Europe, lacked adequate managerial and technical skills.[75] The EB approved the loan unanimously. After the vote, former Economy Minister Alsogaray sent Knapp a personal message of gratitude. He conveyed his belief that Argentina had been on the verge of forsaking Western democratic and capitalist values and expressed his relief and appreciation for the opportunity presented by the loan. As he wrote: "In 1956 [when the country joined the Bretton Woods institutions], Argentina was a strongly socialist country with an interventionist and totalitarian type of economy, but, in less than three years, they completed a significant change."[76] Like Alsogaray, many in Argentina understood, rightly, that collaboration with the WB meant full alignment with the US-led bloc and leaving the door open to Western influence in domestic affairs.

The signing of a loan agreement with the Bank marked the beginning of its increased engagement in the country. The agreement outlined rigorous monitoring by WB staff, entailing phased withdrawals from the loan account contingent upon compliance with loan conditions and project progress. It mandated that funds from the WB were to be exclusively utilized for the designated project. Additionally, it included an intrusive and highly contentious requirement for *Vialidad* to "employ or cause to be employed engineering consultants acceptable to [. . .] the Borrower [*Vialidad*] and the [World] Bank." The agreement also established that *Vialidad* would furnish the WB with any relevant information it might request and "shall afford all reasonable opportunity for accredited representatives of the Bank to visit any part of the territories of the Borrower for purposes related to the Loan."[77]

In fact, a conversation that took place between Brignone and Schmidt days after the first loan was approved reflects the snowball effect that WB lending had on Argentina's economic liberalization. Seeking to convince Schmidt that Frondizi's policy met the WB's economic preconditions, Brignone pointed out that the government had already ordered the retirement of 22,000 workers and removed about 4,000 km of railways from service—falling somewhat short of Larkin's recommended 15,000 km reduction—out of a total of 43,000 km. The railway was indeed in dire condition. Ever since its nationalization under Perón, it had been overstaffed; the number of workers rose from 158,000 in 1947 to 220,000 in 1959, and the ratio between payroll and revenue increased from 79.5 percent in 1953 to 134 percent in 1958.[78] For the WB, like the IMF, the railways symbolized the worst of Peronism: an inflated and inefficient management created by political and clientelist motivations, and combative workers represented by allegedly communist unions. The draconian steps aimed at rationalizing the railways, and consequently at depoliticizing them by weakening the unions, were stipulated in Decree 4061 of May 1961, which was promoted by the new Minister of Economy, Roberto Alemann (who replaced Alsogaray upon his resignation), and by Arturo Acevedo, the new minister of public works and services (an orthodox economist from the private sector).[79] The decree established that any wage increase not commensurate with an increase in productivity would automatically incur an increase in tariffs. It also stipulated that the overall number of personnel would be drastically reduced, including the layoff of 75,000 workers; that complementary services such as the cleaning of train cars and stations, cafes, and train car restaurants would be privatized; and that a new study would determine the technical and economic prospects of a full or partial privatization of the railway repair shops.[80] As shown in this and other chapters, even though the WB advocated for extensive job cuts primarily based on economic rationales, its initiatives were in line with and bolstered US Cold War agendas. These actions stemmed from concerns over the powerful Peronist movement and the falsely assumed communist sway over Argentina's workers.

Ideological proximity notwithstanding, Argentina doubted the WB's intentions to engage in further loan negotiations. Therefore, with the aim of securing financial support from the United States and backing in their dealings with the WB, Krieger Vasena arrived in Washington with a trade delegation. The mission first presented a request to the Kennedy administration for a $200 million loan for projects in the domains of electricity, airports, steel mills, and railroads. Next, they met with Black and Schmidt at the WB.[81] Krieger Vasena expressed his dissatisfaction with the decreasing ability of Argentina to export, attributing it to circumstances beyond the country's control. He argued that at the very moment Argentina was moving towards liberalizing its foreign trade, European countries were intensifying government intervention in international trade. Even worse, he protested, Argentine meat had already been banned from international markets due to foot and mouth disease, and the imposition of new tariffs further reduced the prospects of selling wheat to the US market.[82] Black responded that if Frondizi's administration took the necessary steps to solve the railroad problem and continued to improve the economy, the WB "would be prepared to lend [. . .] large amounts of money." Nevertheless, he warned that Argentina's foreign debt was already too large and, therefore, it would be unwise for Frondizi's administration to borrow money it did not need just because the US administration made such loans available.[83] On one hand, Black was attempting to persuade the Argentines not to seek loans from the US and the Eximbank in order to maintain the WB as the country's primary lender. On the other hand, he cautiously avoided making any firm commitments until Argentina carried out the requested economic reforms and launched a far-reaching railway rehabilitation plan. It seems that Black was trying to consolidate the WB's status vis-à-vis a new, promising borrower, without rocking its status with its strongest member-state. It is also evident that, while the intensifying Cold War in Latin America and its implications, such as the establishment of the Alliance, motivated the Bank to initiate operations in Argentina, once engaged in the country, it prioritized economic criteria.

The WB and Argentina Under the Shadow of the Alliance for Progress

After the unproductive negotiations conducted by Krieger Vasena's delegation in Washington, the UN General Assembly in late September 1961 served as the backdrop for two significant meetings between Argentina's delegation and US representatives. During their initial meeting, Frondizi told US Ambassador Stevenson that it was the first time ever that Argentina's foreign policy had turned away from European aid in favor of US assistance. Frondizi noted that this transition had encountered considerable opposition within Argentina on nationalist grounds. According to Stevenson, Frondizi's "attitude came close to being an intimation that Argentine cooperation with the United States on the Cuban matter could be had only after a down-payment of economic assistance by the United States."[84] US aid was discussed in greater detail during a subsequent meeting between the presidents of Argentina and the United States. Frondizi asked Kennedy for loans totaling $1 billion.[85] Such a significant sum was intended to complement several loans that Argentina aspired to negotiate with the WB. Kennedy, however, was more interested in discussing Argentina's stance on pressing Cold War matters, such as the situation in Cuba and the events unfolding in Berlin, than focusing on lending possibilities.[86]

Following the Frondizi-Kennedy meeting, Minister Alemann met with Black and Knapp at the WB.[87] Perhaps aiming to demonstrate that Frondizi's administration was the best possible partner in Argentina, Alemann stressed that in 1958, Frondizi had issued a decree ordering a comprehensive reform of the electric sector. The decree established a new electric company, *Servicios Eléctricos del Gran Buenos Aires* (SEGBA), and provided for the purchase of the shares of *Societe d'Electricite* (SODEC), an affiliate of the Spanish-Belgian-owned company *Société Financiere de Transports et d'Entreprises Industrielles* (SOFINA), the foreign group that had invested in SEGBA. Alemann also noted that the government had not yet integrated the fourteen municipalities in the northwestern area of the Buenos Aires Federal District into SEGBA, as the WB had repeatedly urged them to do, nor had it assembled an adequate management team for the company. Yet, extending a blank check to the WB staff in an attempt to please it, Alemann assured them that "the Government would propose names shortly" to hear the WB's opinion on the different candidates being considered for management positions in SEGBA.[88] He also explained that the transference of the municipalities was unlikely because it required the approval of Congress, where the government lacked a majority. Knapp dismissed Alemann's rationale for postponing the transfer of the municipalities to SEBGA—a measure that the Bank considered imperative in order to improve the efficiency of the electric sector.[89] At this point, Black turned to an even bigger problem—the railways.

Regarding the railways, Alemann claimed, the Argentine government had attempted to implement an extensive rehabilitation plan that was derailed by a railway union strike. Knapp was certainly aware of the strike. In early June 1961, maintenance workers demonstrating in the city of Rosario had attacked members of the WB-Larkin mission as they were touring railroad repair shops.[90] Alemann argued that many people in Argentina's governmental and military circles thought the moment was inopportune to push the unions.[91] Nevertheless, in late October 1961, when the government shut down hundreds of kilometers of railway lines and dozens of repair facilities, a longer and more violent strike erupted in Buenos Aires and other provinces.[92] Black and Knapp remained intransigent, and this tense meeting ultimately proved unsuccessful. Due to the lack of results, Frondizi wrote to Kennedy requesting his personal involvement in the negotiations with both the Eximbank and the WB.[93] Once again, Frondizi assumed that the road to WB loans passed through the White House. His assumption certainly made sense. However, rather than responding to Frondizi's request, Kennedy asked him to support Colombia's proposal to convene Latin American foreign ministers to deliberate on the expulsion of Castro's Cuba from the OAS.[94] While Frondizi talked economics and development, Kennedy was thinking Cold War politics.

On December 24, 1961, Kennedy, along with Assistant Secretary of State Robert Woodward, held a second meeting with Frondizi. The newly appointed foreign minister, Miguel Carcano, and the Argentine ambassador to Washington, Donato del Carril, were also present. Similar to the WB negotiations, the discussions focused on Argentina's railways, a subject widely viewed in Washington as a litmus test for Frondizi's new policy. Frondizi highlighted the resolution of the railroad strike and the dismissal of 40,000 railroad workers, who were compensated in full. He also mentioned the possibility of laying off an additional 40,000 workers if funds became available, unveiling an economic approach that was unconceivable in Argentina before 1958. He stressed that his government was in urgent need of funding to develop the railway system and to prove that the stringent measures had not been implemented in vain. Kennedy vaguely responded that the Eximbank expected the WB to consider a loan for the railway system.[95] Then, rather than discussing specific credits as Frondizi wished, Kennedy asked about Argentina's stance on Cuba. The meeting ended without results.

The WB's Temporary Seizure of Argentina's Development Project: The Second Loan

In January 1962, Black circulated to the EDs his recommendation on a proposed $95 million loan to SEGBA.[96] This loan was of singular importance for Frondizi's development plans, as the expansion of SEGBA through the completion of the *Dock Sud* project in the Buenos Aires province was expected to solve the energy shortages that hindered industrialization efforts. In his report, Black explained that since the first mission to Argentina in 1957, the WB had identified the development of the electric power sector, especially in Buenos Aires, as a top priority. Black's recommendations not only detailed the technical aspects of the project, but also emphasized the impact that the loan might have on the ongoing liberalization of Argentina's economy. Black stressed that a reformed SEGBA, able to meet its debt services out of its own earnings, could gradually attract private capital. This, he clarified, was important because Frondizi was ready "to return power properties to the private sector as rapidly as possible."[97]

The SEGBA loan, aimed at co-financing the completion of the *Dock Sud*'s construction, was discussed in the EB meeting of January 18, 1962. Following standard procedures, WB staff presented different aspects of the project.[98] Notably, six years after Perón's removal from power, WB staff continued to blame him for Argentina's problems. For instance, it was argued that Perón's nationalism had resulted in the expropriation of foreign-owned utilities and the founding of a state agency, *Agua y Energía Eléctrica,* that functioned purely as "a political instrument" without any "reasonably sound organization."[99] Other comments referred to the "weak economic and financial condition in which Argentina was left in 1955 by the dictatorial regime [of Perón]" and the problems that the Perón dictatorship had created in the power sector. However, the WB-WHD staff claimed, Frondizi's administration had achieved "real improvements" which justified the provision of financial assistance to the power and transportation sectors.[100] The questions that the EDs posed focused on technical matters, but also on the impact of a $95 million WB loan on Argentina's already large external debt and its deteriorating balance of trade and payments. Despite these questions, the loan was unanimously approved.[101]

After the second loan was approved, the WB gained a greater sense of authority to persuade Frondizi to implement deeper policy changes, extending beyond the stringent conditions outlined in the existing agreements. In February 1962, Black sent Frondizi a letter containing the most recent WB report on Argentina's economy. The letter focused on "fundamental economic problems," especially energy shortages and deficient transportation infrastructures, which the two valid loans were expected to alleviate.[102] As if this was not enough, Black recommended raising agricultural output and exports and called, in what became a routine admonishment, that a stop be put to "the drain on the economy from losses by state enterprises, particularly the railroads." He stressed that the WB would decide on additional loans to Argentina "only within the framework of a sound overall investment plan."[103]

On March 18, 1962, Argentina held legislative elections. Although exiled in Spain and banned from returning since the 1955 coup, Perón supported parties led by his closest allies, primarily the *Unión Popular.*

The election results were unfavorable to Frondizi, indicating that Peronism was still the dominant political force in Argentina. Without delay, the military issued an ultimatum calling on Frondizi to resign or be removed. On March 19, in light of the economic crisis, and just one day after the elections that triggered a worsening political crisis, the IMF decided to deny Argentina the right to continue drawing money within the framework of the SBA that had been signed three months earlier, arguing, supposedly neutrally, that Argentina had not fulfilled the loan conditions.[104] Undoubtedly, the IMF decision contributed to the widespread sense that a coup was imminent. Nevertheless, Frondizi's ouster had more to do with political than economic factors, such as his authorization of Peronist participation in the elections and his adoption of a pragmatic stance towards Cuba. Although Frondizi was not particularly concerned about Cold War issues, his meeting in Buenos Aires in August 1961 with the Argentine Che Guevara, Cuba's minister of industry, as well as Argentina's strengthening of commercial and diplomatic ties with the Soviet bloc, sparked harsh opposition among right-wing groups and the military and caused many of them to suspect him of communist leanings.[105] This ultimately led to his downfall.

To conclude, the initial loans granted by the WB to Argentina contributed to the growth of foreign investment in critical sectors such as transportation, energy, and oil, accompanied by a rise in the Bank's intervention in the national economy. In this sense, WB loans had what economists call a "catalytic effect," meaning that agreements with international institutions like the WB and the IMF help attract foreign investment, thereby accelerating a country's recovery during crises.[106] In any case, combined, these steps deepened the economic dependence of Argentina on powerful economic players in the Western bloc: the Bretton Woods institutions, the US administration, commercial banks, and US corporations. Even though the WB never conducted serious discussions with Frondizi regarding his *developmentalist* approach, the meetings, negotiations, and accords described above indicate that he was the right person at the right time to put WB-Argentina relations in motion. Frondizi's *developmentalism,* and certainly the more orthodox approach that he adopted as his economic team underwent personnel changes, provided ample justification for the WB to grant him loans. Moreover, fearing that the Kennedy administration would become Argentina's primary source of development assistance to the country, the Bank could no longer afford to wait. In the same vein, the WB's traditional lending portfolio and its request to rationalize the transport and energy sectors not only fit well with Frondizi's development priorities, but also helped him justify the implementation of controversial reforms. These reforms marked an initial yet significant attempt to move away from the protectionism, interventionism, and clientelism deeply embedded in Argentina—practices that US administrations viewed as incompatible with Western principles of capitalism and democracy. As explained below, the WB granted no new loans to the provisional regime that deposed Frondizi.

PART 3: THE WB AND JOSÉ M. GUIDO: FREEZING LENDING TO A WARM COLD WAR ALLY

Following the military coup of March 1962, a confrontation broke out in Argentine military circles between two main factions: the Reds, a reactionary group that perceived Peronism as close to communism and therefore aspired to be a continuation of the Liberating Revolution (1955–1958), and the more moderate Blues, who sought to pursue a limited democracy. Both factions defined themselves as anti-communist, Christian, and Western in political and cultural terms. In the battle between the two camps, it was finally decided to establish a semi-constitutional regime and to appoint José M. Guido as president. Guido, a lawyer and member of the UCR like Frondizi, had served as president of the Senate under the recently deposed president. Remaining in power until October 1963, Guido was unable to effectively stabilize Argentina's political and economic situation.[107] While the Kennedy administration repeatedly expressed its commitment to promoting democracy in Latin America, it swiftly recognized the new *de facto* regime.[108]

From the outset of his rule, Guido had no alternative but to make concessions that left power in the hands of the military. Subsequently, he annulled the March 1962 elections, dissolved Congress, retained the ban on the Peronist Party, and established an anti-Peronist and anti-Frondizist cabinet.[109] Guido adopted a distinct pro-US stance, perhaps the most decisively US-friendly stance in Argentina since the beginning of the Cold War. This included playing a decisive role in blocking Cuba's entry into the Latin American Free Trade Area (LAFTA) in August 1962, aligning with the Kennedy administration in the OAS during the Cuban Missile Crisis of October 1962, and deploying forces in the Caribbean when the US requested the region's support.[110] Kennedy did not remain indifferent to these visible expressions of partnership.[111] Economically, Guido's administration abandoned the *developmentalist* approach of Frondizi and adopted a plan that was even more in line with monetarist principles prevalent in Washington. It sought to achieve monetary stability, curb inflation, reduce the fiscal deficit, stop the devaluation of the *peso*, improve the balance of payments, and reschedule debt repayments. Guido's team was unstable, with five different economic ministers—Jorge Wehbe, Federico Pinedo, Álvaro Alsogaray, Eustaquio Méndez Delfino, and José Alfredo Martínez de Hoz—serving in succession over just 562 days in power.[112] Instability was bad news for WB-Argentina relations. As we saw in Chapter 1 and will see in the following chapters, the WB's willingness to support Argentina diminished as the country's political instability increased, regardless of the nature of the regime in power.

As noted above, at the time of the coup of 1962, the WB had granted two loans to Argentina and was, albeit reluctantly, considering a third one. However, after the coup, the WB discontinued its lending to the country, and was not to resume doing so until 1967. According to the WB, the official reasons for non-lending included Guido's failure to develop investment plans compatible with WB requests, the eruption of a financial crisis, the inability to repay external debts, and the poor implementation of the WB-supported highway project that had been approved in 1961. Despite Guido's strong alignment with the United States in the context of the Cold War and the eagerness of his team of liberal economists to cooperate with the WB—even if it meant implementing unpopular austerity measures and repressing labor movements—the Bank remained unconvinced. The WB's choice to withhold loans from Guido's authoritarian government contradicts the widespread fallacy that the Bank preferred non-democratic regimes, often mistakenly believed to be more capable of enforcing severe austerity measures than democratic governments. In practice, the determining factor had been not the type of regime but rather the economic policies endorsed by it. This does not necessarily mean that ideological affinity on economic matters alone has ever been *enough* to secure WB's assistance. The temporary nature of Guido's regime and its inability to put national finances in order were the main obstacles to WB lending.

History Repeats: Too Many Meetings, Too Little Support

The WB's interactions with Guido's administration began shortly after the coup. On April 28, 1962, Chaufournier and Schmidt, representing the WB at the annual IDB gathering in Buenos Aires, met with Alsogaray at his home on his first day as minister of economy under the new regime—a sign of the close professional and personal relationship they had built over the years.[113] They updated Alsogaray on the details of the two WB-supported projects in progress and asked him to prepare a list of additional high-priority projects. Alsogaray enthusiastically agreed and stressed that Argentina had embarked on too many projects without sufficient preparatory studies and had signed too many contracts without proper financing. Explicitly detaching himself from Frondizi's *developmentalist* priorities, he claimed that the *Chocón* hydroelectric project and other "fantasies" should be dropped. He then commented that he had accepted, once again, the position of minister on the condition that he have overall control of the economy, which meant that he served as the Minister of Economy as well as the chairman of the Economic Council (comprising the ministries of economy, labor, and public works). Knapp and Alsogaray decided that once the study of the power sector was completed, Alsogaray would ask the WB "to check the conclusions and advise the Government as to the appropriate next step."[114] When questioned about the stability of the political situation, a matter of serious concern among WB staff, and whether it was sufficient for him to implement his economic plans, Alsogaray responded by stating that he had the support of the armed forces. Emphasizing his profound affinity with WB policies, he committed himself to work on a railway rehabilitation plan because "the railroads problem had to be settled once and for all, even at the cost of a long strike." Schmidt thus recommended that a WB staff member be stationed in Argentina as long as needed to help the planning council produce comprehensive development plans.[115] The WB-WHD appears to have perceived the new regime as a window of opportunity to intensify its influence in Argentina, even in the absence of new loan agreements. In the meantime, given that the US ambassador to Argentina had been unsuccessful in convincing the State Department to support Alsogaray's financial requests, many WB personnel speculated that the minister might turn to the Bank for assistance in restructuring Argentina's foreign debt.[116] Since the WB did not allow the rescheduling of debts owed to it, as a precaution to safeguard its creditworthiness, there was no possibility that it would consent to any form of debt restructuring. Seeking to avoid default, the US Treasury granted Argentina a $50 million loan and the IMF approved a new $100 million SBA to improve the country's financial solvency—the first to the Guido regime.[117]

On July 19, 1962, Alsogaray met with Knapp and Schmidt at the WB headquarters.[118] Alsogaray assured them that he would be able to stabilize Argentina's economy within the framework of a free enterprise system and articulated his belief that President Guido was determined "to preserve both the form and substance of democracy in Argentina." Comparing Peronism to Nazism and Fascism, Alsogaray stated that the general elections scheduled for July 1963 would "be closed to totalitarian groups both of the right and the left."[119] Following these Cold War-related comments, Alsogaray referred to the *Dock Sud* project, *ACINDAR*, and the transport sector, explaining that due to Argentina's financial difficulties, investments in the railroad had been kept to a minimum. He assured them that fuel prices and bus fares had already been adjusted upwards and that railways tariffs would also be increased. He proudly announced that, with the exception of the subways, which were still government-owned, all buses and tramlines in Buenos Aires were already privatized.[120] Alsogaray clearly wished to convey to the WB staff that he was their loyal, sympathetic interlocutor in Argentina's government. Several days later, still in Washington, Alsogaray met with WB president Eugene Black.[121] Argentina, Alsogaray stated, would not embark on any new projects in the public sector until the financial situation improved and a new development plan was elaborated. He stressed that it was time for the WB to send a mission to Argentina to study the steel project and urged Black to approve the requests that Argentine private firms had already submitted to the IFC.[122]

In light of the WB's ambiguous responses, in early August, Roberto Alemann, who had assumed the role of the Argentine ambassador to Washington, extended an invitation to Schmidt for a lunch meeting at the embassy.[123] Alemann addressed the same concerns that Alsogaray had raised, particularly various strategies to reduce Argentina's external foreign debt obligations. Trying to make the WB an intermediary in rescheduling negotiations with the banking system, Alemann said that he would like to see the WB sponsoring a meeting of the chief non-US creditors immediately following the annual meeting of the Board of Governors, when all the relevant actors would be in Washington. Schmidt responded that the US government had already agreed to support Alsogaray vis-à-vis the European creditors.[124] Rejecting Alemann's request, Schmidt insisted that Argentina assemble a plan of high-priority projects and investments. Alemann replied that first, Argentina's government would have to decide on the future status of SOMISA (the state-owned steel mill that Guido's administration intended to privatize) and *Yacimientos Petrolíferos Fiscales* (YPF), the government oil company, which Guido intended to privatize as well. Several US and European private firms—including the US Steel Company, the world's largest steel producer at the time—were interested in investing in SOMISA stock.[125] Despite his best efforts, Alemann was unable to secure a promise of WB support. Interestingly and somewhat counterintuitively, the more US-friendly and orthodox the administration was, the freer the WB felt to demand deeper reforms and better economic results. What is clear is that the authoritarian character of Guido's regime did not influence the WB's decisions.

Argentina's efforts continued, but in vain. In late September, a delegation headed by Ricardo Pasman (president of the BCRA) and Alemann met with Black, Knapp, and Schmidt. Knapp maintained that the WB was concerned about the delays in the ongoing highway project. He nervously inquired as to the transfer of the fourteen municipalities from the Ministry of Power and Energy to SEGBA and complained that the decree authorizing SEGBA to import equipment and materials duty-free for the project had not yet been issued.[126] As the minutes of this tense meeting reveal, the WB's appraisal of Argentina continued to deteriorate. With a lending break already in place, the Bank did not rule out a unilateral interruption of disbursements on the two projects already in progress.

Despite the slim chance of reaching an agreement, a WB steel mission headed by Horst Eschenberg arrived in Argentina in October 1962.[127] Many parties worked to enable this mission. WB files show that several foreign companies, in particular the German company *Ferrostaal* and the US Steel Corporation, exerted pressure on the Bank staff to promote a steel loan that would allow them to buy shares of SOMISA.[128] Argentina, however, was still in the midst of a financial crisis which, in itself, was enough to block loan negotiations. In 1962, the gross national income (GNI or GNP) fell by 7 percent, and the budget deficit reached 48 million *pesos*. The private sector was suffering from severe illiquidity and numerous factories had closed down or were working at only partial capacity. In his report, Eschenberg stated that the economy suffered "a lack of direction and orientation," with virtually no planning, and urgently recommended providing technical assistance. To that end, he suggested that the IMF press Alsogaray to formalize a request for WB's technical assistance.[129] As to the study of the steel sector, the mission explained to the Argentine authorities that they "should in no way expect a commitment on the part of the Bank as a result of the mission."[130]

Meanwhile, Argentina's political and economic stability continued to deteriorate. Industrial production decreased by 9 percent and per capita consumption by 11 percent. Investments in equipment and machinery fell by 30 percent.[131] On December 10, 1962, Alsogaray was replaced by Méndez Delfino. With a new economic team in office, notwithstanding the halt in lending, the WB continued its studies and coordination with other possible sources of financing for future projects in Argentina.[132] Throughout 1963, with no new loans on the horizon, the WB continued to oversee the two projects still in progress while severely reducing interactions with Guido's administration.[133] The IMF, for its part, began to lose patience. However, fully aware that Argentina needed its seal of approval to open debt-rescheduling negotiations with the Paris Club (an informal group of official creditors, created in 1956, whose role is to find coordinated solutions to the payment difficulties experienced by debtor countries), in March 1963, the IMF approved a new SBA worth $100 million.[134] Yet, following this SBA, the IMF signed no new agreements with Argentina until May 1967. The political and economic instability gripping the country was so off-putting that both the WB and the IMF decided to take a step back from Argentina. The abandonment of interventionist and *developmentalist* policies, a fuller alignment with Washington's economic precepts, and their clear support for the US stance on Cuba and other sensitive issues—such as LAFTA and privatizations—were not enough to convince the WB to lend to Guido's regime. Ideological affinity mattered—but the WB also wanted actions, stability, and warranties.

CONCLUSIONS

The WB's long-awaited launching of lending to Argentina took place in 1961, merely two years after the Cuban Revolution of 1959, which exacerbated Cold War tensions in Latin America. This timing also coincided with President Kennedy's announcement of one of the most ambitious initiatives for the region: the Alliance for Progress. Intended to promote development as a means to contain the advance of communism in the region, the Alliance, at least in principle, overlapped with the main mandate of the WB. The growing prominence of development on the global stage, initially seen as advantageous for the Bank, eventually became a double-edged sword. The conceptualization of development aid as an instrument to build alliances and propagate a Western model of progress and modernization meant that the United States sought to grant direct development assistance at its sole discretion. The realization that the WB's performance in Latin America had hitherto fallen short of expectations led Kennedy and his advisors to step in and address what they perceived as a vacuum in the realm of development.

This US decision brings to mind the launching of the Marshall Plan in 1948, which formally rendered European countries receiving "Marshall dollars" ineligible for WB support. Although, unlike the Marshall Plan, the Alliance did not entirely supplant WB assistance, it did send a threatening message to the Bank. The Kennedy administration not only questioned the WB's capacity to fulfill its Cold War mission in the Western Hemisphere but also aimed to maintain a strategic advantage by closely controlling its options. This strategy enhanced the administration's ability to impose political conditions, such as joining US initiatives against Cuba, in exchange for critically needed development assistance.

Faced with these challenging circumstances, WB President Black initiated a comprehensive organizational reform with the goal of enabling the expansion of the Bank's operations in developing nations. Reforms encompassed the establishment of the IDA and the inclusion of new sectors in the WB's lending portfolio. Afraid of losing influence in Latin America, the WB commenced operations in Argentina—one of the largest economies in the region that could easily turn into a chronic client of the Bank. The fact that Argentina was governed at the time by Frondizi—whose *developmentalist* vision translated into concrete policies welcomed by the WB, including legislation protecting foreign investments, a willingness to pursue privatizations despite conflicts with organized labor, and a readiness to adopt IMF and WB policy recommendations—convinced the Bank that the moment had come to begin operations in Argentina. These operations, in turn, were expected to serve as a solid platform for urging Frondizi to expedite his economic reforms and strengthen ties with the US private sector. However, the WB soon encountered difficulties in sustaining a consistent pattern of interactions with a country characterized by continuous political and economic instability.

As this chapter has shown, the economic and political situation in Argentina pushed the Bank in opposing directions. On one hand, the unprecedented, albeit moderate economic liberalization advocated by Frondizi, and even more so by Guido, acted as a magnet for WB financial and technical assistance. On the other hand, the combination of soaring inflation, mounting foreign debt, political instability, and deficient managerial capabilities of the state and state-owned enterprises repulsed the Bank from Argentina. At the end of the day, neither the partial ideological affinity with Frondizi nor the pressure exerted by the United States and the Third World resulted in the Bank working against its organizational interests. The WB's management and staff found themselves zigzagging, looking for pretexts to renew and then cease lending to the country.

This chapter has highlighted the existence of shifting levels of agreement and coordination among Washington-based institutions, particularly between the WB, the IMF, and the US administration. It has also demonstrated that Frondizi, as well as his predecessors and successors, approached their relationship with the WB under the assumption that the Bank was an integral part of a broad Washington-based apparatus. Thus, meetings that took place between Frondizi or members of his government with representatives of the US administration almost always included an appeal of some sort to intercede with the WB to increase the chances of its lending to Argentina. In the same manner, discussions conducted by Argentina's representatives with WB management and staff brimmed with references to potential US and Eximbank loans to Argentina. Clearly, the existence of a WB-Argentina-US triangle was one of the basic assumptions informing the Argentine leadership when they came knocking on WB doors.

Finally, the cases of Frondizi and the authoritarian regime that followed show that although the WB did its best to operate on the basis of economic criteria alone, the establishment of fruitful bilateral ties involved more than agreements on economic ideas. Political instability in Argentina, characterized by a tragic sequence of weak democratic regimes deposed by military coups in favor of often equally unstable dictatorships, emerged as one of the main obstacles to WB lending and to Argentina's capacity to implement long-term development plans. Moreover, the fact that the two regimes analyzed in this chapter, similar to many of the regimes analyzed in other chapters, were unable to adhere to their stated economic policies posed a significant additional obstacle to the WB-Argentina-US triangular relationship. As we shall see in the next chapter, political instability in Argentina continued to worsen during the late 1960s, and the WB continued to limit its lending to the country.

3 THE WORLD BANK AND ECONOMIC NATIONALISM

DURING THE 1960S, ECONOMIC NATIONALISM emerged as a prominent source of tension in US-Latin American relations. US efforts to confront economic nationalism, whether by imposing sanctions or by co-opting leaders who advocated it, had a direct impact on the triangular dynamics that evolved between the US administration, the WB, and its Latin American borrowers, Argentina among them. Although economic nationalism was a feature of both classical populism and *developmentalism*, it took a radical turn in the early 1960s. This radicalization was translated into laws aimed at curtailing dependence on foreign capital. Of key interest to the US administration and the WB—albeit for different reasons—was that economic nationalists in Latin America were expropriating and nationalizing foreign firms. In response, Congress passed the Hickenlooper Amendment to the Foreign Assistance Act of 1962, which prohibited economic assistance to any country that expropriated US property without making restitution. The bill also called upon US representatives to multilateral organizations such as the WB, the IMF, and the IDB to vote against loans to countries that expropriated or in any other way acted against US firms operating within their territory.

By examining WB-Argentina relations during the administration of President Arturo Illia (October 1963–June 1966), known for his economic nationalism,[1] this chapter sheds light on the strategies that the WB developed to address the nationalist challenge without endangering its status vis-à-vis Argentina or the United States. This balance became increasingly difficult in November 1963, when Illia canceled the contracts between Argentina and foreign oil companies working in the country. To what extent was the WB able to navigate between US Cold War interests, the expectations of US businesses—so decisive in determining the Bank's own creditworthiness—and Argentina's need for development assistance? What was the WB's stance towards expropriations? These questions are crucial given the differing interpretations of expropriations within the WB-Argentina-US triangle. To the Bank, expropriations were considered a legitimate economic measure as long as compensations were provided. However, for the US administration, particularly under the shadow of the Cuban Revolution, expropriations were not only viewed as an economic issue but also as a sign of communist leanings in Latin America. For leaders like Illia, by contrast, expropriations had little or nothing to do with the Cold War. Furthermore, they were not seen as imitations of the large-scale expropriations carried out by Fidel Castro in Cuba, which led the US administration to regard nationalism and socialism as two sides of the same coin.[2] For Illia, expropriations were a means to attain self-sufficiency in energy, foster economic development, and achieve economic independence. While looking at the workings of the WB in Argentina under the shadow of the oil dispute, this chapter invites us to revisit questions central to a broader understanding of the role played by the WB in the Cold War in Latin America in three main areas: the promotion of liberal capitalism in developing nations, neutrality regarding the nature of the regime in power, and the WB's Sisyphean struggle to increase its autonomy vis-à-vis the US administration.

On November 15, 1963, Illia, barely one month in office, fulfilled one of his key electoral promises and voided contracts with private oil companies working in Argentina—ten for production and four for exploration. Nine of these companies were US-owned, including Esso

Argentina, Tennessee Argentina S.A., Ohio Oil Company, Pan American Argentina, and Union Oil Company of California.[3] The Johnson administration (1963–1969), in response, immediately called for the interruption of assistance to the country, including highly sought-after WB loans.[4] This US response was further triggered by the fact that, in addition to annulling the aforementioned contracts, Illia also enacted laws that were detrimental to foreign investors and firms operating in Argentina. Moreover, Illia actively sought to distance Argentina from the IMF and to diversify trading ties with countries outside the Western bloc. The signing of a barter deal between Argentina's state oil company YPF and the Soviet Union—according to which Argentina would import oil in exchange for wool, leather, and linseed oil—was particularly alarming.[5]

Illia was well aware of the pressure that the US administration was exerting on the WB to withhold lending to Argentina until the oil dispute was resolved. Seeking to keep the Bank uninvolved in this conflict, Illia's economic team avoided discussing this problem in talks with WB representatives. The WB, with the same goal in mind, adopted the same strategy and remained silent. Matters were more complicated, however. First, even if the US administration refrained from enacting the Hickenlooper Amendment, it still could use its veto power in the WB's EB to impede lending to Argentina and other administrations that expropriated US assets. Second, the WB viewed the settling of disputes with foreign companies as a central pre-condition for lending—during and after the Cold War. It was already in the early 1950s that the WB had formulated policies on two issues that would soon become prerequisites for lending: the borrower's debt repayment record and the fulfillment of international obligations, especially concerning compensation for expropriations.[6]

A wide array of primary sources, including recently declassified WB records, unveil a counterintuitive picture of the nationalist challenge in WB-Argentina-US triangular dynamics. Although the WB had good reasons of its own to address the problem of compensation, it refrained from doing so out of concern for being perceived by its borrowers as an arm of US foreign policy and Cold War goals. The WB thus evaded discussing the oil dispute not only with the Argentines, but also with representatives of the US State Department, the Eximbank, and the IDB, signaling that it could not be compelled to engage in a sensitive political issue. This strategy was somewhat straightforward to implement, as the Bank had additional justifications to support its decision not to lend to the Illia administration. These included non-compliance with certain controversial conditions stipulated in the SEGBA loan accord of 1962 and the implementation of policies that were at odds with WB efforts to reduce state intervention in the economy.

An examination of WB-Argentina-US dynamics in the 1960s sheds new light on a particular historical moment for all parties involved. For the WB, the 1960s was a time of impressive growth. During George Woods's presidency (1963–1968), the Bank's membership increased from 81 to 106 member-states, the list of borrowing nations surged from 21 to 51, and the annual count of approved loans nearly tripled, rising from 44 in 1959–1960 to 103 in 1968–1969.[7] Woods also founded a new affiliated institution of the WB Group—the International Centre for Settlement of Investment Disputes (ICSID). As its name indicates, the ICSID was an attempt on the part of the Bank's management to play a formal role in the settlement of disputes over compensations—disputes whose solution was vital in order to allow it to continue lending. This was particularly important given the wave of expropriations in Latin America and other Third World countries at the time.

From the vantage point of the United States, the 1960s was a tumultuous era. Three political assassinations rocked the country and the world—President John F. Kennedy in November 1963, Martin Luther King Jr. in April 1968, and Senator Robert Kennedy in June 1968. President Kennedy was succeeded by Vice President Lyndon Johnson, the architect of the Great Society[8] and the so-called War on Poverty.[9] Johnson sought to improve the performance of the Alliance for Progress on the one hand, while increasing US military intervention in Latin America on the other.[10] Seeking to contain the advancement of Communism in Latin America, the Johnson administration supported the military coup that deposed Brazilian President João Goulart in April 1964, the CIA intervened in the elections in British Guiana in December 1964, and US marines landed in the Dominican Republic in April 1965.[11]

For Latin America, the 1960s were characterized by increasing political mobilization. Cuba's ongoing radicalization, the proliferation of guerrilla movements, and the expansion of urban, student, indigenous, and women's movements all shaped and reflected the escalating Cold War in Latin America.[12] This was a time when democracy, considered vulnerable to communist infiltration, lost its luster not only in the eyes of military officers, but also among the local elites and middle classes.[13] This decade also saw the advent of contradictory ideas. On one hand, Dependency Theory—advanced by theoreticians such as André Gunder Frank, Enzo Faletto, and Henrique Cardoso—gained prominence in the region. According to this theory, countries in the periphery of the world economy could develop only by creating non-capitalist economies.[14] On the other hand, the National Security Doctrine (NSD), promoted by the United States, was influential, and tragically so. Inspired by the NSD, a new wave of military regimes that Guillermo O'Donnell defined as "Bureaucratic-Authoritarian states" (BAS) multiplied throughout the region. With regards to Argentina, the NSD was publicly adopted in August 1964, when General Juan Carlos Onganía, the commander-in-chief and leader of the coup that would depose Illia in 1966, publicly endorsed it.[15]

The chapter opens with a brief discussion of economic nationalism in general and Illia's independentist nationalism in particular. Then it offers an analysis of the goals and constraints that impacted the Illia administration, the WB, and their relations with the United States. The next section examines the WB's interactions with Illia's administration. The chapter shows that despite the lack of lending operations, the WB managed to exert influence on economic policy and administrative reforms in Argentina, inevitably serving US Cold War interests in the country. Yet, in June 1966, days before Illia's anticipated deposal by a military coup, the WB decided to renew lending to Argentina.

PART 1: CLASHING INTERESTS

Economic nationalism is a highly contested term in scholarship.[16] Robert Gilpin defines it as a doctrine of state-building that subordinates the economy to the pursuit of state interests. States, he maintains, whether weak or strong, always try to change the rules of international economic relations to their benefit.[17] The study of the WB's relations with its Latin American borrowers, however, shows that economic nationalism has shaped relations not only between states, but also between states and foreign banks, multinationals, and multilateral institutions, including the Bretton Woods twins.

Throughout the Cold War, every Argentine government promoted its own vision of economic nationalism. Juan Perón (1946–1955), for instance, nationalized the railways and the telephone companies by purchasing them from foreign companies and making them state-owned enterprises. In contrast, the military regime that deposed him (1955–1958), and later Arturo Frondizi (1958–1962), promoted an economic nationalism that treated foreign capital as a valued element in national development efforts. This chapter is in line with the analysis of Eric Helleiner, who claims that economic nationalism extends beyond protectionism and other non-liberal practices. It is also compatible with many kinds of economic policies, including neoliberal ones that became popular in the 1980s and 1990s.[18]

The chapter is also informed by the recent and seminal work of Marvin Suesse and his notion of the "nationalist dilemma." According to Suesse, nationalists are driven by two main motivations: isolation and expansion. Isolationism seeks to restrict the inflow of foreign influence, goods, capital, and people, thereby allowing the nation, its farmers, and merchants to prevent foreign competition. To achieve these goals, isolationists employ protectionist measures. Expansionism, by contrast, seeks to attain national economic development for reasons of national security, collective prosperity, and reputation. Achieving this requires a mix of export-led growth, foreign capital, and new technologies. For Suesse, developing policies that reconcile these two conflicting motives is what sparks the nationalists' dilemma.[19] Suesse's analytical framework provides useful tools to explore the intricacy of Argentina's fluctuating relations with the WB and the international financial community at large. Yet, given the centrality that the aspiration to reach economic independence has had in the region since it reached political independence in the early nineteenth century, and taking into consideration the emergence of Dependency Theory in the 1960s, I suggest that Illia's response to the nationalist dilemma be defined as "independentist economic nationalism." To be sure, Illia did not aim to detach Argentina from the Western bloc or to create an autarkic economy. Rather, his goal was to promote Argentina's development and economic independence. Although he rejected contractual terms that allowed foreign companies to reap excessive profits in Argentina, and refused to accept the intrusive conditions imposed in IMF and WB agreements, he did not view foreign capital as intrinsically harmful to the national interest.[20]

The dilemmas and difficulties that the WB confronted in dealing with the Illia administration transcended national boundaries. During the 1960s, Illia was not the only Latin American leader who, disappointed by the lack of economic progress under US auspices, contested US hegemony. Like many of his counterparts in the region, he expressed solidarity with the Third World,[21] resisted collaboration with the IMF, and opposed the growing intervention of US corporations in the national sphere. Remarkably, between 1968 and 1976, in twenty-two separate instances, twelve Latin American nations seized or forced the sale of US-owned companies in their territory.[22] Among the best-known cases were the nationalization of the Gulf Oil company in Bolivia in 1969 by the dictator Alfredo Ovando Candia, the partial nationalization of copper mines in Chile under President Eduardo Frei and their full expropriation by Salvador Allende in 1971, the expropriation of the International Petroleum Corp. (IPC, a subsidiary of Standard Oil of N.J.) in Peru by military dictator Velasco Alvarado in 1968, and the frequent seizure of US tuna boats by Peruvian and Ecuadorian authorities in their territorial waters.[23] The WB, for its part, endeavored to find the justification to continue lending to most of these regimes even while the US administration expected it to do otherwise.

Beyond the Bank's semi-autonomy, its operations and institutional survival were at stake. Lending operations have always been the most vital of all the WB's activities. Therefore, it is not surprising that except in the cases of Salvador Allende—the socialist president of Chile between 1970 and 1973, who refused to compensate foreign copper companies—and Illia, as long as he had not been able to resolve the conflict with the oil companies, the WB continued lending to administrations that took conciliatory steps or, at least, pledged to do so.[24] The WB, for instance, granted seven loans to Frei's administration, even though in January 1966, his government passed Law 16425 that established the purchase by the Chilean state of 25 percent of the shares of US-owned copper mines—a percentage that increased to 51 percent in 1969.[25] In the case of Bolivia, the WB (through the IDA) granted a livestock loan to Ovando Candia's regime, though only after he assured the Bank's president, Robert McNamara (1968–1981), that his administration "intends to pay adequate compensation for the nationalized properties."[26] In Peru, the WB renewed lending only after Velasco Alvarado secretly confirmed his intention to pay compensation to the IPC, thereby fulfilling WB's preconditions for lending.[27]

As elaborated below, Illia's negotiations with the oil companies were not enough to obtain WB loans. Unlike presidents Frei and Velasco Alvarado, whose readiness to solve disputes with foreign companies secured them WB loans, Illia also had to demonstrate that he was ready to comply with Argentina's previous commitments to the Bank, repay foreign debts, and implement strict economic and administrative reforms. In other words, the dispute with the oil companies was not the only obstacle on Illia's road to the Bank's negotiation table. As we will see, during his last weeks in office, as the economic situation improved, the WB decided to unfreeze lending to the country.

The Illia Administration: The Price of Independentist Economic Nationalism

Arturo Humberto Illia won the general elections of July 1963 with 31 percent of the votes as the candidate of the *Unión Cívica Radical del Pueblo* (UCRP). Elections were held while Perón's *Justicialist* Party, as well as the Communist Party, remained outlawed, and former president Frondizi was under arrest.[28] Illia and Vice President Carlos Humberto Perette, whom the US State Department regarded as ultranationalist, took office on October 12.[29] From day one, Illia's political position was precarious. Although his economic plans were intended to benefit the working class, the powerful Peronist-led unions actively fought the government, organizing strikes and factory occupations.[30] The union's activism further intensified the resentment among businessmen and industrialists, who were already opposed to Illia's economic policies, particularly those concerning wages and prices.[31]

Illia advanced two heterodox and expansionist plans: a short-term plan designed to restore monetary stability and promote consumption and growth, and a five-year National Development Plan (NDP).[32] Combined, the two plans were expected to solve the structural disequilibrium between the agricultural and industrial sectors, which Illia perceived as a major cause of inflation, and reduce foreign indebtedness from $2.6 to $2 billion within five years.[33] These goals were to be achieved through interventionist and protectionist measures such as maximum prices, exchange rate controls, and import ceilings. In order to reduce the fiscal deficit, the plans promoted tariff increases and the expansion of the agricultural sector—two measures that the WB supported. The NDP, formulated by the *Consejo Nacional de Desarrollo* (CONADE—National Council of Development) in consultation with CEPAL and prestigious economists such as Simon Kusnetz and Richard Mallon (Harvard University), had four main goals: 1) ensure the full employment of a growing population; 2) improve the real salary and general standard of living; 3) achieve a 5.7 percent growth of the GDP and a 20 percent increase of exports by 1969, as well as balanced growth across all regions in the country; and 4) help curb inflation by increasing the availability of goods and services, and improve public and private finances as a result of the increase in economic activity and more efficient administration.[34] Although Argentina's economic performance significantly improved under Illia, the plan fell short in generating sufficient financial resources to undertake major development projects without foreign assistance. So Illia's administration persisted in meeting with the Bank in the hope that eventually they would see tangible results.

Illia's independentist economic nationalism was a determining factor in his foreign economic policy. As mentioned earlier, he was successful in increasing the number of Argentina's trading partners, thereby reducing the country's overwhelming reliance on the United States and Western European countries. However, the most contentious measure he undertook was the annulment of the contracts that former President Frondizi signed with foreign oil companies in 1958. Illia asserted that he nullified the contracts due to their illegality, citing three primary reasons: they were not the result of competitive bidding, they were not ratified by Argentina's Congress, and the foreign oil companies remitted excessive profits out of Argentina.[35] The main problem, at least from Washington's perspective, was that the cancellation decrees made no mention of compensation. Instead, they mandated the appointment of a federal attorney who would be charged with initiating action to recover economic losses that had resulted from the "irrational exploitation" of the oil fields by the foreign companies, and from shortages in petroleum due to inadequate storage facilities and unpaid taxes.[36] In addition, Illia's administration established a parliamentary committee to investigate any illegal aspects of contract approvals. However, during this fact-finding period, the oil companies were permitted to continue their operations in Argentina. The special committee announced its conclusions on August 31, 1964. It determined that the contracts were effectively canceled. Not less significant, it announced that joint committees composed of representatives of YPF and the foreign oil companies would settle the disputes over compensation and that new bids would be arranged.[37] The reactions of the oil companies were varied. Tennessee and a few other companies soon reached an agreement on compensation. The largest corporations—including Shell, Transworld Cadipsa, and Union Oil—adopted a more confrontational stance. They continued arguing the annulment terms with Argentina's authorities at the same time that they successfully lobbied in Washington to enlarge the definition of expropriation under the Hickenlooper Amendment.[38] The oil companies were not alone. Lobbyists of other US enterprises operating in different sectors across Latin America—such as IT&T, the United Fruit Company, and several copper companies—also campaigned to legislate sanctions against countries where their interests were at risk.[39]

The companies' campaign in Washington was understandable. The abrupt termination of the contracts raised concerns both among US officials and private oil companies that Argentina's precedent might be replicated by more oil-rich nations such as Peru and Venezuela. As historian Dustin Walcher claims, the cancellation of the contracts sparked heated debates in the US Senate regarding the obligations of countries receiving US aid to respect US economic activities, whether private or governmental, within their borders.[40] The Hickenlooper Amendment to the Foreign Assistance Act of 1962 addressed these concerns and constituted a partial response to the massive confiscations carried out by Castro in Cuba and by the expropriation, without full compensation, of IT&T properties in Rio Grande do Sul (Brazil) in February 1962.[41] This amendment was just the beginning. The conviction that the mere threat of the Hickenlooper Amendment was a useful tool of US foreign policy led to its further revision in 1963 when the US Congress, partially in response to Illia's actions, broadened its definition of expropriation to include contract nullification.[42] With this amendment in place, the WB's ability to lend to Illia's administration was, at least in theory, nullified.

The Political Neutralization of WB Lending

George Woods, former chairman of the First Boston Corporation, one of the largest investment banks in the United States at the time, served as WB president from January 1963 to March 1968. According to Woods, lack of development was a chronic economic problem whose solution depended on the opening to foreign trade and investments—which conflicted with independentist economic nationalism prevalent in Latin America—and on the modernization and downsizing of the state apparatus. Developing countries, he argued, confronted several problems. Their exports were limited due to trade barriers, their external debt was hard to repay, and their economic and financial policies failed to support effective resource mobilization and allocation.[43] Aspiring to equip the WB to better solve these problems, Woods reshaped its lending practices and staff composition, while also enhancing coordination—though not necessarily cooperation—with the IMF and the State Department. From the perspective of Latin American member-states like Argentina, Woods did not bring with him any new medicine to cure their chronic economic ills.

Considering the Bank's strategy to steer clear of politicized issues in Latin America, such as compensations, Woods proactively worked to nurture constructive, or at least non-confrontational, relationships with economic-nationalist leaders in the region, even when lending operations were highly improbable. He likely wanted to avoid a situation in which Latin American countries perceived the WB as entirely aligned with US Cold War policies and the interests of US private firms, to the detriment of its relationship with its largest group of clients. During his speech at the inaugural meeting of the United Nations Conference on Trade and Development (UNCTAD) in Geneva, held from March to June 1964, Woods declared that the WB, traditionally opposed to postponing debt repayments by its member-states, was ready to refinance loans already sanctioned for a "few countries now caught in an acute cash squeeze." Although Woods did not specify which debtors were under consideration for debt adjustments, many speculated that he was referring to Brazil (whose annual repayments to the WB reached $15 million a year) and Argentina (due to problems in its balance of payments). Concessions, however, were not unconditional. Woods clarified that the WB would contemplate adjustments to members with long-term obligations only if they refrained from accumulating substantial short-term debts to other lenders.[44] He also stated that it was imperative to help developing countries escape their "overdependence on the export of primary goods," which the Latin American nations had been saying for decades. Woods acknowledged that achieving modernization and economic development necessitated a vigorous local industry alongside a dynamic agricultural sector. However, diverging from the prevailing *statist* and nationalist ideas in Latin America at the time, he argued that industrialization should be achieved through private investments, national and foreign. Since the WB had always seen the private sector, and certainly foreign firms and investors, as key actors in development efforts, its punitive stance on expropriations was aimed at granting foreign actors the warranties needed to invest in Latin America. The WB typically granted only a fraction of the funds needed to advance development projects, so it relied heavily on partnerships with private firms that finance and execute the projects. As discussions between Argentina and the WB over international bidding indicate, the WB had a longstanding preference of working with foreign or, namely, US companies and contractors.

As noted, under Woods, there were high expectations for the *techno-cratization* and neutralization of the Bank's decision-making process. When Woods became Bank president, some twenty economists could be counted among the institution's staff. By the end of his term, their number had surged to two hundred, with the total staff count reaching approximately eight hundred members. One of Woods's most pivotal appointments was Irving S. Friedman, who transitioned from his role as the director of the IMF's Exchange Restrictions Department to become the first economic adviser to the WB president.[45] Friedman's responsibilities included supervising the new Economics Department, which rapidly became the second-largest department in the Bank. He also held key roles as the director of Special Economic Studies and overseer of the Economic Program Department, the Computing Activities Department, and the Development Research Center. As 25 percent of the Bank's staff were economists, Woods could portray their decisions as professional and unbiased. From a constructivist perspective, staffing procedures and professional training lead bureaucrats to develop their own policies and preferences, with international organizations evolving into autonomous centers of authority due to their bureaucracies' legitimate authority and control over expertise.[46] In his professionalization of the WB staff, Woods aimed not only to improve its decision-making processes and establish economic and neutral lending criteria but also to bolster the Bank's reputation among its borrowers and its autonomy from the United States.

According to Woods's directive, in addition to the Loan Committee's review (which focused on the economics of each project), every loan proposal was scrutinized by the Economic Committee (which discussed the economics of the borrowing country) before being presented to the EB for a vote.[47] In Illia's case, it was the Economic Committee that, in June 1966, approved a new lending program to Argentina based on the country's economic performance. As elaborated later in this chapter, this decision appeared, at least outwardly, to be detached from Argentina's political crisis.

Last, Woods placed significant emphasis on aid coordination. The proliferation of consultative groups led by the WB increased, and coordination with the IMF was further systematized.[48] Woods also expanded coordination with the US administration, which, autonomist aspirations aside, has always been crucial to the Bank's financing. Interactions with members of the US administration, and particularly with the State Department, undermined the Bank's assertions of political neutrality and likely heightened the probability that its staff would become more aware of, and ultimately serve, US Cold War interests. During the Bank's formative period, it was mostly staffed by former US government officials who brought the values and worldviews that they had internalized in their previous jobs. Naturally, then, the Bank's bureaucrats would have been interested in these joint meetings. Coordination with the US administration took place in mutual visits at the WB headquarters and the State Department, located within walking distance from each other, as well as in multiorganizational forums. One of them, created in August 1963 by President Kennedy, was the Inter-American Committee of the Alliance for Progress (CIAP). The CIAP was a multilateral organ of the Inter-American Economic and Social Council of the OAS, whose mandate was to review, on an annual basis, the economic policy, plans, and performance of countries receiving Alliance assistance.[49] CIAP reviews were generally attended by representatives of the country in question, as well as by high-ranking staff of the WB, IMF, USAID, and the IDB. Like all other Bank presidents, Woods sought to navigate between the Bank's need to secure good relations with its main principal and its desire to portray itself as an autonomous and reliable institution. Results were mixed.

PART 2: THE NATIONALIST TRAP

The initial interactions between Illia's team and the WB staff occurred shortly after the July 1963 general elections. Following Illia's invitation,[50] John Loftus, an economist from the WB-WHD, met the president-elect in Buenos Aires. Striking a pessimistic tone, Loftus stated that the economic indicators were insufficient for a well-grounded assessment of

Argentina's economy. He also expressed concern about the slow progress of the highway project that the WB approved in 1961.[51]

Nevertheless, he noted, the Bank was content with the outstanding performance of the ongoing WB-supported SEBGA project initiated in 1962. Wasting no time, Illia asked about the assistance the Bank was prepared to offer Argentina. Loftus responded, in a professional and apparently neutral manner, that the unfavorable ratio between debt repayments and the value of exports rendered Argentina ineligible for additional WB credit. Perhaps seeking to prepare the ground for future bilateral cooperation, he noted that the Bank might be ready "to play some major coordinating role in the management and adjustment of the existing [foreign] debt."[52] Given that Illia had not yet revealed the economic plan he intended to implement upon taking office, Loftus refrained from committing to initiating loan negotiations.

Illia, keen to access needed WB development funds, assured Loftus that CONADE would soon present a detailed investment plan in line with the WB's requests and working standards. Illia's priorities were to increase exports and expand energy and transport infrastructures—areas that were at the core of the WB lending portfolio. Loftus responded that, as a prerequisite for lending, the railways and *Agua y Energía* (AyE), both state enterprises, needed to improve their technical and administrative capacities, for which the WB might agree to provide technical assistance. According to Loftus, Illia's response was that although he recognized the limitations under which the WB operated, "[he] begg[ed] [the Bank], [. . .] that [it] would not invoke too stringently [its] banking and economic norms."[53] This comment can be understood in at least two ways. The first echoes the plea from Latin American countries for the WB to adopt a more flexible approach towards developing nations. The second interpretation is that Illia was concerned that the imminent cancellation of oil contracts would be used to justify non-lending to Argentina. If this was the case, Illia expected the Bank not only to remain politically neutral but also to abandon its well-established practice of rejecting loan requests coming from countries that refused to pay compensations to private firms operating in their territory. Illia's expectation that the WB would avoid political considerations and focus on Argentina's overall economic performance was reasonable, particularly given Woods's emphasis on economic criteria. Additionally, Illia likely understood that the Bank's policy on disputes arising from expropriations or contract annulments left the institution some maneuvering room. Notably, the Bank recognized that nations have the right to conduct expropriations, which in themselves were not necessarily a barrier to WB lending. Problems arose when governments refused to negotiate compensations. Thus, if a government expressed its intention to negotiate compensations, and if its economy was in good shape, the WB would approve loans. In the case of Argentina, the hiatus in WB lending during the 1960s started not with the contract's annulment in November 1963 but in 1962, due to the poor economic situation in the country and Argentina's failure to comply with the conditions stipulated in previous agreements.[54]

Concerns among WB staff and, more broadly, in Washington circles grew following Illia's inauguration in October 1963. These concerns were fueled by the nationalist and *statist* positions held by several of Illia's most influential ministers, notably Eugenio Blanco and Félix Gilberto Elizalde, as well as by the newly appointed president of the Central Bank, Bernardo Grinspun.[55] Illia, however, pragmatically adopted different positions towards each of the Bretton Woods institutions. He unilaterally reduced the IMF's contentious role in Argentina, canceling pre-arranged IMF missions and breaching obligations outlined in the last SBA signed by the previous regime.[56] However, he also promoted reforms aimed at bringing the design and implementation of a comprehensive development plan in line with WB standards. For instance, in November 1963 and January 1964, echoing WB recommendations, he passed two decrees that facilitated the reorganization of the Technical Secretariat of the National Development Board.[57] In light of the delays in the implementation of the already approved SEGBA project, however, these decrees did not convince the Bank to lend to Argentina. While the WB-WHD waited to see whether Illia would fulfill his electoral promise concerning the oil contracts, the WHD's staff outlined a strategy to proceed with non-financial operations in the country. Among other ideas, it began contemplating the possibility of creating a comprehensive mission or a series of small missions tasked with studying Argentina's external debt, offering recommendations on the economic policy that the new administration should pursue, and helping to formulate a program for public investments.[58] Clearly, the WHD had no intention of curtailing its operations in Argentina.

Notwithstanding the goodwill of both the Bank staff and Illia's economic team, tensions between the parties began to emerge in mid-November 1963. On the surface, these seemed unrelated to the oil crisis. Not wishing to be caught in the crosshairs between Illia, the oil companies, and the Johnson administration, the WB did not mention the oil conflict in meetings with the Argentines. Illia, hoping for Bank neutrality, also kept silent on the issue.

What the WB did was raise other obstacles for lending, all of them procedural, starting with Argentina's non-compliance with certain conditions stipulated in the SEGBA and railroads loan agreements of 1962. The most controversial of those conditions were the transfer of assets located in the fourteen districts of Greater Buenos Aires to SEGBA's control, sharp tariff increases, the sale of SEGBA's shares (which meant its partial privatization), and the appointment of SEGBA's top officials which required, as specified in the loan agreement, WB's prior consent.[59] In December 1963, Woods contacted Blanco and urged him to comply with the SEGBA agreement. Blanco responded that while the issue would be reconsidered, Argentina would ultimately have the final say.[60] Woods then sent a warning letter to Illia stating that a satisfactory resolution of the problems related to the SEGBA loan was a prerequisite for any additional assistance to the country.[61] In other words, although the WB management sought to maintain an appearance of non-involvement in the highly politicized oil conflict, its non-lending to Illia's administration served US Cold War interests. While the immediate interests and motivations of the WB's management and staff and the US administration differed, their actions were mutually reinforcing. Even when the Bank refused to grant new loans to Illia's administration, thereby allegedly aligning with the US administration's anti-Illia stance, the decisive factor was not Washington's ability to impose its preferences on the WB but rather internal WB policies and lending terms. Of course, in some cases, such as the requirement to pay compensation to expropriated US firms, WB and US policies coincided.

In mid-February 1964, Knapp, Loftus, and Mario Piccagli (WB Public Utilities Division) visited Argentina.[62] Upon their arrival, Knapp held a press conference at the airport, a sign of the great expectations that potential WB loans raised in Argentina.[63] Meetings with Blanco and high-ranking officials focused, however, not on potential loans, but on unresolved problems regarding SEGBA's rates, the transfer of the fourteen municipalities to SEGBA's responsibility, and the WB's right to veto the appointment of SEBGA's executive vice president—the most interventionist clause of the 1962 WB loan agreement.[64] Soon after Knapp's visit to Buenos Aires, an Argentine delegation visited the WB headquarters in Washington. During a meeting with Woods, Minister Elizalde conveyed optimism, most likely influenced by Woods's announcement at the UNCTAD assembly about flexibility for highly indebted Bank member-states. Responding to Woods's questions about the foreign debt, which stood at around $2.6 billion at the time, Elizalde emphasized that he intended to pursue debt rescheduling. He stressed that projected payments to service existing debts would amount to about $500 million in 1965, $400 million in 1966, and $250 million in 1967.[65] Woods evasively responded that any economic development program required the endorsement of the IMF, with which Illia's administration had no intention to collaborate.[66] The meeting, like the previous one in Argentina, ended without results.

The WB's Political Neutralization of the Oil Conflict

From the beginning, Illia's administration signaled that it intended to settle the disputes caused by the annulment of the oil contracts. Anxious to attract foreign investments and protective of Argentina's reputation for honoring its debts, Illia stressed that he was prepared to repay capital invested by nine US oil companies whose contracts he had annulled.[67] These were by no means empty words. By January 1964, Facundo Suárez, President of YPF, had begun talks with the oil companies whose multimillion-dollar contracts were canceled two months earlier.

Negotiations on new contracts advanced well at the time, particularly with two US-owned companies, the Cities Service Company and the Tennessee Gas Transmission Company of Houston, as well as with the Italian Company Ente Nazionale Idrocarburi. Other companies had already presented their answers to the government's legal actions against them, and the rest were still working on their responses.[68] However, given the violations of the SEGBA agreement and the delays in the railroads project, the WB refrained from considering new loans.

As time passed and the oil conflict remained partially unsolved, the WB found itself increasingly isolated in its attempts to maintain a neutral stance amid the crisis in US-Argentina relations. The US administration, meanwhile, grappled with the old dilemma of whether to pursue a hard or flexible line towards Argentina. Although the State Department sought to avoid an overt conflict with Argentina, it was reluctant to "leaving relations entirely to discussions between private oil companies and the Argentine Government."[69] Additionally, there was concern that imposing economic sanctions might intensify domestic opposition to Illia, potentially triggering a military coup against him. Furthermore, there was the added risk that US sanctions could be counterproductive, exacerbating anti-Americanism and economic nationalism in Argentina. Due to these and other considerations, the State Department was leaning towards a middle-ground approach. Such an approach meant refraining from invoking the Hickenlooper Amendment, which, in principle, left the WB room for semi-autonomous action. It also implied retaining the flexibility to "quietly reduce aid, including military assistance."[70] In any case, as expropriations of US assets became a popular practice in the region, the US administration and the WB recognized that any decision regarding Argentina could influence the actions of more important oil producers in Latin America and the Middle East.

Many Washington-based institutions faced dilemmas in their relations with Illia. Their positions were colored by their composition—whether exclusively US or regional and multilateral institutions. This heterogeneity became particularly evident in May 1964, when David Knox (WB-WHD) took part in a meeting organized by the recently established Inter-American Development Assistance Coordinating Group, consisting of representatives from the State Department, USAID, Eximbank, IDB, IMF, and the WB. The delegates of USAID and the Eximbank, both US institutions, were, naturally, in full accord with US foreign policy. They stated that they were not contemplating any significant business in Argentina as long as the oil conflict remained unresolved. The IDB representatives, as could be expected in a regional organization, were the most supportive of Argentina's requests.[71] Similar discrepancies regarding assistance to Argentina were observed two months later, when Knox attended another multiorganizational meeting to present an updated WB report on Argentina's development plan.[72] Although the WB sought to relegate the oil expropriation to near-invisible status, the reality remained that, much like US-owned financial institutions, it did not contemplate any loan proposals for Argentina, claiming this was based on technical and impartial grounds. Notably, even if the Bank had decided to grant loans to Illia's administration, it would have faced the almost insurmountable challenge of overcoming the US executive director's veto at the EB. Hence, even without invoking the Hickenlooper Amendment, the US administration could still constrain the WB's already partial autonomy.

Despite these adverse financial circumstances, the Illia administration, maintaining that the cancellation of oil contracts was a legitimate economic decision, sought sources of foreign financing. Independentist nationalism did not blind Illia to Argentina's economic needs. In late June 1964, in light of the undeclared but factual halt in WB, IMF, USAID, Eximbank, and US lending, Elizalde (President of BCRA) and Roque Carranza (Director of CONADE) headed a mission to Washington, Western Europe, and Japan for talks on assistance needed to finance Argentina's five-year economic plan. The mission expected to persuade the WB to undertake the coordination of all creditors.[73] Apparently, the Argentines believed that the WB was impartial enough (or more than all other institutions) to serve as mediator and successfully navigate among contradictory interests of all parties involved. Remarkably, this mission took place shortly after Blanco's announcement of nationalist and protectionist economic measures that were at odds with the WB's efforts to promote a free-market economy. The new measures included restrictions on the use of imported spare parts in the automotive industry and the approval of special credits for national companies that reduced their reliance on imported raw materials. These measures were accompanied by legislation that reflected the government's commitment to promote economic independence and a more socially oriented domestic economic policy. This encompassed the 1964 Supply Law, aimed at ensuring the availability of basic products at reasonable prices; the Minimum Wage Law of June 1964, intended to secure a fair income for all workers, particularly the poor; and the Law of Pharmaceutics of August 1964, which mandated state control over prices and all activities related to the production, import, and commercialization of medicines by the pharmaceutical industry, most of which were in foreign (mainly US) hands.[74] Seen in this context, Argentina's nullification of oil contracts was by no means an anomaly. Rather, it was a crucial feature of a broader shift towards independentist economic nationalism and self-sufficiency in energy and other critical sectors.

Despite the lack of significant progress in negotiations with the WB, and with undeclared US economic sanctions against Argentina still in effect, bilateral interactions continued to take place both in Washington and Buenos Aires. While Argentina hoped that these talks would ultimately pave the way to WB loans, the WB strove to gain time. In early August, following an exploratory WB-WHD mission which discussed the status of the 1965–1969 development plan with CONADE, two additional WB missions arrived in Buenos Aires.[75] One was an eight-week-long mission focusing on economic matters, while the other, led by Knox, was slated to help CONADE in formulating an investment program and was scheduled for three months.[76] The fact that the WB maintained its influence over Argentina's economic policy and development programs even in the absence of new lending activities explains why, from its standpoint, buying time was not considered a waste of time. It also attests to the efforts made by WB staff to remain active. However, from Argentina's perspective, this interim period without loans had unfavorable consequences. On September 8, for instance, Knox wrote a disparaging report in which he argued that discussions with Argentina's Federal Council of Investments had been "abortive" because it was "incapable of producing any data beyond 1961."[77] He also claimed that although several state agencies had prepared investment programs in the areas of transport, power, and fuel, their respective financing plans were partial, unclear, and at times nonexistent.[78] The mission, which remained in Buenos Aires and continued to advise Argentina's economic team, recommended that the WB's highest authorities take any new loan considerations off the table.[79]

In the meantime, the WB continued its meetings with the State Department. A look at US-WB bilateral meetings about Argentina unveils a somewhat ambivalent picture. On one hand, as Henry Hoyt—director of the Office of Argentine, Paraguayan, and Uruguayan Affairs—told Knox on December 23, 1964, the State Department (like Argentina's administration) saw the Bank as a privileged and useful actor in relations with Illia's administration. He realistically explained that, as a multilateral organization, the WB was better positioned than US officials to handle Illia's nationalism.[80] On the other hand, however, the US State Department disapproved several actions that the WB took because they clashed with its own stance towards Illia.

For instance, in January 1965, Anthony Solomon (Assistant Secretary of State for Economic Affairs), Palmer and Bloomfield (State Department), Oakes (Eximbank), and Constanza (US Treasury Department) visited Gerald Alter (Director WB-WHD, 1964–1970) to discuss the draft of the WB economic report on Argentina.[81] Solomon raised three main objections. First, he noted that the report did not explicitly state that improved economic performance and policies were necessary preconditions for debt rescheduling. Second, he argued that the document gave a misleading impression by suggesting an overall rescheduling of 85 percent of all government debt due in 1965, which included $75 million to the IMF, $18 million to the US Treasury, and $5 million to US private banks. Third, Solomon expressed concern that the report made far-reaching recommendations on the postponement of debt repayments until 1970. Alter brushed off Solomon's criticism and assured him that as far as the WB was concerned, satisfactory economic performance was a key precondition for debt rescheduling.[82] This was obviously true.

Solomon seems to have read the WB report as a sign of the WB's initial rapprochement towards the Illia administration. In February 1965, just one month after the completion of the report on Argentina, the WB began to consider potential projects.[83] As detailed in the next section, it did not take long for other Washington-based institutions to loosen up their stance towards Argentina. The ongoing improvement in Argentina's economic performance and Illia's constructive negotiations with the oil companies left no further "neutral" reasons to postpone lending to Argentina.

Between Economic Nationalism, Economic Performance, and Political Instability

In light of the improvement in Argentina's economy and the government's endeavors to reach an agreement with the oil companies whose contracts Illia had annulled, in 1965, several institutions began a restart of operations in Argentina. In February, the Eximbank approved $20 million for two steel projects in Argentina (SOMISA and Santa Rosa).[84] In the meantime, the IDB, which continued to be the most pro-Illia organization, granted Argentina two loans worth $15 million each, one to the industrial sector and the other to the Argentine Industrial Bank.[85] On March 5, 1965, representatives of the WB, IMF, IDB, USAID, and US State Department (but not of Argentina) attended another CIAP meeting in Washington, in which Knox played a more prominent role than in previous consultations.[86] Two weeks later, Knox contacted USAID representatives in Buenos Aires to ask about the US attitude towards Argentina. They explained that some US bankers and businessmen were frustrated by financial restrictions in Argentina and were therefore "opposed to any official U.S. assistance to [the country] at [the] time."[87] They also told Knox that the US government was not considering new loans to the country due to the oil contracts situation.[88]

In late March, Knox held two meetings with Elizalde and Pugliese. In these meetings, a slight improvement in the WB approach towards Argentina became apparent. The parties agreed that the WB would dispatch three missions: one to assess the ACINDAR steel project, another to obtain an update on SEGBA's situation, and the last to evaluate a potential agriculture-related project.[89] Knox made it clear that in light of several delays in the execution of the SEGBA project and the wage increases that Illia had recently approved, Argentina could not expect new WB loans in the near future. As in prior bilateral meetings, no mention was made of the oil contracts. In the meantime, the triumph of the *Unión Popular* (a political party made up of Peronists who could not run under the umbrella of their own *Justicialist* Party because it was still banned) in the legislative elections of March 14, 1965, as well as Illia's refusal to join the OAS forces in the Dominican Republic as the Johnson administration expected, further debilitated his political legitimacy at home and abroad, and, therefore his capability to obtain new loans.[90] Conditions in Argentina thus continued to be unfavorable for WB lending. On one hand, the country's economic indicators were improving, and negotiations over oil contracts were progressing positively. On the other hand, Argentina had still failed to fulfill its obligations under the loan agreements signed in 1962. In addition, political instability—which the WB, as a rule, perceived as an impediment to lending—was on the rise. As explained below, aware of Illia's fragile political situation, the WB became increasingly pessimistic about his ability to resolve conflicts with the labor unions or fulfill the WB's loan conditions.

In May 1965, Woods accepted an invitation from Argentine Ambassador Norberto Barrenechea to visit the country. This visit, to be sure, clashed with the US anti-Illia stance. The WB-WHD briefing prepared for his trip stated that the most delicate issue in relations with Argentina was the cancellation of the oil contracts and the unresolved matter of compensation to the foreign oil companies.[91] This statement further underscores the WB's efforts to remain impartial in the oil dispute. The WHD staff viewed the oil conflict as a significant factor in their dealings with Illia's administration, yet they consistently avoided discussing it with Argentina's and US representatives. Unveiling the challenges that the WB confronted at the time, and its growing focus on economic parameters, the briefing additionally recognized that during its first fifteen months in office, Illia's government accomplished a notable 8 percent increase in real income and a reduction in unemployment.

The document also highlighted inflation, challenges in repaying external debts, and a substantial increment in petroleum imports as Argentina's most pressing economic problems. The surge in imports, which was attributed to the annulment of oil contracts, led to a drain on foreign exchange earnings.[92] As the briefing stressed, WB's operations were lagging behind. The WB staff considered that the low levels of disbursements on the highway loan that was approved in 1961 were the result of "*Vialidad*'s administrative inefficiency." The delays in the project were so significant that a WB transport mission recommended that the loan be canceled. In any case, the SEGBA loan, despite various unresolved problems, was proceeding as planned.[93]

In mid-May, already in Buenos Aires, Woods and Schmidt met Pugliese and the Central Bank management. In what appears to have been a mere courtesy meeting, Woods stated that he had "no specific business to cover," which was a diplomatic way to say that no loans would be negotiated.[94] Then, Woods and Schmidt met Illia, Pugliese, and other ministers.[95] Woods began by highlighting positive aspects of Argentina's economy, particularly the increase in tax revenues and the raising of utility tariffs, mainly the telephone, power, railroad, and subway. He then addressed more controversial issues. First was Illia's wage policy, which, so Woods claimed, pushed up costs and prices. Second was the need to limit the supply of money and credit if the government aimed to control inflation. Third was the importance of permitting the exchange rate to adjust to ongoing changes in the Argentine cost-price structure. Woods stated that as long as Argentina persisted in accumulating deficits on the railways, the WB would refrain from engaging in discussions regarding any new loan requests.[96] The Argentines were notably concerned about the significant railway losses and understood the importance that the WB attributed to the reorganization of the railway system. Hence, when Woods was still in Argentina, the Minister of Public Works and Services announced that he would present, in forty-five days, a detailed plan to reactivate and rationalize the railways.[97] Exerting pressure on Illia, Woods criticized the government's attempts to avoid conflict with powerful unions when seeking to reduce budget deficits. According to Schmidt, Illia responded that his team would seek to solve the railroad problem, suggesting that this would involve, at the very least, tariff increases. Woods, rather than promising to consider new loans, expressed concern about the stalled implementation of the WB-supported highway and SEGBA projects.

Towards the end of the meeting, Woods referred, for the first time in bilateral talks, to the impact of the oil dispute on WB lending. He chose his words carefully, remarking that "he would not say that settlement with the oil companies would be a prerequisite for Bank lending to Argentina but he would say that if the matter were settled it would make some of the World Bank's directors feel more comfortable."[98] While WB management and staff were not conditioning lending on the resolution of the oil disputes, the politicized EB would not give its consent to lend to Argentina until the disputes with foreign oil companies were settled. Woods was most probably referring to the US executive director, who could use his *de facto* veto power to prevent the WB from acting against US interests. This makes sense as other Latin American member-states that were at the time conducting expropriations of foreign assets would surely have supported lending to Argentina, and expected reciprocity. Pugliese responded that an agreement with the powerful US companies Esso and Shell would likely be reached in the near future.[99]

Despite the improbability of receiving WB financial assistance, in June 1965, Pugliese launched a National Development Plan. The plan was designed "to achieve, within a framework of growing monetary stability, a high and sustained growth in national production, as well as to solve the structural problems that have impeded the economic development of the country for years [. . .]."[100] As Pugliese explained, the plan was "compatible with free private initiative" which shared, with the state, the responsibility to promote economic growth.[101] The plan also referred to the reform and rationalization of the railways, which was a constant source of friction with the railway worker unions (and the WB).[102] The cost of the plan was estimated at $1.74 billion, of which $1 billion would come from the private sector and only about 10 percent of the total would be provided by foreign creditors and investors.[103] Given the improvement in Argentina's economic performance, and the progress in debt rescheduling discussions, it was not unrealistic to assume that Argentina could recruit the funds needed to put such an ambitious plan in motion. Illia's representatives successfully concluded a round of negotiations to refinance $300 million of Argentina's debt to Western European nations, Japan, and the United States. IMF and WB representatives, as had by now become routine, participated in all negotiations and helped Argentina reach an agreement with the Paris Club.[104] This time, even the WB consented to a modest postponement of $6.7 million in repayments due in 1965, compared with the IMF's agreement to reschedule $67 million of debts owed it.[105] At the end of the negotiations, the creditors agreed to reschedule 60 percent of Argentina's foreign debt—a significant achievement of the Illia administration, which promised a certain degree of financial stability.[106]

The WB's Hypocrisy

When it seemed that the WB and Argentina had reached a loan-less *modus vivendi,* Illia's team continued to press the WB to open loan negotiations. In late August 1965, San Miguel, Argentina's new ED to the Bank, called Knox to discuss the status of WB operations in Argentina and asked about a potential road loan.[107] Although Knox's response was generally discouraging, he did acknowledge that the decision by *Vialidad* (the government agency in charge of roads and railroads) to change the consultants it worked with appeared to be a step "in the right direction." This is significant because, as Knox stressed, he had sent *Vialidad* the contact information of two consultant firms that were acceptable to the WB.[108] Simply put, as it did during the Peronist era, the WB—despite mutual disagreements with Argentina and the absence of lending activities—continued pushing the country to implement economic reforms and promote the shift in mentality it sought to achieve among developing nations. This is noteworthy because working with foreign consultants was at odds with Illia's economic nationalism. Illia's administration, then, was ready to take important steps in order to please the Bank and access its development funds.

In early September 1965, economist Irving Friedman, one of the most influential members of the WB management at the time, visited

Argentina, Brazil, and Chile. The visits to Brazil and Chile were easily justifiable. In February 1965, with the military in power since April 1964, the WB renewed lending to Brazil after a six-year break. Following Friedman's visit, WB lending to the country saw a substantial increase. In 1966 alone, for example, the WB extended Brazil seven loans.[109] In Chile, Friedman met with President Eduardo Frei Montalva, a member of the Christian-Democrat Party. Though he showed no socialist leanings, he launched a moderate land reform and a so-called "*Chileanization* of the copper industry"—a sector that had been dominated by US private firms.[110] Despite these interventionist and nationalistic steps, taken between 1965 and 1970, the WB granted Frei's administration seven loans. Unlike the oil contracts, which Illia unilaterally canceled, the issue of compensation was irrelevant here because Chile bought shares in the mining companies. The visit to Argentina was a different story. Friedman's gloomy report on the country's economy underlined expectations of continued inflation, wage increases, and capital flights.[111] According to Friedman, state enterprises, particularly the railroad, "continue[d] to be a mess." He expressed concern that, despite the advanced stage of negotiations, agreements with the oil companies had not been finalized. In meetings with Illia, Pugliese, and Elizalde, Friedman claimed that economic recovery could not succeed without the goodwill of the business community and without good relations with the IMF, the WB, and foreign creditors and investors. He believed, correctly, that Argentina's business community had little confidence in Illia's government, and so did not expect any significant economic improvement in the near future.[112] The question thus arises: why did Friedman include the country in his itinerary in the first place? One possible explanation is that, in line with Woods's stance, he wanted to avoid offending Illia and sparking tensions with one of the largest economies in Latin America. Another possibility is that he wanted to create the impression that WB lending could soon be resumed, using this as leverage to pressure the administration to continue to implement economic and administrative reforms in *Vialidad* and SEGBA and resolve the ongoing disputes with all the oil companies. Moreover, by imparting a sense that lending would resume, the Bank could portray itself as a neutral institution, rejecting the punitive stance taken by the United States towards a regime that made independentist economic nationalism its guiding principle. In any case, the visit was futile.

In mid-November 1965, another WB mission, staffed by Murray Ross and Hans Wyss, visited Argentina to review its economic and financial plan for 1966.[113] The mission's report indicated that the GDP target of at least 5 percent, set in early 1965, had been met. There was a notable increase in agricultural production and manufacturing output, particularly in the automotive industry. Construction, primarily in the private sector, was also experiencing growth, and unemployment rates had declined from 8.8 percent in July 1963 to 4.6 percent by late 1965. The petroleum sector, grappling with the repercussions of the oil disputes, exhibited the weakest performance, with a 2 percent reduction in output compared to 1964.[114] The trade balance for 1965 was $20 million short of the $300 million surplus projected at the beginning of the year. Estimates from the Central Bank indicated a 35 percent increase in the cost of living during 1965 and wage increases of approximately 36 percent. According to the mission, Illia's team acknowledged that its wage policy was the weakest element in the 1965 financial program. In an effort to tackle this issue, the government announced that, in 1966, all public sector wage agreements would be capped at a maximum average increase of 15 percent—a measure expected to encounter resistance from the Peronist unions.[115] In sum, as the WB report confirmed, Argentina's economy was showing signs of recovery, and the government was becoming more willing to enact unpopular measures, such as those concerning wages.

The economic recovery was not felt on the streets of Argentina. By late 1965, the prevailing feeling among Argentines was that the country was on the brink of another military coup. In stark contrast to the mood on the domestic front, however, Washington-based institutions such as Eximbank saw in the improving economy a window of opportunity to de-freeze lending to the country. Not only was Argentina's economy recuperating but, as US Secretary of State Dean Rusk stated, Illia's administration was proceeding in good faith with oil negotiations—which meant that "the Hickenlooper amendment [was] not being violated in letter or spirit."[116] A key obstacle to lending for the WB and other financial institutions had been removed. Nevertheless, it was only in early March 1966 that the WB began to contemplate resuming operations in Argentina. With this goal in mind, the WB dispatched a new economic mission to Buenos Aires, which recommended proceeding with loan negotiations.[117]

In early 1966, in an attempt to prevent an economic crisis stemming from massive debt repayments in the upcoming months, and seeking to placate opponents at home, including the military, Argentina requested financial assistance from the IMF. This request conveyed a message of pragmatism, if not of a gradual abandonment of independentist economic nationalism. Under these circumstances, and following assurances from Pugliese that he would promote the liberalization of the exchange market, the IMF granted authorization for Argentina's Central Bank to purchase $30 million.[118] This, the smallest amount ever transferred to Argentina by the IMF, represented an almost automatic purchase of dollars within the framework of the so-called "gold tranche."[119] Nonetheless, it signaled the beginning of a bilateral rapprochement that went beyond the IMF itself and encompassed other Washington-based institutions.

Even more significantly, in March 1966, the WB Economic Committee deliberated on a new report on Argentina and Friedman deemed the country creditworthy for a modest $15 million livestock loan. He also instructed the committee to review Argentina's creditworthiness for potential loans for SEGBA and ACINDAR.[120]

In light of this significant shift in the WB's attitude towards the Illia administration, Knox and Roger Chaufournier, Deputy Director of Operations (WB-WHD), visited Argentina in April.[121] In June, the WB-WHD handed Friedman a detailed report on Argentina's economic policy that could serve as the basis for future loan discussions.[122] Within this context, Alter, head of the WB-WHD, determined that Argentina was creditworthy for loans to the areas of livestock, energy (SEGBA), and steel (ACINDAR). He also said that a satisfactory economic performance during 1967–1968 could make Argentina eligible for additional lending for high-priority projects of about $100–130 million annually.[123]

However, in light of the rumors flooding Argentina about an imminent military coup, one wonders about the good faith with which Alter and Friedman and their staffs engaged in these discussions. As we have seen, political instability has consistently hindered WB lending.

On June 9, 1966, the Economic Committee reconvened to discuss the WHD's economic report. Besides Friedman and other committee members, Jorge del Canto (Head of the IMF-WHD) was present.[124] The committee concluded that the country's economic and financial policies for 1966 "were along the right lines" and therefore they would consider lending to the country in 1967.[125] This was, or could have been, good news for Illia. The question, however, concerned the true motivation or urgency behind the decision to renew lending to Argentina, especially considering that Illia's overthrow seemed inevitable. To begin with, it should be stressed that the many meetings that WB staff had held with members of the State Department left no room for doubt—the WB staff knew that Illia's political era was about to end. In the first week of June 1966, for instance, Edwin Martin, the US ambassador to Argentina, and the State Department exchanged correspondence regarding the approaching coup. They assumed that, considering US support for the coup in Brazil in 1964, Argentina's military probably anticipated a similar response to theirs.[126] Given that, as previously mentioned, the WB staff met on a regular basis with members of the State Department, it is reasonable to assume that they discussed Argentina's political situation. Moreover, in the first days of June, reports about looming political upheaval began to appear in the US media, including in leading newspapers like *The New York Times*.[127] It was thus impossible that WB staff were unaware of the risks they were incurring when they decided to restart lending to Argentina. It seems that by feigning political neutrality and attempting to avoid accusations of not supporting Illia's democratic regime when it most needed international backing, the WB was seeking to safeguard its own reputation. Moreover, by opting to renew lending at a time when signing loan agreements was practically impossible, the Bank was laying the groundwork for the resumption of lending after the coup. Ironically, Illia's efforts to reach a compromise with labor unions—a fundamental aspect of a democratic society—were viewed as problematic by the Bank's team (and also by the US administration, but for Cold War reasons). However, this does not mean that the WB preferred to collaborate with dictatorial regimes. As argued in this book, during the Cold War, the Bank did not hold any specific preference for either democracies or dictatorships. The years of activity in Latin America in general and in Argentina in particular taught the Bank that there was nothing more stable in the region than political instability.

Less than three weeks after the WB's Economic Committee decided to resume lending to Argentina, Illia's government suffered a significant political setback while attempting to pass a budget proposal in Congress. Beyond causing financial difficulties, the setback underscored the fragility of Illia's political situation. On June 27, 1966, just one day before the coup, US Ambassador Martin, accompanied by other representatives of the State Department, met Alter and Knox at the WB headquarters.[128] As if nothing extraordinary were happening in Argentina, Martin asked about the WB's position on the *El Chocón* hydroelectric project. Without addressing the question, Alter asked Martin if he could explain the political urgency that Argentina's government attached to the project. Martin responded that the governing Radical Party placed a high value on the success of the project. Perhaps subtly pointing to the military regime that was expected to take power soon, Martin added that the project also appealed to the military, which viewed the development of Argentina's Patagonia as a crucial strategy to prevent encroachment by the Chileans on the disputed southern border between the two countries.[129]

On June 28, 1966, Illia's government was overthrown. Illia was opposed by the trade unions, political parties (including factions within the ruling party), the military, the media, the agricultural export sector that opposed the government's involvement in regulating beef prices, and the Industrialist Association (UIA), which opposed the minimum wage bill.[130] The military, for its part, presented itself as a modern, professional, and more capable alternative to the Illia regime.[131] News of a Castroist guerrilla group in the Northern Province of Salta (led by Che's ally, the Argentine journalist Jorge Massetti), along with the increasing radicalization of the Peronist-dominated labor unions, served as additional pretexts for the army to seize power and adopt a fierce anti-communist and anti-Peronist stance. It also led the armed forces to adopt the US-supported NSD, which became a central component of the Cold War in Latin America.[132]

Criticism of Illia aside, his attitude towards the WB and the IMF—along with acts such as the annulment of the controversial oil contracts, the passage of the minimum wage bill, the launch of a development plan, and refusal to dispatch armed forces to Santo Domingo—show him to have been unafraid to take political risks which he believed could secure Argentina's political and economic independence.

CONCLUSIONS

Shortly after assuming office in October 1963, and setting forth an independentist nationalist economic policy, President Arturo Umberto Illia annulled contracts with foreign oil companies, refused to negotiate new conditional accords with the IMF, and passed a series of laws that were aimed at restricting the impact of foreign capital in Argentina's industrial sector. Under the shadow of the Cuban Revolution and Castro's widespread expropriations of foreign assets, among them US banks and influential firms like the United Fruit Company, the US administration identified Illia's economic nationalism as a critical Cold War matter. In order to compel Illia to compensate the oil companies, the US administration applied economic sanctions against Argentina. The sanctions, which were not publicly announced, included suspending US direct assistance to the country and halting multilateral aid from institutions where the United States held a dominant position. The WB, whose development loans Illia was particularly eager to access, was among them.

The US stance posed a serious challenge to the WB. On one hand, the Bank could not allow itself to be perceived by its main clients as an arm of US Cold War policy, particularly at a time when expropriations of foreign firms were on the rise in Latin America. Doing so would have sparked concern that disappointed borrowing states would rescind membership—as Poland did in 1949 when the Bank, succumbing to US pressures, interrupted loan negotiations with Warsaw. On the other hand, the WB could not support Illia's loan requests because the Bank had always conceived the payment of compensations to expropriated firms as an inviolable prerequisite for lending. Aware of this state of affairs, Illia's administration refrained from discussing the oil dispute with WB staff and management. As a close examination of WB-Argentina interactions unveils, the WB used its principle of political neutrality in two main ways: first, to resist US pressure to escalate the oil dispute and openly repudiate it, and second, to remain engaged and influential in Argentina even in the absence of financial operations. This approach proved to be a prudent one, as the WB's own subsistence depended on both financial contributions from the United States and the willingness of its borrowers to enter into conditional loan agreements with it.

As this chapter has shown, the WB was partially able to distance itself from sensitive Cold War issues, such as conflicts with US private enterprises, because it had strong technical and ostensibly neutral reasons to render Illia's administration ineligible for lending. These reasons included Argentina's non-compliance with agreements that had been made with the WB and were still in force, substantial wage increases in the public sector, and a series of protectionist and nationalist measures aimed at restricting the freedom of action of foreign companies operating in the country. In effect, it was the resolution of these issues, alongside the settlement of the oil conflict in May 1966, that led to the decision to resume WB lending to Argentina. By refusing to lend to Illia until then, the WB had, albeit reluctantly, aligned itself with the US administration's retaliatory stance towards his nationalist government. In mid-1966, when Illia's regime settled the disputes with the oil companies, the WB moved to reward Argentina by approving a lending program to the country and, once again, found itself fulfilling US expectations. The nuanced portrayal of the WB's endeavors to pursue its own interests rather than acting as an agent of its strongest principal reinforces this book's argument that the WB was neither fully independent nor merely a tool of the US administration, but rather a semi-autonomous institution. To be sure, although the Bank withheld financial assistance from Illia as the US expected, it also engaged in intense bilateral interactions with his administration, including an official visit to the country by the WB president. In other words, autonomy, and in this case semi-autonomy, cannot be judged solely based on WB lending or non-lending.

The WB's decision to restart operations in Argentina only when Illia's government reached an accord with the oil companies highlights the institution's role in the economic Cold War in Latin America. It underscores its impact as a promoter of Western economic liberalism, as well as a facilitator of the expansion of US business abroad. Furthermore, it shows that, in addition to being motivated by the needs of its borrowers and the will of the United States, the Bank responded to pressures from other lending institutions with whom it competed for influence in Latin America. The WB learned lessons from past mistakes in Argentina, where its neglect created a void in development assistance that was filled by other institutions with partially overlapping mandates, in particular the Eximbank, the IDB, and the Alliance for Progress.

As we shall see in the next chapter, with a military regime installed in Argentina, the WB finally resumed lending to the country. The intransigence of the WB regarding this regime would come as a surprise, given its own liberal economic policy.

4 THE WORLD BANK AND AUTHORITARIANISM

FOR ROBERT MCNAMARA, WHO SERVED as US Secretary of Defense (1961–1968) and then as President of the WB (1968–1981), development and security were fundamentally intertwined with Cold War issues.[1] As he stated in a speech delivered in May 1966:

> "In a modernizing society security means development. Security is not military hardware, though it may include it; security is not military force, though it may involve it; security is not traditional military activity, though it may encompass it. Security is development, and without development there can be no security. [. . .] But by emphasizing that security arises from development, I do not say that an underdeveloped nation cannot be subverted from within, or be aggressed upon from without, or be the victim of a combination of the two."[2]

Less than a month after McNamara delivered these words—though unrelated to his speech—a military coup in Argentina deposed President Arturo Illia and established the self-proclaimed "Argentine Revolution" (1966–1973). Upon seizing power, the military dissolved the national Congress, provincial legislatures, and political parties. They replaced all provincial governors and members of the Supreme Court, took control of the universities, applied censorship, sought to dismantle labor unions, and enacted additional repressive measures. In contrast to past military regimes, including the Liberating Revolution (1955–1958), the leaders of the "Argentine Revolution" rejected the label "provisional" and announced their intent to maintain power indefinitely. Argentina's modernization and development demanded detailed mid- and long-term planning and, therefore, time. As Onganía claimed, development should not be seen as a mere technical and economic process that relegates to the sidelines social, cultural, and spiritual problems. The transformation of Argentina's economy required a disciplined society, order, and security.[3] As a result of the professionalization process the Argentine military had undergone in the 1960s (with US guidance and financial support), the senior military echelon perceived itself as the sole entity capable of improving the nation. Following the model of the dictatorship established in Brazil in April 1964 and guided by the infamous National Security Doctrine (NSD)—which encompassed concepts of the state, geopolitics, counterinsurgency warfare, development, and security[4]—the regime, like McNamara (though not influenced by him), maintained that national security and development were two sides of the same coin. The heads of the Argentine Revolution contended that communism, guerrilla movements, and social unrest were all rooted in underdevelopment. In pursuit of development, the military adopted two complementary strategies. Domestically, they fought a bloody war against what they identified as subversive "internal enemies" allegedly associated with international communism.[5] This war not only targeted political parties, labor unions, and universities, but also extended to areas central to the WB's lending portfolio which had the potential to stimulate development and draw a significant workforce, thereby reducing unemployment. This included promoting industrialization, mechanization of the agricultural sector, and the construction of large infrastructure projects.[6] Internationally, the leaders aimed to tighten ties with foreign capital. They viewed the WB and the IMF not only as providers of financial aid and international legitimacy, but also as Western institutions whose professionalism, working norms, and efficiency Argentina needed to emulate and adopt for its modernization efforts.[7] To what extent did the shared understanding of the link between security and development, so central to Latin America's Cold War since the Cuban Revolution, influence the WB's decisions regarding Argentina? How did the Bank navigate the challenge posed by an authoritarian regime that enforced its policy prescriptions while simultaneously employing brutal repression against those impacted by them? What were the factors that led the Bank to adopt a stricter stance towards the economically liberal military regime compared to the Peronist administration that followed? To what extent did the WB's stance towards both regimes align with US Cold War priorities? Was this a case where the WB's and US's stance on Argentina fully coincided?

This chapter addresses these questions as it explores WB's complex interactions with Argentina between 1966 and 1976. This period comprised two main phases. The first opened with the military coup of June 29, 1966, which ousted President Illia and installed the Argentina Revolution. It ended with the election of the Peronist Héctor Cámpora as president on March 11, 1973. During these years, Argentina was governed by a pro-Western and authoritarian regime that was determined to contain the advancement of communism, eliminate the last vestiges of Peronism, and liberalize the economy. The second phase covered the so-called Third Peronism, which extended from the investiture of Cámpora on May 25, 1973 until March 24, 1976, when President Isabel Perón was overthrown by a military coup. Recently declassified files from the WB archives and other primary sources unveil an ambivalent picture of WB-Argentina-US dynamics during this turbulent period in Latin America's Cold War. To begin with, and contrary to what could be expected from an institution that, since the mid-1960s, put social concerns high in its agenda, the WB acknowledged but remained indifferent to the authoritarian character of the Argentine Revolution.

Despite the regime's systematic use of repressive methods, surpassing those of previous dictatorships, neither the Bank's politicized EB nor its professional staff reconsidered the WB's neutral position towards the country. Like in previous and later periods, the political neutrality enabled the WB to play a proactive role in Latin America's economic Cold War by supporting administrations, such as the Argentine Revolution, that strove to pursue economic liberalization, downsize the state apparatus, privatize state enterprises, reduce the fiscal deficit, and increase the influence of foreign capital and investors. Nevertheless, despite shared economic ideas and alignment with the Western bloc, these factors alone were not enough to ensure continuous access to WB assistance. As political instability grew and fulfilling WB commitments became harder, the Bank ceased lending to Argentina.

Between 1966 and 1976, when the fear of Castroism swept across the region, Argentina's military was not the only one that, prompted by the Pentagon, prepared itself for counter-revolutionary war. Amidst widespread fear of communist infiltration, a series of military coups unfolded across the region, including three in Argentina (1962, 1966, and 1976), one in Peru in 1962, and others in Ecuador, the Dominican Republic, and Honduras in 1963. Additionally, coups took place in Brazil in 1964, Bolivia in 1964 and 1971, and Chile and Uruguay in 1973. Hence, examining the triangular dynamics between the WB, Argentina, and the United States during these tumultuous years invites us to reconsider three understudied and interconnected issues with implications beyond Argentina's borders. The first relates to the widespread but erroneous view that the WB preferred military to democratic regimes. Although the WB extended seven loans to the dictatorship and none to the Peronist administration that followed, its relations with both regimes were equally ambivalent. The second issue refers to the Bank's semi-autonomy and the influence that the US administration could exert on an institution whose president had always been a US citizen, in which only the US enjoyed *de facto* veto power, and whose staff was largely composed of US nationals and/or professionals trained at US universities. If we are to judge by Argentina's case, the appointment of McNamara as WB president, a political figure who moved from the Pentagon directly to the WB, did not necessarily result in greater Bank alignment with US Cold War goals. Notably, during the period from 1966 to 1976, there was a relatively low level of US interference in WB-Argentina relations. The third point concerns the idea that Argentina, like other Latin American nations, exhibited greater agency in its relations with the WB and the international financial community at large than its economic dependence may have warranted.

For Argentina, as noted, the 1966–1976 period was marked by political instability, polarization, and violence. The Argentine Revolution, which lacked a coherent and consensual economic plan, had three consecutive presidents and seven ministers of economy. Instability continued with the transition to democracy. The short-lived presidencies of Héctor Cámpora, Raúl Lastiri, Juan Perón, and Isabel Perón brought back ministers that reinstated old populist policies, but also introduced young economists who advocated alternative plans, closer to the monetarist principles promoted by the Bretton Woods institutions. The opening towards foreign capital, however, was not enough to access WB funds.

For the Bank, this was a time of impressive growth. Under McNamara, the Bank's staff grew rapidly, credits to low-income countries more than quintupled, and loans to mid-income countries increased from $847 million in 1968 to $8 billion in 1978.[8] However, lending to Latin America relatively declined, mostly because McNamara prioritized support to the underdeveloped countries of Asia and Africa. Though McNamara strove to increase the WB's autonomy, the Bank remained dependent on voluntary contributions by its wealthiest members, especially the United States, and on selling bonds in capital markets, mainly Wall Street. From 1973 onward, however, a domestic recession, the Watergate scandal, President Nixon's resignation in August 1974, the oil shocks of 1973–1974, escalating opposition to the Vietnam War, and the US withdrawal from Vietnam in March 1973 made Washington—especially the US Senate—increasingly reluctant to support the WB.[9]

In terms of the US administration, its overall Latin American policy reverberated its determination to avoid Marxist contagion. This included US support of both democratically elected and military regimes, as long as they were anti-communists. Additionally, as elaborated in Chapter 3, during the 1960s and early 1970s, Washington was concerned about the seizure of US property in the region.[10] In March 1972, with the aim of stopping expropriations, US Congress passed the González Amendment—an updated version of the 1962 Hickenlooper Amendment that tied US assistance to the protection of US overseas assets.[11] It required the US president to instruct his representatives to international financial institutions, including the WB, to veto loans to countries that expropriated US investments without compensation. Actions taken by President Alejandro Agustín Lanusse's regime (March 1971–May 1973) against Swift International, a US meatpacking company in Argentina, and Juan Perón's declarations on potential nationalizations certainly prompted US concerns.[12] As this chapter aims to show, the US administration, grappling with internal challenges, opted to decrease direct financial aid to Latin America and instead prioritize its relations with the Soviet Union and China during superpower détente. Likewise, it dedicated less attention to WB-Argentina relations.

To better understand the WB's zig-zagging relations with Argentina during this period, the chapter first outlines the interests of the parties involved. Next, it reconstructs the fluctuating relations between the Bank and the right-wing, economically liberal Argentine Revolution. Finally, it analyzes the intense, if ultimately fruitless, negotiations between the WB and the Third Peronism.

PART 1: CLASHING INTERESTS?

The World Bank: McNamara's New World (Bank) Order

Former Secretary of Defense Robert McNamara had been appointed WB president in April 1968 by President Lyndon B. Johnson (1963–1969), on George Woods's recommendation. He would serve in this capacity until June 1981. Unlike previous Bank presidents, all of whom came from the world of banking, McNamara began his career at the Ford Motor Company. In 1960, he was appointed president of the company, a post he held until 1961, when he accepted then-President John F. Kennedy's invitation to join his government as Secretary of Defense. From the moment of his arrival in Washington, McNamara showed himself to be a devoted Cold War warrior and an enthusiastic proponent of international development and foreign assistance, which he considered important tools in the US strategic arsenal.[13] He brought these ideas to the Bank, where he formulated a more comprehensive vision of development.

Influenced by the bitter experience of the Vietnam War,[14] McNamara also brought to the Bank the conviction that the threats of violence and warfare in developing countries demanded resolution. He believed that communism was intimately tied to poverty, with the despair and hopelessness it caused driving people to choose violence and armed conflict.[15] Under McNamara's leadership, then, existing ideas about social needs, standards of living, and poverty alleviation were explicitly embedded into WB's mission.[16] The Bank's expanding agenda, in turn, served as justification to increase the size, function, and influence of its bureaucratic apparatus. McNamara's first goal was to grow the Bank's financial resources and staff, and to reduce the power of its inherently politicized EB. The staff grew from 767 in 1968 to 1,654 in 1973, 2,000 in 1976, and to over 5,700 in 1981.[17] Like Woods before him, McNamara hired many economists, including Hollis Chenery (who replaced Irving Friedman as the Bank's Chief Economist), a former professor of economics at Harvard University who had worked for USAID throughout the 1960s.[18] McNamara also redesigned the Bank's administrative procedures by establishing, in 1968, the Programming and Budgeting Department, which aimed to entrench the use of statistics in the WB. In that same year, the WB introduced the Country Program Paper (CPP), which served as the basis for the design of five-year lending programs.[19] After a first wave of reforms, in 1972, McNamara hired McKinsey & Company to recommend further changes, resulting, among others, in the establishment of five regional departments.[20]

As for lending, during McNamara's term, the IBRD (the WB's institution focusing on middle-income countries like Argentina) and IDA (the WB's affiliate devoted to low-income countries) approved, co-financed, and supervised some 1,600 projects in over one hundred borrowing nations.[21] IFC commitments to the private sector increased from $50.4 million in 1968 to $111.8 million a year by the end of the 1970s.[22] One of McNamara's main accomplishments was the diversification of the Bank's lending portfolio. Since its inception, the WB had focused on financing economically oriented infrastructure projects. However, McNamara also introduced support for socially oriented projects in areas such as medium- and small-scale agriculture, education, health, and water supply.[23] In September 1973, at the WB and the IMF Joint Board of Governors meeting in Nairobi, Kenya, McNamara announced the Bank's "War on Poverty" as well as its Rural Development Strategy (RDS).[24] In addition, since McNamara considered excessive population growth to be a significant contributing factor to poverty and underdevelopment, many WB loans during this period supported birth control and family planning programs.[25] As historian Patrick Sharma claims, in addition to being based on the Cold War perception of poverty as a security threat, McNamara's anti-poverty strategy was also a means to confront growing criticism being leveled by developing nations against the WB and the US-centered economic order it promoted.[26] This criticism paved the way to the adoption, on May 1, 1974, of the Declaration for the Establishment of a New International Economic Order (NIEO) by the UN General Assembly.[27] The NIEO called, among other things, for an increase in the voting power of Third World countries in multilateral organizations like the WB and the IMF, something that Latin Americans had been demanding since the 1950s.[28] Additional demands focused on the role of the state in promoting economic growth, international aid flows, the regulation of multinational corporations working in developing countries, preferential treatment for developing-country exporters in international markets, the creation of an international fund to stabilize commodity prices, debt relief through a moratorium on debt payments, and poverty alleviation. Following the NIEO resolution, developing nations expected the WB to introduce some of these elements into its agenda. McNamara, however, deemed the requests too politically charged and consequently declined to integrate them into the Bank's objectives.[29] The war on poverty, as noted above, was the only exception.

McNamara faced criticism from both the WB's borrowing member-states and the United States. Under Nixon's administration (1969–1974), US efforts to influence the Bank's lending decisions became more systematic. The US Congress passed legislation conditioning and eventually restricting US financial contributions to the Bank.[30] Simultaneously, in June 1971, Henry Kissinger, National Security Advisor and Secretary of State under President Nixon, issued National Security Study Memorandum 131, directing that loans already in the pipeline within US agencies and multilateral institutions could proceed until the US government completed a study on the policy to be adopted towards countries that expropriated US assets without fair and proper compensation.[31]

In January 1972, National Security Decision Memorandum 148 directed the Secretary of the Treasury to "use the influence of the United States with the management of the World Bank to induce the Bank to effectively apply its stated policy on compensation [. . .] on withholding assistance to countries not taking reasonable steps to meet compensation obligations in cases of expropriation." Moreover, it instructed the Treasury and State Department to seek the deferral of new loans in multilateral institutions and to abstain or vote negatively if a vote was required.[32] In March 1972, as mentioned, the US Congress passed the González Amendment.[33]

McNamara initially assumed that the Bank could count on Nixon's support, but this proved not to be the case—likely because, on a number of occasions, he took positions that seemed to contradict those of the United States. For example, in 1971, McNamara refused to withdraw loan proposals for Guyana and Bolivia, which had expropriated US companies without compensation. However, the Bank's US ED vetoed both proposals.[34] During the 1971 South Asian crisis, when India entered into war against Pakistan, a US ally, McNamara, backed by several executive directors from Third World nations, outvoted the US, and the Bank continued lending to India. Later, however, the Nixon administration—while never losing control over the Bank's policy towards India and Pakistan—managed to freeze WB loans to India while swiftly directing funds to keep Pakistan afloat.[35] In short, during the early 1970s, the Bank more than once sought to ignore US instructions, though with mixed results. Nevertheless, as was already mentioned, WB's operations in Argentina during 1966 and 1976 did not lead to tensions in WB-US relations, and WB's actions and non-actions hardly contradicted US expectations.

Argentina: Between the National Security Doctrine and the Return of Peronism

Upon taking power, the Argentine Revolution was supported by the Catholic Church and Catholic organizations like the Opus Dei, important figures in the media and the press, members of landed elites, industrialists, and even Perón from exile. The military remained in power for seven years with three different presidents: former Commander in

Chief of the Army, Juan Carlos Onganía (June 1966–June 1970), General Marcelo Levingston (June 1970–March 1971), and General Alejandro Agustín Lanusse (March 1971–May 1973). The military was split into two factions: one, led by Lanusse, leaned liberal, while the other, to which Onganía belonged, was nationalist, Catholic, pro-fascist, and Francoist.[36] Unlike Illia's independentist nationalism, the dictatorship's nationalism asserted that Argentina needed to integrate more effectively into the global economy to realize its full potential. This did not imply, however, that Argentina should restrict its trade and financial connections to the Western bloc only.[37] While the regime expected the US government and its related financial institutions, the WB among them, to provide it with financial assistance in recognition of its Cold War stance, Onganía's team was careful to send the message to the US administration that Argentina should not be taken for granted.[38]

Although under the shadow of the Cuban Revolution the United States grew increasingly inclined to support authoritarian and democratic regimes that displayed pro-Western tendencies, it took the US administration more than two weeks to officially recognize Onganía's regime.[39] During the Johnson administration (1963–1969), there were reservations about Onganía's team. However, the turning point came with the appointment of the orthodox economist Krieger Vasena in January 1967. A pivotal moment in the bilateral rapprochement between the United States and Argentina was the enactment of the Hydrocarbons Law 17.319 on June 23, 1967. This legislation, exceeding US expectations and erasing every remnant of Illia's oil policy, granted preferential treatment to US oil companies at the expense of the state-owned company YPF.[40] This rapprochement, however, was fragile. Even while the Nixon administration (1969–1974) viewed Onganía's regime as anti-communist and close to US values,[41] bilateral relations soon deteriorated, especially after Onganía refused to adhere to Washington's plans to de-nuclearize Latin America. Relations worsened further under Lanusse when an economic crisis in the United States pushed Argentina's agricultural-export sector to look for new markets in the Soviet Union and its Eastern European satellites.[42]

Onganía and his successors had, in principle, good prospects for securing WB support. Although the regime's economic team was heterogeneous, it was keen, notably under Minister Krieger Vasena, to adopt the orthodox models that the WB and other Washington-based institutions promoted.[43] Yet common ground between the WB and the Argentine Revolution extended beyond specific economic measures. It also encompassed a shared commitment to state reform and the adoption of working norms prevalent in developed Western countries and promoted by the Bretton Woods institutions. This involved prioritizing planning and the *technocratization* and depoliticization of economic affairs. The regime established what political scientist Guillermo O'Donnell termed a bureaucratic-authoritarian state.[44] It was *authoritarian* because it considered liberal institutions associated with democratic systems incompetent, and because the war against the enemy from within was inexorably violent. The Bank, as mentioned, tried to ignore this central aspect of the regime. The Argentine Revolution was *bureaucratic* because Argentina's "unpostponable modernization" required that the management of the economy and of state affairs be based on technical, scientific, and allegedly de-politicized and de-ideologized criteria[45]—which coincided with the WB's efforts to promote development and modernization among its borrowers.

Onganía was overthrown by opposing factions of the armed forces on June 9, 1970. In order to stabilize the economy, appease the workers, and end strikes, the new president, Alejandro Lanusse, implemented an expansionary plan which clashed with the WB's policy recommendations. To finance the plan, he requested between $500 million and $1 billion in economic aid from the Nixon administration, threatening to turn to the Soviet bloc for help if US assistance was not forthcoming. On Kissinger's recommendation, the US administration did not offer Lanusse direct financial assistance, suggesting instead that Argentina apply to the IMF and the WB for loans.[46] This approach to foreign aid was not exclusive to Argentina. Following the actual termination of the Alliance for Progress with Johnson's invasion of the Dominican Republic in 1965, US financial aid to Latin America was dramatically downgraded. Peaking at $888 million in 1966, it plummeted to just $190 million by 1977.[47] It is worth noting that the reduction of financial assistance to Latin America should not be read as US disapproval of military regimes, which the US identified as legitimate Cold War partners. As Nelson Rockefeller, Nixon's special envoy to the region, claimed in 1969, the military regimes that seized power in Latin America in the 1960s were not comparable to the old-style dictators. In fact, he claimed, they were necessary to secure stability and prevent radicalization—something that democratic governments proved incapable of doing.[48]

PART 2: THE WB AND THE MILITARY REGIME: NEITHER FRIENDS NOR FOES

The WB's relations with Onganía's government started a month after the coup d'etat of June 1966. Initially, efforts were concentrated on resuming lending activities that had been suspended since January 1962, when President Frondizi was in power. The first official interaction—a meeting between Argentine Ambassador to Washington Álvaro Alsogaray, Angel Caram (financial counselor at the Argentine embassy), Burke Knapp (WB Vice President of Operations), Gerald Alter (Director, WB-WHD) and David Knox (WB Projects Department)—took place in late July.[49] Alsogaray admitted that the military still lacked an economic program. Nevertheless, he maintained, all parties agreed that the basic goals were to curb inflation, solve the railway problem (which caused serious economic losses), and raise energy and transport tariffs. Aware that several days before the military takeover the WB had decided to renew lending to Argentina, Alsogaray requested that the WB-WHD continue to advance with several projects already under consideration. Knapp and Alter responded positively but clarified that before presenting any loan proposal to the EB, they would need to evaluate the economic measures taken by the government. Alsogaray, in an attempt to justify the absence of a well-designed economic policy and to demonstrate that the new regime merited WB assistance, handed Knapp a memorandum explaining Argentina's recent political developments.[50] The document depicted the Argentine Revolution as a departure from three decades of *statism*, interventionism, and totalitarianism and stressed that the armed forces were preparing themselves to fight against an eventual Castro-Communist attack.[51] This first meeting was symptomatic of the bilateral dynamics that soon evolved between the parties. While the WB staff used economic criteria to postpone lending, Alsogaray sought to use Cold War arguments, particularly the anti-communist and anti-Peronist nature of the regime, to access WB funds. Notably, Alsogaray employed these same Cold War rationales in discussions with officials from the US State Department, a more suitable venue for such political claims than the WB. For instance, while meeting with Lincoln Gordon, Assistant Secretary of State for Inter-American Affairs, Alsogaray claimed that the military had no choice but to intervene in light of Argentina's deteriorating economy, the shift towards socialism, and a possible Peronist victory at the polls.[52]

Two weeks later, Alsogaray and Caram paid a second visit to Alter. They urged him to dispatch a mission to Argentina in October and revealed their plans to soon request two loans—one for a livestock project and another one for SEGBA.[53] Obviously, the presence of a WB mission in Argentina and the approval of loans after over four loan-less years could be interpreted as an official endorsement of the military regime by the Western bloc. For all these reasons, the Argentines were keen to access both loans. Hence, Luis Gotelli, Secretary of Power and Fuels, met Woods, Knapp, Alter, and Knox and asked them to increase the value of the SEGBA loan proposal from $50 to $70–75 million. Despite Knapp's rejection of Gotelli's request, they all concurred that any potential energy loan, akin to the SEGBA loan approved in January 1962, would require prior consultation with the WB staff regarding the appointment of SEGBA's vice president and general manager, as they "should be mutually acceptable to the Bank and SEGBA."[54] Since SEGBA's appointments had been an ongoing cause of friction between the WB and Illia's administration, Gotelli's consent marked a clear departure from the independentist economic nationalism of the deposed administration—a policy shift that would be further crystalized with the Hydrocarbons Law of June 1967. It also reflected the bureaucratic mindset of the regime. Discussions then turned to labor relations, which both the WB (due to economic reasons) and the US administration (due to concerns over communist infiltration) had always considered a high priority in negotiations with Argentina. Gotelli argued that there was no justification for the Argentine Revolution if it were unable to resolve the labor problem. Moreover, he promised to reduce SEBGA's personnel by 10 percent (about 2,500 workers) within ten months. The parties also referred to the situation of the railways and to the as yet not entirely resolved conflicts with the foreign oil companies.[55]

As time went on and Onganía struggled to formulate a cohesive economic strategy, the WB grew increasingly worried about the internal divisions within Argentina's government. Ideological disagreement became evident to Alter when he met the Minister of Economy and Labor, Jorge Néstor Salimei, a liberal businessman and fervent Catholic, and the President of Argentina's Central Bank, Felipe Tami, who supported a gradualist approach to inflation.[56] Yet, while meeting Woods, Knapp, and Friedman, Salimei asserted that an economic plan acceptable to the WB would soon be announced.[57] In light of this assurance, a WB mission made its way to Argentina.[58] Alter reported from Argentina that the economic performance in 1966 fell far short of WB expectations, thus providing no grounds for initiating loan negotiations.[59] WB lending to the Argentine Revolution was, in any event, out of the question given the State Department's determination that no new loans would be granted to Argentina until disputes with all oil companies were all settled. This included the potential enactment of the Hickenlooper Amendment and the consequent US negative vote on WB loans to Argentina.[60] During a conversation between former Ambassador to the United States Roberto Alemann and US Ambassador to Argentina Edwin Martin, Alemann blamed the State Department for the delays in WB lending. Despite Martin's denial of this accusation, Alemann remained steadfast in his position.[61] Undoubtedly, Alemann did not believe that the WB was an autonomous institution.

Seeking to reach a consensus over economic policy, so crucial to attracting foreign aid and investments, in January 1967 the orthodox economist Adalbert Krieger Vasena replaced Minister of Economy Salimei.[62] This appointment was well received among Washington circles.[63] In March 1967, the new minister announced the first Stabilization and Development Plan for 1967–1969. The plan's main components were privatizations, fiscal austerity, a reduction of the monetary expansion, the end of the deficit of public enterprises, and reforms of the state administration. Reflecting the heterogeneity of Onganía's team, the plan also contemplated several heterodox measures, such as a freeze in wages and salaries and the signing of a price agreement between the government and large industrial firms.[64] While launching the plan, the military regime, following NSD principles, warned the Peronist-led General Confederation of Labor (CGT) that strikes and protests would be considered a threat to national security and would not be tolerated. Initially, the CGT opted to collaborate with Krieger Vasena. This cooperation, however, ended abruptly in mid-1968 when workers resumed salary demands. The same applied to certain sectors of the business community and the most reactionary factions of the military and media, whose initial support of Onganía soon turned into critique. The opening to direct foreign investments, they claimed, would lead to a denationalization of the economy, especially in the industrial and banking sectors.[65] They were right. Under Onganía's rule, a series of local companies were acquired by foreign corporations which, from a Washington perspective, was a promising step. For instance, the tobacco company *Massalin y Celasco* was acquired by Philip Morris, and *Imparciales* by Reval. The *Banco Argentino de Comercio* became the Chase Manhattan Bank, and Citibank bought up *Banco Argentino del Atlántico* and *Banco de Bahía Blanca*. The automobile plant *Acinfer* was taken over by Ford.[66]

With Krieger Vasena's program in place, Alter traveled to Argentina. His visit coincided with an IMF mission that was negotiating a new SBA worth $125 million aimed at supporting the stabilization plan.[67] Based on the data Alter obtained from the IMF mission, and the favorable impression left on him by Krieger Vasena, he concluded that the moment was propitious to resume lending.[68] Following the approval of the Hydrocarbons Law in June, there were few impediments to moving forward. Moreover, the WB and IMF extended an invitation for Krieger Vasena to serve as chairman of their joint Board of Governors for 1968–1969—an honor bestowed upon only a select few Latin Americans.[69] This honor was just the beginning. In 1974, Krieger Vasena joined the WB as director of the WB's Country Programs Department in charge of operations in several Latin America countries. In February 1975, McNamara appointed him WB Regional President for Latin America, replacing Gerald Alter.[70]

In tandem with the growing optimism about WB's operations in Argentina, relations between the US administration and the military regime somewhat improved. In April 1967, President Johnson and Walt Rostow met Onganía, who assured them that the Argentine Revolution was working "within the framework of a democratic system" and that "Argentina's main problem [was] political and not economic."[71] Although this claim was debatable, the State Department considered that "Onganía's anti-Communist leanings will continue to be a force of close cooperation with the U.S."[72] Nevertheless, the State Department was by no means blind to the weaknesses of Onganía's regime. On the economic front, as the Embassy in Buenos Aires acknowledged, the main problems were inflation, recession, capital-labor relations, and the failure to implement coherent economic policies. In the political sphere, the military failed to widen its base of support.[73] Political instability remained a real concern.

The Renewal of WB Lending to Argentina: The Victory of Political Neutrality?

After a hiatus of over five years, in June 1967, Alter recommended presenting to the WB's executive directors (EDs) three potential loans for Argentine ventures: livestock, SEGBA, and the steel company ACINDAR. He also suggested submitting to the EB, in early 1968, a $60 million loan for the long-awaited *El Chocón* hydroelectric project.[74] Woods immediately sent to the EDs his enthusiastic recommendation regarding a new loan to Argentina.[75] The loan was intended to provide $15.3 million out of the $39 million total cost of the *Balcarce* Livestock Project, with the rest to be covered by the Argentine government, private banks, participating farmers, and machinery contractors. While presenting the project, members of the WB staff explained that it would enhance Argentina's agricultural production and exports, especially of beef. They stressed that the economic program for 1967 reflected "the firmness of the government's commitment to a truly comprehensive approach to control inflation, and an approach which [gave] top priority to fiscal and wages policy."[76] Remarkably, no ED queried the morality of providing assistance to an illegitimate and repressive regime, and the loan was unanimously approved on July 18, 1967. A week later, the IDB followed in the WB's footsteps and extended Argentina a $17.5 million credit for the construction of grain elevators in six ports.[77]

Encouraged by these developments, in September 1967, while heading Argentina's delegation to the IMF-WB annual joint meeting, Krieger Vasena met with Woods, Knapp, and Alter. The minister presented what he considered the success of Argentina's stabilization efforts. Then, in stark contrast to deposed President Illia, he discussed the new petroleum policy, which enabled the government to solicit international bids and explore the potential for privatizing the oil sector. Krieger Vasena also reported about certain reforms that Onganía's administration was undertaking, knowing that the WB had long been advocating for Argentina to implement them. This involved an extensive reform of the national administration and public agencies, especially the railways, including an initial 70 percent tariff increase and the "reintroduction [of] order into the system" by putting an end to strikes.[78] Finally, he requested that the WB approve a large pipeline of future projects.[79] With such a sympathetic interlocutor serving as Minister of Economy, the Argentina-WB collaboration soon improved. Table 2 below shows the seven loans that the WB ultimately granted to the Argentine Revolution.

On December 15, 1967, the WB Economic Committee, headed by Irvin Friedman, held a meeting to which Jorge del Canto, head of the IMF-WHD, was also invited. The committee concluded that Argentina's economic performance and prospects justified assistance to SEGBA and ACINDAR, as well as a $50–100 million increase in WB lending for the upcoming year.[80] Additionally, it was decided that lending during 1968 would be conditioned on a decrease in inflation rates, an increase in public savings, the formulation of a detailed program to rationalize public finance, the expansion of exports, the reduction of export retentions, and a more effective management of the country's foreign debt.[81] Following this decision, an economic mission headed by Peter Wright (WB-WHD) arrived in Argentina in mid-January 1968, just as an IMF delegation was negotiating a new SBA.[82] Wright recommended moving ahead with a lending program of some $100 million a year.[83] In early January 1968, Woods sent to the EDs his recommendations on the

Table 2: World Bank Loans to the Argentine Revolution, 1966–1973.

	Project Title	Project ID	Commitment Amount (in million US dollars)	Executive Board Approval Date
1	**Balcarce Livestock Project**	P005934	15.3	July 31, 1967
2	**Buenos Aires Power Project (02)**	P005933	55	January 25, 1968
3	**El Chocón Power Project**	P005932	82	December 17, 1968
4	**Road Project (02)**	P005931	25	June 24, 1969
5	**Buenos Aires Power Project (03)**	P005930	60	October 7, 1969
6	**Highway Project (03)**	P005928	67.5	March 30, 1971
7	**Railway Project**	P005929	84	March 30, 1971
	TOTAL AMOUNT		**388.8**	

Source: Data from World Bank Group Site, Projects by Country, Argentina (https://projects.worldbank.org/en/projects-operations/projects-summary?countrycode_exact=AR&title=Argentina)

long-awaited $55 million proposed loan for a power project in Buenos Aires, emphasizing that the economic program that Krieger Vasena launched in March 1967 provided a suitable climate for Bank operations in Argentina. He noted that SEGBA had finally appointed a new management in line with WB requirements, thereby removing a longstanding obstacle to WB operations.[84] On January 25, 1968, the EB unanimously approved the loan. Shortly after its approval, Alter traveled to Argentina. In Buenos Aires, Krieger Vasena provided him with a list of projects that Onganía hoped to advance with WB financial support, the majority of which were aimed at sectors requiring institutional reforms.[85] Clearly, the government viewed WB assistance as a legitimate source of financing as well as a stamp of political and economic approval that could help it defend unpopular reforms. For the WB, this represented an opportunity to leave its own imprint on the modernization of the state and the liberalization of Argentina's economy—a clear indication of its role in the economic Cold War in Latin America.

Under these promising circumstances, in October 1968, Argentina's delegation to the joint meeting of the IMF and WB, led again by Krieger Vasena, had their first meeting with McNamara, the newly appointed WB president. As Krieger Vasena put it, Onganía's regime offered a golden opportunity to embed Washington-promoted ideas in Argentina. He highlighted significant disparities between the economic policies advocated by Onganía and himself, Perón, and Illia, commenting that "it was interesting to see how a government could destroy an economy through inflation, nationalization, and expropriation."[86] Furthermore, he asserted that Argentina's late entry into the WB in 1956 was a grave mistake. He added that the WB "should not be blamed for this [mistake], [as] it was Argentina's fault that she did not pursue correct policies."[87] Untouched by the minister's flattery, McNamara turned to the railways problem. Trying to assess Krieger Vasena's capability to pursue unpopular economic reforms, he wondered to what extent the railway's deficit was "a political problem resulting from the opposition by the population in the affected areas to the closing of uneconomic lines."[88] Krieger Vasena responded that political opposition to railway reorganization had come from the powerful railway union, but now the railways were under the direction of military engineers who deactivated the union's harmful interference—*depolitization* at its best. Therefore, he insisted, "reducing personnel and closing lines no longer presented political problems."[89] The government's unwavering commitment to economic reforms, regardless of their social cost, further fueled the ongoing radicalization of the labor movement—an especially concerning development during the Cold War. Student and worker protests, such as the uprising that commenced in the city of Córdoba in May 1969, debilitated Onganía and ultimately led to his removal from power in 1970.

After this initial summit, McNamara paid a four-day visit to Argentina,[90] during which he met ministers and other high-ranking officials and visited several provinces, factories, and farms.[91] McNamara's visit was a great achievement for the Argentine Revolution, both in the international and domestic spheres. It was rare for a WB president, and particularly a high-profile figure like McNamara, to visit a Latin American country. Yet the visits to Argentina of Presidents McCloy (1954), Woods (1965), and McNamara (1968) underscored the Bank's determination to engage with such a large economy and influential regional power. Among the many meetings McNamara held in Argentina, the one with President Onganía was perhaps the most significant, as it revealed little-known aspects of the WB's alleged political neutrality. Onganía took the opportunity to share his political vision, shaped by the NSD, expanding "at length on his conception of the important role that the military had to play at this critical juncture in the development of Argentina's national spirit and its political and economic integration."[92] According to Onganía, Argentina's most pressing need was "a reordering and transformation of its economic life so that, at a later stage, political institutions could be restructured and representative government re-established." Unfortunately, the WB documents that I could access omitted McNamara's response to Onganía's exposition. Nevertheless, they indicate that McNamara and Alter, who accompanied him, had strong doubts about the President's ideas. They considered that Onganía's "mystical conception of the role of the military may well lead to irrational and costly expenditures for military purposes," and that there was no assurance that the population would be ready to accept an indefinite time schedule to restore democratic rule.[93] This was not the only occasion in which McNamara was informed about delicate domestic issues from Argentine representatives. This underscores that, although he was cognizant of the situation, he opted to maintain the façade of a neutral stance. As McNamara once explained to the new Minister of Economy, Moyano Llerena, in September 1970, his concern over political and social developments stemmed from, and was limited to, the potential negative reaction of private foreign capital to political uncertainties in Argentina, given investor need for predictability in the treatment of foreign capital.[94]

Political concerns aside, McNamara fulfilled his promise to Onganía.[95] In December 1968, he submitted to the EDs his recommendations on the *El Chocón* hydroelectric project in the Neuquén Province.[96] While presenting the project to the EB for approval, McNamara emphasized the success of Onganía's stabilization plan and the ongoing rationalization of state enterprises—with the exception of the railways. As in previous votes, the EDs asked no questions about the nature of the regime in power, unanimously approving the $82 million loan on December 17, 1968.[97] In light of McNamara's focus on social issues, it was surprising that WB staff and EDs made no inquiries regarding the social implications of this mega-project. That this should have been a concern was made clear in December 1969 and again in March 1970. Workers constructing the *Chocón* dam and close village organized two violent strikes demanding a 40 percent wage increase and protesting the poor working conditions that had already resulted in injuries to several workers and a number of deaths. Onganía's dictatorship declared the strikes illegal, arrested union leaders, and brutally repressed the workers.[98] Remarkably, recently declassified WB records reveal no instances of WB remonstration to the Argentine authorities, nor even any debate among WB staff regarding the substandard working conditions in a WB co-financed project. By acting as if it were really neutral, the WB not only steered clear of political considerations such as the type of regime in power or its repressive methods, but it also avoided getting involved in the defense of workers' basic rights. This stance was particularly delicate under the shadow of the NSD, which identified organized workers as an internal enemy and a menace to national security. This was not unique to Argentina. For example, under McNamara's leadership, the WB funded several projects in Africa that involved the forcible removal of people from their ancestral land without adequately addressing the significant harm caused to those displaced.[99] The WB's archival records show that in the case of the *Chocón* project, the WB staff not only avoided voicing concerns about working conditions, but it even referred to the workers as an obstacle that hindered the reform and rationalization of state-owned enterprises.

In any event, in early June 1969, McNamara sent his recommendations to the EDs on a new road loan to Argentina. Although McNamara stressed that the transport sector was still showing deficient managerial capacities and vast overstaffing, he claimed that the project was justifiable because the government was in the process of stabilizing and reactivating the economy.[100] The $25 million loan, approved on June 24, 1969, was aimed at supporting the improvement of 800 kilometers of access roads in the greater Buenos Aires area, deemed vital to promote economic activity and exports. While presenting the project, McNamara referred to the correlation between inflation, economic growth, and labor unrest, as if unrest were a mere economic parameter.[101] Since part of McNamara's introductory remarks and conclusions were blacked out during the declassification process of the transcript, it is impossible to determine whether McNamara overtly referred to the political circumstances in Argentina or the ongoing repression of strikes and protests being carried out there. What is certain is that WB lending to the country continued steadily.

Barely three months later, in late September 1969, McNamara recommended granting a third loan to SEGBA worth $60 million. This loan, as McNamara explained to the EDs, was necessary to build a 120-kilometer-long transmission ring around Buenos Aires, connect the transmission lines from *Chocón* and the atomic plant *Atucha*, and extend the distribution network in the greater Buenos Aires area. He noted that the new management of SEGBA, which the WB had approved in advance, had successfully increased efficiency levels—including the layoff of 1,140 workers.[102] This action once again demonstrated a significant indifference towards social issues, especially concerning a social group that, within the context of the Cold War, many viewed as a Trojan Horse. Whether intentionally or not, McNamara ultimately supported the weakening of labor unions, which was a significant goal of Onganía's security doctrine. In any case, EB discussions stressed Argentina's improving economy and the government's ability to implement a coherent economic policy.[103] It is worth noting that this flow of WB loans to the Argentine Revolutions was made possible with the full support of the Nixon administration, which believed that the best way to support Argentina's groundbreaking economic reforms was through multilateral organizations like the IMF and the WB, rather than through US direct assistance.[104] As discussed below, it did not take long for growing political instability and social unrest in Argentina to endanger WB lending to the country.

A Renewed Break in Lending: When Alignment with the Western Bloc is Insufficient

Onganía was ousted on June 9, 1970, a mere two weeks after the kidnapping and assassination of former President Pedro Aramburu (1955–1958) in a terrorist act that shocked the nation.[105] His deposal was a response from groups within the armed forces to his failure to quell violence and social and labor unrest. From June 1970 onwards, Argentina entered a period of growing instability. The new president, General Roberto Levingston (June 1970–March 1971), appointed Carlos Moyano Llerena as Minister of Economy and Labor (June–October 1970). However, due to ideological differences within the military regime, Levingston soon replaced him with the renowned economist Aldo Ferrer. Ferrer, a former disciple of Raúl Prebisch who was associated with Latin America's *developmentalism* and structuralism, was well-known in Washington circles for his involvement in a consulting group for Kennedy's Alliance for Progress. Additionally, he was a founding member of UNESCO's Latin American Social Science Council (CLACSO).[106] Ferrer launched an expansionary plan that sought to develop the national industry and increase the export of manufactured goods as a means to improve Argentina's entry into international markets. He advocated an industrialization process based on domestic capital, although he was aware of the need to attract foreign investors.[107] His plan soon exacerbated inflation, however, leading to salary adjustments and tariff increases—actions that the WB objected. On March 22, 1971, General Alejandro Agustín Lanusse deposed Levingston. Lanusse, the last president of the Argentine Revolution, kept Ferrer in office until May 1971, when he dissolved the Ministry of Economy and established a Ministry of Finance in its place. Lanusse appointed three Ministers of Finance: Juan Quilici (May–October 1971), Cayetano Licciardo (October 1971– October 1972), and Jorge Wehbe (October 1972–May 1973). While Ferrer and Quilici implemented expansionary policies, Licciardo and Wehbe focused on improving the balance of payments and curbing inflation. Nevertheless, the annual rate of inflation accelerated from 12.5 percent in June 1970 to 78.8 percent in May 1973.[108]

On March 30, 1971, with Lanusse in power for barely a week and Argentina roiling from unrest, the WB EB approved two new loans to the country. These were the last loans granted until September 1976. One loan, amounting to $67.5 million, was to co-finance a highway project.[109] The other, worth $84 million, was intended to support a controversial five-year modernization plan of the railways.[110] McNamara, avoiding any reference to worsening social and political conditions in Argentina, justified the loans by emphasizing the crucial importance of transport infrastructure to a vast country such as Argentina. He also explained that the Argentine government was committed to supporting the rationalization of the existing services, establishing realistic tariffs, and basing investment decisions on sound economic criteria.[111] The EDs, as was routine, asked only technical questions. However, Latin American representatives urged the WB management to expand the participation of local contractors in WB-supported projects, far beyond the mere 15 percent that the WB permitted at the time. They argued that increased involvement of local contractors was essential, especially in Argentina, a country with a substantial cadre of skilled professionals.[112] This demand mirrored the escalating criticism from Third World countries regarding the conditions attached to WB loan agreements, particularly those favoring foreign companies, consultants, and experts at the expense of local ones. All these issues were, naturally, central to the demands of the NIEO advocates.

Disagreements between the WB and Lanusse's administration were quick to emerge. In April, Ferrer found himself out of his post, thereby raising concern among WB-WHD staff over governmental instability and what they perceived as Argentina's weakening technical capacity.[113] In May 1971, Alter completed an ambivalent report on Argentina,[114] and in June, a WB mission landed in Buenos Aires to collect information on the functioning of the Central Bank's regulatory powers and on problems in the balance of payments.[115] Concerns increased as inflation was expected to reach a 40 percent annual rate by the end of 1971.[116] As the economy worsened, rumors became widespread in Argentina regarding an aid package of around $1 billion over five years, which, so Lanusse claimed, the US administration was arranging. The US State Department, however, denied any involvement in such an initiative.[117] It should be noted that here too the State Department took the position that Argentina's economic problems should be dealt with through IMF and WB assistance.[118] However, according to available WB records, during the 1971–1976 period, when the Bank was not seriously considering any loans to Argentina, the State Department made no overt attempts to persuade it to lend to the Argentine Revolution. Lanusse, like Onganía and Alsogaray before him, threatened a turn to the Soviet bloc in the absence of assistance from the United States.[119] Given that these warnings originated from a regime staunchly opposed to communism, they apparently seemed unconvincing.

By September 1971, it became evident that Lanusse's prospects of reaching additional agreements with the WB were steadily diminishing. The main reason was that Argentina had implemented certain economic measures that contravened the loan agreements signed in 1971. Among these measures, the most problematic were wage increases negotiated with labor unions and a sixty-day freeze on all prices and tariffs, including those pertaining to SEGBA and the railways.[120]

Notwithstanding the concern over mounting instability, in October 1971, several WB missions arrived in Buenos Aires.[121] They all reached the same conclusion—that Lanusse lacked the political power and legitimacy needed to implement unpopular austerity measures. In an effort to avert a recession and seemingly aware that the WB would cease lending due to non-compliance with the conditions outlined in still valid loan agreements, Lanusse sought Nixon's assistance by requesting the dispatch of a US special envoy to Argentina. Nixon agreed. On August 30, 1971, Assistant Secretary of Treasury John R. Petty arrived in Buenos Aires, where he met President Lanusse, Central Bank President Carlos Brignone, and others. Lanusse told Petty that "Argentina [was] fighting not only for her own future but for a way of life which is the free, Western-style way of life." He warned that the eyes of all the other Latin American countries were on Argentina, and if the economic situation continued to deteriorate, the country would turn to socialism. Petty skeptically suggested that Argentina seek help from multilateral lending institutions.[122] The WB, however, chose to prioritize its own organizational interests rather than backing a regime that, despite its threats, remained firmly aligned with the Western bloc. After all, non-compliance with the terms and conditions stipulated in its loan agreements had always justified non-lending. Thus, rather than increasing assistance to Lanusse's regime as the Nixon administration apparently expected (but did not actively promote), the WB began to curtail it. It refused to engage in negotiations for new loans and suspended disbursements for previously approved projects. Certainly, McNamara's motivations went beyond his efforts to secure the Bank's partial autonomy vis-à-vis the US administration. They also involved considerations related to the Bank's operational standards, economic criteria, and credibility.

By December 1971, given Argentina's deteriorating economy and the unsatisfactory outcomes in sectors receiving WB financing, WB-WHD personnel suggested delaying, once more, the initial disbursement of the railway loan, initially slated for April 1971. It also suggested suspending disbursements on the SEGBA loan approved in 1969.[123] A few days later, a WB inter-departmental forum decided to advise Lanusse's government, the railways, and SEGBA against submitting withdrawal applications for their already-approved loans—a decision that set off alarm bells in Argentina. The forum also determined that the WB would not approve any further loans until the tariff and wage issues were resolved.[124]

In January 1972, IMF and WB missions once again arrived in Argentina.[125] Although Lanusse did not intend to sign a new SBA with the IMF, he aspired to open negotiations that could pave the way to agreements with US and European creditors.[126] Gunter Wiese, the Head of a WB-WHD mission, considered that Lanusse's economic plan for 1972 was insufficient to address the budget deficit, halt the escalating inflation, and mitigate reserve losses, which had reached $65 million monthly. Additionally, Wiese questioned SEGBA's ability to meet two fundamental requirements stipulated by the WB: implementing tariff increases of at least 25 percent and undergoing substantial reorganization.[127] Since Argentina could not guarantee that SEGBA and the railways would fulfill their contractual obligations, Alter recommended, once again, suspending disbursements on already-approved loans.[128]

Initially, the WB hesitated to make an official announcement regarding the suspension of disbursements. Halting disbursements was viewed as a punitive measure. Moreover, doing so entailed acknowledging that the Bank had provided loans to an unreliable borrower. Instead, the WB opted to await the final version of the economic program Lanusse was negotiating with the IMF, giving Argentina time to conclude negotiations also with US and European banks.[129] In March 1972, Argentina opened loan talks with the IMF, for the first time since 1968. However, due to the IMF's skepticism regarding Argentina's capacity to reactivate its economy, negotiations were halted.[130] A few months later, in July 1972, the WB officially declared the suspension of disbursements on the $84 million railroad loan to Argentina, citing its failure to follow the plan agreed upon at the time of signing. Despite the 1971 loan agreement stipulating that revenues should at least cover labor costs, only 70 percent of such costs were covered during 1972. Lanusse's government justified this noncompliance by arguing that any tariff increase would raise inflation rates. Although the WB was contemplating a complete cancellation of the loan, it did not rule out the possibility of renewing disbursements if SEGBA improved its income levels.[131] Nevertheless, Lanusse, fearing the social and political impact of additional adjustments, did not raise tariffs. Even though the regime aligned itself with the US-led bloc and filled an active role in efforts to contain communism in the region, it did not receive the significant financial support it expected from Washington. In the case of the WB, the period of cooperation between the parties was shorter than anticipated. From August 1972 until the March 1973 general elections, interactions between the Bank and Argentina were practically non-existent. Following the elections, it was the turn of Peronism to rebuild ties with the Bank. However, as we shall see below, this goal was only partially accomplished.

PART 3: THE WB AND THE THIRD PERONISM: POPULISM AS AN OBSTACLE

Juan D. Perón returned to Argentina on November 17, 1972, following eighteen years of exile. During his brief first stay in the country and before returning to Madrid, he established a broad coalition, the *Frente Justicialista de Liberación* (FREJULI). From Spain, Perón negotiated with

Lanusse the transition to democracy.[132] Because Perón was officially banned from running in the general elections of March 11, 1973, he chose Héctor Cámpora, a left-wing Peronist, and Vicente Solano Lima, a member of the Popular Conservative Party, as FREJULI's candidates for President and Vice President.[133] In the first round, FREJULI won 49.5 percent of the votes. In light of the results, Ricardo Balbín, the candidate of the UCR, bailed out of the second round and FREJULI was proclaimed the winner. In the meantime, violence continued to grow. Between the elections and Cámpora's investiture on May 25, the number of terrorist attacks, kidnappings, and murders increased. On June 20, 1973, Perón returned to Argentina for good. President Cámpora's brief tenure was characterized by political and economic decline, leading to his resignation after just seven weeks in office. New elections were held in July 1973. This time, FREJULI obtained 61.9 percent of the votes. Between July 13 and October 12, Raúl Lastiri, the chairman of the Chamber of Deputies and a FREJULI member, ruled as interim president. In October 1973, Lastiri delivered the government to Perón and his vice president, María Estela Martínez de Perón (Isabel), Perón's third wife.

WB expectations, already at record lows under Lanusse, plummeted even further with the return of Peronism to power. This situation appears related to the Bank's previous experience with Peronism (1946–1955), which WB economists still blamed for the "deep damage" Perón caused to the national economy.[134] Negative perceptions of Perón held by influential actors in Washington contributed to this pessimistic outlook. For instance, *The New York Times* often referred to Perón as a former dictator identified with urban guerrilla movements like *Montoneros*,[135] and to Peronism as a movement associated with repression, class hatred, corruption, economic manipulation, and demagogy.[136] Official US agencies were even more critical. Seeking to characterize Peronism, the CIA stated: "It claims to be anti-Communist, yet many of its young members have a certain Marxist-Leninist tinge. It claims that it is not fascist, yet among older adherents there is a significant current of right-wing ultra-nationalist fanaticism."[137]

With Cámpora in office, WB-Argentina interactions were perhaps more cordial than under Lanusse but equally fruitless. Cámpora appointed two old Perón allies associated with classic populism (see Chapter 1) to key economic positions: Alfredo Gómez Morales as Central Bank President and Minister of Economic Affairs, and José Ber Gelbard as Minister of Economy (in charge of the Ministries of Finance, Industry, Commerce, Agriculture, and Public Works, and the Planning Office). Employing the same strategy he had applied while serving under Perón in the 1940s–1950s, Gómez Morales, whom WB-WHD staff deemed a moderate,[138] openly criticized the IMF but avoided complaining about the WB, whose funds he wished to access.[139] Gelbard, who had been allied with the Communist party and who remained in office also under Lastiri, Péron, and Isabel, continued to support interventionism and economic nationalism. His policy, which implied a clear departure from the more orthodox approach implemented by Krieger Vasena and other liberal economists, emphasized short-term goals, a more equitable distribution of income, and lower inflation.[140] In June 1973, Gelbard promoted a foreign investment law stipulating that all new foreign investments be conditioned on the participation of at least 51 percent domestic capital, and that existing investments undergo gradual nationalization. He strove to strengthen the national industry and state-owned enterprises and reverse privatizations carried out by the Argentine Revolution.[141] In short, the WB had plenty of economic justifications to forgo lending to the Cámpora administration. If this was not enough, the WB-WHD staff predicted that consensus over economic policies would soon vanish due to friction within the government, as the Peronist movement "include[d] virtually all shades of political opinion, from the extreme Marxist views of certain youth groups to the positions of some of the most conservative segments of Argentinean society."[142] In the view of the WB-WHD team, Perón himself, behind the scenes, had taken charge of the political process with Cámpora playing a secondary role. Despite this appraisal, Gerald Alter, head of the WB-WHD, intended to send a mission to establish initial relations with Cámpora and Gelbard. Gelbard, who, unlike Gómez Morales, had publicly condemned the WB "for letting political considerations influence its lending strategy vis-à-vis Argentina," asked for a postponement of the mission until the government defined its economic policy.[143] The mission ultimately landed in Argentina in June 1973. Its findings were discouraging. According to its report, although the railways' rates had increased by 20–25 percent, the company's earnings for 1973 were well behind those specified in the 1971 loan agreement. The mission criticized Argentina's reluctance to reduce railway staff and close unprofitable lines, as if these were mere technical issues.[144] As in previous occasions, and despite the social turn under McNamara, the WB continued to show indifference to the social costs inherent in many of its *ex-ante* conditions.

Following Cámpora's resignation in July 1973, the WB-WHD began to work on a tentative lending plan for 1974–1975.[145] On August 1, 1973, Gómez Morales, Central Bank President, met McNamara, Knapp, and Wiese. He described his efforts to curb inflation and declared that the government and the labor unions had reached an agreement on wage controls. In his view, Argentina's economy was imperiled by the prospect of a severe energy shortage—an issue that had been central in Argentina's discussions with the WB since the 1950s. The minister spoke about Argentina's over-reliance on importing substantial amounts of petrol and revealed that the government was exploring the feasibility of using natural gas, which would require additional pipelines and auxiliary facilities.[146] He added that Argentina needed to expand its hydroelectric facilities, emphasizing that development in these areas would require WB assistance. McNamara, rather than responding to Gómez Morales's request for loans, asked whether the government intended to raise tariffs. The minister answered that SEGBA and all other public enterprises would have to improve their efficiency. Closing the meeting, McNamara stressed that the WB "st[ood] ready to engage in detailed discussions as soon as the Government is ready, and to assist the Government in its development efforts."[147] From McNamara's perspective, ready meant when Argentina complied with WB policy prescriptions.

Perón in Power: A Second Chance for a First Impression?

Perón was invested as Argentina's president on October 12, 1973. A few days later, the WB-WHD reported that Argentina was preparing a three-year plan aimed at accelerating economic and export growth, reducing inequality, and decelerating the annual inflation rate to 10–15 percent.[148] Wiese opined that "with his mandate from the voters (62% of the votes), it should be possible for Perón to extract sacrifices from the people."[149] The same month, a mission visited Argentina to evaluate ongoing WB-financed projects.[150] Wiese told McNamara that he would ask Perón's team to confirm their willingness to work with the Bank. He added, "Should we receive such confirmation, we are prepared to send a small economic and operational mission [. . .]. We would then also consider whether we should appraise the fourth SEGBA power project."[151] To the WB's surprise, in December 1973, Alejandro Orfila, the new ambassador to Washington, assured McNamara that Perón was very interested in establishing good working relationships with the international financial institutions.[152]

In January 1974, during their second meeting, Orfila expressed gratitude to McNamara for the WB's flexibility regarding disbursements related to the highway loan signed in 1969. In a rare move, the WB agreed to redirect the remaining balance of the loan to other projects—a decision starkly different from the suspension of disbursements to the Argentine Revolution.

Orfila then stated that "speaking for President Perón, Minister Gelbard and the whole economic team, he wished to convey their very strong interest in working closely with the World Bank."[153] He added that Argentina hoped to obtain $300–$350 million per year in WB loans and expressed satisfaction that WB missions were already working in Argentina. Orfila went on to say that "he hoped that the World Bank would appreciate that Argentina faced an image problem in the outside world."[154] The Perón administration had more than an image problem, however, as its economic policy and performance disqualified it from WB lending. McNamara diplomatically responded that he was pleased that the new authorities were interested in strengthening bilateral cooperation. He then suggested that they first concentrate on reaching an agreement on the de-freezing of disbursements of the 1971 loans.[155] Following this meeting, several ministers prepared proposals for future projects.[156] Perón's administration was ready to make concessions for the sake of development loans and, not less significant, of the Bank's seal of approval. Nevertheless, its path to multilateral aid was still plagued with pitfalls.

Perón, as Argentina's Foreign Minister Alberto Vignes conveyed to US Secretary of State Kissinger, sought to improve relations with the US administration. Vignes emphasized Argentina's desire to cooperate with the United States and added that although the country had credit arrangements with Cuba, "Cuba kn[ew] that Argentina [was] '*justicialista*' [referring to the official name of the Peronist Party] and anti-Communist [. . .]."[157] The State Department became increasingly convinced that Perón was indeed interested in cultivating relations with Washington.[158] However, Argentina's reestablishment of diplomatic and commercial relations with Cuba in 1973, and terrorist attacks against US firms operating in the country, precluded a full rapprochement with the United States.[159]

Perón, who died of a heart attack on July 1, 1974, after a mere nine months in power, missed a second chance to work with the WB. Perón's widow and vice president, Isabel, succeeded him.[160] Isabel, though, was unsuccessful in her attempts to quell violence and stabilize the economy. On October 21, 1974, she appointed Gómez Morales as Minister of Economy. One of his first steps was to turn to the IMF for a loan, partially out of the conviction that this would pave the road to WB loans. His term, which ended in June 1975, represented a transition between Gelbard's isolationist nationalism and economic interventionism and the "shock policy," detailed below, that was advanced by Celestino Rodrigo, Minister of Economy from June 5 until July 17, 1975.[161]

The WB-WHD staff closely followed Argentina's political and economic deterioration. The briefing that Alter sent to McNamara ahead of his meeting with Gómez Morales shed light on the Bank's view of Argentina's situation at the time. To begin with, Alter assumed that "the re-imposition of military rule remain[ed] a possibility."[162] Regarding the WB's operations in the country, he asserted that bilateral relations had deteriorated since 1971 for two main reasons. The first was political instability and the declining quality of Argentina's economic management. The second reason was that "the slow and painful transition from military rule to civilian government and the eventual return of Mr. Perón totally absorbed the attention of top officials in Buenos

Aires and the dialogue between the Bank and the Government practically came to a standstill."[163] According to Alter, with Peronism back in power, and parts of the Peronist movement retaining their old distrust of the international financial institutions, Argentina's rulers showed little interest in working with the Bank. However, he stressed, this attitude changed significantly after Perón's death. Against the backdrop of Argentina's uncertain situation, the meeting between Gómez Morales and McNamara on January 17, 1975, focused on potential projects and on SEGBA's decision to increase tariffs, thereby fulfilling WB requests. In a further gesture of goodwill, shortly after this meeting, the WB EB approved a $100 million line of credit for a four-year lending program to Argentina.[164] The plan's approval at a time when WB lending to Argentina was deemed unfeasible due to the economic crisis is intriguing. It recalls the approval of a package of potential projects shortly before President Illia's overthrow in June 1966. In both instances, it seems that the WB's decision had more to do with its efforts to present itself as politically neutral and prevent tensions with Argentina than with a concrete lending program. By endorsing lines of credit to collapsing democratic regimes shortly before military coups, the Bank aimed to secure the legitimacy necessary to collaborate with the dictatorships that succeeded them. In any event, Alter informed Gómez Morales that he intended to submit to the EB, at an undefined date, a new highway and a new SEGBA loan.[165]

Gómez Morales did not give up and took significant steps to attract foreign investments and credits. In 1975, he signed accords with private US banks and multinationals, including the General Motors Corporation, Ford Motor Company, and Chrysler Corporation.[166] In the meantime, the economic and political situation continued to worsen.[167] In June 1975, trapped between irreconcilable pressures from opposing Peronist factions, Gómez Morales resigned and was replaced by Celestino Rodrigo. When Rodrigo entered office, Argentina was expected to repay $2 billion in debt to commercial US and European banks, the WB, and the IDB. Attempting to avoid default, Rodrigo opened negotiations with the IMF.[168] At the same time, he implemented a "shock plan" in line with IMF and WB requests (known as the "*Rodrigazo*"), which included a 160 percent devaluation of the national currency, a doubling of the tariffs charged by public utility companies, and a 50 percent limit on wage increases. In contrast to economic policies associated with classic populism, Rodrigo deregulated the prices of most basic consumption products. The unions responded with a general strike. In mid-June 1975, new collective labor agreements granted an initial wage increase of 45–100 percent. The furor that erupted in response to Rodrigo's plan led to his resignation. His successor, Pedro José Bonanni, was in office for less than a month (July 22–August 11, 1975) and was replaced by Antonio Cafiero, an old-school Peronist who, in the 1940s, opposed Argentina's joining the Bretton Woods institution, which he depicted as arms of US foreign policy.[169]

In December 1975, the IMF, after a seven-year break in lending to Argentina, approved a drawing of $126 million under the Compensatory Financial Facility (CFF). This credit program, which typically had no binding conditions, was approved almost automatically by the IMF as emergency assistance to countries facing a sudden shortfall in export earnings or a rise in the price of imports due to fluctuating global commodity prices.[170] The partial renewal of IMF lending had the potential to facilitate WB lending—but it did not. Argentina's creditworthiness remained low. Cafiero, constrained by conflicting pressures from within Peronism, resigned on February 3, 1976. The new minister, Emilio Mondelli, was a liberal economist and a technocrat with no political affiliation. On February 25, he submitted his plan to Isabel and to the commanders of the Navy, Air Force, and ground forces, an indication of the immense pressure that the military exerted on Isabel's government.[171] Mondelli's shock plan enacted harsh austerity measures, including new tariffs for public services, maximum prices for basic products, and wage increases. With widespread rumors of an imminent coup, the WB-WHD continued monitoring Argentina's situation. It identified the wage increases as a major cause of inflation. The government granted an 18 percent wage increase to private sector workers on January 1, 1976. Public employees were paid the remainder of a 160 percent increase that had been approved in June and received another 40 percent increase. Since price increases averaged 10 percent per month, demands for wage increases were constant.[172] To make things worse, adverse climatic conditions harmed crops, reducing exports and aggravating existing problems in the balance of payments. Once again, Argentina opened negotiations to access IMF funds.[173] On March 24, 1976, Isabel was deposed by a military coup (see Chapter 5).

Less than two weeks later, with a new military dictatorship in power, IMF and WB missions arrived in Argentina to negotiate new loans.[174] In June 1976, Wiese informed McNamara: "It is difficult to overestimate the degree of damage suffered by the Argentine economy during the final months of the Peronist era. During the Presidency of Isabel Perón the country was virtually leaderless. [. . .] The Congress was in total disarray [. . .]. With unbridled, irresponsible unions. Encouraged by demagogic leaders, and highly protected, oligopolistic industry engaged in a struggle over wages and prices, with total lack of monetary control and fiscal discipline."[175]

CONCLUSIONS

The military regime that replaced Illia, the self-proclaimed "Argentine Revolution" (1966–1973), seemed to possess the necessary requisites for cultivating a fruitful partnership with the WB. The new regime, despite important internal ideological disagreements, advocated a free-market economy, economic stabilization, and the establishment of a highly qualified bureaucratic apparatus able to manage the state in line with the standards promoted by Washington-based institutions. Inspired by the US-backed NSD, the regime was staunchly anti-Peronist, anti-Communist, and pro-Western. Its threats to seek assistance from the Soviet bloc stemmed more from pragmatism, nationalism, and disappointment with the lack of significant Western backing than from any wavering in the regime's Cold War stance.

Like WB President Robert McNamara (1968–1981), the heads of the Argentine Revolution saw national security and economic development, as well as poverty and communism, as two sides of a single, integrated process. Unlike the WB, Onganía believed that fostering economic growth required disciplining Argentina's society. In practical terms, this meant that in order to promote development and modernization, it was necessary to depoliticize, and even eliminate, potential sources of resistance. Chief among these were the politicized universities and the *Peronized* unions. The WB, for its part, focused only on those economic parameters that it established as preconditions for lending to explain its assistance to the Argentine Revolution. Although the WB management and staff, as well as members of its EB, were aware of the repressive methods implemented by the military regime, they did not let the state violence jeopardize Bank operations in the country.

In July 1967, six months after the appointment of the orthodox economist Adalbert Krieger Vasena as Minister of Economy, the WB resumed lending to Argentina after a five-year halt that began during Arturo Frondizi's presidency (see Chapter 2). Krieger Vasena, keen to reinstate Argentina's relations with the US administration and the Western financial community, launched a rigorous stabilization plan, promoted a new Hydrocarbons Law granting US oil companies more favorable conditions than those of the state-owned company YPF, and adopted a non-conciliatory stance towards the labor movement. However, as time passed, the regime found it increasingly difficult to comply with the conditions specified in already approved loan agreements. Under such circumstances, and in light of escalating political instability and economic deterioration, the loans that the Bank granted to the country in March 1971 became the last ones until September 1976.

Examining the WB's relations with the Argentine Revolution and with the Peronist administration that followed, this chapter has challenged the widespread notion that the Bank preferred military over democratic regimes. Although the WB approved seven loans to the dictatorship but refrained from providing any new loans to the Peronist government, it imposed a stricter approach towards the pro-market Argentine Revolution than towards the more socially oriented Peronism. The picture is counterintuitive: the higher the ideological affinity between the WB and the regime in power, whether democratic or dictatorial, the more stringent the conditions set forth by the Bank. In effect, both the WB and the US administration believed that the Argentine Revolution would remain anti-Communist and pro-Western with or without Western support. They also knew, based on their experience in Argentina, that the Peronist administration would be overthrown in any case, with or without financial assistance from Western creditors.

Finally, this chapter has complicated the widespread view of dictators as actors able to implement painful shock policies. It has also shown that authoritarian regimes vary with respect to the freedom of action they have regarding opponents both within government circles and society at large. The WB was aware of these constraints. As Alter noted in an interview when asked about the Bank's stance vis-à-vis countries that experienced high political instability during the 1960s and 1970s:

> "*. . . to be absolutely frank with you, I don't think the Bank at that period [1960s–1970s] was attaching any great importance to the questions of democracy versus dictatorship, human rights versus oppression, these strictly what we might call 'political aspects.' We definitely were interested in the economic impacts of the political changes that were taking place [in Latin America]. [. . .] One of the lessons I think that we [the WB management] learned was that dictatorships were not necessarily any more decisive in resolving difficult economic problems than democracies were. The old saw that it takes a dictatorship to resolve these problems just turned out to be completely false. And we recognized that, I think, at a very early stage.*"[176]

5 THE WORLD BANK AND HUMAN RIGHTS

IN THE 1970S, AT THE same time that the Cold War between the superpowers underwent a period of détente, and tensions between Eastern and Western Europe eased, conflicts intensified in Latin America and other Third World areas.[1] Struggles stemming from Latin America's own political instability, economic stagnation, and radicalization converged with the pressures that the United States was still exerting on the region to contain communism. It was this interplay between domestic conflicts and the Cold War which helped create the conditions for a wave of right-wing and anti-communist military dictatorships in Latin America.[2] These regimes, many of which came to power with US support, considered the United States and the multilateral financial institutions that it created, in particular the Bretton Woods institutions, allies in their crusade to erase any trace of populism and communism. Their efforts to promote a free-market economy were in line with neoliberal precepts that were on the rise in the region—especially in Pinochet's Chile—and also in the United States under Ronald Reagan, Britain under Margaret Thatcher, and Germany under Helmut Kohl. Thus, two apparently opposing processes were at work in Latin America. On one hand, there was a profound opening and (neo)liberalization of the economy—goals that the WB had pursued since initiating operations in the region in 1948. On the other hand, military dictatorships enforced censorship, repression, and state terrorism, targeting, among others, opponents of this economic shift, including the labor movement and a growing population falling below the poverty line.

The military regime that governed Argentina between the coup of March 24, 1976 and the transition to democracy on December 10, 1983 was emblematic of this phenomenon. Argentina's dictatorship revoked civil and political rights and systematically violated human rights. These dark years took a devastating toll, with between 9,000 and 30,000 forced disappearances (depending on the source), thousands of political exiles, the seizure of hundreds of babies from mothers kept in captivity, the creation of blacklists, and other egregious acts. Not without reason, by mid-1976, Argentina became central to US debates on human rights. It also emerged as a focal point for a transnational human rights movement and a key site for the implementation of shifting versions of US human rights diplomacy during the Ford, Carter, and Reagan administrations.[3] Of course, the topic of human rights was hardly new in the international sphere.[4] It had played a prominent role in East-West rivalries throughout the Cold War, particularly during the so-called human rights booms of the 1940s and 1970s, and again towards the conflict's end.[5]

Based on new evidence, this chapter examines the difficulties the WB faced and the opportunities it found while cultivating ties with Argentina's dictatorship. Zooming in on the WB's involvement in Argentina from 1976 until 1983 provides fertile ground for a more critical assessment of a central question in this book: whether the WB preferred to work with dictatorships or democracies. Scholars remain divided, with some supporting the "democratic advantage" theory and others advocating the "democratic disadvantage" approach. Supporters of the former argue that the WB favored collaboration with democratic regimes due to their higher accountability and determination to avoid default,[6] while those of the latter contend that the WB favored authoritarian regimes for their ability to enforce strict austerity measures, ensuring debt repayment.[7] This binary reading, which implies a direct correlation between the type of regime and its economic performance (rather than its economic ideology), is indeed relevant to the study of WB-Argentina relations. Yet the case of Argentina's last dictatorship adds a new dimension to core questions concerning the Bank's relations with authoritarian regimes. The junta that took power in 1976 committed unprecedented atrocities for which the Carter administration (1977–1981) expected the Bank to interrupt lending to Argentina. The WB, however, reflecting its traditional indifference regarding the nature of the borrowing regime, and seeking to secure its own organizational interests, showed a lack of concern for human rights violations.

This chapter, it is worth noting, does not seek to join legal or normative debates on whether human rights should have been a criterion for WB lending.[8] Instead, it explores the Bank's concrete engagement, or lack thereof, with human rights during the Cold War,[9] contributing to the growing scholarship on their history and impact on multilateral organizations.[10] A number of scholars have argued that human rights concerns influenced the WB's lending criteria.[11] Argentina's case refutes this claim. The WB is not a signatory to any major human rights convention and, formally, is not obliged to apply internationally recognized human rights standards in its operations. Nonetheless, as a specialized UN agency since 1947, it is required to conform to the UN Charter. Historically, the Bank has treated human rights violations that are not directly connected to its operations as beyond its jurisdiction.[12] The WB's relationship with Argentina's junta followed this pattern.

Examining the triangular dynamics between the WB, Argentina's dictatorship, and the US administration, this chapter provides a new prism through which to explore the role that the WB played in the Cold War in Latin America at a particular historical moment of increased WB-US tensions, when the United States strove to bring the Bank in line with its human rights policy. In this regard, the Carter administration acted proactively, enacting laws that conditioned the provision of WB assistance on improvements in the area of human rights.

To prevent the erosion of its semi-autonomy and safeguard its operations in Argentina and other countries that were under repressive regimes, the WB formulated various strategies. As was already mentioned, seeking to repel US pressures, the WB management asserted that human rights were beyond the organization's purview. This did not necessarily mean, however, that by focusing solely on economic criteria and by granting assistance to dictatorial regimes that abused human rights, the WB did not serve US Cold War interests. In fact, it was precisely the ability of a multilateral institution like the Bank to assist brutal dictatorships that allowed it to promote Western capitalism in Argentina and beyond, while freeing the US from the need to directly undertake such a contentious mission. Ultimately, the WB would extend thirteen loans to Argentina's dictatorship by December 1981, and an additional one in May 1983, shortly before Raúl Alfonsín entered the presidential office in December 1983.

Chilean General Augusto Pinochet (1973–1990) also managed to obtain WB support despite US opposition on human rights grounds.[13] The same applied to other Latin American regimes with poor track records on human rights. The Brazilian dictatorship (1964–1985), for instance, received 116 WB loans, and Uruguay's military regime (1973–1985) thirteen. Argentina's junta, for its part, took significant steps to avoid a US veto on WB loans, spreading false promises of improvements in the human rights arena. Furthermore, Argentina's ED to the Bank cautioned its staff that straying from economic matters into the political realm could jeopardize the WB's reputation.

In order to understand the dynamics that facilitated WB lending to Argentina's dictatorship, this chapter identifies five stages in their bilateral relations. The first is from the coup of March 1976 until August 1976, when José Alfredo Martínez de Hoz, Argentina's Minister of Economy (1976–1981), launched his first stabilization plan with IMF support. The second stage comprised the first two loans that the WB granted to Argentina's dictatorship in September 1976 and March 1977. The transition from the Ford to the Carter administration in January 1977, and the increasing centrality of human rights in US foreign policy, did not substantially affect WB lending to the junta, and these initial loans were made with US approval. In the third stage, from April 1977 to late 1980, the United States abstained, on human rights grounds, from all EB votes on loans to the country, allowing the Bank to secure its operations in Argentina. The fourth stage started with the inauguration of President Reagan in January 1981. In July 1981, the replacement of WB president

McNamara by Tom Clausen signaled a crucial turning point for the WB. The fifth stage began in January 1982 and ended with the transition to democracy in December 1983. This period coincides with a series of game-changing events both in Argentina (especially the Falklands/Malvinas War against Britain in mid-1982) and the eruption of Latin America's debt crisis in August 1982 (elaborated in detail in Chapter 6).

PART 1: CLASHING INTERESTS

Argentina: Between Economic Neoliberalization and Human Rights Violations

Following the coup of March 24, 1976, Argentina was ruled by a military junta with General Jorge Rafael Videla as president (1976–1981). Upon seizing power, the junta launched what it called "The National Reorganization Process" (*Proceso de Reorganización Nacional* or just *Proceso*) that included the liberalization of Argentina's economy, the reorganization and modernization of the state, and an alignment with the Western bloc in the Cold War.[14] These goals would be achieved by dissolving the parliament and placing severe limits on political activity, declaring a state of siege, prohibiting the activities of labor and professional organizations, abolishing the right to strike, intervening in universities and courts, applying strict censorship on the press, and more. The cultivation of ties with the US administration and with the international financial community constituted a significant keystone of the *Proceso*. Keen to restore relations with the Bretton Woods institutions, as well as with international banks and investors, the regime reformed Argentina's investment law to attract foreign capital. Additionally, it settled disputes with US companies that had been expropriated by the Peronist regime,[15] removing a sizable obstacle to the WB negotiation table.

Videla, like many other presidents, regarded economic success as crucial to the survival of his regime. Along with ensuring that the control of the economy remained in the hands of skilled professionals aligned with the junta's goals, appointing "sympathetic interlocutors" to Washington-based institutions was essential to strengthening ties with the WB, the IMF, and the broader international financial community.[16] Martínez de Hoz, Minister of Economy between March 1976 and March

1981, was one such figure. A graduate of Cambridge University from a landholding family associated with the elitist *Sociedad Rural Argentina* and, until the coup, president of the Board of Industrialists, he was instrumental in fashioning the image of self-discipline that the regime sought to attribute to itself.[17] As a liberal and fervent anti-Keynesian,[18] he sought to transform Argentina's economy through the dismantling of state interventionism and the promotion of a free-market economy, privatizations, deregulation, fighting against inflation, correction of price distortions, expansion of the industrial infrastructure, and diversification of the export sector. Although the regime's slogan was "Shrinking the State to Widen the Nation," the minister engaged in the construction of costly public projects, some of them with WB support.[19]

Despite the existence of an ideological affinity on economic matters, human rights violations jeopardized US-Argentine relations and heightened the risk of generating cracks in the WB-Argentina-US triangular dynamics. Jimmy Carter's presidential win in November 1976 was a defining moment for US foreign policy, marking a shift from the Cold War security concerns that had dominated US relations with the developing world to a growing, albeit not exclusive, focus on human rights issues. While the junta's anti-communist campaign fully aligned with US Cold War security interests, the ruthless methods that the armed forces employed conflicted with Carter's human rights diplomacy.

This conflict soon reached the WB's doorstep, as Carter sought to link the provision of US bilateral assistance, as well as multilateral lending, to advances in the human rights arena. For its part, the military regime attempted to persuade its detractors, including human rights supporters in the US Congress and State Department, of its alleged moderation, while, in fact, it repressed what it perceived as leftist subversives. Videla also warned that if his government fell, a harder-line junta would replace it. However, beginning in May 1976, as reports of arbitrary detentions, torture, and disappearances mounted, the US ambassador to Argentina, Robert Hill, started to doubt Videla's moderation. Hill demanded that Videla's regime reduce its human rights violations,[20] but his efforts were undermined by Secretary of State Henry Kissinger, who strove to avoid conflicts with the new Cold War ally of the United States in the Southern Cone.[21]

The junta sought to conceal the magnitude of state terrorism by diverting US attention to economic reforms and anti-communist measures. Time and again, Argentine officials assured US representatives that the government would soon release detainees and allow international organizations to visit detention centers to verify the well-being of the prisoners. Trying to justify its repressive methods, it also announced that the Secretary of Economic Coordination, Guillermo Walter Klein, and his family were the target of a terrorist attack,[22] as was the case with other government figures such as Martínez de Hoz, Juan Alemann, and even Videla.[23] Attempting to show that repression would soon be abandoned, the junta issued a statement in December 1979 outlining vague principles and guidelines that would form the basis for a return to constitutional governance at an unspecified time in the future.[24]

In addition to promising the Carter administration that he would safeguard human rights, Videla took advantage of the president's difficulties in conciliating between moral concerns and US economic and security interests. In effect, following the Soviet invasion of Afghanistan in December 1979 and the end of détente, it became increasingly hard for Carter to prioritize human rights concerns in relations with the junta. Argentina's strategic significance for Washington increased when Carter imposed a grain embargo on Moscow. Fearing that Videla would violate the embargo, Carter pursued a rapprochement with the junta,[25] reducing both US-WB potential tensions and the likelihood of a US veto on WB loans to Argentina.

If, by late December 1980, the junta had secured ten WB loans (compared to a total of nine before the coup of 1976), some with US support and others thanks to US abstention, the prospect of expanding WB assistance grew even stronger with President Ronald Reagan's arrival at the White House in January 1981. During his first year in office, Reagan's foreign policy was largely guided by the fervent anti-communism of key policymakers like Jeane Kirkpatrick, his foreign policy adviser during the presidential campaign and US Ambassador to the UN since

February 1981. Reagan's officials sought to dismantle the human rights policy of the Carter administration and to reaffirm fruitful relations with anti-communist and neoliberal Latin American dictators that had been the targets of Carter's team.[26] As historian Vanessa Walker argues, the Reagan administration did not entirely neglect human rights but approached them within a reinvigorated Cold War context, viewing communism as the foremost global threat due to the greater violations committed by communist regimes. This approach justified downplaying human rights violations of Cold War allies in Latin America, framing military aid to right-wing dictatorial regimes as a crucial element of both hemispheric defense against communism and the promotion of human rights.[27] In 1982, Reagan's staff began to reorient policy towards democracy promotion, a factor in the fall of Argentina's dictatorial regime in 1983.

The dictatorship's last years in power were marked by a deepening economic and political crisis. Argentina struggled to repay its mounting foreign debt and confronted instability and tension within competing military factions. The situation worsened when General Roberto Viola replaced Videla in March 1981. In November 1981, the military deposed Viola and replaced him first by interim presidents Horacio Liendo and Carlos Lacoste, and eventually by Leopoldo Galtieri, who assumed the presidency on December 22, 1981.[28]

As Minister of Economy, Galtieri appointed the lawyer and liberal economist Roberto Alemann. In the period 1979–1981, Argentina's external debt had tripled, reaching some $27 billion. Alemann aspired to an even more orthodox policy than Martínez de Hoz by curbing inflation, privatizing state-owned companies, and implementing deregulation and wage freezes—all of which triggered social unrest. Fearful of losing control, Galtieri embarked on a dangerous military adventure by invading the Falkland/Malvinas islands in the South Atlantic Ocean, which led to a deadly war with Britain that lasted from April 2 to June 14, 1982. Argentina's painful defeat in the war, under the shadow of a vicious power struggle among members of the military, spurred unprecedented political and social turmoil which left Galtieri with no choice but to resign. On June 18, 1982, he was replaced by interim president Alfredo

Oscar Saint-Jean, and on July 1, 1983, Reynaldo Brignone became the last president of the dictatorship.

McNamara's WB: Between Political Neutrality and Human Rights

Through most of the period analyzed in this chapter, the WB was headed by Robert McNamara, in office since 1968. In late 1980, a compromise between President Carter and President-elect Reagan led to the appointment of Alden W. Clausen, nicknamed "Tom," the former head of Bank of America, as the new president of the WB. Clausen succeeded McNamara in July 1981. The repercussions of this transition did not escape Argentina.

Under McNamara, the WB achieved impressive growth. It quadrupled its staff (which grew to 2,500 members in 1980)[29] and quintupled the amount of its lending (totaling $12 billion per year by 1980 for the IBRD and IDA combined). Towards the end of McNamara's term, the WB was supervising over 1,600 projects in more than one hundred developing member-states. Lending to Latin America declined, however, because McNamara, as well as Clausen later on, prioritized support to the poorer countries in Sub-Saharan Africa.[30]

During McNamara's tenure, United States-World Bank tensions were on the rise. This reflected Washington's reconsideration of its foreign aid policy and its growing discontent with McNamara, who took significant steps to try to enhance the WB's autonomy and adopted several positions that conflicted with US expectations. In Argentina, McNamara sought EB approval on loans that the United States opposed on human rights grounds. During the 1970s, the WB approved all loans that the US ED objected to on such grounds.[31] As historians Patrick Sharma and William Schmidli argue, US efforts to influence WB decisions on human rights grounds were often counterproductive, causing resistance among EDs from other countries and ultimately weakening Washington's position.[32]

The WB's eagerness to assist Argentina's dictatorship transcended McNamara's autonomist aspirations and reflected pressures exerted by the Bank's clientele. At the time, many developing countries, including several Latin American republics, joined the NIEO initiative, which criticized the economic order orchestrated by the WB and the IMF. As mentioned in Chapter 4, the NIEO, promulgated by the UN declaration in 1974, called for the redirection of a greater proportion of the benefits of the global economy towards developing nations. More than a set of economic-legal proposals, the NIEO was a political initiative. In essence, the NIEO challenged the conventional division in Cold War politics. Instead of framing the central divide as between Western and Eastern blocs, it posited a distinction between a wealthy and hegemonic North and an impoverished and neglected South that called for a fairer distribution of wealth.[33] While the WB tried to respond to these demands without irritating the United States, Secretary of State Kissinger (1973–1977) saw the WB as a means to blunt southern demands and co-opt NIEO supporters.[34] By the time that Reagan assumed the presidency, the NIEO had been debilitated due to internal disagreements.

As WB records show, US abstentions during the Carter administration and favorable votes under Ford, Carter, and Reagan demonstrated the Bank's determination to remain active in Latin America despite changing political circumstances in the region and US stances. However, more than the Bank's semi-autonomy, they reflected US internal contradictions. The US decision to refrain from exercising its veto power in the WB's EB does not imply that the United States ceased to view the Bank as an arm of its foreign policy. In fact, as stressed, the US government struggled to navigate between its human rights policy and its strategic and economic Cold War interests in Latin America. While the Bank refused to get involved in human rights diplomacy, it enthusiastically acted in the economic Cold War, which was enormously beneficial to the United States. WB-supported projects, as well as the policy conditions attached to its loan accords, helped foster economic stability and growth, keep international markets open to US exports, provide lucrative opportunities for US contractors and investors, and promote a capitalist model of development and progress.[35] To be sure, developing countries experiencing economic growth were more likely to remain aligned with the Western bloc.

The difficulties that the United States confronted while engaging in human rights diplomacy were reflected in several pieces of legislation.

Human rights legislation passed in the US Congress in 1974 established human rights issues as a binding precondition for US direct security assistance.[36] These laws were further solidified in September 1975, with the approval of the Harkin Amendment or Section 116 of the Foreign Assistance Act of 1961, which established that no assistance (of any kind) should be provided to governments that engage in a consistent pattern of gross violations of internationally recognized human rights. The only exception was aid that would directly benefit the needy sectors of society.[37] These laws, however, were not binding on the US executive branch. During both the Nixon and Ford administrations, the executive sharply opposed the human rights legislation and resisted enforcement measures passed by Congress. To overcome this resistance, Congress gradually reduced the executive's freedom of action with regard to the granting of direct US aid to countries that violated human rights.[38] On April 6, 1977, the House of Representatives approved the International Financial Act of 1977 subsection (a), which required US representatives to all IFIs, including for the first time the WB, to vote against loans to countries that violated human rights. A country was considered to be in violation of human rights if it practiced torture, cruel treatment, or prolonged imprisonment without charges—crimes that Argentina's regime was committing at the time.[39] The US president maintained his prerogative in determining policy towards multilateral development banks, however, arguing that these were nonpolitical institutions.[40] It was precisely this prerogative which allowed the Carter and Reagan administrations to make decisions on a case-by-case basis and avoid focusing only on human rights concerns.

Notably, during McNamara's tenure, tensions between the WB and the US administration were centered on human rights but also on the WB's anti-poverty programs, which Reagan strongly criticized. However, with Clausen in office, a new source of friction emerged, related to what Reagan's conservative team perceived as the Bank's support for the public sector in developing countries, particularly in the oil sector. There was little ground for this tension. To begin with, Clausen was an avid supporter of the private sector. He redirected the Bank's focus from the distribution concerns that defined McNamara's era back to the prioritization of economic growth. These policies were positively received by the Reagan administration and Argentina's dictatorship, both of which were manifestly neoliberal. In light of the oil shocks of 1973 and 1979, Clausen announced a 25 percent increase in energy lending—a sector that was considered crucial to Argentina's development. Lending for oil and gas exploration and development, however, soon became a matter of contention between the WB and the Reagan administration, which wanted oil and gas left in private hands. Clausen, who agreed that private entrepreneurs were the best possible choice, considered that the most urgent goal was to reduce the dependence on oil imports, even if, in order to reach this goal, the Bank would assist state-owned oil companies.[41] This was good news for Argentina. As detailed below, the first two loans that the Bank granted to Argentina when Clausen took office were to the energy sector.

PART 2: ARGENTINA'S DICTATORSHIP AND ITS AMBIVALENT RELATIONS WITH THE WB

Phase 1: Paving the Road to Renewed WB Lending to Argentina (March-August 1976)

President Videla, as previously mentioned, made it a priority to restore relations with the international financial community. Since IMF lending had ceased in 1967 and WB lending in March 1971, he could present the renewal of assistance from both institutions not only as an economic achievement but also as a sign of Argentina's improved status in the international sphere. The day of the coup, while tanks were still surrounding the presidential palace, General Joaquín de las Heras, the incumbent Minister of Economy, contacted the IMF to inform them of Argentina's intention to secure an SBA.[42] Martínez de Hoz, who replaced him five days later, promptly intensified efforts to reinstate ties with the Bretton Woods institutions. However, despite the significance of these ties, the new minister asserted that he would approach the IMF only after a stabilization program had been enacted into law.[43] This postponement, as Martínez de Hoz explained several years later, represented part of the challenges he encountered while trying to assemble a "coherent and uniform economic team" capable of "breaking the doctrinarian line [the statism and interventionism associated with Peronism] that had been dominant in Argentina since 1945."[44]

Martínez de Hoz filled the senior positions on his team with economists who belonged to two types of liberals: the old guard or traditional liberals (like himself), and the young technocrats or "Chicago Boys."[45] Despite disagreements over anti-inflationary policies and the proper pace of reforms, these two groups shared radical anti-populist and anti-*statist* stands and enthusiastically promoted the establishment of a free-market economy.[46] Among the most influential Chicago Boys were Adolfo Diz, a former ED to the IMF (1967–1968), who in 1976 was appointed president of the Central Bank, and Guillermo Walter Klein, Martínez de Hoz's secretary of planning, who had been involved in negotiations with the Bank since the late 1950s.[47]

Martínez de Hoz's plan was launched on April 2, 1976. It was designed to reduce inflation, improve the balance of payments, deregulate the economy, promote competition, and bring about "liberalization, openness, and modernization of the economy."[48] The plan earned the minister supporters in Washington, particularly Secretary of State Henry Kissinger and William Rogers, the assistant secretary of state for Latin America.[49] It also reinforced the regime's ties with the domestic private sector, where Martínez de Hoz identified, as he recalled, "a valid interlocutor"[50] who historians like Horacio Verbitsky and Juan Pablo Bohoslavsky describe as "economic accomplices to the dictatorship."[51]

The opening of Argentina's economy and the professionalization of its economic management increased the IMF's and WB's readiness to work with the junta. The Bretton Woods institutions, invoking their political neutrality, did not let the regime's illegitimacy or its crimes against humanity jeopardize their involvement in transforming Argentina's economy. In May 1976, the first IMF and WB missions landed in Argentina. In meetings with Diz and Martínez de Hoz, David Green (head of the WB Financial Evaluation Department) stated that the mission was evaluating "how the WB can contribute to Argentina's progress and recuperation."[52] In June, Gerald Wiese (WB country programs director, WHD) explained: "During the Presidency of Isabel Perón the country was virtually leaderless. [. . .] Encouraged by demagogic leaders, and highly protected, oligopolistic industry engaged in a struggle over wages and prices, with total lack of monetary control and fiscal discipline."[53] Wiese considered that Martínez de Hoz's philosophy can "be broadly classified as economic liberalism, i.e. a moving back from the nationalist-*statist*-populism which characterized Peronism to a more market and private sector-oriented approach."[54]

The mission report focused only on economic issues. Yet the staff, which spent weeks in Argentina, must have had some sense of the atrocities going on around them. Vito Tanzi, a senior IMF economist who participated in several of the missions between 1976 and 1978, often in coordination with the WB, referred to "the atmosphere of fear and constant danger" rampant in Argentina, the armed bodyguards that accompanied the mission during its stay, and the beggars that appeared in the streets since the coup. Attempting to justify the IMF's support of a deadly dictatorship, Tanzi stated that "as long as a government is firm in power, the Fund was expected to be indifferent to its political nature. It was expected to be politically neutral."[55] McNamara, like Tanzi, showed little concern over human rights violations in Argentina. Martínez de Hoz needed the Bank's assistance to facilitate the liberalization of Argentina's economy. McNamara, for his part, needed Martínez de Hoz to showcase that the WB had succeeded in imparting its economic vision and development model to a significant Latin American country like Argentina. Certainly, there were two to tango.

The Bretton Woods institutions were not the only ones backing the junta. In June 1976, Martínez de Hoz and Diz met with IMF and WB staff, but also with Secretary Kissinger, Secretary of the Treasury William Simon, and high-ranking Eximbank officials.[56] The Eximbank confirmed that it would resume lending to Argentina, which had been suspended in October 1975. The IMF announced that it would open negotiations on a new SBA for the country.[57] Private banks in the United States, Europe, Japan, and Canada agreed to grant credits worth $850 million.[58] Under these rosy circumstances, Martínez de Hoz met McNamara, Burke Knapp (WB Senior Vice President of Operations), and the Argentine Adalbert Krieger Vasena, Head of the WB-WHD. During the meeting, Martínez de Hoz referred to "the chaotic economic circumstances" that preceded the coup. He rightly stressed that "the military takeover had been greeted by almost the entire population, including parts of the Peronist movement, with a sigh of relief."[59] He then explained that "inspired by economic and political developments in neighboring countries, particularly in Peru and [Pinochet's] Chile, the military rulers had gradually developed a strong economic philosophy favoring the re-creation of a relatively free-market economy and a disciplined and efficient management of the public sector." Aware that the WB viewed wage increases as a major driver of inflation, he highlighted that wages had been reduced by 20 percent during his first weeks in office. He expected inflation to continue declining and assured that no further real wage reductions would be implemented. As if poverty reduction were not a fundamental goal of the so-called "War on Poverty" that McNamara announced in Nairobi in 1973, Martínez de Hoz went on to assert that the plan's success depended on the government's ability to keep real wages down. Doubting its ability to do so, McNamara asked about the labor unions' willingness to cooperate. The minister avoided responding to this question—probably because the regime had violently dismantled the unions and was cruelly repressing the labor movement. In any case, Martínez de Hoz asked for McNamara's support in restoring confidence in Argentina's economy by initiating projects related to agricultural storage, credit, and industrial exports—projects that a WB mission to Argentina was already evaluating. McNamara, demonstrating a high level of political neutrality yet also a degree of social indifference, expressed agreement with the need to restore confidence in Argentina. He stressed that "the Bank would like to support the Government's efforts which fully met [the WB's] assistance standards."[60]

Following these encouraging meetings, Martínez de Hoz considered that the time had come to obtain the IMF's seal of economic and political approval, which certainly increased the already high chances of reaching an accord with the WB. On July 8, 1976, Martínez de Hoz and Diz officially requested an SBA worth $300 million,[61] which was soon approved.[62] This SBA constituted the largest loan ever granted by the IMF to a Latin American country, underscoring the considerable magnitude of the IMF's support.[63] As Martínez de Hoz claimed years later, "Our economic program was even more severe than what the IMF demanded. There were no disagreements or debates with the IMF. It was easy."[64]

The SBA paved the way for additional loans. In October 1976, Argentina received $800 million from private banks in the United States, Canada, Switzerland, Britain, Holland, Scandinavia, France, Belgium, Spain, and Germany.[65]

In sum, barely two months of meetings with representatives of the international financial community were enough to restore lending to Argentina after years of minimal activity. Human rights concerns were not even mentioned during this first phase of Argentina-WB negotiations. As shown below, the IMF loan was a significant contributing factor in reestablishing WB lending.

Phase 2: The Beginning of WB Lending to the Junta: Human Rights as a Non-Issue (September 1976–March 1977)

By the end of 1976, accounts of forced disappearances in Argentina, alongside Carter's presidential campaign push to infuse a stronger moral dimension into US foreign policy, brought increased focus on human rights to the Ford administration and public sentiment. By the end of the year, WB staff and EDs could no longer ignore the situation in Argentina. Nevertheless, in September 1976, when McNamara submitted to the EB the first loan proposal to Argentina's dictatorship, worth $115 million, for an energy power project in Buenos Aires, no reference was made to the repression conducted by the armed forces. McNamara explained that loans to Argentina had been sporadic due to concerns about creditworthiness and disagreement on specific projects. Besides several comments on "the economic chaos inherited by the military government," McNamara's report was strictly technical.[66] After all, the regime was doing everything the Bank could hope for: halting hyperinflation, liberalizing the economy, and precluding default on Argentina's external financial obligations that had reached $3.2 billion by December 1975, including debts owed to the WB. As McNamara explained, the junta "undertook the twin task of breaking the wage-price spiral and eliminating price controls," two steps that previous regimes had refused to take.[67] By May 1976, real wages had reached their lowest level in years—about 80 percent of the average for 1971–1975. Paradoxically,

McNamara, the person who brought social issues to the top of the WB agenda, did not mention, even in passing, the social impact of decreasing real wages on the workers.

The EB discussed the loan at its meeting of September 21, 1976. The US ED (still under the Ford administration) voted in favor, and the loan was approved unanimously. However, a few days later, US Ambassador Hill warned Videla that he saw the positive vote at the WB "as probably [the] last time [that] the U.S. would be able to avoid invoking [the Harkin] Amendment against Argentina unless G[overment] o[f] A[rgentina] moved quickly to demonstrate [that] it [was] taking measures to get [the] human rights situation in hand."[68] Hill's threats aside, Argentina-WB negotiations advanced without real interference on the part of the United States.

Goodwill in the WB abounded. It led to the approval, on March 22, 1977, of the second WB loan to Argentina's dictatorship, this time totaling $105 million to carry out a highway project. The decisive EB meeting took place barely two months after Carter's inauguration and shortly before the passing of the legislation that established, for the first time, that US representatives to the WB should vote against loans to countries that violated human rights. But McNamara, arguing that human rights were not part of the Bank's mandate, continued working with Argentina's dictatorship. In September 1976, McNamara's report to the EB omitted any reference to the dictatorial nature of the regime or human rights concerns and conveyed, instead, a subtle message of political impartiality. McNamara stressed that Argentina's government had already achieved the goals of the first phase of its "economic reconstruction program" and had embarked on reforms necessary to lay the foundation for strong, self-sustained economic growth.[69] As on previous and later occasions, the potential effects of economic liberalization on the poor were also overlooked. During the EB meeting, Einar Magnussen, the ED who represented Denmark, Finland, Iceland, Norway, and Sweden, was the only participant who asked whether the highway project would benefit the poor. Segura, representing the WB-WHD, answered that ". . . since the roads are located in different parts [of Argentina], [the project] will help the rural population to a great extent."[70] Wiese added that road construction would require a significant labor force, including unskilled workers from the poor sectors.[71] These evasive answers seem to indicate that the liberalization of Argentina's economy was the main, or even the only, goal of the WB in the country at the time. It becomes evident that the WB played a crucial role in Latin America's Cold War dynamics by backing a brutal dictatorial regime that was resolute to ensure Argentina's full integration into the capitalist bloc.

Notwithstanding Carter's human rights policy, the United States's vote in the WB did not change. In March 1977, Hal Reynolds, the US ED to the WB, actively supported the highway loan. However, during the decisive Board meeting, he stated: "I wouldn't wish my support of the project be interpreted as any lessening on [US] concern [with human rights in Argentina]. But I do look upon the project as economically justified and supportive of general economic policies aimed at restoring stability and sound economic growth to the Argentina economy."[72] Reynolds went on to criticize McNamara's apathy regarding human rights violations in Argentina, saying: "I think the goals and purposes of the Bank properly encompass a broad range of human concerns, including freedom from physical and mental abuse as well as freedom from economic privation and want." These harsh words reflected Carter's understanding of human rights, which identified three basic rights: the right to be free from governmental violations of the integrity of the person, such as torture and lack of a fair trial; economic and social rights, that is, the right to be free from government action or inaction which inhibits individuals from meeting basic needs like health care, education, and shelter; and the right to enjoy civil and political liberties.[73] In any event, Reynolds concluded by saying that he hoped other WB members would join the United States in that regard. Magnussen responded that nobody would doubt that the Nordic countries were sympathetic to Reynolds's view. However, attempting to artificially de-politicize the discussion, he added, human rights "should not be stressed as an argument against the present loan proposal."[74]

Towards the end of the meeting, Argentina's representative Eduardo Conesa thanked the EB for supporting the loan and responded to Reynolds's remarks, declaring: "My Argentinian authorities [. . .] are second to none in the defense of human rights. Precisely the first goal of my authorities is to establish human rights in Argentina." He then argued that the WB's prestige among developing countries resulted from its "economic and technical analyses" and "the professional excellence" of its staff. Conesa stressed that the WB Articles of Agreement posit that "the Executive Directors cannot judge whether a given country respects human rights or is engaged in a flagrant denial of the right to life, liberty, or security of the person." Without trying to conceal his criticism of Carter's pressures on the WB, he stressed that ". . . history tells us that all the preliminary legal work on the [WB's] Articles of Agreement was done within the US Government by US lawyers," therefore, the United States should support them." He concluded: "Nobody questions [. . .] the undisputable right of any Executive Directors to vote for or against any given loan, but such a vote must be cast on economic grounds, not on political grounds. Any order or instruction of any member country directing his own Executive Director to vote in the WB on political grounds is illegal and unconstitutional."[75]

The deliberations at the EB reveal two central points. First, contrary to prevailing scholarly approaches, the United States was not always able to impose its views on the EB of the Bank. Second, by invoking the WB Articles of Agreement, which were largely authored by US delegates to the Bretton Woods conference, Conesa sought to utilize the WB political neutrality as a means to evade political and moral questions regarding the systematic violation of human rights by Argentina's armed forces. Conesa not only exerted direct pressure on the Bank, but also delegitimized the US attempts to subordinate the grant of WB loans to human rights criteria. As shown below, the situation changed only slightly following the April 1977 US legislation on human rights. The table below summarizes WB lending to the dictatorial regime.

Phase 3: Human Rights on the Rise? (April 1977–December 1980)

In April 1977, as noted previously, the House of Representatives approved the International Financial Act of 1977, which, in subsection (a) required US representatives to all IFIs, including, for the first time,

Table 3: World Bank Loans to the National Reorganization Process, 1976–1983.

	Project Title	Project ID	Commitment Amount (in million US dollars)	Executive Board Approval Date
1	**Buenos Aires Power Project (04)**	P005931	115	September 21, 1976
2	**Highway Project (04)**	P005932	105	March 22, 1977
3	**Industrial Credit Project**	P005930	100	June 16, 1977
4	**Grain Storage Project**	P005934	105	February 21, 1978
5	**Agricultural Credit Project**	P005933	60	May 9, 1978
6	**Railways Project (02)**	P005935	96	March 27, 1979
7	**Yacyretá Hydroelectric Project**	P005937	210	October 16, 1979
8	**Oil and Gas Engineering Project**	P005936	27	June 24, 1980
9	**Vocational Training and Technical Education Project**	P005938	58	October 7, 1980
10	**Coal Exploration Project**	P005939	10	December 9, 1980
11	**Refinery Conversion Project**	P005942	200	July 7, 1981
12	**Oil and Gas Credit Project**	P005941	100	July 7, 1981
13	**Industrial Credit Project (02)**	P005940	100	December 1, 1981
14	**Highway Project (05)**	P005943	100	May 31, 1983
	TOTAL AMOUNT		**1,386**	

Source: Data from World Bank Group Site, Projects by Country, Argentina (https://projects.worldbank.org/en/projects-operations/projects-summary?countrycode_exact=AR&title=Argentina)

the WB, to vote against loans to countries in violation of human rights. Shortly after the act's approval, the US Secretary of the Treasury Michael Blumenthal (1977–1979) met Martínez de Hoz at the Annual Assembly of the IDB. Blumenthal cautioned him that "when [the US] casts [its] vote in an international organization, such as [the IDB], [it] will take into account whether the money is being used to benefit the people, and whether there is a respect for human rights."[76] He emphasized that the same principles would apply to the US vote in the WB. Linking financial assistance to human rights criteria, however, proved to be difficult as it required the agreement and adherence of other member states that held voting power in multilateral organizations. For example, when the US delegation to the IDB endeavored to garner support for the human rights cause among representatives from Europe, Japan, Israel, Canada, and Latin America, many of them insisted that financial aid should be evaluated solely on economic grounds.[77] This stance, as WB's EB meetings demonstrated, was particularly pronounced among representatives of Latin American dictatorships, which expected reciprocal support from Argentina and sought favorable votes on loan proposals for their own nations in return. Reciprocity proved to be successful. Suffice it to mention that while the WB granted thirteen loans to the Uruguayan dictatorship, six of them received approval during Carter's tenure. Similarly, out of the 116 loans granted to the Brazilian dictatorship (1964–1985), thirty-two were approved under Carter.

Although Carter's human rights legislation did not prevent WB lending to the junta, the mere act of US abstention—and more significantly, the potential threat of a negative US vote in the WB's EB—posed a significant risk to Argentina's image both domestically and internationally. The same applied to the Bank's management which, as a rule, refrained from submitting to the EB's vote loan proposals whose approval the US objected. In early June 1977, for instance, given the risk of a potential unfavorable US vote due to human rights concerns, the WB-WHD staff wondered about the wisdom of bringing to the EB's table a proposal for a new loan to Argentina. Martínez de Hoz, trying to convince the Bank to follow agreed-upon plans, told Knapp that "the Argentine Government expected to take some significant action to improve their 'human rights' image before June 16 [the scheduled date of the EB meeting]."[78] Moreover, recognizing that the main obstacle was a potential US negative vote, Argentina's ambassador to Washington reached out to the State Department and asserted that the junta had already implemented sufficient human rights actions to warrant lending to the country. Yet, as reports on human rights violations persisted, the State Department persevered in its efforts to persuade Argentina to withdraw its loan application.[79]

Notwithstanding US pressures, McNamara brought the loan proposal to the Board as originally scheduled. It is clear that McNamara was confident that the proposal would encounter little to no significant opposition. In contrast to prior positive votes, the US ED abstained this time, and the loan was approved on June 16, 1977.[80] During the decisive EB meeting, US ED Reynolds stated that his abstention "underscore[d] the very serious commitment of [his] Government to human rights worldwide." He further remarked that the US government had discussed the issue with Argentina's authorities and that President Carter hoped that improvements in the human rights area "will make it possible for [the United States] to support future loans to Argentina."[81] Colombian ED Ramón Martínez Aponte, adhering to the strategy used by the Argentines and in line with NIEO dmands, replied that projects should be considered only on their financial and economic merits.[82] Likewise, Said El-Naggar, the Egyptian ED, declared: "the question of human rights, as much as it is important, should not be a criteria for considering any project in this Board."[83] Closing the meeting, Argentina's ED Conesa stated that Argentina "strongly supports the technocratic professional integrity of the World Bank staff against any intent of politicization," emphasizing that "it is essential to decide whether we are going to be in the future an international bank for human rights or we are going to be an international bank for reconstruction and development."[84] Unfortunately, McNamara's response to this provocative statement was blacked out during the declassification process at the WB Archives.

Although the US abstained on this specific loan, Argentina could not afford to sit back and rest on its laurels. President General Videla himself took part in efforts to persuade the US administration that the level of repression was decreasing. In his only meeting with Carter, on September 9, 1977, Videla stated that he would welcome missions from international organizations to assess the status of human rights. Additionally, he gave his word that the human rights situation would be normalized by Christmas. Carter, in response, showed Videla a list of 3,000 political detainees that the Washington-based Argentine Committee for

Human Rights had handed him and asked about the Soviet-born Argentine journalist Jacobo Timerman and the Deutsch family, among the best-known detainees at the time.[85] Nevertheless, eager to showcase Argentina as a success of his human rights policy, Carter desisted from taking a tough stance against the junta. Ultimately, he mixed sanctions and concessions, resulting in inconsistent US voting on assistance to Argentina from various institutions. For example, in 1977, the United States opposed three loans from the IDB to the junta,[86] abstained on WB loans, and approved the allocation of Eximbank credits. The fact that the Carter administration supported the granting of credits solely from the Eximbank, the only US and non-multilateral institution among the three, requires an explanation as it runs counter to Senate legislation regarding US bilateral aid. On the surface, statements by the military regime that it would make certain concessions, including an on-site investigation by the Inter-American Human Rights Commission, provided Carter sufficient legitimacy for approving direct assistance. After all, the junta was a loyal Cold War ally—but loyalty came with a price, and loans were the preferable instrument of payment. Eximbank loans were designed to boost US exports by providing borrowing states with the necessary funds to purchase US goods. Therefore, it seems that Eximbank's lending to the dictatorship largely, or at least partially, stemmed from pressures exerted by the US business sector and its advocates in Washington. They argued that the United States should not bear the cost of human rights violations abroad through the loss of markets or jobs.[87]

As the risk of a US veto gradually diminished, WB-Argentina collaboration became routine. In early October 1977, during the IMF and WB Annual Meeting in Washington, Martínez de Hoz met McNamara and Knapp for the first time. He thanked McNamara for the Bank's assistance and then referred to three projects for whose realization he sought WB funding: railways, *Yacyretá* (a hydroelectric project), and *El Pachón* (a copper project). Discussions regarding the railways reveal not only the scope and impact of Martínez de Hoz's economic reforms, but also the ideological affinity between the parties.[88] Contrary to the Peronist administration, which nationalized the railways in 1948 and refused to shut down unprofitable train lines, Martínez de Hoz was fully committed to transforming the railways into "an economically viable institution." He claimed that 4,000 km of unprofitable lines were already approved for closure and another 4,000 km would be soon authorized. The railway company, he added, cut its personnel by 28,000 workers and reduced uneconomic inter-city passenger traffic by 36 percent. By the end of 1979, the length of the railway system was expected to be down to 20,000 km, a reduction of 50 percent. One can imagine the impact these draconian closures and layoffs had on both workers and the poor.[89] Yet, rather than asking about the social consequences of these cuts, McNamara expressed satisfaction with the impressive progress towards rehabilitating the railway system, which reflected the entrenchment of a free-market economy in Argentina.[90] At the close of the meeting, Martínez de Hoz invited McNamara to visit Argentina—a visit that could improve the regime's reputation among Western democracies.

In late November 1977, Secretary of State Cyrus Vance visited Argentina. Videla promised him that he would release 500 detainees and allow the International Red Cross to visit detention centers. However, in December, a series of high-profile kidnappings and additional disappearances, including one of the founders of *Madres de Plaza de Mayo*, tarnished Videla's image in Washington—this in the very month when the junta, in an effort to get loans approved, sent the State Department a report stating that there was some progress in the area of human rights, including the release of 440 prisoners.[91] By Christmas, the State Department affirmed that the number of missing people had risen to 15,000–20,000, and that Videla's promises to Carter and Vance were empty.[92]

The impact that these unfulfilled promises had on WB lending to Videla's regime was marginal. In February 1978, McNamara submitted to the EB yet another loan proposal for Argentina—this time for a grain storage project. In addition to the importance of agriculture for Argentina's exports, McNamara justified the loan by praising the considerable progress that Martínez de Hoz had made in stabilizing the economy.[93] Edward Fried, the new US ED to the WB, repeated a statement that became a watchword: "Under instructions from my authorities, I wish to be recorded as having abstained on this loan."[94] While this abstention reflected Carter's expectation that Videla's assurances on human rights would be honored, WB documents suggest this was only a partial explanation.[95] Fried understood that WB loans to the junta would likely be approved even without his support, and that a negative vote at the EB could prove counterproductive. The US abstention thus obscured its inability to exert substantial influence over other members of the Bank's EB and, to a certain extent, over the Bank's staff, while also reflecting its apparent willingness to protect the WB's image as an institution that served the interests of both its donors and debtors—an important goal at a time when Third World countries were demanding reforms to the international economic order. Once again, thus, the loan was approved without opposition.

In May 1978, McNamara recommended the granting of an additional loan to Argentina. In the report that he circulated among the EDs, he praised the junta for its "considerable progress in stabilizing the economy," and for putting aside "the protectionist import-substituting industrial development strategy" associated with Peronism. He stressed specific measures demonstrating that Argentina's economy was transforming. This included privatizations, the imposition of additional taxation, the rationalization of the tax administration, and foreign debt repayments.[96] The decisive EB meeting regarding a loan for an agricultural credit project worth $60 million took place on May 9, 1978.[97] This time, ED Magnussen from Scandinavia focused on social issues. He argued that although the Bank was intended to promote social justice, the project seemed "not at all to direct itself to the lower income strata." He also claimed that the Bank was subordinating social goals to economic figures. Several EDs representing Third World countries shared Magnussen's criticism. Disregarding the existence of human rights violations in Argentina, and perhaps even more worryingly, acting as if the regime did not exhibit a clear indifference towards the needs of the most vulnerable sectors of society, Lerdau, a staff member of the WB-WHD, responded that the main social problems derived "from the efforts of the [Argentine] government to bring the economy back into some sort of equilibrium which ha[d] involved a series of measures which ha[d] hit all classes of society, but which includes also the reduction in real wages." US ED Fried declared that he was instructed to abstain, but the loan was approved all the same.[98] At the same time that human rights violations did not obstruct WB lending to the junta, they hampered US military assistance to it. In September 1978, as Argentina failed to make a persuasive case for human rights improvements, a US embargo on arms sales to the country entered into effect.[99]

WB-Argentina cooperation progressed until the end of 1979 despite the ambivalent message the United States sent on human rights. In March, for instance, Viron P. Vaky, Assistant Secretary of State for Inter-American Affairs, met the Argentine Ambassador to Washington, Jorge Aja Espil, to express deep concern over the lack of progress on human rights. Vaky warned "that in the absence of substantial improvement [the US] will shift to negative votes on Argentine non-BHN [basic human needs] loans in the IFIs."[100] Despite Vaky's considerable skepticism regarding Argentina's promises, he advised against implementing a more restrictive policy towards the junta, among others, on WB loans. In his view, it would have been "tragic and ironic" to punish the regime just when it "had begun to move and respond to our [human rights] concerns."[101]

The EB meeting about the railways loan on March 27 illustrates the WB's resolve to leave its imprint on the most profound transformation of Argentina's economy up to that point, even if doing so implied relegating human rights matters to a second place. Seeking to convey that the loan's significance extended beyond being a mere component of Argentina's liberalization plan, Martínez, the WB staff member who presented the loan proposal to the EB, claimed that the railways symbolized "the damages that decades of political turbulence and economic disorder ha[d] brought to [Argentina]."[102] He blamed "governments and labor unions [who] had for many years arbitrarily interfered with the management of the railways."[103] He contended that "the high political cost" of the actions needed to reform the railways had "prevented previous governments from carrying them out," which had led to the partial cancelation of a railways loan that the WB had approved in 1971. Nevertheless, he continued, the current government decided "to attack this intractable problem at its roots" by "using the economic and financial criteria that any enterprise, public or private, needs to apply if it is to be viable."[104] Martínez's presentation seemed to suggest that addressing issues "at their roots" solely involved reforming the railways company. However, this approach also involved acting against the workers and shutting down rail lines that were essential for socially and geographically peripheral communities. In any case, Martínez stressed that the WB had played "a delicate and important role in the efforts to rehabilitate the railways [as] the Government and the railways respect the technical competence and neutrality of the Bank and ha[d] relied frequently on Bank advice."[105] He further stated that Argentina concurred with the WB in the belief that railways should function as a commercial enterprise, engaging in free competition with other modes of transportation. Following Martínez's presentation, several EDs asked questions regarding the likelihood of Argentina successfully implementing the project. No questions regarding the dictatorial nature of the regime or human rights were raised, and the loan was approved despite—and in part because of—US abstention.[106]

A few months later, the EB discussed yet another large loan to Argentina whose approval the WB had delayed for years—a $210 million loan to the *Yacyretá* hydroelectric project to be constructed on the border between Argentina and Paraguay. This binational project involved Argentina compensating Paraguay for using the energy generated on the Paraguayan side and for the planned flooding of adjacent Paraguayan territory. The flooding was contentious because it required the relocation of approximately 33,000 people residing in the affected areas, which both the WB and the IDB were already planning.[107] In any event, as McNamara started to announce the project's approval, Bill Bradley, the US ED, interrupted him and declared that he had been instructed to abstain.[108] As in the previous votes since June 1977, the US abstention did not impede the loan's approval.

During 1980, WB lending to Argentina continued at a stable pace. The US voiced concerns, but the Argentine-WB financial caravan kept moving forward. In June, McNamara recommended the approval of a loan to the oil company YPF. He stressed that the loan would allow the WB to support Argentina's efforts to reform its economic structure, strengthen public institutions, and address "some social problems" which he did not specify.[109] During the relevant EB meeting, WB staff explained that the loan was necessary because Argentina still had to attain self-sufficiency in energy.[110] They also claimed that to attract foreign companies to the energy sector, Argentina required a robust banking system with strong private banks. Hence, so they claimed, the WB was already assisting Argentina in advancing the reform of its banking system. Before closing the meeting, McNamara asked the new US ED, Colbert I. King, if he had any comments. King responded, in a way which was to become ritual, that he would like to be recorded as having abstained on this project.[111] Once again, the loan, worth $27 million, was approved without opposition.

In early December 1980, the WB approved a $10 million loan for a coal exploration project in Argentina. These energy loans signaled the fruitful collaboration that had evolved between the dictatorship and the WB, but also the Bank's renewed focus on the energy sector in response to the oil crises of 1973 and 1979. Against the backdrop of these crises, in 1980, McNamara suggested creating a new specialized WB affiliate to focus on the oil sector. This proposed affiliate would have an initial budget of $12 billion, supplementing the existing $13 billion WB energy development plan already underway in Third World countries dependent on oil imports. However, President Reagan would reject this proposal in 1981, arguing that Bank lending to state-owned oil companies abroad (like YPF) was a mistake, as this sector should remain in private hands.[112] In addition to these two loans, the WB provided a first loan to Argentina's educational sector, worth $58 million.[113] As in previous instances, the US abstained, and the loan was approved without difficulty.

Phase 4: The Turning Point (January–December 1981)

The year 1981 was a turning point for all the relevant actors. In January, Ronald Reagan, a Republican, assumed office, succeeding the Democrat Jimmy Carter. In March, following the end of President Videla's term, the military regime, and consequently the entire country, entered a period of growing instability. As mentioned above, WB President McNamara was replaced by Tom Clausen in July. Despite these important transitions, WB lending to Argentina remained steady.

The Carter administration, as detailed above, had abstained on all WB loans to Argentina, with the exception of one that it actively supported in March 1977. With the advent of a new administration that was determined to reorient Carter's human rights diplomacy and solidify US relations with anti-communist regimes in Latin America, the situation became more auspicious for the junta, as the risk of losing support due to human rights violations decreased. Correspondence between Stephen E. Palmer, the acting Assistant Secretary of State for Human Rights, and Secretary of State Alexander Haig (1981–1982) regarding US votes on multilateral development banks' (MDBs) loans to Argentina, Chile, and Uruguay offers valuable insights into the motivations that prompted the Reagan administration to relax the US stance on WB loans to Latin American dictatorships. Palmer argued that till then, the US had considered MDBs' loans on a case-by-case basis. However, now the State Department aimed to actively support loans while making it clear that the United States did not abandon, but instead redefined, its human rights concerns.[114] The Reagan administration claimed that human rights abuses in Latin America stemmed not from violent military rulers but rather from communist subversion. Consequently, in its initial years of governance, it favored assisting military regimes that supposedly protected their populations from potential communist infiltration from abroad. In other words, with Reagan in office, the United States defined a new balance between human rights, Cold War security concerns, and economic interests.

In June 1981, the Reagan administration began supporting Argentina's requests for MDBs' loans "in recognition of the fact that the human rights situation then was markedly improved from the period of the so-called 'dirty-war', when disappearances and torture were common occurrences."[115] Further indications of Washington's favorable disposition towards the junta included the July 1981 visit to Argentina by J. William Middendorf, the US Ambassador to the OAS. In meetings with President Viola, Middendorf underscored Reagan's commitment to enhancing relations between the United States and Argentina. He also explained that Reagan's approach to economic development in the Third World—fully in line with WB policy—centered on the necessity to cut back government spending and to strengthen the private sector at the expense of the public sector.[116] Viola, in return, promised to support US initiatives in the OAS, including US calls to fight terrorism in Latin America.[117] The deal was clear: the United States would back the provision of multilateral loans to Argentina, and in return, the regime would align itself with the Cold War security and economic interests of the Reagan administration.

The US shift to positive votes in the MDBs did not alter WB lending to Argentina, which remained as stable as it had been since September 1976. The only discernible difference pertained to the international legitimacy that the US votes granted the dictatorship. Amidst these favorable circumstances, on July 7, 1981, the EB, led by the WB President Clausen, considered two loan proposals for Argentina's energy sector. One of the loans, amounting to $100 million, was designated for *Banco Nacional* for an oil and gas credit project. The other, totaling $200 million, was allocated to YPF for a refinery conversion project.[118]

Sullivan (WB-WHD) presented both projects to the EB and referred to the unstable trajectory of YPF. Reiterating the arguments that the WB used when approving the railways loan in 1979, he claimed that YPF used to operate "along nationalistic and political lines, more than on economic and development ones." Yet, he went on, Argentina's "reform-minded economic team" was determined to rationalize petroleum development and to give "a meaningful role to the private sector."[119] During this period, WB loans to major state enterprises such as the railways, YPF, ENTEL, and SEGBA were facilitated by their continuous structural reforms, new private sector participation, and partial privatization. In turn, WB loans spurred additional and more profound reforms due to the conditions attached to its loan agreements.

Like in 1978 and 1979, none of the EDs raised questions concerning the regime's dictatorial nature or its human rights violations. Instead, their remarks centered exclusively on oil prices and the country's capacity to meet its debt obligations. Interestingly, one of the EDs asked whether the Bank was potentially encroaching on the domain of private companies that could participate in Argentina's petroleum sector.[120] This question was significant because members of the Reagan administration complained that the WB supported the public sector at the expense of private enterprise. Sullivan rejected this claim, saying that "it seem[ed] very unlikely that the [oil] project could have materialized if the Bank had not been involved." He rightly added that the WB's intervention extended beyond the project's economic aspects and encompassed institutional objectives, including the shaping of YPF's project and the YPF company itself. This time, the US ED voted favorably and both loans were unanimously approved.[121]

Encouraged by the improving stance of the United States towards Argentina, Lorenzo Sigaut, the Minister of Economy during Viola's term, submitted to the WB a request for an Industrial Credit Project of $100 million to the *Banco Nacional de Desarrollo* (BANADE, National Development Bank). While introducing the project to the EB, Robert Kanchuger (WB-WHD) explained that BANADE had become a key supporter of the government's trade liberalization policies. The proposed loan was aimed at mobilizing provincial resources for industrial development and at providing technical assistance for further institutional reforms.[122] The loan was approved unanimously in late December 1981.[123]

Phase 5: Ideological Affinity is Not Enough (January 1982–December 1983)

Just when it seemed that WB lending to the junta had become routine, a series of events in Argentina disrupted the WB-Argentina-US triangular dynamics. From January 1982 and until the end of the dictatorship in early December 1983, as described below, the WB granted only one additional loan to the country, in May 1983.

When General Galtieri was sworn in as president on December 22, 1981, Argentina was grappling with an evolving political and economic crisis. The WB nonetheless expected that Galtieri would accelerate and expand the economic liberalization plan that was launched in 1976. The WB's expectations were fueled by Galtieri's appointment of the liberal-minded Roberto Alemann as Minister of Economy. Alemann, who resigned in June 1982, assembled a team of liberal economists, among them Manuel Alberto Solanet as the Treasury Secretary, Raúl Salaberren as the Secretary of Agriculture and Livestock, and Elvio

Baldinelli as the Secretary of Industry and Mining.[124] Yet ideological affinity with Galtieri's government proved not to be enough to secure a smooth flow of WB loans to Argentina.

Besides the political and economic crisis in Argentina, and despite Reagan's decision in early 1981 to support multilateral lending to a series of South American dictatorial regimes, the United States, due to a variety of factors, reversed its course of action. Some of these factors are related to Reagan's negative perception of foreign aid in general and WB development assistance in particular. According to Reagan's conservative team, the focus on poverty alleviation that (at least in theory) characterized McNamara's tenure had turned the WB into a welfare organization and, consequently, into a waste of money from US taxpayers.[125] US officials also complained that the WB not only failed to advance US interests on a global scale but also assumed a role that US enterprises could have played in the construction of expensive development projects in nations like Argentina and Colombia.[126] Partially because of these reasons, and seeking to restrict the WB's capability to misuse financial resources, in October 1981, the Reagan administration declared Argentina and Brazil, the largest economies in the region and two heavy clients of the WB in Latin America, as sufficiently developed countries to fend for themselves without relying on WB assistance.[127] In this manner, the Reagan administration retained the authority to provide direct assistance to its right-wing allies, with political support for its Cold War interests as a stipulated condition. However, in the face of strong objections from both Argentina and Brazil—who were by no means ready to cut off borrowing from the WB—and considering the Bank's need to remain active in Latin America, WB President Clausen proposed a compromise. In February 1982, he announced that Argentina and Brazil would still be eligible for development loans for at least another six months, which allowed the Bank to continue operating in the region without escalating tensions with the Reagan administration.[128]

Despite the WB's temporary extension of Argentina's eligibility for lending, and although human rights concerns were suddenly relegated to the margins, the volatile situation in the country emerged as a tricky obstacle to overcome. In March 1982, the US Embassy in Buenos Aires reported that "Argentina [was] showing more political ferment that at any time since 1976."[129] During the Falklands/Malvinas War in mid-1982, US Treasury Secretary Donald Regan stated his expectation that Argentina would continue making payments on its $35 billion foreign loans, despite the "side-effects" of the war. These side effects, far from trivial, included not only the block of Argentina's assets in Britain (worth about $1.3 billion), but also the US imposition of economic sanctions in May 1982, comprising a continued ban on military exports and an unusual suspension of Eximbank's credits and guarantees. Making things even harder for the junta, the same month President Reagan instructed US EDs to the MDBs, the WB among them, to consult with him if Argentina applied for new loans.[130] Argentina, now deprived of US and European backing and fearing a risky political setback in multilateral banks, did not request any WB loans during 1982.

After the war ended, Argentina's situation further deteriorated. By July 1982, its foreign debt totaled about $37 billion (compared to $8 billion in 1975). Debt services in the second half of 1982 were expected to be over $7 billion or even more if creditors refused to reschedule payments.[131] Economic difficulties came hand in hand with political instability. In late August 1982, a few weeks after succeeding Alemann, Minister of Economy Dagnino Pastore resigned and was replaced by Jorge Wehbe.[132] Notwithstanding the worsening crisis, the US Embassy considered that it would be counterproductive to force Argentina into default. The Embassy warned that there were "real dangers that economic pressures from Western countries would force Argentina towards the Soviet and to the radical Nonaligned [countries] (Libya, Iran, etc.)."[133] Not for the first time, thus, the Reagan administration adopted a pragmatic and ambivalent stance towards Argentina.

In the meantime, a lack of political legitimacy and an increasing incapability to implement unpopular economic measures pushed Wehbe to use Washington's Cold War concerns as leverage to obtain financial assistance from different actors in the Western bloc. In September 1982, he declared that Argentina would not sign a new agreement with the IMF because there were other sources of finance available and even with fewer conditions, implicitly referring to Eastern creditors.[134] The same month, Clausen met Wehbe at the Annual Meeting of the IMF and WB Board of Governors. Aware that the risk of a potential default was a real cause of concern in the international financial community, Wehbe assured him that Argentina had a tradition of paying its debts which was not about to be broken.[135] A few days later, echoing Wehbe's early declarations, an IMF mission visited Argentina to negotiate a new SBA that could prevent it from defaulting on its foreign debt.[136] In January 1983, two months after the military announced the transition to democracy (but not because of this announcement), the IMF granted Argentina a CFF aimed at compensating for the temporary fall of national exports.[137] Almost simultaneously, the IMF approved a $2 billion SBA to the country.[138] With the IMF back in Argentina, international private banks began to discuss a special rescue package.[139] Despite the IMF's return to Argentina, negotiations for new development loans with the Bank were not underway, given the country's weak creditworthiness and growing difficulties in repaying its debts.

On February 9, 1983, a financial mission headed by Wehbe met Clausen at the WB headquarters.[140] Aware that development loans were not a viable option, Wehbe requested a special assistance loan (rather than a project-related loan). This request reflected the significant diversification of WB operations at the time. Amidst the debt crisis, when the WB found itself under increasing pressure from the Reagan administration to play a more active role in seeking solutions to avoid bankruptcy and default among Latin American debtor-nations,[141] the WB reinterpreted the scope of "emergency" assistance. Until that point, the Bank had included natural catastrophes or wars. From the 1980s onwards, however, it incorporated also acute economic and financial crises. Somewhat surprisingly, Clausen responded to Wehbe that there was already a long queue of applicants for such assistance (as other Latin American countries had declared default) and the Bank's funds were limited.[142] The mission left empty-handed.

Back in Argentina, Wehbe sent a letter to Clausen summarizing Argentina's requests from the Bank: to negotiate a loan to develop foreign trade, increase the amount allotted to Argentina's Lending Program, and send a mission to prepare a study on Argentina's economy.[143] Clausen confirmed that the WB would soon dispatch an economic mission to identify the type of assistance that the WB could offer.[144] The mission, which arrived in April 1983, prepared a list of recommendations not for the junta but for the soon-to-be-elected democratic government. Although the mission, like the US State Department, wrongly assumed that the Peronist party would win the elections, it expected it to correct the problems emanating from the "inconsistencies involved in the recent experiment in partial liberalization" advanced by the dictatorship.[145] This comment is illuminating. First, it shows that it was only when the WB staff realized that the military regime was marching towards its end that they felt free to criticize the junta's economic policy—a policy that they had actively promoted but, so they claimed, the regime only partially applied. Second, considering the history of WB relations with the Peronist administrations of 1946–1955 and 1970–1973, it is ironic that the mission expected that a Peronist administration would implement a free-market economy more decisively than a right-wing and pro-market dictatorship. When the dictatorship breathed its last breath, the WB endeavored to detach itself from its economic failure. This action should not come as a surprise, given that the WB had previously taken a similar opportunistic approach towards the downfall of other regimes, whether democratic or dictatorial.

In May 1983, the WB reactivated, albeit briefly, its lending program to Argentina and approved a $100 million Highway Project Loan. This loan, the first approved since December 1981, and the last before the presidential elections in October 1983, did not signal the reactivation of collaboration between the parties but was instead the exception that proved the rule. As on previous occasions, declining to provide a loan to Argentina at that critical moment could have been interpreted as an acknowledgment, on the part of the WB, of involvement in the failure of Argentina's economic policy—a policy that the Bank had fervently supported. The decisive EB meeting took place on May 31.[146] Ebiri (WB-WHD) opened his presentation by saying that Argentina was in its third year of deep economic recession. He argued that during this period, "which ha[d] been accompanied by serious political uncertainties and several changes of government, the Argentine economy fell back to the output levels of the early 1970s with the industrial sector contracting 25% and unemployment doubling."[147] Ebiri stressed that following the economic crisis sparked by the war, Argentina adopted an IMF-supported stabilization plan aimed at reducing inflation in 1983 to 110 percent (compared to 360 percent in late 1982), cutting the balance of payments deficit from $5.5 billion in 1982 to $500 million in 1983, and reaching a 5 percent GDP growth in 1983. The loan was approved unanimously.[148]

In December 1983, the democratically elected President Raúl Alfonsín inherited an economy in crisis. Inflation soared to 433.7 percent, GDP barely surpassed that of 1970, and investments dropped by 30 percent compared to the previous decade. Despite this legacy, Alfonsín fulfilled one of his crucial electoral promises by initiating an unprecedented process to address the crimes against humanity committed by the dictatorship. With Alfonsín in power, the WB—as well as the IMF, the US administration, and the international community at large—had to find a new balance between rescuing Argentina from economic collapse and the moral imperative to support a democratic regime—the new Cold War focus of the Reagan administration.

CONCLUSIONS

The dictatorship that governed Argentina between 1976 and 1983 posed a unique challenge to the WB and to the intricate WB-Argentina-US triangle. While Argentina's neoliberal dictatorship was an enthusiastic client of the WB and an eager Cold War ally of the United States, it was not necessarily an ideal partner for either of them. On one hand, the junta aligned with US Cold War security interests and with Western and WB efforts to advance a free-market economy, leaving behind decades of interventionism and economic nationalism. On the other hand, the human rights violations that it committed, under the pretext that repression was necessary to combat communism and labor resistance to economic reform, conflicted with Carter's human rights policy. This contradiction was eased when Ronald Reagan took office in 1981, as he understood human rights differently than his predecessor. While, for Carter, human rights included not only the right to be free from governmental violations of the integrity of the person but also economic and social rights, along with the right to enjoy civil and political liberties, Reagan was more focused on "classic" Cold War considerations. Given that, in Reagan's view, communist regimes were the main violators of human rights, supporting anti-communist military regimes in Latin America was a legitimate strategy to advance Cold War interests in the region. Nevertheless, the escalating instability in Argentina and the Falklands/Malvinas War against Britain in mid-1982 had adverse effects on the junta's relations with key players in the Western bloc. When President Reagan aligned with his closest ally, British Prime Minister Margaret Thatcher, and distanced himself from his anti-communist and neoliberal partner in South America, the military regime recognized that its ties with the conservative US administration were more fragile than it had hoped. For the WB, it was the economic crisis, worsened by the war, that resulted in it stepping back from Argentina. In addition, although it does not appear in the documents, it is probable that the WB management realized that, with the United States and Europe implementing economic sanctions against Argentina, the prospect of approving loans was essentially nil.

As this chapter has shown, the WB and the shifting military administrations managed to maintain productive relations despite significant challenges, signing a total of fourteen loan agreements over seven years. These loans supported large-scale projects central to Argentina's economic development—particularly in oil, coal, and electricity—and played a key role in the Bank's lending strategy in the wake of the 1973 and 1979 oil crises. This was a notable achievement for the junta, especially considering that from 1961, when the Bank launched lending to Argentina, until the coup of 1976, the country had received only ten WB loans. Thus, the military regime secured an average of two loans per year, contrasting sharply with the preceding fifteen years, when Argentina received an annual average of 0.66 percent loans. For the Bank, lending to *de facto* regimes that kidnapped, tortured, and killed their own citizens and foreigners, while following WB policy recommendations to the letter, was "neutrally" acceptable.

As was argued here, part of the Bank's success in dealing with opposing pressures from its donors and borrowers in the violent 1970s in Latin America can be attributed to the US's failure to translate its moral discourse into concrete and consistent human rights policies. As Argentina's case demonstrates, US attempts to force the WB to incorporate human rights considerations into its decision-making process were tinged with ambivalence, internal contradiction, and hypocrisy. Hence, rather than using its *de facto* veto power to impede the flow of WB assistance to Argentina and other Latin American dictatorships, the Carter administration often abstained in WB votes. These abstentions involved the implicit approval of WB lending. Argentina's dictatorial regime, aware of the clash between the conflicting agendas of the US and the WB over human rights, developed effective mechanisms to obtain WB loans. Among others, it scattered false promises about the fates of the detainees and missing people. In other cases, Argentina's government threatened to turn to lenders outside of the Western bloc if the United States and the Bretton Woods institutions did not provide support.

Besides taking advantage of US ambivalence, the WB also developed proactive strategies that allowed it to continue lending to the junta. Although the WB's organizational structure was designed to secure the United States a hegemonic position on its EB (the Bank's chief decision-making body), it also allowed other donors—such as the Scandinavian nations—and borrowers—such as Egypt, Chile, Mexico, and Peru—to exert pressure. The involvement of these countries through the building of ad-hoc coalitions in the EB votes helped Argentina's military regime access not only WB loans but also its much-needed seal of approval. Argentina's dictatorship was not alone. Chilean General Augusto Pinochet (1973–1990) also managed to obtain WB assistance despite US opposition on human rights grounds.[149] The same applied to other Latin American dictatorships guilty of human rights violations. Among others, the WB granted 116 loans to the Brazilian dictatorship (1964–85) and thirteen loans to Uruguay's military regime (1973–85).

The United States's inability to fully impose its stance on the Bank—at least regarding brutal dictatorships in Latin America—echoes historian John Gaddis's argument that during the Cold War, the two superpowers "were not all that super."[150] Argentina's case shows that weak and/or peripheral states, and to a large extent also the Bank's bureaucratic apparatus, could, under certain circumstances, increase their influence and leverage US foreign policy to their advantage.[151]

Undoubtedly, the WB was an influential actor in the economic Cold War in Latin America, including during the deadly period analyzed in this chapter. Its loans and technical assistance provided the dictatorship the international legitimacy and professional backing needed to demonstrate to its opponents, at home and abroad, that the new economic policy contributed to restore Argentina's reputation in the international scene. Moreover, through its lending and interactions with members of the military regime as well as with the professional economists that filled key positions in the Central Bank, the Ministry of Economy, and specialized agencies, the WB contributed to shape the rhythm and content of the reforms. Aware that the multilateral composition of the WB allowed it to play a crucial and allegedly non-coercive role in the promotion of US-style economic ideas and policies, the United States had sufficient reason to let the WB fulfill its "civilizing" and liberalizing mission in countries like Argentina, despite the fact that it did not fulfill all its expectations. Even President Reagan, who initially criticized the WB due to what he perceived as its ineffectiveness in promoting US interests, soon changed his approach and pushed the Bank to enter into new areas, especially with regard to the acute Latin American debt crisis of the early 1980s (analyzed in detail in Chapter 6).

Finally, in their effort to remain active in Argentina and other Latin American countries, McNamara, Clausen, and the Bank's staff at large ignored not only the non-democratic constitution of the regime and its human rights violations, but also the impoverishment and marginalization of segments of Argentina's population—outcomes of both political repression and those same economic programs that the WB so "neutrally" supported, including the closing of railways lines and wage freezes. As detailed in the next chapter, shortly after the transition to democratic rule in December 1983, the WB increased its involvement in Argentina, attempting to deal with the poverty, foreign debt, and lack of energy infrastructure that had marked the dictatorship. As Alfonsín claimed, such problems posed a serious threat to democracy.

6 THE WORLD BANK, LATIN AMERICA'S LOST DECADE, AND THE END OF THE COLD WAR

THE 1980S MARKED THE FINAL phase of the global Cold War. The precise factors and actors that facilitated the peaceful conclusion of this conflict and its exact termination date still remain subjects of scholarly debates. As historian Fritz Bartel argues, the war ended with the convergence of four processes: the cessation of the nuclear and conventional arms race between the two superpowers, the end of the global ideological competition between democratic capitalism and state socialism, the collapse of the Soviet Union and communist states in Eastern Europe, and the reunification of Germany.[1] What is certain is that US President George W. Bush and Soviet Secretary General Mikhail Gorbachev jointly announced the end of the Cold War at the Malta Summit on December 2–3, 1989, a few weeks after the fall of the Berlin Wall.[2] Two years later, in December 1991, Gorbachev dissolved the Soviet Union. The global Cold War was over, and the United States had won it. Capitalism, in its updated and neoliberal version, became the dominant economic paradigm worldwide.

The 1980s also constituted a critical juncture for the Cold War in Latin America. During this period, sometimes referred to as Latin America's Lost Decade, Argentina, Brazil, Peru, and Uruguay, among others, experienced three momentous processes. The first was the debt crisis that began in 1982, when states in the region found themselves unable to service huge debts owed to Western creditors, among them the WB, the IMF, and commercial banks (two-thirds of them, US banks). The second process was the end of dictatorial regimes and the subsequent transition to democracy. While the demise of military rule concurred with the outbreak of the debt crisis, the stability of newly democratic regimes was endangered by the burden of debt repayments and the harsh adjustment programs that they implemented to prevent default. This was the case in Argentina, where the debt crisis loomed large over the entire term of Raúl Alfonsín (1983–1989), the first president of the reestablished democracy. The third process was the *grand finale* of a protracted and non-linear economic liberalization that had started not with Argentina's entry into the Bretton Woods institutions in 1956, but since the early postwar era, when President Juan D. Perón (1946–1955) took the first economic steps needed to qualify for WB and IMF membership (see Chapter 1). As the staff of the WB-WHD claimed in 1986:

> "The main institutions, policies, programs and priorities in Argentina's social sector are hybrid products of the application during the last 50 years, to the country's socioeconomic system, of three quite different models and structures, i.e.: a) a type of semi-fascist corporativism reminiscent of Italian and Spanish practices in the mid-1930s; b) state capitalism, promoted by governments seeking to create and strengthen a national industry (Perón, some military regimes, and Frondizi's '*desarrollismo*'); and c) liberalism, paradoxically pushed in the past by authoritarian governments. As might be expected, the hybrid is quite inefficient and reflects the deficiencies of each model, with the resulting loss of their best qualities. Moreover, its working is impaired by heterogenous, often conflicting objectives."[3]

In effect, since the 1980s, Argentina and many of its neighbors ceased to be, or at least were prepared to stop being the hybrid entities described by the WB's staff. The debt crisis, and to some extent the WB, left them with no choice but to take sides—no more state intervention in the economy, no more state-owned enterprises, no more protectionism, no more progressive taxation and subsidies, no more powerful labor unions.

Scholarship commonly associates the 1980s with the rise of the so-called "Washington Consensus," a term coined in 1989 by British economist John Williamson to describe a series of policy reforms linked with neoliberalism. These reforms, encompassing the privatization of state enterprises, deregulation, liberalization of trade and capital flows, and anti-inflationary stabilization, were heavily promoted by influential Washington-based institutions in Latin America and other developing regions.[4] However, a close examination of WB-Argentina relations since the early Cold War demonstrates that the policy recommendations that made up the Washington Consensus of the 1980s were hardly new. Thus, this book is in line with revisionist approaches that view neoliberalism as a context-dependent phenomenon, whose roots extend back several decades before.[5] For the WB, which had played a pivotal role in planting the seeds of neoliberalism in Argentina and other countries in the region since the 1940s, the 1980s convinced it that the time had come to cultivate a purer version of neoliberalism not only in Latin America and other Third World regions, but also among the former Soviet states. With the end of the Cold War, the WB turned global and, as sociologist Sara Babb claims, the Washington Consensus emerged as a transformative transnational policy paradigm.[6]

This chapter delves into the opportunities and the challenges encountered by the WB while it was involved with the administration of Raúl Alfonsín, president of Argentina from December 1983 to July 1989. When Alfonsín took office, Argentina was one of the most heavily indebted nations in the region, alongside Brazil and Mexico. The country's external debt stood at $45 billion, a figure five times its total annual exports. The study of the WB's relations with Argentina from 1983 to 1989 shows that the debt crisis, which stemmed from the country's longstanding dependence on financial assistance from powerful financiers in the Western bloc, impelled Alfonsín and other leaders to embrace a neoliberal and more radical version of capitalism. Furthermore, this chapter unveils that, with the exception of Cuba, the Cold War in Latin America ended in the early 1980s with a crisis that originated from, and symbolized, Latin America's ultimate alignment with Western capitalism. Although primarily anchored in the economic dimensions of the Cold War, the debt crisis served as a catalyst for the fall of anti-communist dictatorships that were aligned with US Cold War security concerns.

In the 1980s, the WB played a central role in the global and regional Cold War. In 1980, it opened relations with the People's Republic of China, followed by the approval of Hungary's membership in 1982 and the readmission of Poland in 1986. Especially since 1989, the Bank, and also its former president Robert McNamara, became involved in negotiations with Soviet advocates of *perestroika* (economic restructuring), providing advice in the transition from socialism to capitalism.

As far as Latin America is concerned, during this decade, the WB witnessed the most comprehensive adoption of its neoliberal policies till then by the recently installed democratic regimes. The WB's agency in the entrenchment of neoliberal ideas and practices in the region should be understood in light of the fact that the debt crisis was seen, both in Latin America and Washington, as a problem of long-term growth. As the argument ran, some countries were not developed enough to increase their exports and attain the earning levels needed to repay their debts. Hence, the solution lay in growth-oriented policies that could help the region meet its debts. The WB, thus, took the lead in addressing a problem that had persisted despite decades of lending to the region.

Until the debt crisis, WB lending was restricted to co-financing development projects and extending technical assistance. The crisis provided the justification needed to diversify and expand its operations. In the 1980s, the Bank began to grant non-project loans aimed at supporting structural adjustment plans conditioned on the implementation of more complete neoliberal reforms. The use of new lending instruments enabled a steep escalation in WB lending volume. Argentina was a case in point. Over a period of twenty-two years, from 1961 when the Bank approved its first loan to the country to Alfonsín's inauguration in late 1983, the WB granted twenty-four loans to Argentina, averaging about one loan per year. However, during Alfonsín's five-and-a-half-year term, it approved eighteen loans, marking an average of three loans per year—until then, an unimaginable rate.

Notably, what is termed the Lost Decade was not lost in all spheres. During this decade, almost all Latin American dictatorial regimes fell, and the region returned to democracy. This turn of events provides another opportunity to assert that the WB showed no preference for collaborating with dictatorial over democratic regimes. The Argentine case is particularly revealing given Alfonsín's view of democracy and human rights, and the somewhat unrealistic expectations that the return to democracy sparked in Argentina. For Alfonsín, democracy encompassed not only political rights but also the right to eat, work, study, and live a decent life. Although Alfonsín's socio-economic priorities coincided with basic WB development objectives, these were rarely addressed in joint discussions. Moreover, new evidence indicates that the democratic character of Alfonsín's regime played only a marginal role in the WB decision-making process. The chapter thus advances the claim that the Bank displayed a similar indifference to Alfonsín's endeavors to solidify democracy as it did towards human rights violations in the 1970s (see Chapter 5).

Taken together, the WB's strengthening during this period, as manifested in its relationship with the Alfonsín administration, and the increasing reliance of highly indebted Latin American countries on WB assistance demonstrate that the WB was among the main beneficiaries of the debt crisis. Despite the initial concern that its Latin American borrowers, grappling with a severe economic crisis, would not qualify for WB lending, thereby rendering it irrelevant, the opposite happened. Due to strong pressure exerted by Latin American countries and the Reagan administration, the WB ended up in a privileged position to deal with the debt crisis—a crisis that Reagan initially saw as the result of a Soviet-orchestrated destabilization plan aimed at creating the conditions to interfere in the United States's geographically closest sphere of influence.[7] As detailed below, the debt crisis, which initially posed a serious risk to the WB's prestige and operations, turned into fertile ground to design new lending instruments, diversify and multiply its operations, justify its demands to promote policy reforms which blurred the division of labor with the IMF, and, no less significant, overcome the threat posed by Reagan. As we shall see, although the conservative Reagan administration started out as highly critical of the WB, the debt crisis persuaded the US president that the Bank could serve US interests. This involved acting as an intermediary between heavily indebted Latin

American borrowers, such as Argentina, and US commercial banks, thereby freeing the US administration from being seen as promoting controversial economic reforms in the region and letting it devote most of its attention to ending the Cold War and reshaping the global order.

The chapter begins with a discussion of the debt crisis in the Cold War context and its repercussions for the WB, Argentina, and the United States, together and apart. Next, it outlines three distinct phases in WB-Argentina relations, tracing the shift from economic heterodoxy and gradualism to shock treatment and orthodox neoliberalism—a process I associate with the end of the economic Cold War in Latin America. The first phase, from late 1983 to late 1984, was a loan-less period of mutual learning and adjustment. The second phase, between 1985 and 1986, marked the resumption of WB operations in Argentina after a four-year hiatus—interrupted only by a single loan granted in May 1983. It included three groundbreaking developments that took place in 1985: the launching of Alfonsín's first stabilization plan with IMF's backing; the beginning of the WB's structural adjustment lending to highly indebted Latin American borrowers, Argentina being an emblematic example; and the introduction of the Baker Plan as Reagan's main strategy to confront Latin America's debt crisis. The last phase, which began in early 1987 and concluded with the abrupt end of the Alfonsín administration, shows the limits of WB and US efforts to solve Argentina's debt crisis. We will see that as Argentina's economy deteriorated, the WB became its (nearly) sole source of financing. The chapter ends with a brief overview of the early post-Cold War years and the presidency of Carlos Saúl Menem (1989–1999), who became the poster child of neoliberalism in Argentina and beyond.

PART 1: CLASHING OR INTERSECTING INTERESTS? THE DEBT CRISIS AND THE END OF LATIN AMERICA'S COLD WAR

The Debt Crisis: Bad News for Latin America, Good News for the WB

As we have seen, in previous decades, the United States expected the Bank to adhere to its policy towards Argentina and Latin America. However, for a variety of reasons, the WB had often resisted doing so fully or overtly. The debt crisis, in contrast, introduced a different dynamic, one in which there was greater affinity between WB and US interests. Another important change during the Lost Decade concerned Alfonsín's readiness to adopt a more orthodox version of economic neoliberalism. Yet, before embarking on a close examination of the interests of all parties involved, it is essential to elucidate the origins and scope of the debt crisis and contextualize it within the framework of the Cold War.

Although Argentina and other Latin American nations had a long record of borrowing and debt accumulation, the situation became acute during the Lost Decade. In 1970, the outstanding debt of Latin America totaled $29 billion; by late 1978, the number had soared to $159 billion, and in 1982, it stood at $327 billion. What propelled this inundation of foreign lending and indebtedness? The dollar crisis of the early 1970s (the so-called Great Inflation) and the oil shocks of 1973–1974 freed up capital in the developed world and boosted the flow of Eurodollars and petrodollars to developing economies. In the case of Latin America, lending was further eased by the erroneous belief of US and European commercial banks that sovereign nations could not go bankrupt. Hence, rather than realistically assessing whether borrowing nations would be able to repay their debts, bankers seemed to have overestimated the importance of non-economic factors, especially the ideological stance and credibility of ministers of economy and the stability of the ruling regimes.[8] Debtor nations were equally irresponsible. They prioritized the availability of loans while relegating to the sidelines, and to the next administrations, the problems that future repayments might cause. Both creditors and debtors appeared to have operated on the assumption that there would always be fresh funds available to settle old debts, and that loans would be renegotiated as many times as needed.[9] External borrowing by public and private enterprises, at least in the case of Argentina, was further enabled by speculative practices. These practices were motivated by the gap between the interest rates in dollars and *pesos* within a context of hyperinflation, as well as by Martínez de Hoz's infamous *Tablita*—a list of preannounced and gradual devaluations that was in effect between January 1979 and March 1981.[10]

For decades, then, loans had flowed smoothly into Latin America. However, a shift occurred in the late 1970s and early 1980s, driven by increasing fiscal deficits in the United States and the resultant rise in interest rates. This rise, which was intended to bring capital back to the United States, rendered credit scarce and costlier. The capacity of borrowers to access new funds and meet payments on existing debts abruptly declined.[11] The crisis erupted in August 1982, when Mexico's Finance Minister Jesús Silva Herzog informed the FED, the US Treasury, and the IMF that Mexico would no longer be able to service its debts, which at the time totaled $80 billion. Mexico's announcement spread like wildfire throughout Latin America. Sixteen Latin American countries, Argentina among them, along with eleven developing nations in other regions, followed in Mexico's footsteps. In response, banks halted new lending and strived to collect on existing loans and restructure them. Creditors agreed to reschedule debts and offer bailout packages to debtors who signed agreements with the IMF and complied with rigorous reforms. The WB eventually assumed the task of assuring implementation, curtailing a traditional task of the IMF.

Latin America's debt crisis jeopardized the stability of the US banking system. The debts of Argentina, Brazil, and Mexico, the most indebted nations in the region, accounted for 89 percent of the total debts owed to major US banks, including Citibank, JP Morgan, Salomon Brothers, and the Bank of Boston. In addition to negatively affecting the US economy, a bank crash had the potential to reinvigorate West-East ideological rivalry and North-South tensions. In 1982, Reagan claimed that the roots of the crisis were to be found in a Soviet-masterminded destabilization plan. However, it is far from clear that in the early 1980s the Soviets were willing or able to play a significant role in the region. In his first years in power, Gorbachev's policy towards the Third World was limited to ending the war in Afghanistan, protecting Soviet geopolitical gains in Angola and Mozambique, cultivating relations with India and China, and continuing to support Cuba and Nicaragua.[12] Aside from several Central American nations, US hegemony in Latin America was virtually unchallenged. Based on the absence of superpower rivalry over influence in Latin America in the 1980s, historian Duccio Basosi argues that the debt crisis should be seen as a manifestation of a "missing Cold War" in the region. According to Basosi, Moscow, recognizing US supremacy in Latin America, encountered not only serious constraints in the region but also opportunities that it was unable to exploit. Basosi finds support for his argument in the fact that the increase in poverty rates and inequality stemming from Washington-supported austerity measures neither triggered superpower competition nor led to a new cycle of North-South confrontation.

Yet this chapter shows that the debt crisis was a quintessential Cold War issue. Basosi rightly claims that the US administration monopolized the management of the crisis (also, as this book shows, by means of using the WB as an arm of its economic foreign policy). However, the lack of Soviet interference and the exclusive participation of Western actors in solutions to the crisis did not signal a missing Cold War. Instead, this was the precise moment when the economic Cold War in Latin America reached its apex and ended. Despite the negative consequences of the region's dependence on Western financiers, Latin American leaders no longer criticized the capitalist system that had pushed their nations to the abyss but, instead, followed the neoliberal creed to the letter. The debt crisis thus can be understood as the triumph of the West, and certainly of the United States and the financial institutions that it created, in Latin America's Cold War. For Latin America, socialism and Eastern sources of financing were no longer realistic or desired alternatives.

In Search of Neoliberal Solutions to the Debt Crisis: The Baker Plan and the Brady Plan

Reagan's decision to entrust the WB, the multilateral institution that he had threatened to shut down, with a dominant role in the management of the debt crisis had a far-reaching impact on WB-Argentina-US dynamics. In October 1985, at the annual joint meeting of the IMF and WB board of governors, James Baker, US Secretary of the Treasury and Chairman of the President's Economic Council, announced the launch of a US-led initiative to stimulate growth in debtor countries: the "Program of Sustained Growth," also known as the Baker Plan. The plan offered financial assistance in exchange for fiscal discipline (avoiding excessive borrowing and further debt accumulation), reduction of public spending (especially of social programs), increase of tax collection through consumption taxes, liberalization of the financial system and interest rates, liberalization of trade through lower tariffs and abolition of import requirements, and facilities for investments, privatizations, deregulation, and expansion of property rights.[13] Although Argentina and Ecuador were the first to enter it, Alfonsín was not enthusiastic about the Baker Plan because it did not contemplate debt relief.[14] In his view, the resolution of the crisis should be the shared responsibility of negligent debtors and creditors, and debt reduction should be the result.

The Baker Plan marked a watershed in US policy towards Latin America's debt crisis. The Reagan administration accepted the Latin American claim, made also by Alfonsín, that growth-oriented policies would enable the region to meet its debt obligations more effectively than the controversial IMF-promoted austerity programs.[15] The WB welcomed the Baker Plan for two reasons. First, by prioritizing long-term development (the Bank's main goal) over short-term balance of payments stabilization (among the IMF's principal objectives), the plan positioned the WB as the primary institution in charge of debt management.[16] Second, the plan liberated the WB from the need to choose between pressures from its donor and borrowing member-states, as there were no significant clashes. The plan called for debtor countries to adopt adjustment programs; commercial banks to reschedule payments and provide new loans; industrial countries to reschedule credits, provide bridge loans, and increase contributions to MDBs; and international organizations to provide policy recommendations and funding. The goal was twofold: to avoid a breakdown of the international banking system and to facilitate adjustment and development in debtor countries.[17]

The Baker Plan achieved mixed results. In 1984–1985, before the plan's enactment, Latin American growth rates stood at 3.7 percent and 3.6 percent, respectively. Despite a slight improvement to 3.9 percent in 1986, the region's real gross national income (GNI) decelerated to 2.5 percent in 1987 and to 0.7 percent in 1988. These disappointing figures sparked discontent among Latin American countries, which from the beginning had claimed that the $29 billion contemplated for the first stage of the Baker Plan ($9 billion from the WB and the rest from commercial banks) was miniscule compared to the magnitude of the debt.[18] Thus, in March 1989, US Treasury Secretary Nicholas Brady launched a new plan, aimed at restructuring unsustainable debts via the issuance of "Brady bonds." This initiative marked a clear departure from the Baker Plan because it contemplated the reduction of debts owed by heavily indebted nations—as Latin American nations had demanded. Argentina, Brazil, Mexico, Uruguay, Peru, Ecuador, and Costa Rica undertook Brady restructurings beginning in 1990 and continuing through 1998.[19]

Argentina: The Debt Crisis as a Threat to Democracy

The entry of Alfonsín, leader of the UCR, into the presidential palace in December 1983 raised huge expectations in Argentina. Three mayor issues dominated Alfonsín's agenda: the reshaping of civil-military relations,[20] the prosecution of violators of human rights under the last dictatorship,[21] and the debt crisis. As recently declassified WB files demonstrate, the Bank, loyal to its self-imposed principle of political neutrality, focused only on the debt crisis and on the promotion of neoliberal policies to solve it. Democracy promotion and human rights, so central to Reagan's Cold War strategy, were deemed beyond its jurisdiction.

As mentioned, when Alfonsín assumed power, Argentina was in the midst of a severe economic crisis. Inflation surged to an alarming annual rate of nearly 434 percent, and the GDP had stagnated to 1970 levels. The foreign debt had reached $45 billion, compared to $7.8 billion at the time of the 1976 coup. Outstanding payments amounted to $2 billion by the close of 1983.[22] Alfonsín's first economic team, led by Minister of Economy Bernardo Grinspun and Central Bank President Enrique García Vásquez, attempted to alleviate the economic crisis by reintroducing the nationalist and expansionist policies they had implemented in the 1960s while serving in Arturo Illia's administration (see Chapter 3). Grinspun's strategy stipulated price controls, an 8 percent wage increase, and a rise in public spending, mainly via social programs in the areas of housing, health, and nutrition—most notably the National Food Plan, Alfonsín's flagship initiative.[23] Notably, the same heterodox approach was adopted at the time by other democratic leaders, including Alan García in Peru and José Sarney in Brazil.[24]

Alfonsín's condemnation of the international financial community for providing loans to an illegitimate regime (the *Proceso*), and his claim that the debt crisis was a political problem that transcended the national sphere,[25] raised concern among foreign banks and the centers of power in Washington.[26] Alarm bells rang in January 1984, when Alfonsín annulled the SBA that the military regime and the IMF had signed just a few months earlier.[27] However, seeking to access new credits and hoping to initiate debt rescheduling negotiations, in December 1984, shortly after a first trip to Washington where he met also with President Reagan, Alfonsín signed his first SBA.[28] The accord comprised measures aimed at curbing inflation from 1,200 percent annually to 150 percent, removing price controls, reducing the deficit of the private sector, and liberalizing foreign trade. As expected, the SBA, with its so-called catalytic effect, paved the way to negotiations with other creditors. In January 1985, Grinspun discussed the rescheduling of Argentina's external debt service obligations with the Paris Club—a significant achievement given that European banks held almost a third of Argentina's total debt.[29]

The year 1985 marked a turning point in Alfonsín's efforts to deal with the debt crisis. In February, following Grinspun's resignation, Alfonsín appointed Juan Sourrouille, a Harvard-trained economist, as Minister of Economy. In March, commercial banks and the IMF suspended lending to Argentina due to non-compliance with the conditions outlined in the SBA signed in December.

In mid-April, Sourrouille, accompanied by Mario Brodersohn and José Luis Machinea (all advocates of *developmentalism*), presented the draft of the *Plan Austral*, a heterodox stabilization plan,[30] to the IMF, the US Treasury, and the FED.[31] The plan was officially introduced in June 1985 and remained in effect until August 1988. It focused on a temporary price and wage freeze and reversing hyperinflationary trends. The plan also stipulated increased taxation and spending cuts, and created a new national currency, the *Austral*, which replaced the Argentine peso at a rate of 1,000 pesos to one Austral.[32] The results were immediate. Inflation dropped from a daily rate of 1 percent to an annual rate of 2 percent, while the fiscal deficit decreased from the 15 percent level inherited from the dictatorship to 3.6 percent in 1987. The initial success of the *Plan Austral* secured Alfonsín's political gains. The Congressional elections of November 1985 constituted a vote of confidence for his administration, and Alfonsín's approval rating reached 80 percent by late 1985.[33] Nevertheless, the plan's positive outcomes were short-lived, and the economy began to deteriorate in early 1986. Various sectors of society, including the *Sociedad Rural Argentina,* the Argentine Industrial Union, the banking sector, and the combatant CGT, all pressed the government to revise the plan. From the plan's inception until January 1987, the CGT organized eight general strikes to protest the economic policies.[34]

In April 1986, Sourrouille announced a second, more gradual phase of the *Plan Austral,* which included modest wage increases and a reduction in price controls.[35] By early 1987, Alfonsín's political situation deteriorated further when the CGT formed an alliance with the Catholic Church, which opposed his efforts to legalize divorce. At the same time, the government's relations with the military worsened. Under intense pressure from the military and reactionary groups, the National Congress passed the *Ley de Punto Final* (Full Stop Law) on December 24, 1986, effectively halting investigations and prosecutions of armed forces members accused of crimes committed during the last dictatorship. Initially, Alfonsín resisted endorsing the law, but the looming threat of another coup forced his hand. Subsequent military uprisings led him to grant further concessions to the armed forces, fueling widespread social discontent.[36] In August 1988, a new inflationary process prompted the government to launch an orthodox economic program—the *Plan Primavera* (Spring Plan), which failed within weeks, leading to a hyperinflation episode in mid-1989 with grave political and social consequences. Between May 24 and June 1, 1989, food riots exploded in Argentina. Police used tear gas and rubber bullets to repel crowds, hundreds of looters were arrested, and about nineteen people were killed. By the time the riots subsided, the country was under a thirty-day state of siege, and Alfonsín had called for early elections.[37]

Ultimately, despite the significant challenges the country encountered during its transition to democracy and the fluctuations in economic policy, Alfonsín signed eighteen loan agreements with the WB—two immediately after the launching of the *Plan Austral*, four in 1986, four in 1987, seven in 1988, and one in 1989.

The WB: The Big Push

In the late 1970s, the WB's status was in decline. Two oil shocks, elevated interest rates, difficulties in channeling capital to developing countries, contentious lending to brutal dictatorships, and cuts in US contributions to the Bank had eroded its operations.[38] Yet, during the final phase of the global Cold War, the WB experienced momentous growth and transformation. In May 1980, the People's Republic of China joined the Bretton Woods institutions, and the WB soon became involved in economic reforms in one of the largest and most populated countries in the world.[39] Poland, which rescinded membership in 1949, rejoined in 1986. In the late 1980s, the WB opened negotiations with Mikhail Gorbachev. The Russian Federation joined the Bank and Fund in 1992, offering the WB an "absolutely fantastic" opportunity to play a central role in the Soviet reforms.[40] The Bank saw its involvement in the Soviet Union as "a unique opportunity [. . .] to contribute to a critical economic transformation which will have an impact on the global economy and environment for many years to come."[41]

The end of Latin America's Cold War also brought the WB exceptional opportunities. During the 1980s, the Bank underwent three important changes that were related to developments in the region. The first was the establishment, in September 1985, of the fifth and last affiliated institution of the WB Group, the Multilateral Investment Guarantee Agency (MIGA). MIGA aimed to encourage private capital flow to Third World countries by providing guarantees against noncommercial risks and by complementing already existing investment insurance programs.[42]

The second development affected the composition of the WB staff and the subsequent, albeit temporary, abandonment of the WB's anti-poverty agenda. In 1982, Clausen appointed the neoliberal orthodox economist Anne O. Krueger as the WB's Chief Economist and Vice President for Research, the first woman to occupy a WB vice presidency. Krueger was known for her stance on what she perceived as the perverse effects of state interventionism in the Third World. Assembling a team that shared her anti-*statist* position, she fired and hired a relatively high number of economists and shifted the core focus of WB research and publications towards macroeconomics, trade opening, and other liberalizing measures.[43] At the same time, the debt crisis became the WB's main priority. In July 1986, due to still unclear tensions with the Reagan administration, in particular with Secretary of the Treasury Donald Reagan,[44] Clausen resigned. He was replaced by Barber Conable, whose appointment was widely assumed to be linked to the role that the Bank was expected to play under the Baker Plan.[45] Unlike most of his predecessors, Conable was not a banker or a lawyer but a politician, having served as a US Republican Congressman for New York since the 1970s. In 1987, Conable partially revived the battle against poverty, ironically, as a means to alleviate the social consequences of the debt crisis and the WB-supported adjustment programs that were implemented to address it. He served as WB president until August 1991.

The third change, and perhaps the most impactful, was the introduction of the WB's Sectoral and Structural Adjustment Lending (SECAL and SAL), which became the centerpiece of the Bank's response to the debt crisis. The SAL was initially formulated by McNamara in the 1980s, among others, as an internally driven response to a crisis in the Bank's operations, including unsatisfactory outcomes of its anti-poverty programs and limitations on lending to highly indebted countries.[46] First introduced in Africa, the SAL became common in Latin America only with the introduction of the Baker Plan in October 1985—which was indicative of the growing rapprochement between the US administration and the WB. Unlike standard WB development loans, SAL and SECAL loans were not attached to any particular project. They were designed to encourage the tackling of economic reforms that the Reagan administration also considered vital, while facilitating a rapid transfer of resources to debtor nations in order to solve acute problems in their balance of payments.[47] This new lending instrument was highly conditional. As Sara Babb points out, structural conditionality is by far the most intrusive. Unlike financial and macroeconomic conditionality, which primarily focuses on fiscal and monetary adjustments, structural conditionality seeks to reshape the fundamental architecture of national economies and political systems. Moreover, since structural reforms are embedded within national political frameworks, they require approval by national assemblies—a process that is often far from straightforward.[48] A typical structural adjustment plan backed by a SAL involved, among other conditions, the devaluation of the national currency (to decrease the prices of exported goods and attract stronger currencies), an increase in interest rates (to attract foreign capital), a reduction of public expenditure, extensive privatization, elimination of public subsidies, and freezing of salaries (to prevent inflation).[49] Although, as seen in previous chapters, this type of WB conditionality was not entirely new, the growing number of conditions and their expanded scope marked a significant shift. As its relations with Argentina demonstrated, the WB's multifaceted involvement in structural adjustment lending was a double-edged sword. While, as Clausen recalled, this involvement enabled the Bank to increase its lending volume and influence (and therefore to recruit more staff), it also damaged the WB's reputation among Third World countries.[50] The Bank found itself taking over part of the role that had been so harmful to the IMF's reputation in the region. Moreover, it increased the WB's exposure in Latin American debtor nations.

PART 2: THE DEBT CRISIS, THE TRIUMPH OF NEOLIBERALISM, AND THE END OF THE COLD WAR IN LATIN AMERICA

Phase 1: The Loan-Less Last Hybrid Stage (1983–1984)

Following the Argentine general election of October 1983, which marked the return of constitutional rule following seven years of a fierce dictatorship, Peter Scherer and his team at the new Country Programs Department of the WB (WB-CPD) began to evaluate the potential for collaboration with Alfonsín's administration.[51] Notwithstanding the significance of the democratic elections, political considerations were given little attention. The sole political observation, which was not entirely favorable, noted that Alfonsín's party, the UCR, had "a strong liberal and democratic tradition," although occasionally emphasizing "extreme nationalistic goals" in competition with the Peronists.[52] The staff expressed concern about Alfonsín's claim that the debt crisis was "an eminently political problem, both in origin and nature" which, as such, should "be dealt [with] by the governments of the creditors."[53] In other words, Alfonsín expected that leaders of industrialized nations would support debtors' efforts to persuade bankers to provide more favorable terms to Argentina and other countries in the region.[54] Scherer found some relief in Alfonsín's commitment to avoid a moratorium on payments, including on debts owed to the WB, and in his determination to "respect [Argentina's] legitimate commitments, even if those were taken irresponsibly."[55]

Besides those concerns, Scherer was encouraged by Alfonsín's resolve to modernize the public administration, improve the efficiency of obsolete public services, and his stated conviction that "the future of the country depended on the private sector."[56] Scherer believed that privatizations would be a central component of any chosen economic policy, even if their pace would be affected by political pressures, in particular by the way in which Alfonsín would address "the volatile matter" of investigating human rights violations during "the anti-terrorist period."[57] Overall, Scherer expected the new administration "to seek close and harmonious relations with the Bank [. . .]. Yet, [. . .] some of the key players (Messrs. Grinspun, Storni and Brodersohn) will not always make for easy cooperation."[58] As was customary, in early January 1984, shortly upon being sworn in as Minister of Economy, Grinspun met Clausen at the WB headquarters in Washington. Grinspun assured him that Argentina would continue to repay its debts to the Bank.[59]

The initial bilateral interactions laid the foundation for extensive collaboration. Talks focused on the conditions Argentina needed to meet in order to qualify for WB lending, which had been suspended since December 1981, with the exception of a loan granted in May 1983. The path to WB loans, however, was fraught with obstacles. Argentina's low creditworthiness and its persistent delays in the implementation of previously approved WB-supported projects made it difficult to justify the submission of new loan proposals to the Bank's EB.[60] Meanwhile, Argentina requested the WB's technical assistance in formulating a medium-term recovery plan and improving the planning and managerial capacities of central government agencies and public enterprises.[61] This request attested that Alfonsín's administration took seriously its promise to modernize the state and find common ground with the Bank. Additionally, in February 1984, Oscar Oszlak, the Vice Secretary of Research and Administrative Reform, informed Scherer that the government had already established a privatization committee and had advanced several reforms in state-owned enterprises—measures that, he claimed, were appropriate for WB assistance.[62] The WB, in turn, agreed to reactivate a $87 million credit that it had granted to Argentina in 1978 but was never taken up.[63]

While the WB appeared in no hurry to commence operations in Argentina, creditors in the Western world, alarmed by the potential risk of a default, extended emergency assistance to the country. In March 1984, US Secretary of the Treasury Donald Regan announced the consolidation of a $500 million rescue package, put together by Brazil, Colombia, Mexico, Venezuela, and the United States, to assist Argentina in meeting its obligations to foreign banks.[64] Mirroring his political reading of the foreign debt, Alfonsín saw this package as a symbol of regional solidarity.[65] As he stated: "If anyone could think or say that democracy serves only for rhetorical declarations, then what has just happened [the rescue package] is irrefutable proof of the opposite."[66] However, Alfonsín's optimistic statement was misleading. After several months of lobbying for Alfonsín's initiative to create a Latin American debtors' cartel, Mexico, Brazil, Venezuela, and Colombia—each of which was, at the time, individually negotiating the rescheduling of its debt—joined the creditors in calling on Argentina to adopt a case-by-case rather than the collective formula that Alfonsín had proposed. Fearing that an Argentine moratorium would weaken their own talks, these four countries joined the United States in lending to Alfonsín's administration.[67]

In November 1984, on the initiative of the IMF's managing director Jacques de Larosière, the IMF management held a meeting with the newly established Advisory Committee on Argentina. The committee brought together major creditors such as Citicorp, Morgan Guaranty, Bank of America, Chase Manhattan, Lloyds, Royal Bank of Canada, Bank of Tokyo, Credit Suisse, and Dresdner Bank. Paul Volker, Clausen, and Ortiz Mena, president of the IDB, also participated. Discussions on a new loan to Argentina were stormy. European and Japanese banks made it clear that deviations from agreements with Argentina would not be tolerated under any circumstances. The US banks adopted a more accommodating position than their counterparts, who criticized the WB for not releasing funds to Argentina and instead asking them to assume additional risks.[68] Partly due to the lack of a realistic possibility of reaching an accord with foreign banks without first committing to an IMF-backed stabilization plan, in December 1984, Grinspun signed a $1.4 billion SBA and an IMF CFF to offset the decline in exports.[69] Although Grinspun had anticipated that the SBA would open the way for $4 or $5 billion in new credits from commercial banks,[70] the IMF abruptly suspended negotiations, claiming that Argentina had failed to implement the austerity measures that had facilitated the agreement in the first place. Despite this reversal, Argentina began to show signs of economic recovery, including a gradual fall in inflation rates. In light of these modest results, David Knox (WB's Regional Vice President for Latin America and the Caribbean) and Scherer met Alfonsín to discuss potential projects in the areas of water supply, ports, gas, oil, mining, agriculture, and industry.[71] For the first time, the WB was ready to consider assistance to the Alfonsín administration.

Phase 2: 1985 as a Turning Point

In February 1985, Scherer informed Knox about what he perceived as promising changes in Alfonsín's cabinet. Alfonsín, Scherer reported, had dismissed his friend Grinspun and appointed in his stead Juan Sourrouille, who had already recruited Adolfo Canitrot, José Luis Machinea, and Mario Brodersohn, all professional economists.[72] Anticipating that the economy would now be conducted "more professionally, predictably and openly,"[73] Scherer intensified his involvement in Argentina. He conducted several studies to identify bottlenecks in the effective implementation and disbursement of already approved WB-co-financed projects. Next, he recommended the establishment of special accounts for specific projects, the reform of agencies overseeing WB-supported projects, a review of regulations related to competitive bidding for government-awarded contracts, the enactment of new decrees and laws necessary to authorize the contracting of goods and services under WB loans, and the promotion of aid coordination.[74] As in previous cases, the closer affinity the Bank had with Argentina's economic team, the greater the pressures it exerted on them to move forward with reforms.

In March 1985, Alfonsín traveled to Washington, where he negotiated a new SBA with the IMF and a bridge loan of $500 million from the United States. In what unfolded as a new chapter in Argentina's economic policy and a new phase in Argentina-WB relations, Clausen assured Alfonsín that the Bank was determined to support the government's initiatives for enhancing economic management and increasing the WB's financial commitments and disbursements.[75] It is worth noting that the meeting with Clausen, which ended without concrete results, differed significantly from Alfonsín's meeting with President Reagan just days earlier. Unlike the WB, which, according to its Articles of Agreement, was required to avoid political considerations, the Reagan administration focused on sensitive Cold War issues while steering clear of getting trapped in negotiations on Argentina's foreign debt. Thus, rather than discussing Alfonsín's demands that the US administration facilitate negotiations with US private creditors, Reagan renewed his denunciations of the Nicaraguan government. As he put it, "the free people of this hemisphere must not stand by and watch the Communist tyranny imposed on Nicaragua spread to the free lands of the Americas." Reagan stressed that the return to democracy "[was] threatened by Marxist-Leninists who continue with the heavy support of the Soviet Union and Cuba to undermine freely elected governments and democratic movements." Alfonsín, who was committed to the non-aligned movement and had refused to sign a US-sponsored nuclear nonproliferation treaty,[76] stressed the need to establish a dialogue with Nicaragua and underlined the "longstanding principle" of international law opposing foreign intervention in Latin America.[77]

Despite his sidestepping of financial discussions with Alfonsín, Reagan was worried about the debt crisis becoming a source of bilateral friction and a threat to the Western economy. This is understandable, as a default by Argentina could have had a domino effect and sparked a bank crash in the United States. Moreover, the bankruptcy of a Western nation that relied heavily on Western assistance and adopted Western economic models could raise questions about the benefits of capitalism. The State Department still believed that the crisis could be solved without direct US interference. Nonetheless, it recommended providing financial support to Argentina while urging the Alfonsín administration to remove barriers to foreign trade and investments and enhance the efficiency of the public sector.[78]

On June 14, 1985, Alfonsín announced the launch of the *Plan Austral*. The plan, he stated, was not aimed at saving a specific administration but the democratic regime, not at solving a temporary economic problem but at transforming the economy. It was a plan, he emphasized, not just to help the people survive, but to move forward and propel national development.[79] The first steps towards restoring ties with the international financial community were taken when the IMF resumed disbursements on the SBA that it had unilaterally suspended in March.[80] Shortly thereafter, Clausen sent the EDs his recommendation to renew lending to Argentina. In the interim, he reached an agreement with Secretary of Planning José Luis Machinea regarding improvements in the execution of WB-supported projects and the establishment of special loan accounts aimed at facilitating faster disbursements.[81] Pointing to political instability, the only political matter that the WB management had ever mentioned, Clausen stressed (as he did in all subsequent reports and recommendations) that "Argentina has rich natural resources, a highly literate population organized in an export-oriented and diversified agriculture, and a large industrial sector. The economic performance of the country has suffered, however, from the policy instability and distortions of incentives introduced by frequently changing governments."[82]

Political instability, he insisted, had severely harmed the readiness of the private sector to invest in Argentina—a sector that the WB had, since its inception, always considered a crucial motor of development. Clausen stressed that "the promising prospects for political stability and serious efforts of the new Government to tackle Argentina's thorny economic problems provide the Bank with an opportunity to play a key role in the country's economic recovery and future development." The public sector was a wise starting point for the WB, which aspired to modernize and downsize it in favor of private activity.[83]

With no further delay, on June 25 the EB approved a $180 million loan to YPF for a Gas Utilization and Technical Assistance project—the first WB loan to Alfonsín's administration. Not by chance, José Sokol (WB-CPD) opened his presentation at the EB meeting by discussing the "strong economic stabilization program" that Alfonsín had just launched with the IMF's support, highlighting the significant efforts being made to improve economic management. Beyond the standard explanations, the staff stressed that Argentina's government was committed to the reconstruction of its democratic institutions and economy—an unusual political remark. They also mentioned that the WB was helping Argentina through "a notable acceleration of disbursements" and a pipeline of projects to be brought for EB vote in 1986–1987. The EB approved the loan without reservation.[84] At the same time, a WB mission completed a study of the country's public sector and discussed its recommendations with the Minister of Public Works and Services, Roque Carranza.[85] The WB management and staff were confident that Alfonsín's new economic team was eager to follow their advice.[86]

Under these auspicious circumstances, and with the announcement of the Baker Plan in October 1985, WB-Argentina-US triangular dynamics gained momentum. In a meeting with Clausen, Minister Sourrouille commented that he was discussing with Paul Volcker, Chair of the FED, several options regarding what both the US administration and the WB could do to assist Argentina. Sourrouille expressed hope that the Bank could play a "greater role in mobilizing financing from commercial banks" via the SAL.[87] In early December, eager to encourage the Bank to play "a greater role" in managing Latin America's debt crisis, Clausen published a joint statement with the IMF's Managing Director supporting the Baker plan and urging the commercial banks to be more cooperative with this initiative.[88] Signaling the Bank's new role as intermediary between debtor nations and creditors, Clausen visited Argentina—accompanied by Knox and Scherer—where he publicly announced his support of the *Plan Austral*.[89] During a visit to an oil refinery in the Province of Mendoza, accompanied by Rodolfo Otero, President of YPF, Clausen announced that the Bank would grant loans to support the second phase of economic reforms.[90] He also stressed that the WB was "ready to provide strong support for the development of Argentina's hydrocarbon resources if the Government continues with programs and policies that offer adequate incentives for private sector participation."[91] Clausen declared that the WB was ready to support ongoing economic reforms in Argentina through a substantial expansion of lending, with WB commitments of $180 million in fiscal year 1985, between $400–500 million in the fiscal year ending on June 30, 1986, and about $700–800 for fiscal year 1987.[92]

On December 10, 1985, with Clausen still in Argentina, the WB approved its second loan to Alfonsín's administration and the first under the Baker Plan—$60 million for a water supply project.[93] As was the case in the EB meeting of June, the staff began by highlighting the effective execution of the stabilization plan. Their presentation also included a list of the institutional changes that Argentina was implementing in accordance with neoliberal precepts. Such changes were geared towards increasing the efficiency of state-owned enterprises through layoffs and the transfer of specific public entities to the private sector, as well as the restructuring of others. The proposed water sector project followed this approach. The loan was approved without opposition or abstention.[94] As detailed below, this was only the beginning of a series of loans that granted the economic assistance and the political legitimacy needed to advance Argentina's economic transformation.

The First SAL to Argentina and Its Deepening Economic Transformation

The WB was eager to endorse "the courageous decisions taken by the Argentine government to stabilize the economy, increase efficiency, and strengthen the country's export potential."[95] This support quickly translated into the approval of the first SAL to the country—a $350 million loan for the agricultural sector, authorized on April 3, 1986. This SAL resembled those recently provided to Colombia, Costa Rica, Chile, and Ecuador, all intended to encourage policy change. Unlike regular development loans, as previously mentioned, the SAL was not intended to co-finance the construction of projects such as grain elevators or irrigation systems. Instead, it aimed to transfer financial resources in support of policy reforms, some of which were controversial. These reforms included reducing export taxes on agricultural products, increasing domestic producer prices, implementing a structural tax reform through the introduction of a federal land tax, adopting fiscal measures to maintain budget deficits at manageable levels, and revising tariff regulations on the import of agricultural inputs. In the case of Argentina's agricultural sector, the WB estimated that these reforms would generate additional earnings of about $1 billion a year in foreign exchange by 1989, mainly through exports of wheat, maize, sorghum, soybeans, and sunflowers. Apart from providing funds to facilitate policy change, the loan covered technical assistance and studies aimed at fostering institutional improvements.[96]

While presenting the loan proposal to the EB, Sokol detailed the initial results of the stabilization plan, which he described as impressive: monthly inflation decreases from 30 percent in June 1985 to 2.5 percent per month on average from August 1985 to February 1986. Real GDP, however, fell by about 4.5 percent in 1985. According to Sokol, Argentina had the potential to gradually resume growth, but this would depend on the adoption of wide-ranging policy reforms and sustained stabilization efforts embodied in the *Plan Austral*. In addition to the policy reforms commonly associated with standard SALs, this specific loan underscored measures for correcting distortions in the trade regime, modernizing the tax administration, revitalizing viable domestic financial markets, and achieving an "overall improvement of the machinery of government."[97] Most EDs considered it wise to start with an agricultural loan because this sector contributed around 75 percent of Argentina's foreign exchange earnings, and also because it faced multiple distortions.[98]

With a first SAL in the works, Argentina and the WB accelerated negotiations on other projects that were already in the pipeline. In May, Secretary of Economic Coordination Adolfo Canitrot held a series of meetings at the WB headquarters to discuss a technical assistance loan aimed at supporting the modernization of the public sector. The parties also discussed a loan for the industrial sector, which was approved in 1987.[99] At the same time, a WB mission headed by Scherer and Van der Merr (Head of the WB's South America Division) met with the Minister of Economy and the directors of public enterprises that were implementing or negotiating new projects with the WB. The parties agreed that total WB disbursements in 1986 would amount to $400 million, triple the amount in 1985, and would rise to $800 million in 1987. Concurrently, another Bank mission was *en route* to Buenos Aires to discuss other potential projects.[100] WB-Argentina's collaboration was flourishing, and the WB-Argentina-US dynamics were more harmonious than in previous decades. As David Knox explained in an interview with *La Nación*, the improvement in WB-Argentina relations and the rise in the volume of lending was the result of Alfonsín's reforms and the Baker Plan.[101] Since mid-1985, WB lending became stable and diversified, not only in terms of the sectors involved, but also with regard to the type of lending instruments. Table 4 below summarizes WB lending to the Alfonsín administration.

The remarkable increase in WB operations in Argentina during the Alfonsín administration supports the claim, advanced in this book, that the debt crisis presented the Bank with a golden opportunity to redefine its role, diversify its lending portfolio, and restore its prestige, which had been in decline during the long 1970s. Yet the increase in WB lending was not solely due to its own merits. At least until late 1986, and despite initial expectations generated by the Baker Plan, commercial creditors were reluctant to extend new credits to highly indebted nations. Credits by commercial banks dropped from $20.2 billion in 1984 to $4.6 billion in late 1985. The repayment by fifteen developing Baker Plan nations of $4.2 billion in 1985 and $2.9 billion in 1986 was not enough to attract new credits. Nevertheless—in what

Table 4: World Bank Loans to the Alfonsín Administration, 1983–1989.

	Project Title	Project ID	Commitment Amount (in million US dollars)	Executive Board Approval Date	Lending Instrument
1	**Gas Utilization and Technical Assistance Project**	P005949	180.00	June 25, 1985	Specific Investment Loan*
2	**Water Supply Project**	P005945	60.00	December 10, 1985	Specific Investment Loan
3	**Agricultural Sector Loan Project**	P005956	350.00	April 3, 1986	Sector Adjustment Loan
4	**Refinery SUPP Loan**	P005967	116.00	May 20, 1986	Specific Investment Loan
5	**Public Sector Management Technical Assistance Project**	P005961	18.50	June 3, 1986	Technical Assistance Loan
6	**Power Engineering Project**	P005962	14.00	September 16, 1986	Technical Assistance Loan
7	**Small and Medium Scale Industry Credit Project**	P005966	125.00	April 14, 1987	Financial Intermediary Loan**
8	**Bahía Blanca I - Port Project**	P005944	50.00	May 5, 1987	Specific Investment Loan
9	**Trade Policy and Export Diversification Project**	P005970	500.00	May 19, 1987	Sector Adjustment Loan

(Continued)

Table 4: (*Continued*)

	Project Title	Project ID	Commitment Amount (in million US dollars)	Executive Board Approval Date	Lending Instrument
10	**SEGBA V**	P005968	257.66	June 23, 1987	Specific Investment Loan
11	**Municipal Development Project**	P005963	120.00	March 22, 1988	Specific Investment Loan
12	**Banking Sector Loan (BSL) Project**	P005976	400.00	March 29, 1988	Sector Adjustment Loan
13	**Agricultural Credit Project (02)**	P005985	106.50	June 23, 1988	Financial Intermediary Loan
14	**Social Sector Management—Technical Assistance Loan Project**	P005991	28.00	July 26, 1988	Technical Assistance Loan
15	**Housing Sector Project (01)**	P006002	300.00	October 27, 1988	Specific Investment Loan
16	**Electric Power Sector Loan Project**	P005986	252.00	October 27, 1988	Specific Investment Loan
17	**Trade Policy Loan Project (02)**	P005987	300.00	October 27, 1988	Sector Adjustment Loan
18	**Tax Administration Technical Assistance**	P006013	6.50	January 24, 1989	Technical Assistance Loan
	TOTAL AMOUNT		**3,184.16**		

Table 4: (*Continued*)

**Specific Investment Loans:* Supplies borrowing countries with financing for projects in all sectors, especially in infrastructure, human development, agriculture, and public administration sectors. Unlike commercial lending, these loans not only supply borrowing countries with needed financing but also serve as a vehicle for knowledge transfer and technical assistance. This includes support to analytical and design work in the conceptual stages of project preparation, technical support and expertise during implementation, and institution building throughout the project.

***Financial Intermediary Loans:* Called today Financial Intermediary Funds (FIFs), these are financial arrangements that typically leverage a variety of public and private resources in support of international initiatives. FIFs enable funds to be raised from multiple sources, both sovereign and private. The WB's role across FIFs is the provision of financial intermediary services, as trustee of the funds. The WB provides a set of agreed financial services that involve receiving, holding, and investing contributed funds, and transferring them when instructed by the FIF governing body.

Source: Data from World Bank Group Site, Projects by Country, Argentina (https://projects.worldbank.org/en/projects-operations/projects-summary?countrycode_exact=AR&title=Argentina)

was not necessarily good news either for the WB or for the debtors—banks were more prone to extend new credits to nations that were implementing stabilization plans backed by an SBA and monitored by the IMF. The IMF, however, for reasons beyond the scope of this discussion, reduced its disbursements to highly indebted countries from $3.1 billion in 1984 to $1.8 billion in 1985 and to zero in 1986. The WB thus emerged as the main, or even only, powerful financier that filled this vacuum and increased its lending from $3.6 billion in 1984 to $4.2 billion in 1985 and to $4.8 billion in 1986.[102] Baker's and Clausen's efforts to persuade US commercial banks and corporations to more fully cooperate with Argentina were only partially successful.[103] As Figure 1 below shows, the WB's operations expanded not only in Argentina—one of the four main borrowers of the Bank in Latin America. For instance, Brazil, the largest borrower in the region, signed nineteen new loan agreements with the Bank in 1985, seventeen in 1986, twenty-two in 1987, and twenty-one in 1988—far exceeding the number of loans per year approved in earlier periods. A similar pattern was observed in Mexico and Colombia, the second and third largest WB clients in Latin America, respectively.

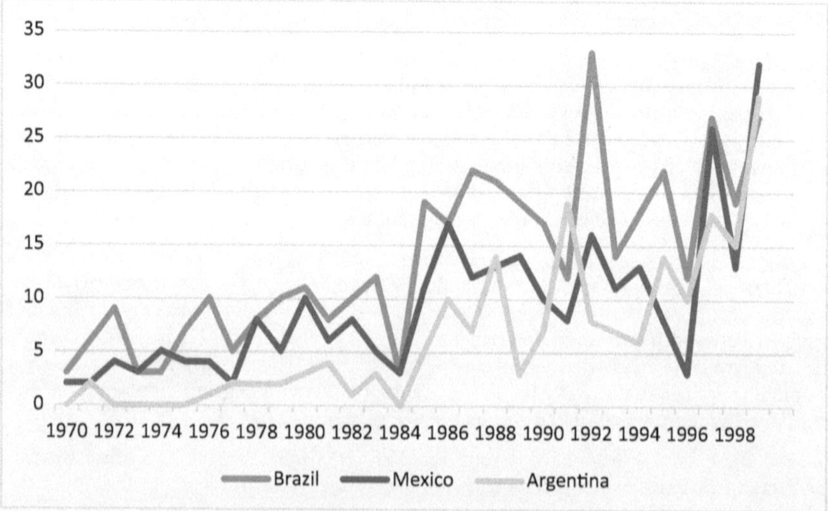

FIGURE 1. Number of World Bank Loans to Argentina, Brazil, and Mexico, 1970–1999.

Source: Data from World Bank Group Site, Projects by Country, Latin America and Caribbean (https://projects.worldbank.org/en/projects-operations/projects-list?regionname_exact=Latin%20America%20and%20Caribbean&title=Latin%20America%20and%20Caribbean&os=0)

Phase 3: The Weaker the Argentine Economy, the More Assistance the WB Granted It (1987–1989)

In the first months of 1987, when Argentina's economy still showed signs of recovery, Alfonsín's economic team obtained new credits from eleven US commercial banks. This achievement was partly facilitated by the efforts of Clausen, Volcker, and Baker, who worked to persuade creditors to take a favorable stance towards the country. Since Argentina had become a test case for the Baker Plan, its success was equally crucial for Baker, Volcker, and the WB. The Argentines, thus, more than once turned to the WB and to Volcker for help in talks with the banks. For instance, when in April, Brodersohn and Sourrouille met Volcker, they asked him to secure for Argentina the political backing it needed in negotiations with bankers and investors.[104] Also, WB President Conable did not miss any opportunity to back Argentina's stabilization efforts. In May 1987, for example, when Brodersohn explained Argentina's economic policy at a special meeting held at the WB with representatives of the creditor banks, Conable, as well as William Rhodes (president of Citibank and chair of the advisory committees of international banks that negotiated debt-restructuring agreements for Argentina, Brazil, Jamaica, Korea, Mexico, Nicaragua, Panama, Peru, and Uruguay), praised Alfonsín's success in reducing the fiscal deficit. To support Argentina's requests to the banks, Conable stated that the WB had already committed $2 billion.[105] These were days of cautious optimism in Argentina. Alfonsín's administration rescheduled debts owed to the Paris Club and obtained $400 million in new credits.[106]

Despite these positive signs, Argentina's political situation deteriorated. In April 1987, members of the *Carapintadas,* a faction within the army, staged a mutiny against Alfonsín in response to the trials of military officials for crimes committed during the dictatorship. Meanwhile, the economy continued to decline. Although the GDP had grown by approximately 3 percent during the first half of 1987, it declined in the second half of the year. Inflation soared to a double-digit rate in July, and the *Austral* underwent consecutive devaluations.[107] On July 20, the Minister of Economy announced a series of short-term price adjustments, various structural reforms in the public sector, and additional privatizations. Simultaneously, Argentina signed two new agreements with the IMF. The first was an SBA,[108] and the second a CFF to address the disturbing decline in export revenues caused by heavy rains that damaged crops.[109] In November 1987, Alfonsín suffered a setback in the legislative elections which jeopardized his ability to ensure governance during the last two years of his term. The Peronists won sixteen of twenty-two gubernatorial races, and the ruling party lost its majority in the Chamber of Deputies. Alfonsín, politically debilitated, not only had to bargain with the Peronists, but also found himself in a weaker position to negotiate with foreign creditors regarding the foreign debt, which had meanwhile reached $53 billion.[110] As we saw in previous chapters, political instability, so linked to Argentina's fluctuating creditworthiness, has always had a negative impact on relations with the WB.

The economic difficulties that began to surface in July 1986 with the surge in inflation to 7 percent intensified in 1987, and became even more pronounced in 1988. The vanishing economic and political stability in Argentina, in turn, had a negative impact on rescheduling negotiations with the IMF and commercial creditors. In early June, while addressing the UN assembly, Alfonsín requested a reduction of interest rates to 4 percent for the next three years—less than half of the interest rates applied by commercial banks. He also demanded an extension of the repayment period of Argentina's foreign debts to thirty years, during which the WB would grant it financial support and warranties. The commercial banks refused.[111] In the absence of viable alternatives, Argentina sought credits from the IMF, the WB, and the IDB.[112] For the first time, the WB management encountered explicit resistance in securing approval for loans to Argentina. In June 1988, during the EB's discussion on releasing the agricultural loan approved in April 1986, the EDs from the United States, Germany, France, Great Britain, and New Zealand abstained. Furthermore, the EB deliberations witnessed serious skepticism regarding Argentina's capacity to meet its financial obligations,[113] implying criticism of the WB's management, staff, and decisions.

In July 1988, a delegation headed by Brodersohn traveled to Washington to meet the new IMF Managing Director, Michel Camdessus, WB President Conable, David Mulford from the US Treasury, and representatives of the creditor banks. The Argentines were particularly interested in the new SBA and WB assistance.[114] The WB was keen to help but was under increasingly stringent provisions. Thus, it formulated an extensive list of macroeconomic conditions for additional structural adjustment lending. Specifically, it requested that Argentina present the 1989 budget to Congress no later than December 31, 1988, reform the General Tax Administration (*Dirección General Impositiva* [DGI]), revise the industrial promotion law and the VAT through progressive elimination of exemptions, substitute many taxes with VAT, and modify income and profit taxes to institute a presumptive tax. It also stipulated the privatization of *Aerolíneas Argentinas* (the state-owned flag carrier of Argentina), ENTEL (the telephone company), ELMA (Argentine Shipping Lines Company), and other state-owned enterprises, and the reorganization of the railways.[115] Notably, the WB was not establishing new conditions. Rather, it believed that Argentina was now ready and willing to fulfill them.

In late 1988, foreign debt stood at $56 billion, and Argentina was $1.2 billion behind in debt payments.[116] As was explained above, the *Plan Primavera,* launched on August 3, 1988, with Conable's strong endorsement (including his visit to Argentina in September 1988[117]), proved ineffective. The drastic cutbacks and stringent measures outlined in the plan—including a 30 percent increase in public service rates and the abolition of price controls—combined with a 27.6 percent inflation rate in August sparked furious protests from labor unions, consumers, and business leaders.[118] A general strike in September ended in violent demonstrations in downtown Buenos Aires. Hundreds entered SEGBA's headquarters, complaining that rates were raised by 200–300 percent instead of 30 percent.[119] The CGT also loudly criticized Conable's presence in Argentina, declaring that "[we] will not accept impositions established by technocrats who had no mandate to define them and that do so with the pretext that they continue to enlarge the spurious indebtedness of the country."[120] The CGT, so it seems, believed that the worse the economic situation, the more the WB was involved.

Although Argentina was in the midst of an internal crisis fueled by an unstable economy and the devastating side effects of the debt problem, the WB's renewed seal of approval facilitated a new round of negotiations with the creditor banks.[121] In contrast to previous negotiations that involved a committee comprising all the banks, this time, Machinea, the Director of the Central Bank, conducted separate meetings with middle-ranking representatives from Citicorp, J.P. Morgan, Chase Manhattan, and Manufacturers Hanover Corp., who lacked the authority to make decisions.[122] Argentina was losing the last shreds of credibility among its major creditors, and the WB emerged, once again, as almost the only financier ready to assist it. In a last attempt to obtain the funds needed to avoid default, the Minister of Economy sent the WB a detailed plan designed to reduce public spending, with the reform of the tax direction as its core component.[123] With this plan in place, and following a meeting between Alfonsín and Conable in New York,[124] the WB approved three loans in October 1988 totaling approximately $800 million, in addition to four other loans approved between March and July of the same year. As Conable declared, these loans reflected WB's support and facilitated the release of a $500 million bridge loan arranged by the United States and other nations via the Bank for International Settlements (BIS). This funding aimed to offset the suspension by the IMF of two loan installments amounting to $500 million, which were initially part of the agreement signed in July 1987.[125] What was remarkable about these three loans is that Conable did not wait for the approval of a new SBA in order to submit them to EB vote. Not only did the Bank provide Argentina with the necessary funds to repay debts that were already overdue, it also sent a powerful message of support for Alfonsín's economic plan.[126] Conable justified the loans, rightly claiming that Alfonsín was determined to implement structural adjustments.[127] The Reagan administration, for its part, supported the approval of WB loans to Argentina as part of its broader endorsement of the country's neoliberal turn. Signaling harmonious coordination between the Bank and the US administration, in September 1988, the House voted, 303 to 90, to authorize US support for a massive increase in WB resources, given that its commitments to developing nations had escalated to nearly $20 billion. The authorization of $420 million for the WB over six years, as *The New York Times* reported, "represented a vote of confidence in Barber B. Conable."[128]

In January 1989, amid political, economic, and social crisis, Argentina and the WB discussed two potential loans. One, motivated by a shortage of electric and water supply, was for an electric plant in Bahía Blanca.[129] Although energy and potable water were central components of the WB's traditional lending portfolio, this project was disqualified because Argentina had used up all the WB funds for which it was eligible.[130] However, the Bank did authorize the deviation of part of the SEGBA loan approved in June 1987 to repair the electric plants that were causing the energy shortages.[131] The second loan, which was the last one that the WB would extend to the Alfonsín administration, was a Tax Administration Technical Assistance Loan valued at $6.5 million. It aimed to accelerate the long-awaited reform of the DGI, which included improving the efficiency of tax collection, the reduction of tax evasion, and the deterrence of fraudulent practices.[132] The loan was unanimously approved in an EB meeting in which no questions about Argentina's fragile political situation were raised.[133]

In early April, following the collapse of the *Plan Primavera* and barely forty days ahead of the general elections, Alfonsín appointed Juan Carlos Pugliese—who had previously served as Minister of Economy during Arturo Illia's presidency—as the new Minister of Economy, replacing Sourrouille. A new cabinet was also announced. In May, determined to curb hyperinflation, Pugliese unveiled a macroeconomic package which included price freezes, tariff increases, the suspension of public works, new agricultural taxes, and an increase in income tax payments.[134] In the meantime, a WB mission visited Argentina. As it reported, the visit "occurred at one of the most difficult moments in recent Argentine history" and at "a desperate time for the new economic team."[135] The new cabinet, upon learning that Argentina was not deemed eligible for debt reduction under the Brady Plan, shared with the WB mission its deep concern.[136] Amidst an economic collapse, the general elections, initially scheduled for October 1989, were brought forward to May 14. The UCR faced slim prospects in elections where the economic crisis took central stage. Carlos Saúl Menem, a lawyer who had served as Governor of La Rioja Province and head of the Peronist Party, emerged victorious in the elections. With Menem as president, Argentina adopted an even more comprehensive form of neoliberalism than under Alfonsín. Although Menem's presidency is beyond the framework of the Cold War, I refer to it briefly to show the long-term results of the WB's efforts to inculcate Western economic models in Argentina and other Latin American countries through the entire Cold War, before it started doing so in former Soviet bloc states.

The Aftermath of the Debt Crisis: President Menem and the Transformation of Argentina's Economy

Following the elections, it became increasingly difficult for Alfonsín to implement economic initiatives, as it had been agreed that President-elect Menem would review them for approval.[137] A sense of paralysis dominated the national scene. On May 29, in the wake of food riots in the cities of Rosario, Quilmes, Bernal, and San Miguel, Alfonsín declared a state of siege that lasted thirty days.[138] On June 12, Alfonsín announced his resignation, to take effect in eight days, allowing Menem to assume office immediately afterward. Taking a different stance than in Argentina's previous political crises, when it had maintained a lower profile, the WB announced that it would send a three-week-long mission to Buenos Aires on June 19.[139] Undoubtedly, Argentina became too big an issue for the WB to let it fail.

Upon assuming the presidency on July 8, 1989, Menem faced a dire economic landscape: projected monthly inflation stood at 200 percent, foreign exchange reserves were virtually exhausted, public spending was dependent on money printing, real wages were meager, prices were sky-high, and non-export sectors had been hit by a severe recession. This critical constellation, as well as the still-fresh memory of the food riots, enabled Menem to implement harsh austerity measures.[140] As Kurt Weyland notes, Fernando Collor de Mello in Brazil (1990–1992) and Alberto Fujimori in Peru (1990–2000) adopted a similar neoliberal approach to deal with the crisis.[141] However, after an electoral campaign centered on promises of a "productive revolution" and a substantial wage increase, President Menem somewhat unexpectedly implemented a sweeping neoliberal economic policy in line with the prevailing economic approach of the Western bloc. His full alignment with the United States extended beyond the economic realm, leading him to break with traditional Peronist foreign policy positions. Under his leadership, Argentina fully embraced Washington's strategic priorities, evident in decisions such as sending troops to the Gulf War, revising its stance on nuclear weapons, and withdrawing from the Non-Aligned Movement in 1991—marking a clear departure from the Peronist previous Third Position of controversial neutrality. Additionally, Menem reestablished diplomatic relations with Britain, which had been severed since 1982.[142]

Upon assuming office, Menem faced an Argentina reeling from the aftermath of the latest dictatorship, the defeat in the Falklands/Malvinas War, the sudden termination of Alfonsín's government, and hyperinflation. These elements provided fertile ground for the application of quick and extensive economic reforms that Menem described as a "major surgery without anesthetic,"[143] recalling the shock treatment which Naomi Klein examines in her book *The Shock Doctrine: The Rise of*

Disaster Capitalism.[144] Although Menem's first months in office were characterized by inconsistency, especially in the economic realm, through a series of key appointments and controversial measures, he soon secured the broad support and power needed to neoliberalize the economy.[145]

Together with his Minister of Public Works, Norberto Dromi, a vocal critic of what he identified as inefficient *statism*, Menem devised a plan "to reform the state and transform the nation."[146] The plan took shape in August 1989, when Argentina's Congress passed the State Reform Law (Law No. 23.696), granting the executive the authority to liquidate or privatize, either partially or entirely, nearly all public enterprises. These included, but were not limited to, telecommunications, airlines, television and radio stations, gas, electricity, subways and railways, petrochemicals, steel, and the federal highway system.[147] Soon after, Congress approved the Economic Emergency Law (known as the Dromi Law), which suspended government subsidies for 180 days and allowed the executive to impose, at its own discretion and by presidential decree, economic measures related to wages, taxes, and tariffs.[148] These laws were translated into some 350 decrees related to privatizations, deregulation, the appointment of judges, and the increasingly limited right to strike, leading to an unprecedented concentration of power in the president's hands.[149] These laws were complemented by the Convertibility Law (Law No. 23.928), promoted by Economic Minister Domingo Cavallo and sanctioned in 1991. This law pegged the exchange rate at one Argentine peso per US dollar and required that the Central Bank back two-thirds of the monetary base with international reserves.[150] Additionally, trade liberalization initiatives were implemented, including reductions in import tariffs and the elimination of export duties, which facilitated a substantial influx of foreign capital to the country.[151] From this point until 1999, Argentina would no longer be characterized by hybrid economic models. Menem managed to solidify the neoliberal shift that Alfonsín attempted but was unable to fully realize due to political, economic, and social constraints.

Menem's reforms, along with improvements in short-term macroeconomic imbalances, soon secured him the support of the WB, the IMF, and the Bush administration (1989–1993). The support was expressed in a long series of loans and honors. In 1998, for instance, Menem was invited to open the annual joint meeting of the IMF and the WB in Washington, DC, together with US President Bill Clinton (1993–2001). The WB, which had been active in Argentina during Alfonsín's term, significantly expanded operations under Menem. This started in December 1990 with three non-project loans that were aimed at promoting the reform of public enterprises and of key sectors like agriculture. In an EB meeting in August 1990 in which disbursements to Argentina were discussed, the WB-WHD staff explained that following two episodes of hyperinflation and a deep recession, the economy began to stabilize in March 1990 thanks to Menem's readiness to implement far-reaching structural reforms. As the staff detailed, these reforms encompassed a major tax reform, the extension of the VAT to most goods and banking services, the strengthening of the tax administration, and a privatization program that resulted in the sale of the telephone company, the national airline, and two TV stations, as well as the auctioning off of central oilfields and the transfer of 10,000 kilometers of roads to the private sector. The government also embarked on a reform of the public administration, closing 80 branches of the National Housing Bank and the Industrial Development Bank. As the WB staff claimed, the government also "took drastic measures" to reduce fiscal costs and correct the economic distortions of the incentive regimes for the industrial sector. In order to do so, the government suspended the Buy National Law, eliminated or reduced tax exemptions for ongoing projects, reduced import restrictions, and more.[152] While Argentina had seen similar measures enacted in the past, Menem implemented all of them in one fell swoop.

WB lending to Argentina reached new heights under the Menem administration, totaling seventy-two loans in ten years. However, while the country's macroeconomic performance looked promising, Menem's reforms had a devastating impact on wide sectors of society. By the end of this presidency in 1999, more than 36 percent of the population—about 13.4 million individuals—were living below the poverty line. Moreover, 8.6 percent of the population (approximately 3.2 million people) lived in extreme poverty.[153] Indeed, during Menem's second term (1994–1999), the number of individuals living under the poverty line rose at a rate of one million people on average per year.[154] Like in previous decades, the worsening social conditions did not impede the WB to continue granting highly conditional loans that actually deepened the reforms. Suffice it to say that the WB approved twelve new loans to Argentina in 1998 and eight in 1999, the last one of them on November 24, shortly before a new elected president took power.

In the meantime, all eyes turned towards the dissolving Eastern bloc. It was the end of the global Cold War and the beginning of a new era. Capitalism, in its neoliberal version, became the dominant global economic paradigm. Former Soviet satellites would enter the Bretton Woods institutions, seeking guidance on transitioning from socialism to capitalism. Eight new member-states joined in 1990–1991, twenty-two in 1992, and seven between 1993 and 1997. The WB, which had played a central role in the economic Cold War, could now reap the fruits of its patience and perseverance.

CONCLUSIONS

In December 1983, President Raúl Alfonsín assumed office, marking the end of seven years of military rule that had resulted in the disappearance of some 30,000 people, an economy in recession, increasing rates of poverty, and a $49 billion foreign debt whose repayments were made at the expense of investment in infrastructure, public services, and social welfare. Alfonsín's inauguration also represented the beginning of an era of hope and confidence in the capacity of democracy to cure all the aforementioned ills. However, mounting economic difficulties posed a significant threat to the fledgling democratic regime, ultimately overshadowing Alfonsín's entire term. Initially, his administration attempted to tackle serious financial issues by relying on traditional heterodox strategies. When these strategies proved ineffective, Argentina became more open to exploring new policy approaches. Put differently, the shift in economic policy was not imposed by the WB or other influential financiers. Instead, it represented a sovereign decision to venture into uncharted territory and seek new formulas to resolve longstanding problems. By the early 1980s, the perceived decline of communism and the Soviet Union's increasing focus on domestic issues had narrowed the range of options available to Argentina and other Latin American countries.

As this chapter has shown, the WB was deeply involved in Argentina throughout Alfonsín's presidency, particularly from 1985 onwards with the appointment of Juan Carlos Pugliese as Minister of Economy and the launching of the *Plan Austral*, which eased the resumption of WB lending to the country in June 1986. The WB's engagement in the national economy became so significant that, for the first time since Argentina joined the Bretton Woods institutions in 1956, the Bank's involvement surpassed that of other powerful actors such as the IMF, the US administration, and foreign banks. Notably, while Alfonsín signed eighteen loan agreements with the WB, the IMF granted his administration only two SBAs (in December 1984 and February 1987) and three CFFs for the fall in exports (in December 1984, January 1987, and February 1989).[155] The WB's operations in the country were multifaceted, encompassing a record average of three loans per year (a record that was only surpassed during Menem's presidency), technical assistance, and intermediation in talks with commercial creditors. Additionally, the WB's activities included an unusually high level of overt political support, manifested through visits to Argentina by senior WB officials, including the Bank's President Clausen, and reportedly neutral statements from WB management endorsing Alfonsín's economic policies. As discussed above, while the debt crisis had devastating political and social consequences for Argentina, for the WB, it was a boon. Under the shadow of the debt crisis, the more severe the economic emergency became, the greater the WB lending and the more profound the neoliberalization process in Argentina.

The analysis of the WB-Argentina-US dynamics during the Lost Decade has shed light on the crucial role that the WB played during the last stages of the Cold War, presenting four interconnected arguments. The first is that Latin America's debt crisis marked the conclusion of the economic Cold War in the region. Essentially, it was a crisis within the capitalist system, to which the majority of Latin American countries had aligned with the support of the WB, among others. By the 1980s, countries like Argentina were no longer seeking ideas, financial resources, or solutions from outside the Western world. The Soviets, for their part, had ceased attempting to exert influence in Latin American countries (with very few exceptions in Central America), which had never been a priority for them in any case.

The second claim is that the WB was a principal beneficiary of a crisis of growth and development that it had been unable to prevent despite decades of operations in Argentina and Latin America more broadly. With the launch of the *Plan Austral* in June 1985 and the Baker Plan in October of the same year, the WB significantly expanded its activities in Argentina, Mexico, Brazil, and other debtor nations. This expansion involved technical advice, assistance in negotiations with commercial financial institutions, and the granting of standard project loans as well as of new structural adjustment loans designed to provide the resources necessary for debt repayment in exchange for substantial policy and state reforms.

A third major argument is that the debt crisis proved constructive for WB-US relations. Despite initially being a strident critic of the WB, President Reagan ultimately shifted his stance and entrusted it with a leading role in managing the debt crisis. This was largely due to the fact that the WB's involvement freed the Reagan administration from direct association with the polemical reforms required to address the crisis. Reagan's focus, in any case, was primarily directed towards winning the Cold War and bringing it to a conclusion. Lastly, the chapter highlighted how the WB, adhering to its longstanding principle of political neutrality, strove to depoliticize the debt crisis. This depoliticization not only involved the Bank's focus on the allegedly pure financial aspects of the crisis but also its deliberate oversight of the crisis's impact on Argentina's fragile democracy. Furthermore, the WB, setting aside its own development mission, largely disregarded the significant social costs associated with the structural reforms and adjustment programs it advocated. The Bank's success in technocratizing the crisis is noteworthy, particularly considering that Latin American leaders, led by Alfonsín, promoted a very different approach. They argued that the burden of the crisis should be shouldered not only by the debtors but also by the creditors, who had engaged in irresponsible lending practices.

Finally, while this chapter has shown a steady *crescendo* in Argentina's readiness and efforts to neoliberalize its economy and reshape and downsize the state, this was not a definitive or irreversible shift. After Menem's presidency ended in December 1999, the UCR, Alfonsín's party, returned to power. The new president, Fernando de la Rúa, faced a new economic crisis marked by a banking panic and the infamous "*Corralito*," which imposed limits on bank withdrawals. De la Rúa resigned on December 20, 2001, just two years after taking office, leaving the presidential palace in a helicopter as protesters blocked the surrounding streets. Following months of institutional instability and multiple interim administrations, Néstor Kirchner, a Peronist, was sworn in as president in December 2003. Topping his agenda was a reversal of the neoliberal legacy left by Menem. In these tumultuous years, marked by one change after another, the significant involvement of the WB in Argentina remained a notable constant.

CONCLUSIONS

THIS BOOK HAS REVEALED THE intricate and hitherto untold story of the World Bank and its dynamic relationship with Latin America during the Cold War. Spanning from the immediate postwar era to the Malta Summit of December 1989, the Cold War coincided with the Bank's first half-century. Through a close examination of the Bank's interactions with Argentina, one of Latin America's largest economies and an influential actor in the region, and their triangular dynamics with the United States, the WB's strongest member-state, the book traced the WB's evolution and consolidation. In doing so, it exposed the impact that the Cold War had on the expansion of its development agenda and operations, as well as the imprint that the WB left in this conflict. Against the backdrop of the Cold War's ideological conflict, the promotion among Third World countries of development models rooted in Western notions of progress and modernization was of crucial significance. *The World Bank and the Cold War in Latin America: The Argentine Challenge* unveiled the multifaceted strategies employed by the Bank to encourage Argentina and other Latin American borrowers to adopt policies aligned with Washington's economic paradigms. As the case of Argentina shows, the WB's strategies complemented and reinforced US efforts to contain communism and ensure that developing countries in Latin America, Asia, and Africa remain anchored within the Western bloc. Thus, although the WB's management and staff strived to comply with the institution's commitment to political neutrality, they frequently found themselves serving US Cold War interests. As WB President Robert McNamara (1968–1981) affirmed, ". . . the [World] Bank can take the lead in various issues relating to the Third World. But at certain times there are rigidities that you can't go beyond, and the Cold War was one rigidity. You could not, the World Bank couldn't break down an action that was stimulated by the Cold War. That was an overwhelming force you couldn't deal with. . . ."[1] Argentina, a country where communism has hardly transcended the confines of a small and relatively uninfluential Communist Party, provides a unique viewpoint from which to monitor the WB's struggle to shield itself from the constraints and risks imposed by the Cold War. As we saw, this struggle was Sisyphean due to the DNA of the WB, which bore the genes of the United States, its primary architect and most influential member-state. Additionally, during the Cold War, the WB depended on US financial support. In a conflict where any departure from economic orthodoxy was perceived as a potential risk to the US-led Liberal International Order, the WB's policy recommendations were an integral component of the Cold War dynamics.

As a wide array of recently declassified files from the WB archives and other primary sources reveal, throughout the Cold War, the Bank was involved in Argentina's gradual—though not always linear—transition from the *statism*, interventionism, and economic nationalism of the 1940s and 1950s towards an orthodox capitalist model associated with the so-called Washington Consensus and neoliberalism. The Bank facilitated this economic transformation from the 1940s, when Argentina was denied entry into the Bretton Woods institutions, until the late 1980s and 1990s, when the country became one of Latin America's four heaviest WB borrowers, alongside Brazil, Mexico, and Colombia. In order to do so, the Bank engaged in both financial and non-financial activities, including dozens of conditional loan agreements, the provision of technical advice, meetings with government officials and private sector representatives, as well as missions, reports, negotiations, area studies, and surveillance procedures. Yet, despite the clear asymmetry of power between the WB and Argentina, the picture that arises from the study of their interactions, along with their triangular dynamics with the US administration, is far from simple. Contrary to what critics of the WB claim, the Bank did not necessarily impose its will on Argentina. Both the democratic and the authoritarian administrations that governed the country during and after the Cold War expressed a willingness to implement the harsh economic and administrative reforms requested by the WB. This was the case also when it became evident—to them and possibly to the Bank itself—that they lacked the political capacity to fulfill their promises.

Argentine leaders viewed the WB alternately as a legitimate partner, as in the cases of the Liberating Revolution (1955–1958) and the Frondizi administration (1958–1962), or as a scapegoat to be blamed for the sometimes-painful social impact of economic reforms, as in the case of the Process of National Reorganization (1976–1983). Furthermore, the relatively reduced political cost attached to agreements with a multilateral institution where Argentina held full membership contrasted with the higher political price of bilateral agreements, particularly those signed with the US government and commercial banks. It was precisely this gap between the political implications of multilateral versus government-to-government lending that nurtured Argentina's eagerness to find common ground with the WB.

An in-depth examination of the Argentine case has shown that the triangular relations between its government, the Bank, and the US administration were an integral component of the intra-bloc Cold War dynamics. To begin with, the WB did not turn its attention to its Latin American member-states until March 1948, nearly two years after its inauguration in June 1946, and following the launch of the Marshall Plan—a plan devised to contain Soviet expansionism and communist appeal in Europe. The WB approved its first loans to a non-European state, Chile—which were also its initial development (rather than reconstruction) loans—after European member-states who were receiving Marshall Plan assistance no longer qualified for Bank lending. Argentina, whose entry into the Bretton Woods institutions had been vetoed by the US government for more than a decade, joined the IMF and the

WB in 1956, following the deposal of President Juan D. Perón (detailed in Chapter 1). The US administration perceived Perón as a fascist and a fervent advocate of Argentina's wartime neutrality. Additionally, they saw him as the proponent of policies that were at odds with its Cold War goals and that many in the US State Department mistakenly perceived as leaning towards socialism. These policies included Perón's initial actions against foreign capital (such as nationalizations and the partial expropriation of the American Foreign Power Company), his solid ties with politicized labor unions, and the adoption of a Third Position in international affairs. However, it was only in 1961 that the WB granted its first loans to Argentina. As elaborated in Chapter 2, the timing of these long-awaited loans was influenced not only by the shift in economic policy under the *developmentalist* President Arturo Frondizi but also by the broader geopolitical context. The Cuban Revolution had heightened the Bank's concerns that a potentially disillusioned Argentine government might lead a regional revolt against the institution. As discussed in Chapter 6, WB-Argentina-US triangular relations remained deeply entwined with Cold War dynamics until the end of the war. In effect, the outbreak of the debt crisis in 1982, in itself a consequence of the success of the Bank and other Western institutions in becoming the sole financiers of a major Latin American economy like Argentina, drove President Raúl Alfonsín (1983–1989) to embrace neoliberalism, thereby solidifying the country's alignment with Western developed nations. The neoliberal turn of the 1980s was further enabled by the absence of expectations of financial assistance from the Soviet Union, expectations which, in any case, had not been viable for most Latin American countries. The ability of a large bureaucratic apparatus like the WB to reinvent itself in order to remain relevant reflected its organizational strength and its confidence that, in the long run, patience, perseverance, and a degree of flexibility were essential for success. The WB's strategy was wise. When, under the shadow of the Debt Crisis of the early 1980s, Argentina and other countries in the region hewed closely to the so-called Washington Consensus, they were not charting an entirely new ideological course. Rather, they were reinforcing economic principles that the WB had been promoting in the region since 1948.

To be sure, the reorganization and reduction of the state apparatus; the large-scale privatizations; the liberalization and de-regulation of trade, finance, and the labor market; the dismantling of labor unions; the opening of the economy to foreign capital and investors; and other liberalizing measures had been at the core of the WB's mission since its foundation. For the Bank, nations that desired to develop had to become "development-minded," or simply put, capitalistic. In this sense, the book is in line with the recent wave of scholarship that traces the roots of neoliberalism to the pre-1980s era.[2]

FROM CONTEXT-DEPENDENT RESPONSES TO KEY PATTERNS OF ACTION

The six chapters in this book have all explored the often-counterintuitive response of the WB to six major economic and political challenges that Argentina, like other Latin American member-states, posed throughout the Cold War. The main challenges were the classic populism of the 1940s and 1950s, *developmentalist* policies in the late 1950s, economic nationalism and authoritarianism in the 1960s, human rights violations in the 1970s and early 1980s, and the so-called Latin America's Lost Decade of the 1980s. By analyzing the WB's responses to these challenges, which ranged from full alignment with US Cold War interests to apparent neutrality and even subtle dissent and semi-autonomy, the book disclosed a complex interplay of factors. These include the WB's own bureaucratic goals, its symbiotic relationship with the United States, and Argentina's proactive efforts to make the Bank serve its national interests.

While the aforementioned challenges were not all directly motivated by the Cold War, they all became central Cold War issues. To begin with, the US administration viewed these challenges, along with the policies and ideas that spawned them, as detrimental to its Cold War objectives in Latin America. Thus, it reassessed its financial and military assistance to Argentina and other countries that pursued similar "problematic" policies. Most significantly, the US administration also pressured the Bank to use its lending and non-lending tools to encourage Argentina to adopt acceptable policies or, alternatively, to abandon unacceptable ones. Second, the WB acknowledged that certain policies implemented by Argentina's unstable governments were incompatible with Western capitalism and political liberalism and, therefore, also with certain Bank policies and lending conditions. However, keen to safeguard its reputation and (semi) autonomy and avoid being seen as an arm of US foreign policy, the Bank strove to neutralize, *technocratize,* and/or altogether omit those contentious issues. Third and finally, Argentine government officials, aware that their policies raised Cold War concerns in Washington, threatened to turn to the Soviet bloc or to other Western financiers if the WB failed to meet their expectations.

Zooming out and taken together, the six challenges analyzed in this book allow us to identify patterns of action whose importance transcends the Argentine case. Notably, during the Cold War, the same staff of the WB's WHD and of the Economic Department followed the same policies, performed the same working routines, and "sold" the same lending instruments to all Latin American borrowers. It is not surprising, then, as Figure 2 below shows, that the WB's lending to Argentina broadly followed the same upward trend as its lending to the entire region. Some of the Bank's repeated and almost habitual actions and reactions had to do with the WB decision-making process and with its capability to navigate the treacherous waters dividing between its main principal, the United States, and one of its prime Latin American borrowers, Argentina. Others related to the strategies used by Argentine governments to access WB development funds, regardless of their affinity or enmity with the US administration. A third type of pattern involved the uneven efforts made by the US administration to influence WB decisions regarding Argentina.

World Bank Main Patterns of Action

Broadly speaking, the WB's patterns of action during the Cold War revolved around three major interconnected areas. The first pertains to the strategies employed by the Bank to fulfill its obligation to avoid political considerations when dealing with member-states. The WB demonstrated notable indifference towards the type of regime in power in

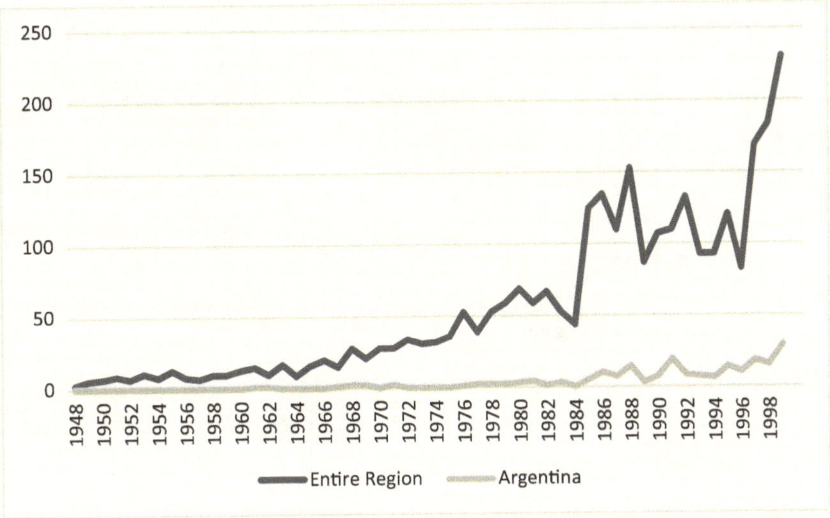

FIGURE 2. Number of World Bank Loans to Argentina and Latin America, 1948–1999.

Source: Data from World Bank Group Site, Projects by Country, Latin America and Caribbean (https://projects.worldbank.org/en/projects-operations/projects-list?regionname_exact=Latin%20America%20and%20Caribbean&title=Latin%20America%20and%20Caribbean&os=0)

Argentina. It was involved equally with both democratic and dictatorial regimes, while consistently expressing serious concerns about political instability and the capability of specific administrations to repay Argentina's foreign debts. The WB was prone to collaborate with stable administrations, regardless of their political nature, and was hesitant to enter into agreements with regimes experiencing economic and/or political crises. The WB's choice to withhold loans from Guido's *de facto* government (1962–1963) and to stop disbursements in the early 1970s when the Argentine Revolution was in power counters the widespread myth that the Bank preferred non-democratic regimes, often erroneously believed to be more capable of enforcing severe austerity measures than democratic governments.

And yet the political neutrality of the WB went beyond its stances towards various types of regimes. It also encompassed the Bank's strategies to prevent political matters from seeping into its daily dealings with member-states. This aspect of the Bank's political neutrality, it is worth noting, pertained not to its politicized EB (in which member-states are unequally represented) but to its bureaucratic apparatus. As noted in the book's introduction, all personnel, from the president to the lowest-ranking employee, were expected to prioritize economic considerations and disregard political aspects of the member-states. Two clear patterns were observed in this front. In some cases, the Bank staff discussed volatile political issues as if they were mere technical problems. This was evident, for example, in the Bank's tense negotiations with the Frondizi (1958–1962) and Alfonsín (1983–1898) administrations. Both administrations, yielding to pressure from Peronist labor unions, ended up authorizing wage increases and price freezes that violated conditions outlined in WB loan agreements. Under such circumstances, rather than evaluating how to alleviate the social and political consequences of the economic reforms that it advocated, the WB insisted that massive layoffs were needed to rationalize the public sector and reduce budget deficits. In other instances, the WB sidestepped reference to sensitive Cold War issues in its interactions with the Argentines or in discussions on Argentina with representatives of the US State Department. This was the case of the annulment of the oil contracts under Illia's administration (1963–1966) and of human rights violations during the *Proceso* (1976–1983). In both patterns, we see that the WB staff used its self-imposed principle of political neutrality as a wildcard and as a pretext to lend or refrain from lending to Argentina without completely disappointing either the United States or the Argentines.

The second area in which patterns of action emerged was in the Bank's efforts to protect and augment its partial autonomy. These at times intersected and at times clashed with its determination to remain politically neutral. For the Bank, to act autonomously implied trying to isolate itself from US Cold War interests and taking decisions that were at odds with US expectations. To be sure, the WB needed to present itself as neutral and at least partially autonomous in order to ensure that Third World nations like Argentina would continue to see it as a legitimate partner in their development efforts. The results were represented on a wide spectrum. At one extreme, the US administration aggressively imposed its will on the Bank. This was the case in Argentina's long exclusion from the Bretton Woods institutions. The US administration vetoed Argentina's entry, and the Bank's hands were tied (see Chapter 1). At the opposite extreme, the WB staff successfully repelled US attempts to impose upon it political considerations. This rare success was notable in the 1970s, when the Carter administration pressured the Bank to halt lending to Argentina's junta due to its systematic violation of human rights. The Bank, as elaborated in Chapter 5, insisted that human rights were beyond its mandate. More than once, WB President McNamara (1968–1981) managed to outvote the US executive director and get the approval of the EB on loans to dictatorial regimes in Argentina, Brazil, Chile, and other countries. Mid-spectrum included numerous cases in which the stances of the US administration and the WB coincided. But while the United States and the WB often agreed on ideological grounds, their short-term goals and interests did not necessarily intersect with each other. As detailed in Chapter 3, for example, while the WB's stance on Illia's annulment of the contracts with US oil companies dovetailed with the US policy on expropriations of US assets abroad, the WB concealed this ideological affinity and sought to publicize that it had its own economic and neutral reasons to refuse opening loan negotiations.

At the core of a third set of patterns of action was the impact that economic ideas had on WB operations in Argentina. The evaluation of WB-Argentina relations in their entirety, beyond just the WB's lending record, has uncovered a consistent and counterintuitive approach: the closer the economic ideological affinity with Argentina's administration was, the more comfortable the WB felt to demand deeper reforms in a shorter time and better economic results. In the context of Argentina, it is evident that the economic stance of the country's administration played a far more decisive role in its relations with the Bank than the specific type of regime in power. This does not necessarily mean, however, that ideological affinity on economic matters alone was ever *enough* to secure WB assistance. The temporary nature of Guido's regime (1966–1970), for example, and its inability to put national finances in order and improve the state's administrative capacity, stood as the main barriers to WB lending. Simply sharing ideological views was insufficient.

Main Patterns of Action: Argentina and the United States

For Argentina, the most obvious pattern of action centered on the effort, across regimes—democratic and authoritarian, left-wing and right-wing, pro- or anti-US—to access highly desired WB development funds and expertise. Moreover, all regimes were ready to take significant political risks in order to reach an agreement with the Bank. The other notable pattern of action has to do with Argentina's proactivity and agency. Most administrations tried to fulfill the WB's preconditions for lending. However, they realized that the WB needed them almost as much as they needed the Bank. Accordingly, Argentina's leaders followed two distinct strategies. First, presidents such as Illia and Alfonsín assumed leading roles in organizing Latin American nations to call, collectively, to make the rules of international finances more favorable towards developing nations. Argentina's support of the NIEO initiative and the efforts to create a debtors' cartel in the 1980s are good cases in point. The second strategy was threatening to turn to the communist bloc if the WB refused to grant them loans. This threat was made by Perón, Frondizi, Illia, and even several anti-communist and neoliberal military regimes. However, nobody in Argentina seriously considered crossing Cold War lines. The ability of the Soviet Union to provide significant assistance to the region (except Cuba and, at times, Nicaragua) was essentially nil. Nevertheless, there was a third strategy: demonstrating a deep understanding of the WB's organizational interests, leaders in the region conveyed to the Bank that its intransigence would push them to alternative Western financiers, such as the IMF and the Eximbank, the Alliance for Progress in the 1960s, and the IDB from the 1950s onwards. Ultimately, it was this more concrete threat that won out.

Concerning the United States, it saw the WB as an agent to which it could delegate a substantial portion of its mission to Westernize other nations. This vision formed the cornerstone of the Bretton Woods institutions and other multilateral organizations whose establishment the United States advanced as a central pillar of the Washington-based postwar global order. With regard to Argentina, specifically in its relations with the Guido and Alfonsín administrations, the United States expected the WB to leverage its multilateral nature to advance policies and solutions that might be more challenging for Argentina to accept if they had been proposed by the US administration. In certain instances, the US administration seemed to lack trust in the WB's loyalties, prompting it to take direct control. This was evident in 1961, when the Kennedy administration launched the Alliance for Progress. Not only did the Alliance largely duplicate the Bank's development objectives, but Kennedy's team also excluded the WB from any official role in this initiative. As it did in the Marshall Plan, the United States aimed to foster development in Latin America at its own discretion. In other cases, such as during the final years of the Argentine Revolution, which was closely allied with the United States, the US administration allowed the Bank to assume a leading role in Argentina. This decision may have been related to the regime's staunch anti-communist and anti-Peronist positions, as well as its determination to implement economic reforms.

Since the Bank's global turn at the end of the Cold War, its relations with Argentina have continued to intensify. One need only consider Argentina's forty-one WB loans during the Cold War compared to the 196 loan agreements it concluded with the Bank since 1989. This increase in loans came hand in hand with the development of new WB lending instruments, which helped deal with the 2008 economic crisis, climate change, the COVID pandemic, and other challenges. These instruments complement traditional project loans to co-finance ventures in areas such as agriculture, transport, energy, health, and other crucial infrastructure, and technical assistance. A wide variety of loans, particularly the SAL, also aim at reforming and downsizing the state apparatus and avoiding default. Over time, all these loans became a significant portion of Argentina's daunting foreign debt burden. Despite its considerable economic potential and its rich natural resources, Argentina continues to grapple with achieving economic development and independence, as well as meeting the needs of its perennially impoverished population. This raises the question of whether the time has come to reassess the WB's governance and development strategy and embark on a more transparent dialogue with Latin American countries regarding their preferred methods for promoting development. As this book has shown, Latin American nations, Argentina in particular, have called for such a dialogue since the early Cold War.

Notes

Introduction

1. The WBG's specialized institutions are: 1. The IBRD, which supports middle-income countries, including most countries in Latin America; 2. The International Development Association (IDA), established in 1961, which provides loans to countries that are not considered "creditworthy" in international markets; 3. The International Finance Corporation (IFC), founded in 1956, which works with the private sector; 4. The Multilateral Investment Guarantee Agency (MIGA), established in 1985, which provides investment through insurance; 5. The International Centre for Settlement of Investment Disputes (ICSID), founded in 1966, which facilitates the settlement of investment disputes between governments and foreign investors.

2. Claudia Kedar, "Economic Neutrality During the Cold War: The World Bank, the United States, and Pinochet's Chile, 1973–1977," *Cold War History* 18, no. 2 (2008): 149–67, https://doi.org/10.1080/14682745.2017.1420056.

3. Eric Helleiner, *Forgotten Foundations of Bretton Woods: International Development and the Making of the Postwar Order* (Ithaca: Cornell University Press, 2014).

4. Michele Alacevich, *The Political Economy of the World Bank: The Early Years* (Stanford: Stanford University Press, an imprint of Stanford University Press and The World Bank, 2009).

5. Patrick Allan Sharma, *Robert McNamara's Other War: The World Bank and International Development* (Philadelphia: University of Pennsylvania Press, 2017).

6. Raúl García Heras, *El Fondo Monetario Internacional y el Banco Mundial en la Argentina: Liberalismo, Populismo y Finanzas Internacionales* (Buenos Aires:

Lumiere, 2008); idem, *Deuda Externa y Crisis Política. Banqueros, Fondo Monetario y Banco Mundial en la Argentina, 1973–1986* (Buenos Aires: Editorial Biblos, 2022).

7. Sara Lorenzini, *Global Development: A Cold War History* (Princeton: Princeton University Press, 2019).

8. Christy Thornton, *Revolution in Development: Mexico and the Governance of the Global Economy* (Oakland: University of California Press, 2021).

9. Agustin E. Ferraro and Miguel A. Centeno, eds., *State and Nation Making in Latin America and Spain: The Rise and Fall of the Developmental State* (Cambridge: Cambridge University Press, 2019).

10. Amy C. Offner, *Sorting Out the Mixed Economy: The Rise and Fall of Welfare and Developmental States in the Americas* (Princeton: Princeton University Press, 2019).

11. Sarah Foss, *On Our Own Terms: Development and Indigeneity in Cold War Guatemala* (Chapel Hill: University of North Carolina Press, 2022).

12. Apart from Odd Arne Westad's seminal work *The Cold War: A World History* (New York: Basic Books, 2017), the most recent publications on the Cold War in the region include: Hal Brands, *Latin America's Cold War* (Cambridge, MA: Harvard University Press, 2010); Thomas Field Jr., Stella Krepp, and Vanni Pettinà, eds., *Latin America and the Global Cold War* (Chapel Hill: University of North Carolina Press, 2020); Tanya Harmer, *Allende's Chile & the Inter-American Cold War* (Chapel Hill: University of North Carolina Press, 2011); Gilbert M. Joseph and Daniela Spencer, *In From the Cold: Latin America's New Encounter with the Cold War* (Durham: Duke University Press, 2008); Stephen G. Rabe, *The Killing Zone: The United States Wages Cold War in Latin America* (New York: Oxford University Press, 2012); Vanni Pettinà, *La Guerra Fría en América Latina* (México: Colegio de México, 2018); and Christopher Darnton, *Rivalry and Alliance Politics in Cold War Latin America* (Baltimore: Johns Hopkins University Press, 2014). To date, only one book focuses on the Cold War in Argentina: William Michael Schmidli, *The Fate of Freedom Elsewhere: Human Rights and the U.S. Cold War Policy Toward Argentina* (Ithaca: Cornell University Press, 2013), which addresses the systematic violation of human rights in the 1970s.

13. Today, Cuba is one of only four countries in the world that are not members of the Bank and the Fund.

14. G. John Ikenberry, *After Victory: Institutions, Strategic Restraint, and the Rebuilding of Order After Major Wars* (Princeton: Princeton University Press, 2001), 163–70.

15. Daniel Deudney and John Ikenberry, "The Nature and Sources of Liberal International Order," *Review of International Studies* 25, no. 2 (1999):179–96, https://doi.org/10.1017/S0260210599001795.

16. Michael J. Mazarr, "The Real History of the Liberal Order: Neither Myth nor Accident," *Foreign Affairs* (2018), https://www.foreignaffairs.com/united-states/real-history-liberal-order.

17. Ikenberry, *After Victory*, 200–2.

18. Eric Helleiner, "The Life and Times of Embedded Liberalism: Legacies and Innovations Since Bretton Woods," *Review of International Political Economy* 26, no. 6 (2019): 1112–35, https://doi.org/10.1080/09692290.2019.1607767; Tom Long, "Latin America and the Liberal International Order: An Agenda for Research," *International Affairs* 94, no. 6 (2018): 1371–90, https://doi.org/10.1093/ia/iiy188; Tom Long and Carsten-Andreas Schulz, "Republican Internationalism: The Nineteenth-Century Roots of Latin American Contributions to International Order," *Cambridge Review of International Affairs* 35, no. 5 (2022): 639–61, https://doi.org/10.1080/09557571.2021.1944983; Juan Pablo Scarfi, "The Latin American Politics of International Law: Latin American Countries' Engagements with International Law and Their Contradictory Impact on the Liberal International Order," *Cambridge Review of International Affairs* 35, no. 5 (2022): 662–79, http://dx.doi.org/10.1080/09557571.2021.1920887; Christy Thornton, "Establishing the Limits of the Liberal International Order: Latin America and the Demand for Development," *Cambridge Review of International Affairs* 35, no. 5 (2022): 680–97, https://doi.org/10.1080/09557571.2021.1937059.

19. There is a debate between scholars who maintain that, from the start, reconstruction and development were of equal importance to the Bank, and those, like myself, who claim that European reconstruction was the main priority. As claimed in this book, the WB began to think seriously about development only after the launching of the Marshall Plan. Among the most recent contributions to this debate, see Helleiner, *Forgotten Foundations of Bretton Woods*; and Thornton, *Revolution in Development*.

20. Under the Bank's Articles of Agreement, each of the five members having the largest number of shares appoints an Executive Director, and the remaining members elect the other Executive Directors, which ended up representing, with very few exceptions, groups of countries.

21. Michael Barnett and Martha Finnemore, *Rules for the World: International Organizations in Global Politics* (Ithaca: Cornell University Press, 2004); Jeffrey Chwieroth, "Organizational Change 'From Within': Exploring the World Bank's Early Lending Practices," *Review of International Political Economy* 15, no. 4 (2008): 481–505, https://doi.org/10.1080/09692290802260498.

22. Darren G. Hawkins, David A. Lake, Daniel L. Nielson, and Michael J. Tierney, "Delegation Under Anarchy: States, International Organizations, and Principal-Agent Theory," in *Delegation and Agency in International Organizations*, eds. Darren G. Hawkins, David A. Lake, Daniel L. Nielson, and Michael J. Tierney (Cambridge: Cambridge University Press, 2006), 3–38.

23. Andrew Cortell and Susan Peterson, "Autonomy and International Organisations," *Journal of International Relations and Development* 25 (2022): 399–424, https://doi.org/10.1057/s41268-021-00243-x; Yoram Haftel and Alexander Thompson, "The Independence of International Organizations: Concept and Applications," *Journal of Conflict Resolution* 50, no. 2 (2006): 253–75, https://doi.org/10.1177/0022002705285288; Daniel Carpenter, *The Forging of Bureaucratic Autonomy: Reputations, Networks, and Policy Innovation in Executive Agencies, 1862–1928* (Princeton: Princeton University Press, 2001); Richard Clark and Lindsay R. Dolan, "Pleasing the Principal: U.S. Influence in World Bank Policymaking," *American Journal of Political Science* 65, no. 1 (2021): 36–51, https://www.jstor.org/stable/45415611.

24. Thomas Barnebeck Andersen, Henrik Hansen, and Thomas Markussen, "US Politics and World Bank IDA Lending," *The Journal of Development Studies* 42, no. 5 (2006): 772–94, https://doi.org/10.1080/00220380600741946; Ashwin Kaja and Eric Werker, "Corporate Governance at the World Bank and the Dilemma of Global Governance," *The World Bank Economic Review* 24, no. 2 (2010): 171–98, https://www.jstor.org/stable/40891365; Axel Dreher, Jan-Egbert Sturm, and James Raymond Vreeland, "Development Aid and International Politics: Does Membership on the UN Security Council Influence World Bank Decisions?" *Journal of Development Economics* 88, no. 1 (2009): 1–18, https://doi.org/10.1016/j.jdeveco.2008.02.003; Erasmus K. Kersting and Christopher Kilby, "With a Little Help from My Friends: Global Electioneering and World Bank Lending," *Journal of Development Economics* 121, no. 3 (2016): 153–65, https://doi.org/10.1016/j.jdeveco.2016.03.010; Christopher Kilby, "The Political Economy of Conditionality: An Empirical Analysis of World Bank Loan Disbursements," *Journal of Development Economics* 89, no. 1 (2009): 51–61, https://doi.org/10.1016/j.jdeveco.2008.06.014.

25. Sarah Babb, *Behind the Development Banks: Washington Politics, World Poverty, and the Wealth of Nations* (Chicago: University of Chicago Press, 2009); Catherine Weaver's *Hypocrisy Trap: The World Bank and the Poverty of Reform* (Princeton: Princeton University Press, 2008); Ngaire Woods, *The Globalizers: The IMF, the World Bank and Their Borrowers* (Ithaca: Cornell University Press, 2006); Kim Moloney, *Who Matters at the World Bank? Bureaucrats, Policy Change, and Public Sector Governance* (Oxford: Oxford University Press, 2022).

26. *Developmentalism* is an economic theory and policy aimed at promoting heavy industry, modernizing agricultural production, expanding infrastructure, and reaching energy self-sufficiency.

27. With the exception of Cuba.

Chapter One

1. According to the distribution of quotas approved at the Bretton Woods conference, the Soviet Union was expected to be the third-strongest member-state

in both the IMF and the Bank with a quota of $1.20 billion. The United States led with a quota of $2.75 billion and the UK was second with a quota of $1.30 billion.

2. Principal-agent theory, which emerged in the 1970s, describes the pitfalls that often arise when one person or group, the "agent," represents another person or group, known as the "principal." This economic theory is widely applied to examine multilateral organizations such as the World Bank. See, among others, Richard Clark and Lindsay R. Dolan, "Pleasing the Principal: U.S. Influence in World Bank Policymaking," *American Journal of Political Science* 65, no.1 (2021): 36–51, https://www.jstor.org/stable/45415611.

3. Yoram Haftel and Alexander Thompson, "The Independence of International Organizations: Concept and Applications," *Journal of Conflict Resolution* 50, no. 2 (2006): 253–75, https://doi.org/10.1177/0022002705285288; Daniel Carpenter, *The Forging of Bureaucratic Autonomy: Reputations, Networks, and Policy Innovation in Executive Agencies, 1862–1928* (Princeton: Princeton University Press, 2001).

4. *Statism* here is understood as a type of state capitalism in which the state has a substantial, necessary, and legitimate role in guiding the major aspects of the economy, either directly through state-owned enterprises and economic planning of production, or indirectly through economic interventionism and macro-economic regulation.

5. National Intelligence Estimate, NIE-66. "Probable Developments in Argentina," June 13, 1952, FRUS 1952–1954, American Republics, vol. 4, 409–18.

6. Tension between Argentina and the United States began long before Perón rose to prominence, partly because the economies of the two countries were competitive (rather than complementary). Tensions increased in light of Perón's aspiration to power on a regional level. See, among others, Joaquín Fermandois, "Entusiasmo y Desconfianza. Populismo y Relaciones Internacionales en el Caso Perón–Ibáñez, 1953–1955," *Ayer* 98, no. 2 (2015): 187–211, https://www.jstor.org/stable/24759518; Loris Zanatta, *La Internacional Justicialista: Auge y Ocaso de los Sueños Imperiales de Perón* (Buenos Aires: Sudamericana, 2013).

7. The term "populism" is often used pejoratively. See, for instance, Cristóbal Rovira Kaltwasser, "The Responses of Populism to Dahl's Democratic Dilemmas," *Political Studies* 62, no. 3 (2013): 470–87, http://doi.org/10.1111/1467-9248.12038. This is particularly blatant in the economic realm, as populist economic policies are often described as irresponsible. See, among others, Luiz Bresser Pereira and Fernando Dall'Acqua, "Economic Populism Versus Keynes: Reinterpreting Budget Deficit in Latin America," *Journal of Post Keynesian Economics* 14, no.1 (2015): 29–381, http://doi.org/10.1080/01603477.1991.11489875; Rudiger Dornbusch and Sebastian Edwards, eds., *The Macroeconomics of Populism in Latin America* (Chicago: Chicago University Press, 1991); Sebastian Edwards, *Left Behind: Latin America and the False Promise of Populism* (Chicago: University of Chicago Press, 2010); and Jeffrey Sachs, "Social Conflict and Populist Policies

in Latin America," *NBER Working Paper Series,* Working paper no. 2897, March 1989, https://www.nber.org/system/files/working_papers/w2897/w2897.pdf. Others stressed positive effects of populist economic policies, such as, among others, Cristóbal Rovira Kaltwasser, "Populismo y Economía: Una Relación Ambivalente," *Perspectivas* 3 (2019): 1–20, https://library.fes.de/pdf-files/bueros/chile/15478.pdf.

8. See, among others, Carlos de la Torre, "Populism and the Politics of the Extraordinary in Latin America," *Journal of Political Ideologies* 21, no. 2 (2016): 121–39, https://doi.org/10.1080/13569317.2016.1150137; Kurt Weyland, "Clarifying a Contested Concept: Populism in the Study of Latin American Politics," *Comparative Politics* 34, no. 1 (2001): 1–22, https://www.jstor.org/stable/422412.

9. Jon V. Kofas, "Stabilization and Class Conflict: The State Department, the IMF, and the IBRD in Chile, 1952–1958," *The International History Review* 21, no. 2 (1999): 352–85, https://doi.org/10.1080/07075332.1999.9640863.

10. Michele Alacevich, *The Political Economy of the World Bank. The Early Years* (Stanford: Stanford University Press, an imprint of Stanford University Press and The World Bank, 2009), 131–35.

11. Eugene Meyer, World Bank website, https://www.worldbank.org/en/about/archives/history/past-presidents/eugene-meyer

12. Transcript of Oral History Interview with Eugene R. Black Held on August 6, 1961, WBGA, https://oralhistory.worldbank.org/transcripts/transcript-oral-history-interview-eugene-r-black-held-august-06-1961-main-transcript.

13. John J. McCloy, World Bank website, https://www.worldbank.org/en/about/archives/history/past-presidents/john-jay-mccloy); Devesh Kapur, John P. Lewis, and Richard C. Webb, eds., *The World Bank: Its First Half Century.* Vol. 1. (Washington, DC: Brookings Institute Press, 1997), 10–11.

14. Jochen Kraske, William H. Becker, William Diamond, and Louis Galambos, *Bankers with a Mission: The Presidents of the World Bank, 1946–91* (Oxford: Oxford University Press, 1996), 53.

15. Transcript of Oral History Interview with Martin Rosen Held on July 12, 1961. World Bank Oral History Project, 15–18, http://documents.worldbank.org/curated/en/658901468161097970; Valerie Assetto, *The Soviet Bloc in the IMF and the IBRD* (Boulder: Westview Press, 1988), 69–75.

16. Louis Galambos and David Milobsky, "Organizing and Reorganizing the World Bank, 1946–1972: A Comparative Perspective," *The Business History Review* 69, no. 2 (1995): 162–64, https://doi.org/10.2307/3117098.

17. Transcript of Oral History Interview with Black, August 6, 1961, WBGA, 4–5.

18. Kapur, Lewis, Webb, *The World Bank*, vol.1, 11–14.

19. Juan Archibaldo Lanús, *De Chapultepec al Beagle: Política Exterior Argentina: 1945–1980* (Buenos Aires: Emecé, 1984), 49–50; Luigi Manzetti, *The International Monetary Fund and Economic Stabilization: The Argentine Case* (New York:

Praeger, 1991), 34; Callum A. MacDonald, "The US, the Cold War and Perón," in *Latin America, Economic Imperialism and the State: The Political Economy of the External Connection from Independence to the Present*, eds. Christopher Abel and Colin M. Lewis (London: Bloomsbury, 1985), 405–14; Mario Rapoport et al., *Historia Económica, Política y Social de la Argentina (1880–2000)* (Buenos Aires: Emecé, 2000), 522.

20. See, for example, Raúl García Heras, *Presiones Externas y Política Económica: El Fondo Monetario Internacional y el Banco Mundial en Argentina, 1955–1966* (Bogotá: Universidad de los Andes, Cátedra Corona, 2003); Manzetti, *International Monetary Fund and Economic Stabilization*; Jorge Marshall, José L. Mardones, and Isabel Marshall, "IMF Conditionality: The Experiences of Argentina, Brazil and Chile," in *IMF Conditionality*, ed. John Williamson (Washington DC: Institute for International Economics, 1983), 275–346.

21. Roberto Frenkel and José María Fanelli, "La Argentina y el Fondo en la Década Pasada," *El Trimestre Económico* 54, no. 231 (1987): 75–131; Norberto Galasso, *De la Banca Baring al FMI: Historia de la Deuda Externa Argentina* (Buenos Aires: Colihue, 2002), 175; Manzetti, *International Monetary Fund and Economic Stabilization*, 34; Rapoport et al., *Historia Económica, Política y Social*, 522.

22. Manzetti, *International Monetary Fund and Economic Stabilization*, 34.

23. Letter from Cordell Hull to the US Embassy in Buenos Aires, April 26, 1943, Bretton Woods Conference Files, Subseries: Year 1940–1947, Box 29, File 276–283, IMF Archives (hereafter: IMFA).

24. Claudia Kedar, "The Beginning of a Controversial Relationship: The IMF, the World Bank, and Argentina, 1943–46," *Canadian Journal of Latin American and Caribbean Studies* 35, no. 69 (2009): 201–30, https://doi.org/10.1080/08263663.2010.10816993.

25. "Non-Recognition of Argentine Regime," *Department of State Bulletin* 11, no. 266 (July 30, 1944): 107–11.

26. "Memorandum of Meeting in Mr. White's Office, January 23, 1946," January 23, 1946, Bretton Woods Conference Files, Subseries: Year 1940–947, Box 35, File 330–342, IMFA.

27. Ibid.

28. Decreto no. 3.185/46, January 31, 1946, *Boletín Oficial de la República Argentina—año LIV*—no. 15.512, published on June 26, 1946.

29. A-C/F—Mr. Collado, CFD—Mr. Young, April 4, 1946, Argentina Subseries, Country File Series, Central Files Box 5, File 1–20, File Title 420–710, IMFA.

30. Andrés Cisneros and Carlos Escudé, *Historia General de las Relaciones Exteriores de la República Argentina*, vol. XIII (Buenos Aires: Nuevohacer, 1998), 202.

31. Assistant Secretary of State (Braden) to Ambassador in Mexico (Messersmith), March 8, 1946, 835.00/2-2846, FRUS, 1946, American Republics, vol.11, 232–33.

32. On the Third Position see, for example, Andrés Cisneros and Carlos Escudé, *Historia General de las Relaciones Exteriores de la República Argentina,* vol. XIII (Buenos Aires: Nuevohacer, 1998), 81–191; Loris Zanatta, "The Rise and Fall of the Third Position. Bolivia, Perón and the Cold War, 1943–1954," *Desarrollo Económico* 45, no. 177 (2006): 1–27, http://socialsciences.scielo.org/scielo.php?script=sci_arttext&pid=S0046-001X2006000100004.

33. On Braden's intervention in the 1946 elections, see Glenn Dorn, *Peronistas and New Dealers: U.S.–Argentine Rivalry and the Western Hemisphere (1946–1950)* (New Orleans: University Press of the South, 2005), 39–58; Alieto Guadagni, *Braden o Perón: La Verdad Documental Norteamericana, Sesenta Años Después* (Buenos Aires: Sudamericana, 2008); C. A. MacDonald, "The Politics of Intervention: The United States and Argentina, 1941–1946," *Journal of Latin American Studies* 12, no. 2 (1980): 365–96, https://doi.org/10.1017/S0022216X00022719.

34. For an analysis of bilateral agreements, see García Heras, *Presiones Externas y Política Económica,* 18–23.

35. On Perón's industrialization policies and ties with the industrial sector, see James Brennan, "Industrialistas y Bolicheros: Business and the Peronist Populist Alliance, 1943–1976," in *Peronism and Argentina,* ed. James Brennan (Wilmington: Rowman & Littlefield, 1998), 79–125; Pablo Gerchunoff and Juan Llach, "Capitalismo Industrial, Desarrollo Asociado y Distribución del Ingreso Entre los Dos Gobiernos Peronistas: 1950–1972," *Desarrollo Económico* 15, no. 57 (1975): 3–54, https://doi.org/10.2307/3466209; Graciela Mateo, "El Gobierno de Domingo Mercante: Expresión Singular del Peronismo Clásico," in *El Primer Peronismo: De Regreso a los Comienzos,* edited by Raanan Rein and Rosalie Sitman (Lumiere, 2005), 211–48; Mónica Peralta-Ramos, *The Political Economy of Argentina: Power and Class Since 1930* (Oxford: Westview Press, 1992), 26–34; Jeffrey Sachs, "Social Conflict and Populist Policies in Latin America," *NBER Working Paper Series,* Working paper no. 2897, March 1989, https://www.nber.org/system/files/working_papers/w2897/w2897.pdf.

36. Perón to Alberto E. Asseff, October 28, 1967, in Juan D. Perón, *Correspondencia,* vol. 1, (Buenos Aires: Corregidor, 1983), 156.

37. Juan D. Perón, *La Hora de los Pueblos* (Buenos Aires: CS Ediciones, 2005), 59. This book was originally published in 1968.

38. The IMF began to develop the principle of "conditionality" in 1952. "Standby" agreements (SBA), characterized by conditional clauses, were created in 1956 and implemented beginning in 1957.

39. "Meeting in Mr. Friedman's Office, August 27, 1947. Subject: Meeting with Economic Counselor and Secretary of the Argentine Embassy," Argentina Subseries, Country File Series, Central Files Box 5, File 1–20, File Title 420–710, IMFA.

40. Ibid.

41. Margaret Garritsen deVries, *The IMF in a Changing World, 1945–85* (Washington, DC: IMF, 1986), 21.

42. Margaret Garritsen deVries, "The Retreat of Bilateralism," in *The International Monetary Fund: 1945–1965: Twenty Years of International Monetary Cooperation,* vol. 2, ed. J. Keith Horsefield (Washington, D.C.: IMF, 1969), 297–316; Johan H. C. de Looper, "Recent Latin American Experience with Bilateral Trade and Payments Agreements," *IMF Staff Papers* 4, no. 1 (1954–1955): 85–112.

43. "Meeting in Mr. Friedman's Office," August 27, 1947.

44. Jon V. Kofas, *The Sword of Damocles: U.S. Financial Hegemony in Colombia and Chile, 1950–1970* (London: Praeger, 2002), 6.

45. Mario Rapoport and Claudio Spiguel, "La Argentina y el Plan Marshall: Promesas y Realidades," *Revista Brasileira de Política Internacional* 52, no. 1 (2009): 5–28, https://doi.org/10.1590/S0034-73292009000100001.

46. *The Washington Post,* May 13, 1948.

47. J. Keith Horsefield, *The International Monetary Fund, 1945–1965: Twenty Years of International Monetary Cooperation, Vol. 1: Chronicle* (Washington, D.C.: IMF, 1969), 217.

48. Letter from Horne to Gutt. Subject: Argentina, dated June 24, 1948. Argentina Subseries, Country File Series, Central Files Box 5, File 1–20, File Title 420–710, IMFA.

49. Letter from Horne to Mendels. Subject: Argentina—approximate terms of membership, June 24, 1948. Argentina Subseries, Country File Series, Central Files Box 5, File 1–20, File Title 420–710, IMFA.

50. *The Wall Street Journal,* November 5, 1948.

51. EBD378, Subject: Gutt's Meeting with Miranda, November 29, 1948. Argentina Subseries, Country File Series, Central Files Box 5, File 1–20, File Title 420–710, IMFA.

52. EBM390, January 5, 1949. Report on Latin America, Argentina Subseries, Country File Series, Central Files Box 5, File 1–20, File Title 420–710, IMFA.

53. Confidential Letter from Mendels to Black, September 8, 1949, Argentina Subseries, Country File Series, Central Files Box 5, File 1–20, File Title 420–710, IMFA.

54. Carlos Escudé, "US Political Destabilisation and Economic Boycott of Argentina During the 1940s," in *Argentina between the Great Powers, 1939–46,* eds. Guido di Tella and D. Cameron Watt (Oxford: Macmillan, 1989), 56–76.

55. Mario Rapoport and Claudio Spiguel, *Estados Unidos y el Peronismo: La Política Norteamericana en la Argentina, 1949–1955* (Buenos Aires: Grupo Editor Latinoamericano, 1994), 75–77.

56. Confidential Official-Informal Letter, E. Miller to Ellsworth Bunker, November 13, 1951. RG 59 General Records of the State Department, Assistant Secretary of State for Latin American Affairs (Edward J. Miller), 1949–1953, A-B, Box 1 of 14, Entry Lot 53D 26, NARA.

57. See, among others, Claudio Belini, "D.I.N.I.E. y los Límites de la Política Industrial Peronista, 1947–1955," *Desarrollo Económico* 41, no. 161 (2001): 97–119, http://dx.doi.org/10.2307/3455966; Raanan Rein, *In the Shadow of Perón: Juan Atilio Bramuglia and the Second Line of Argentina's Populist Movement* (Stanford: Stanford University Press, 2008).

58. Leandro Ariel Morgenfeld, "El Inicio de la Guerra Fría y el Sistema Interamericano: Argentina Frente a Estados Unidos en la Conferencia de Caracas (1954)," *Revista Contemporánea* 1, no. 1 (2010): 75–98, https://ojs.fhce.edu.uy/index.php/cont/article/view/1059.

59. "Visita del Señor Edward G. Miller, Secretario de Asuntos Latinoamericanos del Departamento de Estado de EE.UU.A.," Consejo Económico Nacional. Análisis de la Situación Económica 1950–1952, February 1950, 30–32. BCRA. Biblioteca Prebisch.

60. "Factors in Economic Relations with Argentina," Released to the Press on May 17, 1950, *Department of State Bulletin* 22, no. 569 (May 29, 1950): 860–61.

61. National Advisory Council Doc. No. 88, Action 162, "Proposed Export-Import Bank Loan of $61 million in Argentina," March 1, 1955, RG56 General Records of the Department of the Treasury, Records of the Office of the Assistant Secretary for International Affairs, NAC Actions, August 21, 1945–December 31, 1968, 671–1073 (1954–57), Box 2, Entry 360D, NARA.

62. Confidential Letter Miller to Thorp, "Department's Recommendation that the Export-Import Bank give sympathetic consideration to an Argentine request for financial assistance," November 25, 1949, RG 59 General Records of the State Department, Assistant Secretary of State for Latin American Affairs (Edward J. Miller), 1949–1953, A-B, Box 1 of 14, Entry Lot53D 26, NARA.

63. 120.220/6–1853. Memorandum by the Secretary of State to the President, June 18, 1953, FRUS, 1952–1954, American Republics, vol. 4, 440–41.

64. Letter by Burke Knapp, "International Bank Relations with Argentina," June 9, 1953, File 1514750, Box 193602B, Argentina—General Negotiations 1947–56—I, WBGA.

65. Robert A. Potash, *The Army & Politics in Argentina, 1945–1962* (Stanford: Stanford University Press, 1980), 143–44; Eprime Eshag and R. Thorp, "Las Políticas Económicas Ortodoxas de Perón a Guido (1953–1963): Consecuencias Económicas y Sociales," in *Los Planes de Estabilización en la Argentina,* ed. Aldo Ferrer et al. (Buenos Aires: Paidós, 1974), 64–132; Eduardo Elena, "Peronist Consumer Politics and the Problem of Domesticating Markets in Argentina, 1943–1955," *Hispanic American Historical Review* 87, no. 1 (2007): 111–49.

66. "Radicación de capitales extranjeros. Ley no.14.222, sancionada el 21 de Agosto de 1953," *Memoria Anual del Banco Central 1953—Decimonoveno Ejercicio* (Banco Central, Buenos Aires, 1954), 133–144.

67. Richard Quandt to Knapp, "Sugar Beet Production, and Establishment of Beet Sugar Factories in Argentina," February 19, 1954, File 1514750, Box 193602B, Argentina—General Negotiations 1947–56—I, WBGA.

68. 835.00 TA/6-3054. Memorandum by James F. O'Connor, Jr. of the Office of South American Affairs to the Deputy Director of That Office (Bennett), "Assistance to Argentina," June 30, 1954, FRUS, 1952–1954, American Republics, vol. 4, 469.

69. *El Economista*, March 27, 1954.

70. Office Memorandum, Knapp to Files, "Argentina—Mr. Black's Visit, March 15–17, 1954," File 1514750, Box 193602B, Argentina—General Negotiations 1947–56—I, WBGA.

71. Ibid.

72. Ibid.

73. Argentina—Mr. Black's visit March 15–17, 1954; April 22, 1954, IMFA.

74. Memorandum of Conversation, "U.S.-Argentina Economic Relations," March 15, 1955. RG 59 General Records of the State Department, Assistant Secretary of State for Inter-American Affairs (Henry F. Holland), 1953–1956, Country File Argentina-Bolivia, Box 1, Entry Lot 57D 295, NARA.

75. See, for instance, Juan Perón to Henry Holland, January 17, 1955; April 14, 1955; April 29, 1955, RG 59 General Records of the State Department, Assistant Secretary of State for Inter-American Affairs (Henry F. Holland), 1953–1956, Country File Argentina-Bolivia, Box 1, Entry Lot 57D 295, NARA.

76. "Memorandum of Conversation," US-Argentine Economic Relations, March 15, 1955, RG 59 General Records of the State Department, Assistant Secretary of State for Inter-American Affairs (Henry F. Holland), 1953–1956, Country File Argentina-Bolivia, Box 1, Entry Lot 57D 295, NARA.

77. National Intelligence Estimate, NIE-91–54. "Probable Developments in Argentina," March 9, 1954, FRUS 1952–1954, American Republics, vol. 4, 455–66.

78. "Memorandum of Conversation, Call of Ambassador Paz on Mr. Holland," May 19, 1955, RG 59 General Records of the State Department, Assistant Secretary of State for Inter-American Affairs (Henry F. Holland), 1953–1956, Country File Argentina-Bolivia, Box 1, Entry Lot 57D 295, NARA.

79. "Memorandum of Conversation with President Perón, by the Assistant Secretary of State for Inter-American Affairs (Holland)," December 1954, FRUS 1952–1954, American Republics, vol. 4, 481–85.

80. "Recognition of New Government of Argentina," Released to the Press on September 25, 1955, *Department of State Bulletin* 33, no. 850 (October 10, 1955): 560.

81. Telegram from the Ambassador in Argentina (Nufer) to the Department of State, December 13, 1955, FRUS 1955–1957, American Republics, vol. 7, 398–99.

82. Pablo Gerchunoff and Lucas Llach, *El Ciclo de la Ilusión y el Desencanto: Un Siglo de Políticas Económicas Argentinas* (Buenos Aires: Ariel, 1998), 233; Potash, *The Army & Politics in Argentina,* 214–26.

83. Celia Szusterman, "The 'Revolución Libertadora,' 1955–8," in *The Political Economy of Argentina, 1946–1983,* eds. Guido Di Tella and Rudiger Dornbusch (University of Pittsburgh Press, 1989), 89–103.

84. Norma Silvana Lanciotti, "Inversiones Privadas y Políticas Públicas en el Sector Eléctrico. Argentina, 1920–1958," *XI Jornadas Interescuelas/Departamentos de Historia,* Universidad de Tucumán, San Miguel de Tucumán, 2007. https://cdsa.aacademica.org/000-108/964.pdf.

85. Transcript of Oral History Interview with Robert Garner Held on July 19, 1961, WBGA, 23–27, https://oralhistory.worldbank.org/transcripts/transcript-oral-history-interview-robert-garner-held-july-19-1961.

86. Mario Rapoport et al., *Historia Económica, Política y Social de la Argentina,* 539. For a comprehensive account of Prebisch's life, see Edgar J. Dosman, *The Life and Times of Raúl Prebisch, 1901–1986* (Montreal: McGill-Queen's University Press, 2008).

87. Roberto Cortés Conde, "Raúl Prebisch: His Years in Government," *CEPAL Review* 75 (2001): 81–86; Kathryn Sikkink, "The Influence of Raúl Prebisch on Economic Policy-Making in Argentina, 1950–1962," *Latin American Research Review* 23, no. 2 (1988): 91–114, https://www.jstor.org/stable/i322695.

88. According to Chwieroth, the emergence of domestic interlocutors sympathetic to the IMF staff's policy goals critically shapes the Fund's willingness to supply loans and a government's willingness to request them. See Jeffrey M. Chwieroth, "'The Silent Revolution': How the Staff Exercise Informal Governance Over IMF Lending," *The Review of International Organizations* 8, no. 3 (2013): 265–90, https://doi.org/10.1007/s11558-012-9154-9.

89. Sikkink, "The Influence of Raúl Prebisch," 94.

90. Article XIV Consultations with Argentina, Merle Cochran to Coromina-Segura, March 5, 1957, Argentina Subseries, Country File Series, Central Files Box 6, Files 1–18, File Title 720–810, IMFA.

91. Memorandum of Conversation, "Argentina Economic Mission; United Nations Mission to Argentina," February 2, 1956, RG 59 General Records of the State Department, Records of the Assistant Secretary of State of Inter-American Affairs (Henry F. Holland), 1953–1956, Box 1, Lot 57 D259, NARA.

92. Juan Odisio and Marcelo Rougier, "Swimming Against the (Developmentalist) Mainstream: The Liberal Economists in Argentina Between 1955 and 1976," *PSL Quarterly Review* 72, no. 289 (2019): 91–115.

93. Office Memorandum, Knapp to Black, "Argentina," January 19, 1956, File 1514750, Box 193602B, Argentina—General Negotiations 1947–56—I, WBGA.

94. Office Memorandum, Harold Larsen to Files, "Argentina—Visit by Dr. Raúl Prebisch," March 7, 1956, File 1514750, Box 193602B, Argentina—General Negotiations 1947–56—I, WBGA.

95. Ibid.

96. Ibid.

97. Office Memorandum, Knapp to Black, "Argentina—Dr. Prebisch Mission," March 8, 1956, File 1514750, Box 193602B, Argentina—General Negotiations 1947–56—I, WBGA.

98. Office Memorandum, Knapp to Garner, "Prebisch Report on Argentina," March 7, 1956, File 1514750, Box 193602B, Argentina—General Negotiations 1947–56—I, WBGA.

99. Carlson to Knapp, "Argentina," April 2, 1956, File 1514750, Box 193602B, Argentina—General Negotiations 1947–56—I, WBGA.

100. Acting Secretary to Members of the Executive Board, "Argentina," April 27, 1956, File 1514750, Box 193602B, Argentina—General Negotiations 1947–56—I, WBGA.

101. Office Memorandum, Knapp to Files, "Argentina," May 8, 1956, File 1514750, Box 193602B, Argentina—General Negotiations 1947–56—I, WBGA.

102. Letter, Carl Marks to Black, May 21, 1956, File 1514750, Box 193602B, Argentina—General Negotiations 1947–56—I, WBGA.

103. Alfred Benjamin (Anglo-American Trading Corporation) to IBRD, "Protest against Mission for Loans, of Any Character, Pending Liquidation of Debts," June 25, 1956, File 1514750, Box 193602B, Argentina—General Negotiations 1947–56—I, WBGA.

104. Benjamin to Knapp, July 12, 1956, File 1514750, Box 193602B, Argentina—General Negotiations 1947–56—I, WBGA.

105. Office Memorandum, Knapp to Files, "Argentina," June 4, 1956, File 1514750, Box 193602B, Argentina—General Negotiations 1947–56—I, WBGA.

106. Ibid.

107. Ibid.

108. "Argentina: Membership in the IBRD and the IMF," National Advisory Council doc. no. 88, June 29, 1956, box 2 NARA-NAC.

109. Office Memorandum, Orvis Schmidt to Files, "Argentine Mission Proposal for Discussion with IBRD," July 23, 1956, File 1514750, Box 193602B, Argentina—General Negotiations 1947–56—I, WBGA.

110. Office Memorandum [1], Knapp to Files, "Argentina," August 13, 1956, File 1514750, Box 193602B, Argentina—General Negotiations 1947–56—I, WBGA.

111. Ibid.

112. Ibid.

113. Secretary to Members of the Committee on Membership, "Report on the Admission of the Argentine Republic to Membership in the Fund," August

9, 1956, box 5, files 1–20, file title 420–710, CFC-Argentina, IMFA; "IBRD Board of Governors resolution no. 97: Terms and Conditions on which the Argentine Republic shall be admitted to membership in the Bank," August 8, 1856, WBGA.

114. Ley 15.970, August 31, 1956, *Anales de Legislación Argentina* 16-A (1956): 943–79.

115. Confidential Office Memorandum [2], Burke Knapp to Files, "Argentina," August 13, 1956, File 1514750, Box 193602B, Argentina—General Negotiations 1947–56—I, WBGA.

116. *Department of State Bulletin* 35 (October 1, 1956): 515.

117. Office Memorandum, Sandelin to Schmidt, "Timing of Bank Missions," August 17, 1956, File 1514750, Box 193602B, Argentina—General Negotiations 1947–56—I, WBGA.

118. Ibid.

119. Ibid.

120. Knapp to Coll Benegas, October 9, 1956, File 1514750, Box 193602B, Argentina—General Negotiations 1947–56—I, WBGA.

121. Ibid.

122. Coll Benegas to Knapp, October 22, 1956, File 1514750, Box 193602B, Argentina—General Negotiations 1947–1956-I, WBGA.

123. A. Kamarck to S. Cope, "S.L.C Meeting on Argentina," May 8, 1957, File 1514751, Box 193602B, Argentina—General Negotiations 1957–1961-II, WBGA.

124. Ibid.

125. Office Memorandum, Schmidt to Files, "Meeting of Mr. William Beaulac with Mr. Black," June 13, 1957, File 1514751, Box 193602B, Argentina—General Negotiations 1957–1961-II, WBGA.

126. Ibid.

127. Ibid.

128. Edward Symonds to Files, "Making a (Slow) Start in Argentina—Staff Loan Committee Meeting, August 7, 1957," August 8, 1957, File 1514751, Box 193602B, Argentina—General Negotiations 1957–1961-II, WBGA.

129. Ibid.

130. Ibid.

131. Ibid.

132. Ibid.

133. Schmidt to Files, "Discussions in Argentina on Economic Report," August 16, 1957, File 1514751, Box 193602B, Argentina—General Negotiations 1957–1961-II, WBGA.

134. Knapp to Files, "Conversations with Argentine Government Officials (August 15025, 1957)," September 10, 1957, File 1514751, Box 193602B, Argentina—General Negotiations 1957–1961-II, WBGA.

135. Ibid.

136. Ibid. Today, the IBRD has 189 member-states and the IFC 185 member-states.

137. Ibid.

138. Transcript of Oral History Interview with Eugene R. Black Held on August 6, 1961, WBGA, 26. https://oralhistory.worldbank.org/transcripts/transcript-oral-history-interview-eugene-r-black-held-august-06-1961-main-transcript.

Chapter Two

1. Robert A. Karl, "Reading the Cuban Revolution from Bogotá, 1957–62," *Cold War History* 16, no. 4 (2016): 337–58, https://doi.org/10.1080/14682745.2016.1218848; Renata Keller, "The Latin American Missile Crisis," *Diplomatic History* 39, no. 2 (2015): 195–222, https://doi.org/10.1093/dh/dht134.

2. IDA Articles of Agreement, September 24, 1960, https://thedocs.worldbank.org/en/doc/2a209939e876fdcd0d957036daebff6e-0410011960/ida-articles-of-agreement.

3. Address by Eugene Black to the Investment Bankers' Association, Waldorf-Astoria Hotel, New York City, October 4, 1961. Records of President Eugene Black—1961 Speeches—Speeches 03 Folder ID: 1769197 Dates: 6/6/1960–12/4/1961 Fonds: Records of the Office of the President Sub-Fonds: Records of President Eugene R. Black. WBGA.

4. Claudia Kedar, *The International Monetary Fund and Latin America: The Argentine Puzzle in Context* (Philadelphia: Temple University Press, 2013), 55–93.

5. See, for instance, Matthew Connelly, *Fatal Misconception: The Struggle to Control World Population* (Cambridge, MA: Belnap Press of Harvard University, 2008); Amy L. S. Staples, *The Birth of Development: How the World Bank, Food and Agriculture Organization, and World Health Organization Have Changed the World 1945–1965* (Kent, OH: Kent State University Press, 2006); Nils Gilman, *Mandarins of the Future: Modernization Theory in Cold War America* (Baltimore: Johns Hopkins University Press, 2003); Odd Arne Westad, *The Global Cold War: Third World Interventions and the Making of Our Times* (Cambridge: Cambridge University Press, 2007); Darlene Rivas, "United States-Latin American Relations, 1942–1960," in *A Companion to American Foreign Relations*, ed. Robert D. Schulzinger (Malden, MA: Wiley, 2003); Katherine Marshall, *The World Bank: From Reconstruction to Development to Equity* (New York: Routledge, 2008); Arturo Escobar, *Encountering Development: The Making and Unmaking of the Third World* (Princeton: Princeton University Press, 1995); David C. Engerman and Corinna R. Unger, "Introduction: Towards a Global History of Modernization," *Diplomatic History* 33, no. 3 (2009): 375–85, http://www.jstor.org/stable/44214017; David C. Engerman, ed. *Staging Growth: Modernization, Development, and the Global Cold War* (Amherst, MA: University of Massachusetts Press, 2003); Jochen Kraske

et al., *Bankers with a Mission: The Presidents of the World Bank*, 1946–91 (Oxford: Oxford University Press, 1996); Edward S. Mason and Robert E. Asher, *The World Bank Since Bretton Woods* (Washington DC: The Brookings Institute, 1973); Deborah Shapley, *Promise and Power: The Life and Times of Robert McNamara* (Boston: Little Brown & Co., 1993).

6. "Banco Mundial por fín nos otorgará préstamos," *Clarín*, January 25, 1959.

7. "Duraderas y fructíferas serán las relaciones con la Unión," *La Nación*, January 25, 1959.

8. Devesh Kapur, John P. Lewis, and Richard Webb, eds., *The World Bank: Its First Half Century*, vol. 1 (Washington D.C.: Brookings Institute Press, 1997), 90–94.

9. Charles Dorn and Kristen Ghodsee, "The Cold War Politicization of Literacy: Communism, UNESCO, and the World Bank," *Diplomatic History* 36, no. 2 (2012): 373–98, https://www.jstor.org/stable/44376156.

10. Eugene Black, *The Diplomacy of Economic Development* (Cambridge, MA: Harvard University Press, 1960), 27.

11. Black, *The Diplomacy of Economic Development*, 30–31.

12. Eugene Black, "The World Bank at Work," *Foreign Affairs* 30, no. 3 (1952): 402–11, https://www.jstor.org/stable/20030909; Cristina Rojas, "The Place of the Social at the World Bank (1949–1981): Mingling Race, Nation, and Knowledge," *Global Social Policy* 15, no. 1 (2014): 23–39, https://doi.org/10.1177/1468018114527471.

13. The concept of "economic rationalism" refers to the ability of individuals and organizations involved in business transactions to make logical decisions that yield net positive outcomes. In this particular context, the Bank expected Argentina to put aside political criteria in the management of public enterprises, implying that they expected them to lay off workers, establish realistic tariffs, and make state-owned enterprises and public services more efficient and self-sustaining.

14. "Address by Eugene Black before the 27th Session of the Economic and Social Council of the United Nations, meeting in Mexico, DF," April 10, 1959, Records of the President Black-1959 Speeches. Folder ID 1769195, WBGA.

15. Ibid.

16. Kathryn Sikkink, "The Influence of Raúl Prebisch on Economic Policy-Making in Argentina, 1950–1962," *Latin American Research Review* 23, no. 2 (1988): 91–114, https://www.jstor.org/stable/i322695.

17. Luiz Carlos Bresser Pereira, "Modelos de Estado Desarrollista," *Revista de la CEPAL* 2019, no. 128 (2019): 39–52, http://dx.doi.org/10.18356/5e8f70e1-es; Pablo de San Román, "Conflicto Político y Reforma Estructural: La Experiencia del Desarrollismo en Argentina Durante la Presidencia de Arturo Frondizi (1958–1962)," *Instituto de Estudios Latinoamericanos* (2009), Doc. de trabajo no.

6, https://ebuah.uah.es/dspace/bitstream/handle/10017/6376/Conflicto%20pol%C3%ADtico%20y%20reforma%20estructural.pdf?sequence=1.

18. Among the major writings by Frigerio, see Rogelio Frigerio, *Estatuto del Subdesarrollo: Las Corrientes del Pensamiento Económico Argentino,* (Buenos Aires: Ediciones Librería del Jurista, 1983); idem, *Las Condiciones de la Victoria,* (Montevideo: A. Monteverde y Cia, 1963); and idem, *Desarrollo y Subdesarrollo Económicos* (Buenos Aires: Paidós, 1984). On Frigerio's background, see Hugo Gambini, *Frondizi. El Estadista Acorralado* (Buenos Aires: Editorial Vergara, 2006), 173–78.

19. For an in-depth discussion of *Developmentalism* with a special focus on Argentina, see, for instance, Marcelo Cavarozzi, "El 'Desarrollismo'" y las Relaciones Entre Democracia y Capitalismo Dependiente en Dependencia y Desarrollo en América Latina," *Latin American Research Review* 17, no. 1 (1982): 152–65, https://doi.org/10.1017/S0023879100028569; José Ocampo, "New Economic Thinking in Latin America," *Journal of Latin American Studies* 22, no. 1 (1990): 169–81; Raúl Prebisch, "Five Stages in My Thinking on Development," in *Pioneers in Development,* eds. Gerald M. Meier and Dudley Seers (Oxford: Oxford University Press, 1984), 175–91; Julio E. Nosiglia, *El Desarrollismo* (Buenos Aires: Centro Editor de América Latina, 1983), esp. chaps 2–3; Celia Szusterman, *Frondizi and the Politics of Developmentalism in Argentina, 1955–62* (London: Macmillan, 1993), esp. chaps 4–6.

20. Margarita Fajardo, *The World That Latin America Created: The United Nations Economic Commission for Latin America in the Development Era* (Cambridge, MA: Harvard University Press, 2022), 73–74.

21. Ibid., 11–13, 443–44.

22. Pablo Guido, "Coordenadas Intelectuales de Álvaro Alsogaray," *Procesos de Mercado: Revista Europea de Economía Política* 8, no. 1 (2011): 209–52, https://www.procesosdemercado.com/index.php/inicio/article/view/265/337; Victoria Haidar, "La Polémica Liberal con los Desarrollismos: Un Análisis del Pensamiento de Álvaro Alsogarary y de Federico Pinedo Entre 1958 y 1973," *Nuevo Mundo Mundos Nuevos,* 2015, http://hdl.handle.net/11336/69441.

23. Ruben Marx and Ana Turdo, "Desarrollismo en Argentina y Brasil: Un Modelo y Dos Efectos," *I Jornadas de Economía Política,* December 2007, https://www.ungs.edu.ar/wp-content/uploads/2009/02/Turdo_Marx.pdf.

24. Felipe Pereira Loureiro, "The Alliance for Progress and President João Goulart's Three Year Plan: The Deterioration of US-Brazilian Relations in Cold War Brazil (1962)," *Cold War History* 17, no.1 (2017): 61–79, http://dx.doi.org/10.1080/14682745.2016.1254620.

25. Carlo Edoardo Altamura and Claudia Kedar, "Friends or Foes? Brazil, the IMF, and the World Bank, 1961–1967," *Financial History Review* 28, no. 2 (2021): 205–36, https://doi.org/10.1017/S096856502100007X.

26. Amy C. Offner, *Sorting Out the Mixed Economy: The Rise and Fall of Welfare and Developmental States in the Americas* (Princeton: Princeton University Press, 2019).

27. See, for instance, Artemy Kalinovsky, *Laboratory of Socialist Development: Cold War Politics and Decolonization in Soviet Tajikistan* (Ithaca: Cornell University Press, 2018).

28. Sara Lorenzini, *Global Development: A Cold War History* (Princeton and Oxford: Princeton University Press, 2019), 64–65.

29. "Memorandum Rostow to Kennedy," March 2, 1961, POF, box 64a, 3/61-5/61, Papers of John F. Kennedy. Presidential Papers. President's Office Files, https://www.jfklibrary.org/asset-viewer/archives/JFKPOF/064a/JFKPOF-064a-009.

30. Ibid.

31. Stephany Griffith-Jones. "The Alliance for Progress: An Attempt at Interpretation," *Development and Change* 10, no. 3 (1979): 423–43, https://doi.org/10.1111/j.1467-7660.1979.tb00005.x.

32. The Charter of Punta del Este, Establishing an Alliance for Progress Within the Framework of Operation Pan America; August 17, 1961, The Avalon Project at the Yale Law School, https://web.archive.org/web/20070306162911/http://www.yale.edu/lawweb/avalon/intdip/interam/intam16.htm.

33. Ibid.

34. Charter of Punta del Este. Title I: Objectives.

35. Michele Alacevich, "Paul Rosenstein-Rodan and the Birth of Development Economics," 2020, Working Paper No. 2020–04, Duke University, Center for the History of Political Economy (CHOPE), Durham, NC, https://www.econstor.eu/bitstream/10419/215545/1/169344366X.pdf; Jeffrey Taffet, *Foreign Aid as Foreign Policy: The Alliance for Progress in Latin America* (New York: Routledge, 2007), 32–35; Thomas Tunstall Allcock, *Thomas C. Mann: President Johnson, the Cold War, and the Restructuring of Latin American Foreign Policy* (Lexington: University Press of Kentucky, 2018), 57–59.

36. Charter of Punta del Este, Title III, Art.10.

37. Alliance for Progress: General, July 1962. "Survey of the Alliance for Progress Program in Brazil, Argentina, Chile, and Bolivia (June 16–July 12, 1962)," Papers of John F. Kennedy. Presidential Papers. National Security Files, p. 37. JFKNSF-290-023-p0001.

38. Director of International and Financial Development Affairs (Adair) to the Assistant Secretary of State for Economic Affairs (Mann), memorandum, September 24, 1958, FRUS 1958–1960, American Republics, vol. 5, 510–12.

39. Memorandum, Viron Vaky of the Office of South American Affairs to the Director of the Office of South American Affairs (Bernbaum), August 22, 1958, FRUS 1958–1960, American Republics, vol.5, 500–508.

40. Mario Rapoport, "La Argentina y la Guerra Fría. Opciones Económicas y Estratégicas de la Apertura Hacia el Este, 1955–1973," *Ciclos en la Historia, la Economía y la Sociedad* 5, no. 8 (1995): 91–122, http://bibliotecadigital.econ.uba.ar/download/ciclos/ciclos_v5_n8_05.pdf.

41. Arturo Frondizi, "Mensaje Inaugural," in *Mensajes Presidenciales 1958–1962*, vol. 1, Arturo Frondizi (Buenos Aires: Centro de Estudios Nacionales, 1978), 9–57; Dustin Walcher, "Structuring the Economy in the Periphery: The United States, the 1958 Argentine Stabilization Agreement, and the Evolution of Global Capitalism," in *Foreign Policy at the Periphery: The Shifting Margins of US International Relations Since World War II*, eds. Bevan Sewell and María Ryan (Kentucky: University of Kentucky Press, 2017), 206–28.

42. Walcher, "Structuring the Economy," 212–13.

43. "Argentina Gets 329 Million in Aid," *The New York Times*, December 30, 1958.

44. IMF Office Memorandum, Del Canto to Schmidt, "Argentina," April 24, 1958, File 1514751, Box 193602B, Argentina—General Negotiations 1957–1961-II, WBGA.

45. Confidential Memorandum, "International Bank Relations with Argentina," April 23, 1958, File 1514751, Box 193602B, Argentina—General Negotiations 1957–1961-II, WBGA.

46. "Argentine Seizure Fought by Utility. American & Foreign Power Reports 134,000,000—Peso Loss by Expropriations," *The New York Times*, May 3, 1949.

47. Memorandum of Conversation Between President Aramburu and the Ambassador in Argentina (Beaulac), Buenos Aires, April 23, 1958, FRUS, 1958–1960, American Republics, vol. 5, 475–76.

48. Office Memorandum, Burke Knapp to Files, "Argentina," July 14, 1958, File 1514751, Box 193602B, Argentina—General Negotiations 1957–1961-II, WBGA.

49. Ibid.

50. Office Memorandum, Sandelin to Files, "Argentina—Meeting with Minister of Economy," January 8, 1959, File 1514751, Box 193602B, Argentina—General Negotiations 1957–1961-II, WBGA.

51. Ibid.

52. Ibid.

53. "Argentina—Stand-By Arrangement," EBS/58/76 (December 18, 1958), supp. 2, IMFA.

54. Ibid.

55. Memorandum, the Director of the Office of International Financial and Development Affairs (Adair) to the Assistant Secretary of State for Economic Affairs (Mann), September 24, 1958. FRUS, 1958–1960, American Republics, vol. 5, 510–11.

56. Arturo Frondizi, "Mensaje Radiofónico del Señor Presidente de la Nación Doctor Arturo Frondizi, Transmitido el 19 de Febrero de 1959," *Trabajadores y Empresarios Frente al Programa de Estabilización* (Buenos Aires: Servicio de Prensa de la Presidencia de la Nación), 3–16.

57. Leandro A. Morgenfeld, "Desarrollismo, Alianza para el Progreso y Revolución Cubana. Frondizi, Kennedy y el Che en Punta del Este (1961–1962)," *Ciclos en la Historia, la Economía y la Sociedad* 20, nos. 39–40 (2011–2012): 133–63. https://dialnet.unirioja.es/servlet/articulo?codigo=4053876.

58. Arturo Frondizi to Alberto Lleras Camargo, January 2, 1962, in *La Política Exterior Argentina*, Arturo Frondizi (Buenos Aires: Transición, 1963), 178–213.

59. "Blair House: Posible Escenario para que el Banco Mundial Resuelva Financiar El Chocón," *Clarín*, January 21, 1959; "Argentina Rompe la Inercia del Banco Mundial," *Clarín*, January 23, 1959; "Obtendría Más Créditos Argentina," *Clarín*, January 23, 1959.

60. Schmidt to Files, "Meeting of Mr. Black with President Frondizi," January 23, 1959, File 1514751, Box 193602B, Argentina—General Negotiations 1957–1961-II, WBGA.

61. Ibid.

62. Memorandum of Conversation, White House, January 22, 1959, FRUS, 1958–1960, American Republics, vol. 5, 533–35.

63. Office Memorandum—Draft, Lincoln Sandelin to Files, "Consultation with Delegation to Annual Meeting," October 23, 1959, File 1514751, Box 193602B, Argentina—General Negotiations 1957–1961-II, WBGA.

64. Ibid.

65. Ibid.

66. "Banco Mundial: Propone el Levantamiento de Ramales," *Clarín*, June 16, 1961.

67. Marcelo Coll Cárdenas, "El Plan Larkin Visto Desde los Editoriales y Notas de los Diarios La Nación y El Argentino de La Plata," *Actas de Periodismo y Comunicación* 4, no. 3 (2018), https://sedici.unlp.edu.ar/bitstream/handle/10915/93639/Documento_completo.pdf-PDFA.pdf?sequence=1&isAllowed=y.

68. Office Memorandum, Neil Perry to Files, "Visit of Argentinians to Bank," February 25, 1960, File 1514751, Box 193602B, Argentina—General Negotiations 1957–1961-II, WBGA.

69. Ibid.

70. Confidential, SLC/0/60-24, "Prospective Lending Program for Argentina," June 10, 1960, File 1514751, Box 193602B, Argentina—General Negotiations 1957–1961-II, WBGA.

71. Argentina: Highway Construction and Maintenance Project, Report and Recommendations of the President to the Executive Directors, June 21, 1961, WBGA, http://documents.worldbank.org/curated/en/116691468004206939.

72. Ibid.

73. Transcript of Two Hundred Twenty-Eighth Special Meeting of the Executive Directors of the Bank, Held on Thursday, June 29, 1961, WBGA, http://documents.worldbank.org/curated/en/315731510551291890.

74. *Memoria Anual 1960*, Banco Central República Argentina, 35–36.

75. Ibid (Transcript, June 29, 1961).

76. Alsogaray to Knapp, July 13, 1961, File 1514752, Box 193602B, Argentina—General Negotiations 1961–1964, Vol. III, WBGA.

77. Argentina-Road Project: Loan 0288—Loan Agreement—Conformed, WBGA.

78. Office Memorandum, Schmidt to Files, "Discussion with Mr. Brignone-Points Relating to our Relation with Argentina," July 5, 1961, File 1514752, Box 193602B, Argentina—General Negotiations 1961–1964, vol. III, WBGA.

79. Fernando Ortega, "El Funcionamiento de la Empresa de Ferrocarriles del Estado Argentino (EFEA) Durante el Gobierno de Arturo Frondizi (1958–1962)," Ponencia Terceras Jornadas (2015) de la Asociación Mexicana de Historia Económica, https://old-site.amhe.mx/jornadas/ponencias2015/ARIEL%20ORTEGA%20FERNANDO%20-%20El%20funcionamiento%20de%20la%20Empresa%20de%20Ferrocarriles%20del%20Estado%20Argentino%20(EFEA)%20durante%20el%20gobierno%20de%20Arturo%20Frondizi%20(1958-1962).pdf.

80. Cárdenas, "El Plan Larkin," 2–3.

81. Chaufournier to Files, "Argentina-Meeting with State Department Officials," July 12, 1961, File 1514752, Box 193602B, Argentina—General Negotiations 1961–1964, vol. III, WBGA.

82. Office Memorandum, Schmidt to Files, "Meeting with Krieger Vasena and Black," July 11, 1961, File 1514752, Box 193602B, Argentina—General Negotiations 1961–1964, vol. III, WBGA.

83. Ibid.

84. "Memorandum of Conversation," September 24, 1961, Argentina: Security, 1961–1963. Papers of John F. Kennedy. Presidential Papers. President's Office Files. JFKPOF-111-014-p0005.

85. Telegram, Department of State to the Embassy in Argentina, September 27, 1961, FRUS 1961–1963, American Republics, vol. 12, 358–59.

86. "Text of Communique on Kennedy-Frondizi Meeting," *The New York Times*, September 27, 1961.

87. Chaufournier to Files, "Argentina-Management Meeting with Delegation," September 29, 1961, File 1514752, Box 193602B, Argentina—General Negotiations 1961–1964, vol. III, WBGA.

88. Ibid.

89. Ibid.

90. "US Aides Attacked," *The New York Times*, June 10, 1961.

91. "Argentina-Management Meeting with Delegation," September 29, 1961.

92. Mario Justo López, Jorge Eduardo Waddell, and Juan Pablo Martínez, *Historia del Ferrocarril en Argentina: La Política Ferroviaria Entre 1857 y 2015* (Buenos Aires: Lenguaje Claro Editora, 2016), 176–77; Fernando Ariel Ortega, "De la Modernización a la Racionalización. Políticas Adoptadas por Frondizi Ante la Crisis Ferroviaria (1958–1962), *Revista de Historia de la Industria y el Desarrollo en América Latina* 4, no. 7 (2010): 1–20, https://dialnet.unirioja.es/servlet/articulo?codigo=5009892; Gabriela Scodeller, "La Huelga Ferroviaria de 1961 en la Provincia de Mendoza," in *I Jornadas Nacionales de Historia Social (May 2007)* (Memoria Académica, 2007), (http://www.memoria.fahce.unlp.edu.ar/trab_eventos/ev.9658/ev.9658.pdf); Ariel Ortega, "Modernización a la Racionalización," 3.

93. JFKPOF-111-014-p0005. "Letter Frondizi to Kennedy," November 20, 1961, Argentina: Security, 1961–1963. Papers of John F. Kennedy. Presidential Papers. President's Office Files.

94. Morgenfeld, "Desarrollismo, Alianza para el Progreso y Revolución Cubana," 151–54.

95. Memorandum of Conversation, December 24, 1961, FRUS 1961–1963, American Republics, vol. 12, 359–62.

96. Report and Recommendations of the President to the Executive Directors on a Proposed Loan to SEBGA, Argentina—January 11, 1962, WBGA, http://documents.worldbank.org/curated/en/406171468002422960.

97. Ibid.

98. Transcript of One Hundred Forty-First Special Meeting of the Executive Directors of the Bank, Held on Thursday, January 18, 1962, WBGA, http://documents.worldbank.org/curated/en/829431510552974839.

99. Ibid.

100. Ibid.

101. *Memoria Anual 1962*, Banco Central República Argentina, 65–66.

102. Black to Frondizi, February 7, 1962, File 1514752, Box 193602B, Argentina—General Negotiations 1961–1964, vol. III, WBGA.

103. Ibid.

104. *The New York Times*, March 20, 1962; Kedar, *The International Monetary Fund and Latin America*, 91–93.

105. Daniel Amicci, "La Trayectoria Hacia la Cumbre de Uruguayana: Máxima Expresión de la Aproximación Entre Argentina y Brasil Durante el Desarrollismo," *CONfines de Relaciones Internacionales y Ciencia Política* 8, no. 15 (2012): 133–56. https://www.scielo.org.mx/scielo.php?script=sci_arttext&pid=S1870-35692012000100006; Gambini, *Frondizi. El estadista acorralado*, 277–91; Kathryn Sikkink, *El Proyecto Desarrollista en la Argentina y Brasil: Frondizi y Kubistchek* (Buenos Aires: Siglo XXI, 2009), 44.

106. Ashoka Mody and Diego Saravia, "Catalyzing Capital Flows: Do IMF-Supported Programs Work As Commitment Devices?," IMF Working Paper no. 2003/100. https://www.imf.org/en/Publications/WP/Issues/2016/12/30/Catalyzing-Capital-Flows-Do-IMF-Supported-Programs-Work-As-Commitment-Devices-16443.

107. María Cecilia Míguez, "La Unión Industrial Argentina y el Gobierno de Illia. Los Sectores Civiles y el Golpe de Estado de 1966," *H-Industria* 9, no. 17 (2015): 64–91, https://scispace.com/papers/la-union-industrial-argentina-y-el-gobierno-de-illia-los-2ij2b2vwqo; César Tcach, "Radicalismo y Fuerzas Armadas (1962–1963): Observaciones Desde Córdoba," *Desarrollo Económico* 40, no. 157 (2000): 73–95, https://www.jstor.org/stable/i277205.

108. "Memorandum for Mr. George Bundy. Suggested Message to President of Argentina," April 12, 1963. Argentina: Security, 1961–1963. Papers of John F. Kennedy. Presidential Papers. President's Office Files. JFKPOF-111-014-p0005, https://www.jfklibrary.org/asset-viewer/archives/JFKPOF/111/JFKPOF-111-014.

109. Rapoport et al., *Historia Económica, Política y Social de la Argentina*, 505–507.

110. Felipe Pereira Loureiro, Hamilton de Carvalho Gomes Jr., and Rebeca Guerreiro Antunes Braga, "A Pericentric Punta del Este: Cuba's Failed Attempt to Join the Latin American Free Trade Area (LAFTA) and the Limits of Brazil's Independent Foreign Policy," *Revista Brasileira de Política Internacional* 61, no. 2 (2018): e003, http://dx.doi.org/10.1590/0034-7329201800203.

111. "Memorandum for Mr. George Bundy. The White House," January 21, 1963, Argentina: Security, 1961–1963. Papers of John F. Kennedy. Presidential Papers. President's Office Files. JFKPOF-111-014-p0005, https://www.jfklibrary.org/asset-viewer/archives/JFKPOF/111/JFKPOF-111-014.

112. Raúl García Heras, *Presiones Externas y Política Económica: El Fondo Monetario Internacional y el Banco Mundial en Argentina, 1955–1966* (Bogotá: Universidad de los Andes, Cátedra Corona, 2000), 35–36. On Alsogaray and other liberal economists, see Juan Odisio and Marcelo Rougier, "Swimming Against the (Developmentalist) Mainstream: The Liberal Economists in Argentina Between 1955 and 1976," *PSL Quarterly Review* 72, no. 289 (2019): 91–115.

113. Schmidt to Bill Diamond, From Buenos Aires, April 28, 1962, File 1514752, Box 193602B, Argentina—General Negotiations 1961–1964, vol. III, WBGA.

114. Ibid.

115. Ibid.

116. Office Memorandum, Weiner to Schmidt, "Argentina-Briefing for Minister Alsogaray Visit (July 19–20)," July 16, 1962, File 1514752, Box 193602B, Argentina—General Negotiations 1961–1964, vol. III, WBGA.

117. *The New York Times*, June 8, 1962; *The New York Times*, June 9, 1962.

118. Office Memorandum, Weiner to Files, "Visit of Minister Alsogaray," July 24, 1962, File 1514752, Box 193602B, Argentina—General Negotiations 1961–1964, vol. III, WBGA.

119. Ibid.

120. Ibid.

121. Alsogaray to Black, July 27, 1962, File 1514752, Box 193602B, Argentina—General Negotiations 1961–1964, vol. III, WBGA.

122. Ibid.

123. Office Memorandum, Schmidt to Files, "Discussion with Argentine Ambassador," August 2, 1962, File 1514752, Box 193602B, Argentina—General Negotiations 1961–1964, vol. III, WBGA.

124. Ibid.

125. Ibid.

126. Office Memorandum, Weiner to Files, "Argentina—Meeting with Delegation," September 26, 1962, File 1514752, Box 193602B, Argentina—General Negotiations 1961–1964, vol. III, WBGA.

127. Letter 1, Horst Eschenberg to Chaufournier, November 5, 1962, File 1514752, Box 193602B, Argentina—General Negotiations 1961–1964, vol. III, WBGA.

128. Pedro Pablo Kuczynski to Weiner, "Argentina—Visit of Ferrostaal Representative," July 25, 1962, File 1514752, Box 193602B, Argentina—General Negotiations 1961–1964, vol. III, WBGA.

129. Ibid.

130. Letter 2, Chaufournier to Schmidt, December 2, 1962, File 1514752, Box 193602B, Argentina—General Negotiations 1961–1964, vol. III, WBGA.

131. Daniel Muchnik, *La Patria Financiera: El Juego de la Especulación* (Buenos Aires: Grupo Editorial Norma, 2005), 156–57.

132. Office Memorandum, John Loftus to Files, "Argentina—Agricultural Credit; Meeting at AID Headquarters, Buenos Aires," December 17, 1962, File 1514752, Box 193602B, Argentina—General Negotiations 1961–1964, vol. III, WBGA.

133. Letter No. 2, John Loftus to Files, May 22, 1963, File 1514752, Box 193602B, Argentina—General Negotiations 1961–1964, vol. III, WBGA.

134. Kedar, *The International Monetary Fund and Latin America*, 93–99.

Chapter Three

1. Illia, leader of the *Unión Cívica Radical del Pueblo*, is difficult to categorize. Scholars tend to focus on the nationalist character of his economic policy. However, others consider him a reformist-populist because he promoted the interests of the working class as well as of the urban *bourgeoise*, and because he adopted an anti-imperialist economic stance. See Marcelo Cavarozzi, *Autoritarismo y Democracia* (Buenos Aires, EUDEBA, 2002); Sebastián Settanni and Lucrecia Gringauz, "Un Modesto Galeno Pueblerino. La Construcción de la Figura

de Arturo Illia en Clarín y La Nación," *Questión* 1, no. 18 (2008), https://perio.unlp.edu.ar/ojs/index.php/question/article/view/604.

2. Vanni Pettinà, "The Shadows of Cold War Over Latin America: The US Reaction to Fidel Castro's Nationalism, 1956–59," *Cold War History* 11, no. 3 (2011): 317–39, https://www.scribd.com/document/582943763/pettina2010.

3. "14 Pacts Ended. Illia Decrees are Silent on Compensation to Foreign Concerns," *The New York Times,* November 16, 1963.

4. Although the Kennedy administration recognized Argentina's right to cancel the agreements, it sought to convince Illia's government to refrain from doing so or at least, to announce the payment of compensations. See, among others, *La Nación,* November 15, 1963.

5. "Argentina Maps Deal with Soviet. Wool and Leather May be Bartered for Petroleum," *The New York Times,* November 5, 1964; Mario Rapoport, "La Argentina y la Guerra Fría. Opciones Económicas y Estratégicas de la Apertura Hacia el Este, 1955–1973," *Ciclos en la Historia, la Economía y la Sociedad* 5, no. 8 (1995): 91–122, http://bibliotecadigital.econ.uba.ar/download/ciclos/ciclos_v5_n8_05.pdf.

6. "Testimony of Hon. John Hennessy, Assistant Secretary of Treasury for International Affairs," March 28, 1973, in *Multinational Corporations and the US Foreign Policy* (Washington, DC: US Government Printing Office, 1973), 321–42.

7. Davesh et al., *The World Bank,* vol. 1, 186.

8. The Great Society was an array of domestic policy initiatives, programs, and legislation aimed at ending poverty, reducing crime, abolishing inequality, and improving the environment.

9. The controversial "War on Poverty" drew on two important principles that were deep-rooted in the United States and were transplanted into the WB from its establishment. One is the principle of self-help—an idea that the US administration applied both at home and among aid-recipient nations. The other principle was related to US capitalism and the partnership with the private sector. See, among others, Michael L. Gillette, *Launching the War on Poverty: An Oral History* (Oxford: Oxford University Press, 2010); Romain D. Huret, *The Experts' War on Poverty: Social Research and the Welfare Agenda in Postwar America* (Ithaca: Cornell University Press, 2018); Doug Genens, "Fighting Poverty in the Fields: Legal Services and the War on Poverty in Rural California," *Agricultural History* 94, no. 2 (2020): 251–78, https://doi.org/10.3098/ah.2020.094.2.251; and Annelise Orleck and Lisa Gayle Hazirjian, eds., *The War on Poverty: A New Grassroots History, 1964–1980* (Athens: University of Georgia Press, 2011).

10. Alan L. McPherson, *Intimate Ties, Bitter Struggles: The United States and Latin America Since 1945* (Washington, DC: Potomac Books, 2006), 59–60.

11. Hugo Harvey, "Revisitando el Punto de Inflexión Interamericano en la Guerra Fría: La Crisis Dominicana de 1965, la Intervención de Estados Unidos

y la Fuerza Interamericana de la Paz," *Humanidades* 7 (2020): 25–63, https://doi.org/10.25185/7.2; Stephen G. Rabe, "The Johnson Doctrine," *Presidential Studies Quarterly* 36, no. 1 (2006): 48–58, https://doi.org/10.1111/j.1741-5705.2006.00286.x.

12. See, among others, Aldo Marchesi, *Latin America's Radical Left: Rebellion and Cold War in the Global 1960s* (New York: Cambridge University Press, 2017); Gabriel Rot, *Los Orígenes Perdidos de la Guerrilla en la Argentina: La Historia de Jorge Ricardo Massetti y el Ejército Guerrillero del Pueblo* (Buenos Aires: Ediciones El Cielo por Asalto, 2000).

13. Daniel Kressel, "The 'Argentine Franco'?: The Regime of Juan Carlos Onganía and Its Ideological Dialogue with Francoist Spain (1966–1970)," *The Americas* 78, no. 1 (2021): 89–117, http://dx.doi.org/10.17169/refubium-30531.

14. See, among others, André Gunder Frank, *Capitalismo y Subdesarrollo en América Latina* (Siglo XXI, 1967); idem, *Dependent Accumulation and Underevelopment* (London: Macmillan, 1978); Fernando Henrique Cardoso and Enzo Faletto, *Dependencia y Desarrollo en América Latina* (Siglo XXI, 1977).

15. María Cecilia Míguez, "¿Anticomunistas, Antiestatistas, Antiperonistas? La "Nacionalización" de la Doctrina de Seguridad Nacional en la Argentina y la Legitimación del Golpe de Estado de 1966," *Revista SAAP* 7, no. 1 (2013), https://dialnet.unirioja.es/servlet/articulo?codigo=5119934.

16. While there is a vast bibliography on the political meaning of nationalism, little has been written about its economic aspects. For a debate on the perceptions of economic nationalism, especially in the context of the post-Cold War era, see Andreas Pickel, "False Oppositions: Recontextualizing Economic Nationalism in a Globalizing World," in *Economic Nationalism in a Globalizing World*, eds. Eric Helleiner and Andreas Pickel (Ithaca: Cornell University Press, 2004), 1–17.

The financial crisis of 2008 opened up a renewed scholarly debate on its impact, especially in the United States (with Donald Trump's "America First" approach) and China. See, for instance, Eric Helleiner and Hongying Wang, "The Richness of Financial Nationalism: The Case of China," *Pacific Affairs* 92, no. 2 (2019): 211–34, https://www.jstor.org/stable/48541654; and Weixing Hu, "China as a Listian Trading State: Interest, Power, and Economic Ideology," in *America, China, and the Struggle for World Order: Ideas, Traditions, Historical Legacies, and Global Visions*, eds. G. John Ikenberry, Zhu Feng, and Wang Jisi (New York: Palgrave Macmillan, 2015), 211–44.

17. Robert Gilpin, *The Political Economy of International Relations* (Princeton: Princeton University Press, 1987), 27–29, 31–34.

18. Eric Helleiner, "The Diversity of Economic Nationalism," *New Political Economy* 26, no. 2 (2021): 229–38, https://doi.org/10.1080/13563467.2020.1841137.

19. Marvin Suesse, *The Nationalist Dilemma: A Global History of Economic Nationalism, 1776–Present* (Cambridge: Cambridge University Press, 2023), 1–11.

20. Arturo Illia. Mensaje Presidencial, Cámara de Diputados de la Nación, May 1, 1965, https://www2.hcdn.gob.ar/export/hcdn/secparl/dgral_info_parlamentaria/dip/archivos/1965_Mensaje_presidencial_Ilia.pdf.

21. Hal Brands, *Latin America's Cold War* (Cambridge, MA: Harvard University Press, 2010), 129–31; idem, "Third World Politics in an Age of Global Turmoil: The Latin American Challenge to U.S. and Western Hegemony, 1965–1975," *Diplomatic History* 32, no. 1 (2008): 105–38, https://www.jstor.org/stable/24916057.

22. Hal Brands, "Richard Nixon and Economic Nationalism in Latin America: The Problem of Expropriations, 1969–1974," *Diplomacy & Statecraft* 18, no. 1 (2007): 215–35, https://doi.org/10.1080/09592290601163126.

23. "Rockefeller's Tour: Painful Reappraisal of the Neighbors," *Time Magazine*, November 7, 1969.

24. Claudia Kedar, "The World Bank-United States-Latin American Triangle: The Negotiations with Socialist Chile, 1970–1973," *The International History Review* 39, no. 4 (2017): 667–90, https://doi.org/10.1080/07075332.2016.1239587.

25. *Chile—Fifth Power Project*, World Bank Group, December 14, 1966, http://documents.worldbank.org/curated/en/749301468217451439/Chile-Fifth-Power-Project; *Chile—Second Vocational Training Project*, World Bank Group, March 2, 1970, http://documents.worldbank.org/curated/en/512981468215121764/Chile-Second-Vocational-Training-Project.

26. *Bolivia—Second Beni Livestock Development Project*, World Bank Group, http://documents.worldbank.org/curated/en/876201468016774941/Bolivia-Second-Beni-Livestock-Development-Project.

27. Hal Brands, "The United States and the Peruvian Challenge, 1968–1975," *Diplomacy & Statecraft* 21, no. 3 (2010): 471–90, https://doi.org/10.1080/09592296.2010.508418.

28. César Tcach and Celso Rodríguez, *Arturo Illia: Un Sueño Breve. El Rol del Peronismo y de los Estados Unidos en el Golpe Militar de 1966*, (Buenos Aires: Edhasa, 2006), chap. 1.

29. "The President's Meeting with the Argentine Vice President," Ben Read, State Department, Nov. 15, 1963, 1961–1963, American Republics, vol. 12, 417.

30. "CGT: Más Fábricas Serán Tomadas Hoy," *Clarín*, May 22, 1964; "Illia: Tolerancia Pero no Debilidad," *Clarín*, October 13, 1964.

31. María Cecilia Míguez, "La Unión Industrial Argentina y el Gobierno de Illia. Los Sectores Civiles y el Golpe de Estado de 1966," *H-Industria* 9, no. 17 (2015): 64–91, https://scispace.com/papers/la-union-industrial-argentina-y-el-gobierno-de-illia-los-2ij2b2vwqo.

32. Rapoport et al., *Historia Económica, Política y Social de la Argentina*, 566–68.

33. Tearoti Silvia Aurora, "El Plan de Desarrollo 1965–1969, un Intento de Planificación en la Argentina," in *XIV Jornadas Interescuelas/Departamentos de*

Historia. Departamento de Historia de la Facultad de Filosofía y Letras, (Universidad Nacional de Cuyo, Mendoza, 2013), https://www.aacademica.org/000-010/164.

34. Arturo Illia, *La Política Económica del Gobierno Constitucional* (Unidentified publisher, December 1966) [Biblioteca Ministerio de Economía, Argentina].

35. Alejandro Simonoff, *Los Dilemas de la Autonomía: La Política Exterior de Arturo Illia*, (Buenos Aires: Nuevohacer, 2007), esp. chap. 4.

36. Anulación de los Contratos Petroleros: I. Decretos 744 y 745/63. II. Demandas de la Nación Argentina ante la Justicia Federal. (Buenos Aires: Presidencia de la Nación, December 1963).

37. Leandro Ariel Morgenfeld and María Cecilia Míguez, "La Cuestión Petrolera Durante el Gobierno de Illia: Repercusiones en los Estados Unidos y en las Clases Dirigentes Locales," *Realidad Económica* 271 (2012): 51–75, https://ri.conicet.gov.ar/handle/11336/16173; "Kennedy Aludió al Tema Petrolero," *El Día* (La Plata), November 15, 1963.

38. Morgenfeld and Míguez, "La Cuestión Petrolera," 65–66.

39. Richard B. Lillich, "The Protection of Foreign Investment and the Hickenlooper Amendment," *University of Pennsylvania Law Review* 112, no. 8 (1964): 1116–31, https://doi.org/10.2307/3310530.

40. Dustin Walcher, "Petroleum Pitfalls: The United States, Argentine Nationalism, and the 1963 Oil Crisis," *Diplomatic History* 37, no. 1 (2013): 24–57, https://www.jstor.org/stable/i40178305.

41. Memorandum of Conversation, "The Expropriation of the IT&T Properties in Rio Grande do Sul," February 19, 1962, FRUS, 1961–1963, vol. 12, American Republics, 456–57.

42. Charles H. Lipson, "Corporate Preferences and Public Policies: Foreign Aid Sanctions and Investment Protection," *World Politics* 28, no. 3 (1976): 396–421, https://www.jstor.org/stable/i308696.

43. Jochen Kraske et al., *Bankers with a Mission: The Presidents of the World Bank, 1946–91* (New York: Oxford University Press, 1996), 116–19, 126–34.

44. "World Bank Head Urges Debt Shift," *The New York Times*, March 26, 1964.

45. Mirek Tobiáš Hošman, "Internal Dynamics as Drivers of Change in International Organizations: The Economists' Takeover at the World Bank," *Swiss Journal of Sociology* 49, no. 1 (2023): 41–60, https://doi.org/10.2478/sjs-2023-0004.

46. Michael Barnett and Martha Finnemore, *Rules for the World: International Organizations in Global Politics* (Ithaca: Cornell University Press, 2004); Jeffrey Chwierothz, "Organizational Change 'From Within': Exploring the World Bank's Early Lending Practices," *Review of International Political Economy* 15, no. 4 (2008): 481–505, https://doi.org/10.1080/09692290802260498.

47. Transcript of Oral History Interview with Roger A. Chaufournier Held on July 22, 1986, WB Oral History Program, http://documents.worldbank.org/curated/en/975671468325228694.

48. Davesh et al., *The World Bank,* Vol. 1, 202–205.

49. "Alliance Drafts Wider Latin Role in Channeling Aid," *The New York Times,* August 19, 1963.

50. Alfred Matter to Knapp, "Invitation to Confer with President-Elect Illia," August 27, 1963, File 1514752, Box 193602B, Argentina—General Negotiations 1961–1964, Vol. III, WBGA.

51. Office Memorandum, Loftus to Alfred Matter, "Details of Conversation with President-Elect Illia," September 18, 1963, File 1514752, Box 193602B, Argentina—General Negotiations 1961–1964, Vol. III, WBGA.

52. Ibid.

53. Ibid.

54. Joseph Fajans to Amerasinghe, "Argentina and Bolivia—Past Expropriations," November 18, 1971, Bank Administration and Policy—Expropriation and Compensation—1969–1971. Correspondence. Operational Sector Files, Central Files, Folder 1056931, WB IBRD/IDA ADMCF-07, WBGA.

55. García Heras, *El Fondo Monetario Internacional y el Banco Mundial en la Argentina,* 121–25.

56. Claudia Kedar, *The International Monetary Fund and Latin America: The Argentine Puzzle in Context* (Philadelphia: Temple University Press, 2013), 99–108.

57. Decreto no. 565, Consejo Nacional de Desarrollo, Representación del Ministerio de Defensa Nacional en el Consejo Directivo, Enero 24, 1964, https://www.argentina.gob.ar/normativa/nacional/decreto-565-1964-178771; Decreto no. 566, Consejo Nacional de Desarrollo, Estructura y Reglamentación Interna, Enero 24, 1964, https://www.argentina.gob.ar/normativa/nacional/decreto-566-1964-178780.

58. John Loftus to Orvis Schmidt, "Argentina-Sequence of Future Steps," November 14, 1963, File 1514752, Box 193602B, Argentina—General Negotiations 1961–1964, Vol. III, WBGA.

59. Translation from Spanish 332/64, "Negotiations with the World Bank," *Revista Análisis* (Buenos Aires), March 17, 1964, File 1514752, Box 193602B, Argentina—General Negotiations 1961–1964, Vol. III, WBGA; *La Prensa,* January 14 and 18, 1964.

60. *La Prensa,* January 14, 1964.

61. George Woods to Arturo Illia, December 26, 1963, Box 5, Argentina (1963–1965) file, folder 1, WHD-Argentina, IMFA.

62. *La Prensa,* February 14, 1964.

63. Office Memorandum, Loftus to Files, "Mission to Argentina—February 13–18, inclusive," March 5, 1964, File 1514752, Box 193602B, Argentina—General Negotiations 1961–1964, Vol. III, WBGA.

64. *Argentina—Buenos Aires Power Project: Loan 0308—Loan Agreement—Conformed (English),* WBGA, http://documents.worldbank.org/curated/en

/171481467998525304/Argentina-Buenos-Aires-Power-Project-Loan-0308-Loan-Agreement-Conformed.

65. Office Memorandum, G. Wishart to Files, "Argentina," March 30, 1964, File 1514752, Box 193602B, Argentina—General Negotiations 1961–1964, Vol. III, WBGA.

66. Ibid.

67. "Argentina Plans Oil Payment Deal," *The New York Times,* June 30, 1964.

68. "Argentina Seeks Oil Settlements," *The New York Times,* January 23, 1964.

69. Telegram Department of State to the Embassy in Argentina, June 20, 1964. FRUS, Volume 31, South and Central America; Mexico, 286–87.

70. Ibid.

71. Office Memorandum, Knox to Files, "Meeting of Inter-American Development Assistance Coordinating Group on Argentina," May 12, 1964, File 1514752, Box 193602B, Argentina—General Negotiations 1961–1964, Vol. III, WBGA.

72. Office Memorandum, Knox to Loftus, "Argentina—Meeting of Lending Agencies at the State Department," October 30, 1964, File 1514753, Box 193603B, Argentina—General Negotiations, Vol. IV, WBGA.

73. "Argentina Seeks Expansion Funds," *The New York Times,* June 28, 1964; "Los Caminos que Andará Pugliese," *Primera Plana,* August 25, 1964.

74. Confidential Memorandum, "Argentine Views on the International Financial Agencies," J. del Canto to P. Schweitzer and F. Southard Jr., April 29, 1964, Argentina Subseries, Country Files Series, Central Files, Box 19, Files 1–10, File title 1760, IMFA.

75. Gerald Alter to S. R. Cope, "Argentina—Technical Assistance Mission to National Development Council," July 24, 1964, File 1514735, Box 193601B, Argentina Technical Assistance: National Development Council-1, Vol. 1 (1964–1965), WBGA.

76. Alfred Matter to Andre van Campenhout, "Argentina—Economic Mission and Technical Assistance Mission," July 29, 1964, File 1514735, Box 193601B, Argentina Technical Assistance: National Development Council-1, Vol. 1 (1964–1965), WBGA.

77. Knox to Loftus, "Technical Assistance Mission—Present Position as Regards Data Obtained on Public Investment Plans," September 8, 1964, File 1514735, Box 193601B, Argentina Technical Assistance: National Development Council-1, Vol. 1 (1964–1965), WBGA.

78. Ibid.

79. R. Sheenan to Knox, "Argentina—Technical Assistance Mission," October 19, 1964, File 1514735, Box 193601B, Argentina Technical Assistance: National Development Council-1, Vol. 1 (1964–1965), WBGA.

80. Knox to Alter, "Meeting with Representatives of State Department to Discuss the American Attitude Towards Argentina," December 23, 1964, File 1514753, Box 193603B, Argentina—General Negotiations, Vol. IV, WBGA.

81. Office Memorandum, Knox to Files, "Meeting with US Officials on Policy Towards Argentina," January 7, 1965, File 1514753, Box 193603B, Argentina—General Negotiations, Vol. IV, WBGA.

82. Ibid.

83. Memorandum, "IBRD and Argentina," J. del Canto to Managing Director, February 26, 1965, Argentina Subseries, Country Files Series, Central Files, Box 19, Files 120, nos. 39–40 10, File title 1760, File: 5, IMFA.

84. Office Memorandum, Knox to Files, "Argentina-New Loan by Eximbank," March 1, 1965, File 1514753, Box 193603B, Argentina—General Negotiations, Vol. IV, WBGA.

85. *La Nación,* April 9, 1965; Jorge del Canto to Pierre-Paul Scweitzer and Frank Southard Jr., "Report on the Mission to Argentina," June 4, 1964, Box 7, Files 120, nos. 39–40 33, File title 810, CFC-Argentina IMFA.

86. Office Memorandum, Loftus to Files, "Argentina-CIAP Pre-Country Review Meeting," March 9, 1965, File 1514753, Box 193603B, Argentina—General Negotiations, Vol. IV, WBGA.

87. Office Memorandum, Joseph Fajans to Files, "US Attitude Towards Argentina," March 19, 1965, File 1514753, Box 193603B, Argentina—General Negotiations, Vol. IV, WBGA.

88. Ibid.

89. Knox to Files, "Argentina—Discussion with Minister of Economy", March 24, 1965, File 1514753, Box 193603B, Argentina—General Negotiations, Vol. IV, WBGA.

90. National Intelligence Estimate. "Prospects for Argentina," June 9, 1965. FRUS, Volume 31, South and Central America; Mexico, 294–95. On the crisis over the dispatch of troops to the Dominican Republic, see María Cecilia Míguez, "Illia y Santo Domingo: De las Columnas de *Primera Plana* al Golpe de Estado," *Ciclos en la Historia, la Economía y la Sociedad* 20, nos. 39–40 (2011–2012): 65–192, https://www.scielo.org.ar/img/revistas/ciclos/v20n40/html/v20n40a02.htm.

91. Briefing Paper for Mr. Wood's Visit to Argentina, April 23, 1965, File 1514753, Box 193603B, Argentina—General Negotiations, Vol. IV, WBGA.

92. Ibid.

93. Ibid.

94. Office Memorandum, Murray Ross to Files, "Minutes of Meeting Between Mr. Woods and Minister Pugliese on May 16, 1965, at 6pm," May 25, 1965, File 1514753, Box 193603B, Argentina—General Negotiations, Vol. IV, WBGA.

95. Office Memorandum, Orvis Schmidt to Files, "Woods' Meeting with President Illia of Argentina," May 21, 1965, File 1514753, Box 193603B, Argentina—General Negotiations, Vol. IV, WBGA.

96. Ibid.

97. "Admite Que Aún Se Estudia la Planificación de Ferrocarriles," *Clarín, May 19, 1965.*

98. Ibid.

99. "Pugliese: Una Variante con el Banco Mundial", *Clarín,* May 22, 1965.

100. "Mensaje Dirigido al País el Día 3 de Junio de 1965," Dr. Juan Carlos Pugliese, Ministro de Economía. Printed by the Ministerio de Interior, August 1965, Biblioteca Ministerio de Economía, Buenos Aires.

101. "El Dr. Pugliese Anunció un Plan para Reactivar los Ferrocarriles," *La Nación,* June 4, 1965.

102. "Aplicarán Desde Agosto el Nuevo Plan Ferroviario," *La Nación,* June 25, 1965.

103. *La Nación,* April 28, 1965.

104. "Una Reunión Sobre la Deuda Argentina," *La Nación,* June 1, 1965; "Argentina Finishes Debt Negotiations with 13 Countries," *The New York Times,* June 26, 1965.

105. "Postérgase el Pago de u$s 107 Millones de Deuda Financiera," *La Nación,* June 3, 1965.

106. "Se llegó a un Acuerdo con el Club de París," *La Nación,* June 27, 1965.

107. Office Memorandum, Knox to Alter, "Discussion with Dr. San Miguel," August 23, 1965, File 1514753, Box 193603B, Argentina—General Negotiations, Vol. IV, WBGA.

108. Ibid.

109. Carlo Edoardo Altamura and Claudia Kedar, "Friends or Foes? Brazil, the IMF, and the World Bank, 1961–1967," *Financial History Review* 28, no. 2 (2021): 205–36, https://doi.org/10.1017/S096856502100007X.

110. Felipe Rivero Polo, "¡Ni Capitalistas ni Comunistas! Una Revolución en Libertad en la Guerra Fría," in *Eduardo Frei Montalva: Fe, Política y Cambio Social,* eds. David Vásquez & Felipe Rivero (Chile: Andros Impresores, 2013), 125–56.

111. Office Memorandum, Irving Friedman to George Woods, "Visit to Brazil, Argentina and Chile," September 10, 1965, File 1514753, Box 193603B, Argentina—General Negotiations, Vol. IV, WBGA.

112. Ibid.

113. Alter to Ross, "Mission Terms of Reference," November 15, 1965, File 1514753, Box 193603B, Argentina—General Negotiations, Vol. IV, WBGA.

114. Office Memorandum, Wyss to Files, "Preliminary Comments on 1965 Performance and 1966 Plan," December 13, 1965, File 1514753, Box 193603B, Argentina—General Negotiations, Vol. IV, WBGA.

115. Ibid.

116. Telegram, Secretary of State Rusk to the Department of State, November 17, 1965. FRUS, Volume 31, South and Central America; Mexico, 296–97.

117. Office Memorandum, Gerald Alter to Burke Knapp, "Argentina—Economic Report," March 4, 1966, File 1514754, Box 193604B, Argentina—General Negotiations, Vol. V, WBGA.

118. *The New York Times*, February 17, 1966. For the Argentine request and the Fund's decision on this purchase, see EBM/66/4, January 26, 1966 (Decision no. 1998-66/4), "Argentina—Purchase Transaction," IMFA.

119. "Gold tranche purchase" means a purchase by a member of the currency of another member in exchange for its own currency which does not cause the Fund's holdings of the member's currency to exceed 100 percent of its quota in the IMF. See International Monetary Fund, "1. The Gold Tranche," in *The Reform of the Fund* (USA: International Monetary Fund, 1969), https://doi.org/10.5089/9781451947540.054.

120. EC/M/66-19, "Minutes on Special Meeting on Argentina," May 4, 1966, File 1514754, Box 193604B, Argentina—General Negotiations, Vol. V, WBGA.

121. David Knox to Roger Chaufournier, "Visit to Argentina," April 1, 1966, File 1514754, Box 193604B, Argentina—General Negotiations, Vol. V, WBGA.

122. Confidential EC/0/66–84/1, "Economic Policy Memorandum on Argentina from the Western Hemisphere Department," June 3, 1966, File 1514754, Box 193604B, Argentina—General Negotiations, Vol. V, WBGA.

123. Ibid.

124. Confidential EC/M/66-30, "Conclusions and Recommendations on the Economy of Argentina," June 17, 1966, File 1514754, Box 193604B, Argentina—General Negotiations, Vol. V, WBGA.

125. Ibid.

126. See, for instance, Telegram, Embassy in Argentina to the Department of State, June 4, 1964. FRUS, 1964-1968, Volume XXXI, 298–99; Telegram, Department of State to the Embassy in Argentina, June 7, 1965. FRUS, Volume 31, South and Central America; Mexico, 300–301; Telegram, Embassy in Argentina to the Department of State, June 8, 1964. FRUS, Volume 31, South and Central America; Mexico, 302–303.

127. "Illia Defends Rule, Retains Top Aides," *The New York Times*, June 11, 1961; "Illia Regime Vows Firmness on Reds," *The New York Times*, June 15, 1966.

128. Office Memorandum, Knox to Files, "Argentina—Discussion with US Ambassador," June 28, 1966, File 1514754, Box 193604B, Argentina—General Negotiations, Vol. V, WBGA.

129. Ibid.

130. Catalina Smulovitz, "La Eficacia Como Crítica y Utopía: Notas Sobre la Caída de Illia," *Desarrollo Económico* 33, no. 131 (1993): 403–23, http://doi.org/10.2307/3467088; Tcach and Rodríguez, *Arturo Illia: Un Sueño Breve,* esp. Chap. 3.

131. Smulovitz, "La Eficacia Como Crítica y Utopía," 403–23.

132. María Cecilia Míguez, "La Unión Industrial Argentina y el Gobierno de Illia. Los Sectores Civiles y el Golpe de Estado de 1966," *H-Industria* 9, no. 17 (2015): 64–1, https://scispace.com/papers/la-union-industrial-argentina-y-el-gobierno-de-illia-los-2ij2b2vwqo.

Chapter Four

1. Part of this chapter is based on Claudia Kedar, "The World Bank Lending and Non-Lending to Latin America: The Case of Argentina, 1971–1976," *Revista de Historia Económica: Journal of Iberian and Latin American Economic History* 37, no. 1 (2018): 111–38, reproduced with permission, https://doi.org/10.1017/S0212610918000149. *Copyright © 2018, Cambridge University Press.*

2. Robert S. McNamara, *The Essence of Security* (New York: Harper and Row, 1968), 149.

3. Juan Carlos Onganía, *Directiva para el Planeamiento y Desarrollo de la Acción del Gobierno. Presidencia de la Nación Argentina, Enunciada por el Señor Presidente de la Nación en la Conferencia de Prensa Realizada en el Salón de Gobernadores, el 4 de Agosto de 1966* (Buenos Aires, Argentina: Presidencia de la Nación).

4. Guillermo O'Donnell, "Modernización y Golpes Militares: Teoría, Comparación y el Caso Argentino," *Desarrollo Económico* 12, no. 47 (1972): 519–566, http://repositorio.cedes.org/handle/123456789/2923; David Pion-Berlin, "The National Security Doctrine, Military Threat Perception, and the 'Dirty War' in Argentina," *Comparative Political Studies* 21, no. 3 (1988): 382–407, DOI:10.1177/0010414088021003004.

5. "Ley 17401. Comunismo," August 22, 1967, https://www.argentina.gob.ar/normativa/nacional/ley-17401-260802/texto; Herbert S. Klein and Francisco Vidal Luna, *Brazil 1964–1985: The Military Regimes of Latin America in the Cold War* (New Haven: Yale University Press, 2017), 7–8; James P. Brennan and Mónica B. Gordillo, "Working Class Protest, Popular Revolt, and Urban Insurrection in Argentina: The 1969 'Cordobazo,'" *Journal of Social History* 27, no. 3 (1994): 477–98, https://www.jstor.org/stable/3788983; Darío Dawyd, "El Sindicalismo Peronista Durante el Onganiato. De la CGT de los Argentinos a la Reorganización Sindical (1968–1970)," *Sociohistórica* 33 (2014): 56–76, https://www.sociohistorica.fahce.unlp.edu.ar/article/view/SH2014n33a04; Mónica B. Gordillo, "Los Prolegómenos del Cordobazo. Los Sindicatos Líderes de Córdoba Dentro de la Estructura del Poder Sindical," *Desarrollo Económico* 31, no. 122 (1991): 163–87, https://www.jstor.org/stable/3466830; María Cecilia Míguez, "¿Anticomunistas, Antiestatistas, Antiperonistas? La 'Nacionalización' de la

Doctrina de Seguridad Nacional en la Argentina y la Legitimación del Golpe de Estado de 1966," *Revista SAAP* 7, no. 1 (2013): 65–95, https://dialnet.unirioja.es/servlet/articulo?codigo=5119934.

6. Victoria Zapata, "La Revolución Argentina (1966–1973)," in *La Argentina y el Mundo Frente al Bicentenario de la Revolución de Mayo: Las Relaciones Exteriores Argentinas Desde la Secesión de España Hasta la Actualidad*, ed. Alejandro César Simonoff (La Plata: EDULP, 2010), chap. 11.

7. Claudia Kedar, *The International Monetary Fund and Latin America: The Argentine Puzzle in Context* (Philadelphia: Temple University Press, 2013), 108–109.

8. Edmar L. Bacha and Richard E. Feinberg, "The World Bank and Structural Adjustment in Latin America," *World Development* 14, no. 3 (1986): 333–46, https://doi.org/10.1016/0305-750X(86)90073-2.

9. Gwin, "US Relations," 201–11; Sharma, "The United States, the World Bank," 582.

10. Hal Brands," Richard Nixon and Economic Nationalism in Latin America: The Problem of Expropriations, 1969–1974," *Diplomacy & Statecraft* 18, no. 1 (2007): 215–35, https://doi.org/10.1080/09592290601163126; Hal Brands, "The United States and the Peruvian Challenge, 1968–1975," *Diplomacy & Statecraft* 21, no. 3 (2010): 471–90, https://doi.org/10.1080/09592296.2010.508418.

11. Cynthia Northrup and Elaine C. Prange Turney, eds., *Encyclopedia of Tariffs and Trade in U.S. History*, (Westport, CT: Greenwood Press, 2003), 186–87.

12. Van Der Heijden to Alter, "Swift de la Plata, S.A.," October 4, 1971, File 1514760, General Negotiations-Vol. 11, Argentina-1969–1971, WBGA.

13. Patrick Allan Sharma, *Robert McNamara's Other War: The World Bank and International Development* (Philadelphia: University of Pennsylvania Press, 2017), 27.

14. See, among the most recent publications, Aurélie Basha i Novosejt, "I Made Mistakes," *Robert McNamara's Vietnam War Policy, 1960–1968* (Cambridge: Cambridge University Press, 2019), 186–206.

15. Aurélie Basha i Novosejt, "Breaking Ranks: Robert McNamara, Adam Yarmolinsky, and the Montreal Speech," *Diplomatic History* 43, no 3 (2019): 493–516, https://doi.org/10.1093/dh/dhy091.

16. Jochen Kraske et al., *Bankers with a Mission: The Presidents of the World Bank, 1946–91* (New York: Oxford University Press, 1996), 68.

17. Catherine Weaver, *Hypocrisy Trap: The World Bank and the Poverty of Reform* (Princeton: Princeton University Press, 2008), 84–5.

18. William Clark, "Robert McNamara at the World Bank," *Foreign Affairs* 60, no. 1 (1981): 167–84, http://www.foreignaffairs.com/articles/35520/william-clark/reconsiderations-robert-mcnamara-at-the-world-bank.

19. Devesh Kapur et al., *The World Bank: Its First Half Century*, vol. 1 (Washington, DC.: Brookings Institute Press, 1997), 245.

20. Memorandum for the Record, President's Council Luncheon to Discuss McKinsey Recommendations Regarding the Bank's Organization, July 31, 1972, Records of President Robert S. McNamara President's Council Minutes—Minutes 10, Folder ID 1770823, WBGA; President's Council Meeting to Discuss Organizational Changes, August 7, 1972, Records of President Robert S. McNamara President's Council Minutes—Minutes 10, Folder ID 1770823, WBGA.

21. James Bovard, "The World Bank and the Impoverishment of Nations," in *Perpetuating Poverty: The World Bank, the IMF, and the Developing World*, eds. Doug Bandow and Ian Vásquez (Washington, DC.: Cato Institute, 1994), 59.

22. Louis Galambos and David Milobsky, "Organizing and Reorganizing the World Bank, 1946–1972: A Comparative Perspective," *The Business History Review* 69, no. 2 (1995): 156–90, https://doi.org/10.2307/3117098.

23. See Rob Konkel, "The Monetization of Global Poverty: The Concept of Poverty in World Bank History, 1944–90," *Journal of Global History* 9, no. 2 (2014): 276–300, https://doi.org/10.1017/S1740022814000072; Martha Finnemore, *National Interests in International Society* (Ithaca: Cornell University Press, 1996), 90–91; Edmar L. Bacha and Richard E. Feinberg, "The World Bank and Structural Adjustment in Latin America"; and William Clark, *The McNamara Years at the World Bank: Major Policy Addresses of Robert S. McNamara 1968–1981* (Baltimore: Johns Hopkins University Press, 1981), 9–12.

24. Judith Tendler, "New Lessons from Old Projects: The Workings of Rural Development in Northeast Brazil," in *Banking on the Poor: The World Bank and World Poverty*, ed. by Robert L. Ayres (Cambridge, Mass.: MIT Press, 1983.), chap. 1; Ayres, *Banking on the Poor*, 92–99.

25. Sharma, *McNamara's Other War*, 49.

26. Patrick Sharma, "Between North and South: The World Bank and the New International Economic Order," *Humanity: An International Journal of Human Rights, Humanitarianism, and Development* 6, no. 1 (2015): 189–200, http://dx.doi.org/10.1353/hum.2015.0006.

27. See, among others, Craig Murphy, *The Emergence of the NIEO Ideology* (New York: Routledge, 1984); Robert L. Rothstein, *Global Bargaining: UNCTAD and the Quest for a New International Economic Order* (Princeton: Princeton University Press, 1979).

28. Franczak, *Global Inequality and American Foreign Policy in the 1970s*, 119; Christy Thornton, *Revolution in Development: Mexico and the Governance of the Global Economy* (Oakland, CA.: University of California Press, 2021), 166–89.

29. Sharma, "Between North and South," 191–92.

30. Gwin, "US Relations," 201–11.

31. National Security Study Memorandum 131, "US Policy in Cases of Expropriation," June 23, 1971, Richard Nixon Library and Museum, https://www.nixonlibrary.gov/sites/default/files/virtuallibrary/documents/nssm/nssm_131.pdf.

32. National Security Decision Memorandum 148, "Expropriation Policy in the Multilateral Development Institutions," January 18, 1972, Richard Nixon Library and Museum, https://www.nixonlibrary.gov/sites/default/files/virtuallibrary/documents/nsdm/nsdm_148.pdf.

33. Cynthia Northrup and Elaine C. Prange Turney, eds., *Encyclopedia of Tariffs and Trade in U.S. History* (Westport, CT: Greenwood Press, 2003), 186–87.

34. Patrick Sharma, "The United States, the World Bank, and the Challenges of International Development in the 1970s," *Diplomatic History* 37, no. 3 (2013): 572–603, https://www.jstor.org/stable/44254308.

35. Gary J. Bass, *The Blood Telegram: Nixon, Kissinger, and a Forgotten Genocide* (Alfred A. Knopf, 2013), 267–72.

36. Daniel Kressel, "The 'Argentine Franco'? The Regime of Juan Carlos Onganía and Its Ideological Dialogue with Francoist Spain (1966–1970)," *The Americas* 78, no. 1 (2021): 89–117, http://dx.doi.org/10.17169/refubium-30531.

37. Laguado claims that Onganía promoted an "authoritarian nationalism." See Arturo Claudio Laguado Duca, "Onganía y el Nacionalismo Militar en Argentina," *Universitas Humanística* 62 (2006): 239–59, https://www.redalyc.org/pdf/791/79106210.pdf.

38. "Statement Delivered to Press by Foreign Minister Juan Martín," June 20, 1969, Pol.1. RG59 General Records of the State Department, Central Foreign Policy Files, 1967–1969, BOX1845. NARA.

39. Klein and Vidal Luna, *Brazil 1964–1985,* 40–42; Airgram A-316, AmEmbassy Bs.As. to State Department, "Power Factors in Current Argentine Politics," October 21, 1967, Pol.2. RG59 General Records of the State Department, Central Foreign Policy Files, 1967–1969, BOX1845. NARA.

40. María Florencia Delpino, "El Petróleo Argentino Durante los Años de Onganía: Hacia Una Nueva Ley de Hidrocarburos. Repercusiones Internas y Externas," *Ciclos en la Historia, la Economía y la Sociedad* 25, no. 51 (2018): 107–34, http://scienceopen.com/document?vid=c14fafc0-1bed-4afd-b1ef-34789a8ba1b2.

41. Study Prepared by the National Security Council Interdepartmental Group for Inter-American Affairs, "FY1971-Country Analysis and Strategy Paper-Argentina," October 9, 1969, FRUS, Volume E-10, Documents on American Republics, 1969–1972, 1–11.

42. Leandro Morgenfeld, "Argentina y Estados Unidos, Golpe a Golpe (1966–1976), *Revista SAAP* 8, no. 2 (2014): 521–54, https://www.redalyc.org/pdf/3871/387139302006.pdf

43. Verónica Baudino, "Burguesía Nacional y Estado: La Acción Política de la Unión Industrial Argentina Durante la Revolución Argentina (1966–1969)," *Polis Revista Latinoamericana* 32 (2012), https://journals.openedition.org/polis/6470; Guillermo O'Donnell, *Bureaucratic Authoritarianism. Argentina 1966–1973, in Comparative Perspective* (Berkley: University of California Press, 1988), 93–97.

44. "Acta de la Revolución Argentina con Sus Anexos," June 28, 1966 (Buenos Aires: Secretaría de Estado de Gobierno, 1966), https://www.argentina.gob.ar/sites/default/files/acta_de_la_revolucion_argentina-1966.pdf; Guillermo O'Donnell, "Reflecciones Sobre las Tendencias de Cambio del Estado Burocrático-Autoritario," *Revista Mexicana de Sociología* 39, no. 1 (1977): 9–59, https://www.jstor.org/stable/i282391.

45. Liliana de Riz, *Historia Argentina: La Política en Suspenso, 1966–1976* (Buenos Aires: Paidós, 2000), 36–37, 44–45; María Florencia-Osuna and Esteban Pontoriero, "El Impacto de la Doctrina 'de la Seguridad Nacional' en la Argentina Durante la Guerra Fría (1955–1983)," *Izquierdas* 49 (2020): 352–64, https://dx.doi.org/10.4067/S0718-50492020000100221.

46. Stephen G. Rabe, *Kissinger and Latin America: Intervention, Human Rights, and Diplomacy* (Ithaca: Cornell University Press, 2021), 119–26.

47. Lars Schoultz, *In Their Own Best Interest. A History of U.S. Efforts to Improve Latin Americans* (Cambridge, MA: Harvard University Press, 2018), 218–19,

48. See David F. Schmitz, *The United States and Right-Wing Dictatorships* (New York: Cambridge University Press, 2006), 89–90; and Andrew J. Kirkendall, *Hemispheric Alliances: Liberal Democrats and Cold War Latin America*, (Chapel Hill: The University of North Carolina Press, 2022), 152–58.

49. Confidential Office Memorandum. Murray Ross to Files, "Argentina-Visit of Ambassador Alsogaray," August 1, 1966, File 1514754, Box 193604B, Argentina—General Negotiations, Vol. V, WBGA.

50. Ibid.

51. Memorandum, Delivered by Ambassador Alsogaray on July 28, 1966, Approved by Argentina's Cabinet, File 1514754, Box 193604B, Argentina—General Negotiations, Vol. V, WBGA.

52. Memorandum of Conversation, July 30, 1966, FRUS, 1964–1968, Vol. 31, 326–28.

53. Office Memorandum, Joseph Fajans to Files, "Argentina," August 12, 1966, File 1514754, Box 193604B, Argentina—General Negotiations, Vol. V, WBGA.

54. Office Memorandum, Joseph Fajans to Files, "Mr. Gotelli's Visit," September 16, 1966, File 1514754, Box 193604B, Argentina—General Negotiations, Vol. V, WBGA.

55. Ibid.

56. Office Memorandum, Gerald Alter to George Woods, "Meeting with Argentine Delegation," September 30, 1966, File 1514754, Box 193604B,

Argentina—General Negotiations, Vol. V, WBGA; "Argentine Regime Divided on Loans," *The New York Times*, September 17, 1966.

57. Office Memorandum, Knox to Files, "Meeting Between Minister of Economy and Mr. Woods," October 3, 1966, File 1514754, Box 193604B, Argentina—General Negotiations, Vol. V, WBGA.

58. Confidential Office Memorandum, Knox and Ross to Alter, "Economic Mission October 4-19: Report on 1966 Economic Situation and Prospects for 1967," October 26, 1966, File 1514754, Box 193604B, Argentina—General Negotiations, Vol. V, WBGA.

59. Office Memorandum, Gerald Alter to Burke Knapp and Irving Friedman, "Argentina-Report on Economic Mission," October 28, 1966, File 1514754, Box 193604B, Argentina—General Negotiations, Vol. V, WBGA.

60. Information Memorandum from the Assistant Secretary of State for Inter-American Affairs (Gordon) to Secretary of State Rusk, "Military Assistance to Argentina," February 6, 1967, FRUS, 1964–1968, Vol. 31, 328–29.

61. Airgram A-590, AmEmbassy Bs.As. to State Department, "Views of Dr. Roberto Alemann on Politic-Economic Matters," February 2, 1967, Pol.2-1. RG59 General Records of the State Department, Central Foreign Policy Files, 1967–1969, BOX1845. NARA.

62. "Argentine Reforms Make Haste Slowly," *The New York Times*, January 22, 1968; "Argentina Devalues Her Currency 40% To Draw Investors," *The New York Times*, March 14, 1967.

63. "Argentina Gets Revised Cabinet," *The New York Times*, December 30, 1967; Airgram A-491, AmEmbassy Bs.As. to State Department, "The First Six Months of Onganía's Government; Its Prospects: Political Review," January 7, 1967, Pol.1. RG59 General Records of the State Department, Central Foreign Policy Files, 1967–1969, BOX1845. NARA.

64. Hugo A. Rossi, "La Política Económica de Krieger Vasena y su Participación en el Ingreso de las Empresas Tabacaleras Extranjeras en la Economía Argentina (1967–1969)," *América Latina en la Historia Económica* 29, no. 3 (2022), https://doi.org/10.18232/20073496.1286.

65. Rubén M. Perina, *Onganía, Levingston, Lanusse. Los Militares en la Política Argentina* (Buenos Aires: Editorial de Belgrano, 1983), 99–103; Rouquié, *Poder Militar*, 276–77.

66. Norberto Galasso, *De la Banca Baring al FMI* (Buenos Aires: Colihue, 2002), 200–205.

67. SSM/M/67-11, March 17, 1967, File 1514755, Box 193604B, Argentina—General Negotiations, Vol. VI, WBGA.

68. Office Memorandum, Alter to Knapp, "Argentina—Resumption of Lending," April 3, 1967, File 1514755, Box 193604B, Argentina—General Negotiations, Vol. VI, WBGA.

69. Summary Proceedings Annual Meeting of the Board of Governors, September 30–October 4, 1968, IMFA, https://www.elibrary.imf.org/downloadpdf/display/book/9781475565720/9781475565720.pdf.

70. Announcement of Adalbert Krieger Appointed World Bank Regional Vice President, Gerald Alter Named Senior Adviser on February 25, 1975 (English), Bank News Release, no. 1975–685. WBGA, http://documents.worldbank.org/curated/en/099637011082240895/IDU04af67dca06e9d04ecd0a0e3077dbe73499b4.

71. Telegram from the Department of State to the Embassy in Argentina, April 28, 1967, FRUS, 1964–168, Vol. 31, 330–332.

72. NIE 91-67, Argentina. December 7, 1967. FRUS, 1964–1968, Vol. 31, 332–33.

73. Airgram A-491, AmEmbassy Bs.As. to State Department, "The First Six Months of Onganía's Government; Its Prospects: Political Review," January 7, 1967, Pol.1. RG59 General Records of the State Department, Central Foreign Policy Files, 1967–1969, BOX1845. NARA.

74. Alter to Knapp, "Argentina," June 1, 1967, File 1514755, Box 193604B, Argentina—General Negotiations, Vol. VI, WBGA.

75. Memorandum & Recommendation of the President, Argentina—Balcarce Livestock Development Project, http://documents.worldbank.org/curated/en/851441468207251906/Argentina-Balcarce-Livestock-Development-Project.

76. Ibid.

77. "El BID Acordó un Crédito para Mejoramiento de Nuestro Agro," *Clarín,* July 25, 1967.

78. Cable Address, Boards of Governors, 1967 Annual Meetings, IBRD-IFC-IDA-IMF, September 25, 1967, File 1514755, Box 193604B, Argentina—General Negotiations, Vol. VI, WBGA.

79. Ibid.

80. EC/M/67-33, Economic Committee, Conclusions and Recommendations on the Economy of Argentina, December 15, 1967, File 1514755, Box 193604B, Argentina—General Negotiations, Vol. VI, WBGA.

81. Confidential, EC/O/67-135/1, Economic Policy Memorandum from WHD to Economic Committee, October 27, 1967, File 1514755, Box 193604B, Argentina—General Negotiations, Vol. VI, WBGA.

82. Wright to Daniel Fernandez (Alternate ED for Argentina), "Economic Mission to Argentina," January 9, 1968, File 1514755, Box 193604B, Argentina—General Negotiations, Vol. VI, WBGA.

83. Confidential Letter No. 1, Wright to Alter, January 23, 1968, File 1514755, Box 193604B, Argentina—General Negotiations, Vol. VI, WBGA.

84. Second Buenos Aires Power Project, Report and Recommendation of the President to the Executive Directors, January 8, 1968, WBG, http://documents.worldbank.org/curated/en/274351468002418405/Argentina-Second-Buenos-Aires-Power-Project.

85. Robert Skillings to Files, "Meetings with Minister of Economy, Dr. Krieger Vasena on February 14 and 15," March 1, 1968, File 1514755, Box 193604B, Argentina—General Negotiations, Vol. VI, WBGA.

86. Memorandum for Record, from Fajans, "McNamara's Meeting with Delegation to Annual Meeting," October 4, 1968, File 1514755, Box 193604B, Argentina—General Negotiations, Vol. VI, WBGA.

87. Ibid.

88. Ibid.

89. Ibid.

90. "Proposed Schedule for McNamara's Visit to Argentina, October 18–22, 1968," Travel Briefings: Argentina, Folder 1772477, Records of the President Robert McNamara, WBGA.

91. Office Memorandum, Alter for Records, "Meeting of McNamara with Minister of Economy of Argentina, Dr. Krieger Vasena," October 31, 1968, File 1770940, Contacts with Member Countries-Argentina-Corresp. 01, Records of President McNamara, WBGA.

92. Office Memorandum, Alter for Records, "Meeting of McNamara with President Onganía of Argentina," October 31, 1968, File 1770940, Contacts with Member Countries-Argentina-Corresp. 01, Records of President McNamara, WBGA.

93. Ibid.

94. Office Memorandum, Dragoslav Avramovic for Records, "Meeting of McNamara with the Minister of Argentina, Mr. Carlos Moyano Llerena in Copenhagen on September 24, 1970," September 28, 1970, File 1770940, Contacts with Member Countries-Argentina-Corresp. 01, Records of President McNamara, WBGA.

95. Airgram A-1236, AmEmbassy Bs.As. to Department of State, "Political Highlights—October 1968," November 24, 1968, Pol.2. RG59 General Records of the State Department, Central Foreign Policy Files, 1967–1969, BOX1845. NARA.

96. El Chocon Power Project, Report and Recommendation of the President to the Executive Directors, December 5, 1968, WBG, http://documents.worldbank.org/curated/en/494651468000576923/Argentina-El-Chocon-Power-Project.

97. Transcript of Joint Meeting of the Executive Directors of the IBRD and IDA, Held on Tuesday, December 17, 1968, El Chocón Power Project, WBGA, http://documents.worldbank.org/curated/en/460301510553253166.

98. See, among others, Juan Claudio Quintar, *El Choconazo: 1969–1970* (Argentina: Universidad Nacional del Comahue, 1998); Griselda Fanese and Emilse Kejner, "La Aneida: Una Epopeya de Mujeres en Una Huelga de Obreros. Representaciones de las Mujeres que Participaron en el Choconazo (1969–1970)," *La Aljaba* 11 (2007): 229–48, https://www.scielo.org.ar/scielo.php?script=sci_arttext&pid=S1669-57042007000100011.

99. Sharma, *Robert McNamara's Other War,* 115–16.

100. Second Highway Project, June 9, 1969, WBG, http://documents.worldbank.org/curated/en/529321468205144004/Argentina-Second-Highway-Project.

101. Transcript of Joint Meeting of the Executive Directors of the IBRD and IDA, Held on Tuesday, June 24, 1969, Argentina—Second Road Project, WBGA, http://documents.worldbank.org/curated/en/990801510553688916.

102. Third Buenos Aires Power Project, September 24, 1969, WBG, http://documents.worldbank.org/curated/en/119021468221364987/Argentina-Third-Buenos-Aires-Power-Project.

103. Transcript of Joint Meeting of the Executive Directors of the IBRD and IDA, Held on Tuesday, October 7, 1969: Argentina—Power Project, WBGA, http://documents.worldbank.org/curated/en/834951510554536708.

104. Study Prepared by the National Security Council Interdepartmental Group for Inter-American Affairs, "FY1971-Country Analysis and Strategy Paper-Argentina," October 9, 1969, FRUS, Volume E-10, Documents on American Republics, 1969–1972, 1–11.

105. "Consterna al País el Asesinato de Aramburu,"*Clarín,* July 18, 1970; "Traen el Cadaver: Sería de Aramburu," *Crónica,* July 17, 1970; María O'Donnell, *Aramburu: El Crimen Político que Dividió al País. El Origen de Montoneros* (Buenos Aires: Editorial Planeta, 2020).

106. Marcelo N. Rougier Voilláz y Juan Carlos Odisio, "Del Dicho al Hecho. El 'Modelo Integrado y Abierto' de Aldo Ferrer y la Política Económica en la Argentina de la Segunda Posguerra," *América Latina en la Historia Económica* 19, no. 1 (2012): 99–130, https://www.scielo.org.mx/scielo.php?script=sci_arttext&pid=S1405-22532012000100005

107. Marcelo Rougier, *El Pensamiento Económico de Aldo Ferrer* (Buenos Aires: Manuel Belgrano Ediciones, 2021), 25.

108. Mariano Filippini and María Olcese, "Transitional Economic Policies, 1971–3," in *The Political Economy of Argentina, 1946–83,* eds. Guido DiTella, and R. Dornbusch (Hampshire: Macmillan Press, 1989), 189–212.

109. Legal ISC Files, 1971, Argentina—Third Highway Project: Loan 0734—Loan Agreement—Conformed, WBGA, http://documents.worldbank.org/curated/en/611571468217783704/Argentina-Third-Highway-Project-Loan-0734-Loan-Agreement-Conformed.

110. Legal ISC Files, 1971, Argentina—Railway Project: Loan 0733—Loan Agreement—Conformed, WBG, http://documents.worldbank.org/curated/en/528101467992804970/Argentina-Railway-Project-Loan-0733-Loan-Agreement-Conformed.

111. Transcript of Joint Meeting of the Executive Directors of the IBRD and IDA, Held on Tuesday, March 30, 1971: Argentina—Third Road Project and Railways Project, WBGA, http://documents.worldbank.org/curated/en/552131510557731255.

112. Ibid.

113. Pilvin to Files, "Back-to-Office Report on Mission to Argentina, June 21–25," June 30, 1971, File 1514760, General Negotiations-Vol. 11, Argentina-1969–1971, WBGA.

114. Letter from Alter to Ferrer, May 26, 1971, File 1514760, General Negotiations-Vol. 11, Argentina-1969–1971, WBGA.

115. Lerdau to Yudin, "Mission to Argentina and Santiago," June 8, 1971, File 1514760, General Negotiations-Vol. 11, Argentina-1969–1971, WBGA.

116. "Inflación y Costo de Vida," *Mercado,* August 12, 1971.

117. Backchannel Message from the Ambassador to Argentina (Lodge) to the Assistant Secretary of State for Inter-American Affairs (Meyer), June 30, 1971, FRUS, Volume E-10, Documents on American Republics, 1969–1972.

118. Memorandum from the President's Deputy Assistant for National Security Affairs (Haig) to President Nixon, "Request for Financial Assistance from Argentine President Lanusse," July 14, 1971, FRUS, Volume E-10, Documents on American Republics, 1969–1972.

119. Memorandum from the President's Deputy Assistant for National Security Affairs (Kissinger) to President Nixon, "Request for Financial Assistance from Argentine President Lanusse," August 24, 1971, FRUS, Volume E-10, Documents on American Republics, 1969–1972.

120. Greene to Files, "New Economic Measures," September 3, 1971, File 1514760, General Negotiations-Vol. 11, Argentina-1969–1971, WBGA; "Hacia la Inflación Reprimida," *Mercado,* October 7, 1971; "Un Presupuesto Contra la inflación," *Mercado,* October 28, 1971.

121. Helmers to Frank and Schertz, "Meat Processing Project. Follow-Up. Preparation Mission. Terms of Reference," File 1514760, General Negotiations-Vol. 11, Argentina-1969–1971, WBGA; Van de Heijden and Fajans to Alter, "Report on Recent Mission," November 10, 1971, File 1514760, General Negotiations-Vol. 11, Argentina-1969–1971, WBGA.

122. Backchannel Message from the Ambassador to Argentina (Lodge) to the Executive Secretary of the Department of State (Eliot), August 31, 1971, FRUS, Volume E-10, Documents on American Republics, 1969–1972.

123. Wiese to Knapp, "Power and Railways Rates," December 8, 1971, File 1514760, General Negotiations-Vol. 11, Argentina-1969–1971, WBGA.

124. "Minutes of Special Loan Meeting to Consider 'Argentina-Railways' and 'Argentina-SEGBA' Held on December 13, 1971," December 20, 1971, File 1514760, General Negotiations-Vol. 11, Argentina-1969–1971, WBGA.

125. "Arribarán al País dos Misiones de Estudio del Banco Mundial y el FMI," *La Opinión,* January 15, 1972.

126. "El Gobierno Intentará Obtener Apoyo del FMI con Una Carta de Intención," *La Opinión,* January 27, 1972.

127. Office Memorandum, Alter to McNamara, "Visit by Argentine Delegation," February 3, 1972, File 1770941, Contacts with Member Countries-Argentina-Corresp. 02, Records of President McNamara, WBGA.

128. Ibid.

129. Alter to Files, "Meeting of McNamara with Carlos Brignone," March 14, 1972, File 1770941, Contacts with Member Countries-Argentina-Corresp. 02, Records of President McNamara, WBGA

130. Kedar, *The International Monetary Fund and Latin America,* 115–16.

131. President's Council Meeting, July 3, 1972, Records of President Robert S. McNamara President's Council Minutes—Minutes 10, Folder ID 1770823, WBGA; *Memoria Anual del Banco Central de la República Argentina* (Buenos Aires), 1974, 68–70. Archivo BCRA; "Bloqueó el Crédito el Banco Mundial," *La Nación,* March 26, 1973.

132. María Seoane, *El Burgués Maldito* (Buenos Aires: Editorial Sudamericana, 1998), chap. 6.

133. Mario Rapoport et al., *Historia Económica, Política y Social de la Argentina (1880–2000)* (Buenos Aires: Ediciones Macchi, 2000), 664–70.

134. Argentina—Economic Position and Prospects, November 30, 1967. Western Hemisphere (South America) Series, no. WH 175, WBGA, http://documents.worldbank.org/curated/en/286181468221696174/Argentina-Economic-position-and-prospects.

135. "Peronists Leading With 43% of Vote in Early Returns," *The New York Times,* March 12, 1973.

136. "Triumph for Perón," *The New York Times,* March 14, 1973.

137. Memorandum Prepared in the Office of Current Intelligence, Central Intelligence Agency, "Peronism in Power," June 21, 1973, FRUS 1969–1976, Volume E-11, Part 2, Documents on South America, 1973–1976.

138. Letter, van der Heijden to Alter, May 30, 1973, File 1592285, Argentina—General—Corresp. 1972/1974 Correspondence Vol. 1, WBGA.

139. "Fijó la Argentina su Posición Ante el FMI," *La Nación,* August 2, 1973.

140. Miguel A. Kiguel, *Las Crisis Económicas Argentinas: Una Historia de Ajustes y Desajustes,* (Buenos Aires: Sudamericana, 2015), 91–95; Ricardo Sidicaro, *Los Tres Peronismos. Estado y Poder Económico* (Buenos Aires: Siglo Veintiuno Editores, 2011), 116–17.

141. James Brennan, "Prolegomenon to Neoliberalism: The Political Economy of Populist Argentina, 1943–1976," *Latin American Perspectives* 34, no. 3 (2007): 49–66, https://www.jstor.org/stable/27648022; Marcelo Rougier and Martín Fiszbein, *La Frustración de un Proyecto Económico: El Gobierno Peronista de 1973–76* (Buenos Aires: Manantial, 2006), 64–65.

142. Gonzalez-Cofiño to van der Heijden, "Argentina: The New Economic and Social Policies," June 28, 1973, File 1592285, Argentina—General—Corresp. 1972/1974 Correspondence Vol. 1, WBGA.

143. Skillings to Alter, "Argentina-Bank Group Operations: Present Status and Immediate Outlook," June 28, 1973, File 1592285, Argentina—General—Corresp. 1972/1974 Correspondence Vol. 1, WBGA.

144. Ibid.

145. Office Memorandum, Wiese to McNamara, "Argentina-Visit by Gómez Morales," July 31, 1973, File 1770941, Contacts with Member Countries-Argentina-Corresp. 02, Records of President McNamara, WBGA.

146. Office Memorandum, Wiese to Files, "Argentina-Visit of Gómez Morales with McNamara," August 3, 1973, File 1770941, Contacts with Member Countries-Argentina-Corresp. 02, Records of President McNamara, WBGA.

147. Ibid.

148. Office Memorandum, Wiese to McNamara, "Your Meeting with Ambassador Orfila," November 28, 1973, File 1770941, Contacts with Member Countries-Argentina-Corresp. 02, Records of President McNamara, WBGA.

149. Ibid.

150. "Créditos para Argentina," *La Nación,* October 1, 1973; "Una Misión del Banco Mundial," *La Nación,* November 4, 1973.

151. Office Memorandum, Wiese to McNamara, November 28, 1973.

152. Office Memorandum, AlterFiles, "Meeting of McNamara with Ambassador of Argentina," December 4, 1973, File 1770941, Contacts with Member Countries-Argentina-Corresp. 02, Records of President McNamara, WBGA.

153. Office Memorandum, Alter to Files, "Meeting of McNamara with the Ambassador of Argentina, Orfila," January 15, 1974, File 1770941, Contacts with Member Countries-Argentina-Corresp. 02, Records of President McNamara, WBGA.

154. Ibid.

155. Ibid.

156. Office Memorandum, Wiese to McNamara, "Argentina-Your Meeting with Ambassador Orfila," January 10, 1974, File 1770941, Contacts with Member Countries-Argentina-Corresp. 02, Records of President McNamara, WBGA.

157. Memorandum of Conversation, "U.S.-Argentine Relations," October 5, 1973, Foreign Relations of the United States, 1969–1976, Volume E-11, Part 2, Documents on South America, 1973–1976.

158. Telegram 7789 from the Embassy in Argentina to the Department of State, "U.S.-Argentine Relations: A New Era?," October 25, 1973, Foreign Relations of the United States, 1969–1976, Volume E-11, Part 2, Documents on South America, 1973–1976.

159. Memorandum from the President's Assistant for National Security Affairs (Kissinger) to President Nixon, "Argentina and Our Cuban Denial Policy," January 29, 1974, Foreign Relations of the United States, 1969–1976, Volume E-11, Part 2, Documents on South America, 1973–1976.

160. With Perón's death, a leadership vacuum formed that was eventually filled by José López Rega, the Minister of Welfare. Notorious for his fascist ideology, López Rega established, in November 1973, the paramilitary organization Argentine Anticommunist Alliance (Triple A), instituting a period of violence that was further aggravated after the coup of March 24, 1976.

161. Kiguel, *Las Crisis Económicas Argentinas*, 91–101; Daniel Muchnik, *Argentina Modelo: De la Furia a la Resignación: Economía Política Entre 1973 y 1998*. (Buenos Aires: Manantial, 1998), pp.82–91.

162. Office Memorandum, Gerald Alter to McNamara, "Briefing Paper for Meeting of January 17, 1975 with Gómez Morales to Discuss Bank/Argentina Relations," January 15, 1975, File 1770941, Contacts with Member Countries-Argentina-Corresp. 02, Records of President McNamara, WBGA.

163. Ibid.

164. Office Memorandum, Wiese to Files, "Call on McNamara by Argentine Minister of Finance on January 17, 1975," January 23, 1975, File 1770941, Contacts with Member Countries-Argentina-Corresp. 02, Records of President McNamara, WBGA.

165. Office Memorandum, Alter to McNamara, January 15, 1975.

166. "Argentina Announces Preliminary Pact with Citibank for $250 million Credit," *The New York Times*, June 24, 1975.

167. "The Greatest Violence Has Been Done to Purchasing Power," *The New York Times*, October 19, 1975.

168. Jorge del Canto to Acting Managing Director, "Argentina," Confidential Office Memorandum, June 23, 1975, Box 7, Files 1–3, File title 810, File 33, CFC–Argentina, IMF Archives.

169. Federico Marongiu, "Políticas de Shock en la Agonía del Estado Peronista: El Rodrigazo y el Mondelliazo," 2006, MPRA paper 6338, http://mpra.ub.uni-muenchen.de/6338

170. *Memoria Anual Banco Central de la República Argentina 1975*, 85–88.

171. *El Economista*, February 27, 1976.

172. Office Memorandum, Greene to Wiese, "Argentina-Progress of the Government's Program," January 28, 1976, File 1592307, Argentina—General—Corresp. 1975/1977 Correspondence Vol. 1, WBGA.

173. Ibid.

174. "Argentina," *Latin American Economy & Business*, June 4, 1976, http://www.latinnews.com/search.html?id=80&archive=22605&search=World%20Bank%20AND%20Argentina&content_match=negative.

175. Office Memorandum, Wiese to Krieger Vasena, "Briefing for Your Meeting with Martínez de Hoz, June 16, 1976," June 16, 1976, File 1770941, Contacts with Member Countries-Argentina-Corresp. 02, Records of President McNamara, WBGA.

176. Transcript of Interview with Gerald Alter Held on November 13, 1990, WB Oral History Project, http://documents.worldbank.org/curated/en/921351467988951622/pdf/103395-TRANSC-Oral-interview-Brookings-Alter-PUBLIC.pdf.

Chapter Five

1. Acknowledgment: This chapter is derived in part from an article published in The International History Review on October 25, 2018, copyright Taylor & Francis, available online: http://www.tandfonline.com. https://doi.org/10.1080/07075332.2018.1508052. On superpowers détente, see, among others, Raymond Garthoff, *Détente and Confrontation: American-Soviet Relations from Nixon to Reagan* (Washington, DC.: Brookings Institute, 1985); Jussi M. Hanhimäki, "Ironies and Turning Points: Détente in Perspective," in *Reviewing the Cold War: Approaches, Interpretations, Theory,* ed. Odd Arne Westad (London: Frank Cass, 2000), 326–42; and Jeremi Suri, *Power and Protest: Global Revolution and the Rise of Détente* (Cambridge, MA: Harvard University Press, 2003). On European Détente, see, among others, Oliver Bange and Poul Villaume, eds., *The Long Détente: Changing Concepts of Security and Cooperation in Europe, 1950s–1980s* (Budapest: Central European University Press, 2017); and Jussi M. Hanhimäki, "Détente in Europe, 1962–1975," in *The Cambridge History of the Cold War. Volume 2: Crises and Détente,* eds. Melvyn P. Leffler and Odd Arne Westad (London: Cambridge University Press, 2010), 198–218.

2. Vanni Pettiná, *La Guerra Fría en América Latina* (México: El Colegio de México, 2018), 129–35.

3. Vanessa Walker, *Principles in Power: Latin America and the Politics of U.S. Human Rights Diplomacy* (Ithaca: Cornell University Press, 2020), 1–6, 154–55.

4. The first "boom" is associated with the 1940s and the incorporation of more than a half-dozen references to human rights in the Charter of the United Nations established in 1945, and the signing of the Universal Declaration of Human Rights (UDHR) in Paris in 1948. See, among others, Barbara Keys and Roland Burke, "Human Rights," in *The Oxford Handbook of the Cold War,* eds. Richard H. Immerman and Petra Goedde (Oxford University Press, 2013), 486–502; and Samuel Moyn, "The Return of the Prodigal: The 1970s as a Turning Point in Human Rights History," in *The Breakthrough: Human Rights in the 1970s,* eds. Jan Eckel and Samuel Moyn (Pennsylvania: Univeristy of Pennsylvania Press, 2014), 1–14.

5. Rosemary Foot, "The Cold War and Human Rights," in *The Cambridge History of the Cold War. Vol. III,* eds. Melvyn P. Leffler and Odd Arne Westad (Cambridge University Press, 2010), 445–65; Sarah B. Snyder, "Human Rights and the Cold War," in *The Routledge Handbook of the Cold War,* eds. Artemy M. Kalinovsky and Craig Daigle (London: Routledge, 2014), 237–48.

6. Yong Kyun Kim and Daniel C. O'Neill, "Transparent Motives: Democratic Advantage in International Credit Markets," *Journal of International Relations and Development* 20, no. 1 (2017): 108–32, https://doi.org/:10.1057/jird.2015.1; Kenneth A. Schultz and Barry R. Weingast, "The Democratic Advantage: Institutional Foundations of Financial Power in International Competition," *International Organization* 57, no. 1 (2003): 3–42, https://www.jstor.org/stable/3594824.

7. Sebastian M. Saiegh, "Do Countries Have a 'Democratic Advantage'? Political Institutions, Multilateral Agencies, and Sovereign Borrowing," *Comparative Political Studies* 38, no. 4 (2005): 366–87, https://doi.org/10.1177/0010414004273204; Adam Przeworski, *Democracy and the Market: Political and Economic Reforms in Eastern Europe and Latin America* (New York: Cambridge University Press, 1991); Beth A. Simmons, *Who Adjusts? Domestic Sources of Foreign Economic Policy During the Interwar Years* (Princeton: Princeton University Press, 1997).

8. On legal and moral aspects of WB lending, see, among others, John Ciorciari, "The Lawful Scope of Human Rights Criteria in World Bank Credit Decisions: An Interpretive Analysis of the IBRD and IDA Articles of Agreement," *Cornell International Law Journal*, 33, no. 2 (2000): 330–71, https://www.researchgate.net/publication/290288286_The_Lawful_Scope_of_Human_Rights_Criteria_in_World_Bank_Credit_Decisions_An_Interpretive_Analysis_of_the_IBRD_and_IDA_Articles_of_Agreement; Roberto Dañino, "The Legal Aspects of the World Bank's Work on Human Rights," *The International Lawyer* 41, no. 1 (2007): 21–25, https://www.jstor.org/stable/40708088; Halim Moris, "The World Bank and Human Rights: Indispensable Partnership or Mismatched Alliance?," *ILSA Journal of International & Comparative Law* 4 (1997): 173–200, https://nsuworks.nova.edu/cgi/viewcontent.cgi?article=1117&context=ilsajournal; Joel E. Oestreich, "The Human Rights Responsibilities of the World Bank: A Business Paradigm," *Global Social Policy* 4, no. 1 (2004): 55–76, https://doi.org/10.1177/1468018104040985.

9. In line with Galit Sarfaty's claims, my research shows that the Bank lacks a policy aimed at mitigating the impact of its development supported projects on human rights. Furthermore, its staff has not been required to consider governments' obligations under international human rights law when engaging in loan negotiations, and it has no guidelines to determine when it should suspend operations due to human rights violations. See Galit A. Sarfaty, "Why Culture Matters in International Institutions: The Marginality of Human Rights at the World Bank," *American Society of International Law* 102 (2008): 71–74, https://www.jstor.org/stable/25660269.

10. James Lebovic and Erik Voeten, "The Cost of Shame: International Organisations and Foreign Aid in the Punishing of Human Rights Violators,"

Journal of Peace Research 46, no. 1 (2009): 79–97, https://www.jstor.org/stable/27640800; Sebastian M. Saiegh, "Do Countries have a 'Democratic Advantage'? Political Institutions, Multilateral Agencies, and Sovereign Borrowing," *Comparative Political Studies* 38, no 4 (2005): 366–87, https://doi.org/10.1177/0010414004273204.

11. M. Rodwan Abouharb and David L. Cingranelli, "The Human Rights Effects of World Bank Structural Adjustment, 1981–2000," *International Studies Quarterly* 50, no. 2 (2006): 233–62, https://doi.org/10.1111/j.1468-2478.2006.00401.x.

12. David Bradlow, "The World Bank, the IMF, and Human Rights," *Transnational Law & Contemporary Problems* 6, no. 47 (1996): 47–90, https://digitalcommons.wcl.american.edu/cgi/viewcontent.cgi?article=1942&context=facsch_lawrev

13. "Washington Is Pleased," *The New York Times,* May 22, 1969; Claudia Kedar, "The World Bank-United States-Latin American Triangle: The Negotiations with Socialist Chile, 1970–1973," *The International History Review* 39, no. 4 (2017): 667–90, https://doi.org/10.1080/07075332.2016.1239587.

14. Acta Fijando el Propósito y los Objetivos Básicos para el Proceso de Reorganización Nacional, March 24, 1976. *Documentos Básicos y Bases Políticas de las Fuerzas Armadas para el Proceso de Reorganización Nacional* (Buenos Aires, 1980), 7–8.

15. Klaus Friedrich Veigel, *Dictatorship, Democracy, and Globalization: Argentina and the Cost of Paralysis, 1973–2001* (Pennsylvania: Pennsylvania State University Press, 2009), 48–50.

16. Jeffrey M. Chwieroth, "'The Silent Revolution': How the Staff Exercise Informal Governance Over IMF Lending," *The Review of International Organizations* 8, no. 3 (2013): 265–90, https://doi.org/10.1007/s11558-012-9154-9.

17. Adolfo Canitrot, "La Disciplina Como Objetivo de la Política Económica. Un Ensayo Sobre el Programa Económico del Gobierno Argentino Desde 1976," *Desarrollo Económico* 19, no. 76 (1980): 453–75, https://doi.org/10.2307/3466561; Raúl García Heras, "The Return of International Finance and the Martínez de Hoz Plan in Argentina, 1976–1978," *Latin American Research Review* 53, no. 4 (2018): 799–814, https://www.jstor.org/stable/e26744344.

18. Mario Rapoport, "La Saga de los Martínez de Hoz y el Banquero Arrepentido," *Buenos Aires Económico,* May 5, 2010.

19. José Martínez de Hoz, *Bases para una Argentina Moderna, 1976–1980* (Buenos Aires: Compañía Impresora Argentina S.A., 1981), 17 and chap. 4; Veigel, *Dictatorship, Democracy,* 50–53; Bruno M. Nápoli, Celeste Perosino, and Walter Bosisio, *La Dictadura del Capital Financiero: El Golpe Militar Corporativo y la Trama Bursátil* (Buenos Aires: Ediciones Continente, 2014), 49–51.

20. Stephen G. Rabe, *The Killing Zone: The United States Cold War in Latin America,* (Oxford: Oxford University Press, 2016), 150–55.

21. William Schmidli, "Institutionalizing Human Rights in U.S. Foreign Policy: U.S.-Argentine Relations, 1976–1980," *Diplomatic History* 35, no. 2 (2011): 351–77, https://www.jstor.org/stable/24916482.

22. Secretary of State to Embassy in Buenos Aires, "Secretary's Reply to Foreign Minister's Letter," Oct. 11, 1979, Argentina Project (S200000044) US State Department (AK314); "Atentado Contra un Alto Funcionario de Argentina," *El Día,* September 28, 1979.

23. "El General Videla Escapa a un Nuevo Atentado," *El País,* February 19, 1977.

24. "Argentina Unveils Its Political Plan," Dec. 27, 1979, Argentina Project (S200000044) US State Department (AK357).

25. William Schmidli, *The Fate of Freedom Elsewhere: Human Rights and the U.S. Cold War Policy Toward Argentina* (Ithaca: Cornell University Press, 2013), 4–5.

26. Katherine Sikkink, *Mixed Signals: U.S. Human Rights Policy and Latin America* (Ithaca: Cornell University Press, 2004), 148–51.

27. Walker, *Principles in Power,* 205–207.

28. Alberto Sola (Alternate Executive Director for Chile) to the Office of the President, April 5, 1982, File 1774556, Argentina—General 1981–1986, Correspondence 03, Records of the Office of the President Tom Clausen, WBGA.

29. William Clark, "Robert McNamara at the World Bank," *Foreign Affairs* 60, no. 1 (1981): 167–84, https://www.proquest.com/scholarly-journals/robert-mcnamara-at-world-bank/docview/198248240/se-2.

30. Edmar L. Bacha and Richard E. Feinberg, "The World Bank and Structural Adjustment in Latin America," *World Development* 14, no. 3 (1986): 333–46, https://doi.org/10.1016/0305-750X(86)90073-2; Catherine Weaver, *Hypocrisy Trap: The World Bank and the Poverty of Reform* (Princeton, NJ: Princeton University Press, 2008), 150–57.

31. "Congress Changes Its View on International Lending Agencies," *The New York Times,* May 27, 1979.

32. Sharma, "United States," 596; Schmidli, *The Fate of Freedom Elsewhere,* 26–28.

33. Robert Cox, "Ideologies and the New International Economic Order: Reflections on Some Recent Literature," *International Organization* 33, no. 2 (1979): 257–302, https://www.jstor.org/stable/2706612; Nils Gilman, "The New International Economic Order: A Reintroduction," *Humanity: An International Journal of Human Rights, Humanitarianism, and Development* 6, no. 1 (2015): 1–16, https://www.researchgate.net/publication/276938153_The_New_International_Economic_Order_A_Reintroduction; Jorge Lozoya and Jaime Estevez, eds.,

Latin American and the New International Economic Order (New York: Pergamum Press, 1980), chap. 2.

34. Patrick Sharma, "Between North and South: The World Bank and the New International Economic Order," *Humanity: An International Journal of Human Rights, Humanitarianism, and Development* 6, no. 1 (2015): 189–200, http://dx.doi.org/10.1353/hum.2015.0006.

35. Weaver, *Hypocrisy Trap*, 69–72.

36. David Forsythe, *Human Rights and U.S. Foreign Policy: Congress Reconsidered* (Gainesville: University Press of Florida, 1988), 7–9; Schmidli, *Fate of Freedom*, 59–66.

37. Forsythe, *Human Rights*, 10.

38. Sikkink, *Mixed Signals*, 106–107.

39. "Carter Is Rebuffed by House on Rights," *The New York Times*, April 7, 1977.

40. Babb, *Behind the Development Banks*, 184.

41. Jochen Kraske et al., *Bankers with a Mission: The Presidents of the World Bank, 1946–91* (New York: Oxford University Press and World Bank, 1996), 221–30.

42. EBM/76/52 (IMF Archives).

43. Office Memorandum, "Argentina—New Economic Measures," M. Hardy to J. del Canto, April 5, 1976, Argentina Subseries, Country Files Series, Central Files, Box 8, Files 1–24, File title 810–818, File 1; IMF Archives.

44. Interview with José Martínez de Hoz, 11 Oct. 2005 (Part 1, tape 1), Instituto Gino Germani, University of Buenos Aires (UBA); Paula Canelo, "La Política Contra la Economía: Los Elencos Militares Frente al Plan Económico de Martínez de Hoz Durante el Proceso de Reorganización Nacional (1976–1981)," in *Empresarios, Tecnócratas y Militares. La Trama Corporativa de la Última Dictadura*, ed. Alfredo Pucciarelli (Buenos Aires: Siglo XXI, 2004), 219–312.

45. The term "Chicago Boys" has been used to describe Latin American economists who enrolled in graduate programs and/or identified with the liberal economic theories taught at the University of Chicago by Milton Friedman and Arnold Harberger, although some of them earned degrees at Harvard University or MIT. They advocated widespread deregulation, privatization, structural reforms, and other free-market policies.

46. Mariana Heredia, "El Proceso Como Bisagra. Emergencia y Consolidación del Liberalismo Tecnocrático: FIEL, FM y CEMA," in *Empresarios, Tecnócratas y Militares. La Trama Corporativa de la Última Dictadura*, Alfredo Pucciarelli (Buenos Aires: Siglo XXI, 2004), 313–82.

47. Entrevista a Norberto Galasso, *Página 12*, June 21, 2004, "Observatorio de la Deuda en la Globalización," www.observatoriodeuda.org.; Interview with José Martínez de Hoz, October 11, 2005 (Part 1, tape 1).

48. José Martínez de Hoz, *Quince Años Después,* (Buenos Aires: Emecé, 1991), intro. and chap. 5; Carlos Palacio Deheza, *El Plan Martínez de Hoz y la Economía Argentina* (Buenos Aires: Corregidor, 1981), chaps 2–3.

49. Naomi Klein, *The Shock Doctrine: The Rise of Disaster Capitalism* (New York: Picador, 2008), 108.

50. "Discurso del Dr. Martínez de Hoz, en Ocasión de Celebrarse el Día de la Industria," *Boletín Semanal del Ministerio de Economía,* No. 146, September 10, 1976.

51. These accomplices were businessmen, bankers, and companies that supplied goods and/or services to the dictatorship or obtained benefits from it while they provided political support in return. Horacio Verbitsky and Juan Pablo Bohoslavsky, eds., *The Economic Accomplices to the Argentine Dictatorship: Outstanding Debts* (New York: Cambridge University Press, 2016).

52. "Reuniones con el FMI y el BIRF," *La Nación,* May 28, 1976; "Tono Cordial en Gestiones con el FMI y el BIRF," *La Nación,* May 29, 1976.

53. Office Memorandum, Wiese to Krieger Vasena, "Briefing for Your Meeting with Martínez de Hoz, June 16, 1976," June 16, 1976, File 1770941, Contacts with Member Countries-Argentina-Corresp. 02, Records of President McNamara, World Bank Group Archive (Hereinafter: WBGA).

54. Ibid.

55. Vito Tanzi, *Argentina: An Economic Chronicle. How One of the Richest Countries in the World Lost Its Wealth* (New York: Jorge Pinto Books, Inc., 2007), chap. 2.

56. "Martínez de Hoz con el FMI," *La Nación,* June 17, 1976.

57. "Éxito Global de la Misión en EE.UU.," *La Nación,* June 19, 1976.

58. "Refinánciase la Deuda Externa," *La Nación,* June 22, 1976.

59. Office Memorandum, Wiese to Files, "Visit of Minister Martínez de Hoz," June 18, 1976, File 1770941, Contacts with Member Countries-Argentina-Corresp. 02, Records of President McNamara, WBGA.

60. Ibid.

61. Letter of Intent, Martínez de Hoz and Diz to Witteveen, July 8, 1976, Argentina Subseries, Country Files Series, Central Files, Box 19, Files 1–10, File title 1760, File 7; IMF Archives.

62. EBS/76/340, Supplement 1, Annexed to "Argentina–Stand-By Arrangement," August 9, 1976, IMF Archives; "El Fondo Monetario Otorgó un Crédito a la Argentina," *La Nación,* August 7, 1976.

63. "El Fondo Monetario Internacional Otorgó un Importante Crédito a la Argentina," *Boletín Semanal del Ministerio de Economía,* No. 142, August 13, 1976.

64. Interview with José Martínez de Hoz, October 18, 2005 (Part 2), Instituto Gino Germani, UBA.

65. "Las Gestiones Financieras Internacionales," *Boletín Semanal del Ministerio de Economía,* No. 150, October 8, 1976.

66. *Argentina—Fourth Buenos Aires Power Project,* September 30, 1976. Project Memorandum and Recommendation of the President of the IBRD, http://documents.worldbank.org/curated/en/371551468221411345/pdf/multiopage.pdf.

67. Ibid.

68. Department of State, "Ambassador Discusses US-Argentine Relations with President Videla," September 24, 1976, *Argentina Declassification Project* (1975–1984), https://foia.state.gov.

69. *Argentina—Fourth Highway Project,* March 3, 1977, Project Memorandum and Recommendation of the President of the IBRD, http://documents.worldbank.org/curated/en/159041468001144861/pdf/multiopage.pdf.

70. Transcript of Meeting of the Executive Directors of the IBRD and IDA, Held on Tuesday, March 22, 1977: Argentina—Fourth Highway Project, WBGA.

71. Ibid.

72. Ibid.

73. Michael Franczak, "Human Rights and Basic Needs: Jimmy Carter's North-South Dialogue, 1977–81," *Cold War History* 18, no. 4 (2018): 447–64, https://www.doi.org/10.1080/14682745.2018.1468437.

74. Transcript of Meeting of the Executive Directors of the IBRD and IDA, Held on Tuesday, March 22, 1977.

75. Ibid.

76. Department of State, May 23, 1977, "Argentina—Human Rights,"*Argentina Declassification Project* (1975–1984, https://foia.state.gov; "US Links Aid to Argentina Rights," *The New York Times,* June 1, 1977.

77. Ibid.

78. Knapp to Files, "Argentina—Human Rights," June 7, 1977, File 1592307, Argentina—General—Corresp. 1975/1977 Correspondence Vol. 1, WBGA.

79. Department of State, "Argentina Note Human Rights Improvements in Order to Influence US Votes in IFIs," June 16, 1977, *Argentina Declassification Project* (1975–1984, https://foia.state.gov.

80. "Argentina," June 24, 1977, Latin American Economy & Business http://www.latinnews.com/search.html?id=80&archive=21716&search=World%20Bank%20AND%20Argentina&content_match=negative.

81. Transcript of Meeting of the Executive Directors of the IBRD and IDA, Held on Thursday, June 16, 1977: Argentina—Industrial Credit Project, WBGA.

82. Ibid.

83. Ibid.

84. Ibid.

85. Timerman was a well-known and influential Argentine publisher, journalist, and author, who is most noted for reporting the atrocities of Argentina's last dictatorship. Timerman was persecuted, tortured, and imprisoned by the

junta in April 1977 and was exiled in 1979 with his wife to Israel. See Graciela Mochkofsky, *Timerman: El Periodista que Quiso Ser Parte del Poder (1923–1999)* (Buenos Aires: Editorial Sudamericana, 2003); Jacobo Timerman, *Prisoner Without a Name, Cell Without a Number* (London: University of Wisconsin Press, 2002).

86. Alejandro Avenburg, "Entre la Presión y el Apoyo: La Política de Derechos Humanos de los Estados Unidos y el Gobierno Militar Argentino (1976–1978)," *Desarrollo Económico* 55, no. 215 (2015): 117–18, http://bibliotecadigital.econ.uba.ar/download/toc/2016/Sep/2890-2015_55_215.pdf.

87. Cohen, *Human Rights Diplomacy,* 227–28.

88. Office Memorandum, Schrere to Records, "Argentina—Meeting with Delegation at Annual Meetings in Washington," October 6, 1977, File 1770941, Contacts with Member Countries-Argentina-Corresp. 02, Records of President McNamara, WBGA.

89. Lucas Iramain and Verónica Pérez, "Rieles y Política Económica Durante la Última Dictadura Cívico-Militar Argentina (1976–1983)," *Sociohistorica* 39 (2017), https://doi.org/10.24215/18521606e021.

90. Schrere to Records, October 6, 1977.

91. Department of State, Terence Todman to Deputy Secretary, February 15, 1978, "U.S. Reaction in IFIs to Argentine Human Rights Action," *Argentina Declassification Project* (1975–1984), https://foia.state.gov.

92. Avenburg, "Entre la Presión," 120–24.

93. Grain Storage Project, February 7, 1978, Project Memorandum and Recommendation of the President of the IBRD, http://documents.worldbank.org/curated/en/399671468003314778/pdf/multi-page.pdf.

94. Transcript of Meeting of the Executive Directors of the IBRD and IDA, Held on Tuesday, February 21, 1978: Argentina—Grain Storage Project. WBGA, http://documents.worldbank.org/curated/en/183761510299146672.

95. Avenburg, "Entre la Presión,"124–26.

96. Agricultural Credit Project, April 26, 1978, Project Memorandum and Recommendation of the President of the IBRD, http://documents.worldbank.org/curated/en/609611468212678681/pdf/multi-page.pdf.

97. Transcript of Meeting of the Executive Directors of the IBRD and IDA, Held on Tuesday, May 9, 1978: Argentina—Agricultural Credit Project. WBGA, http://documents.worldbank.org/curated/en/275201510310067477.

98. Ibid.

99. Sikkink, *Mixed Signals,* 130–33.

100. Viron Vaky to Deputy Secretary, "U.S. Initiatives to Effect Human Rights Improvements in Argentina," March 20, 1979, Unclassified US Department of State Case O-2016-16244, Doc. C06305635.

101. Ibid., 3.

102. Transcript of Meeting of the Executive Directors of the IBRD and IDA, Held on March 27, 1979: Argentina—Second Railway Project, WBGA, http://documents.worldbank.org/curated/en/694481510310849885.

103. Ibid., 4.

104. Ibid., 5.

105. Ibid., 6.

106. Ibid., 14.

107. Transcript of Meeting of the Executive Directors of the IBRD and IDA, Held on Tuesday, October 16, 1979: Argentina—Yacyreta Hydroelectric Project, WBGA, http://documents.worldbank.org/curated/en/970591510311218411.

108. Ibid., 21.

109. Report and Recommendation of the President of the IBRD to the Executive Directors on a Proposed Loan to YPF for an Oil and Gas Engineering Project, June 4, 1980, WBGA, https://documents1.worldbank.org/curated/en/166241468002112448/pdf/multi-page.pdf.

110. Transcript of Meeting of the Executive Directors of the IBRD and IDA, Held on Tuesday, June 24, 1980: Argentina—Oil and Gas Engineering Project, June 24, 1980, WBGA, http://documents.worldbank.org/curated/en/977741510311549424.

111. Ibid., 30.

112. "World Bank Call for Action by Oil Exporters," *Latin American Weekly Report*, September 12, 1980, https://www.latinnews.com/search.html?id=80&archive=5233&search=Argentina%20AND%20World%20Bank&content_match=negative.

113. Report and Recommendation of the President of the IBRD to the Executive Directors on a Proposed Loan to the Argentine Republic for a Vocational Training and Technical Education Project, September 18, 1980, WBGA, https://documents1.worldbank.org/curated/en/581481468204558301/pdf/multi-page.pdf.

114. Palmer to Secretary of State, "US on Multilateral Development Bank Loans to Argentina, Chile and Uruguay," June 26, 1981, Case No. /a. Chile Project (#S199900030), U.S. State Department.

115. "Argentina," June 1, 1983, Argentina Project (S200000044), U.S. State Department (AJ002).

116. Secretary of State to Embassy Asunción, "Visit to Argentina of Ambassador J. W. Middendorf," July 25, 1981, Unclassified U.S. Department of State Case O-2016-16244, Doc. C06295275.

117. Ibid., 4–5.

118. Transcript of Meeting of the Executive Directors of the IBRD and IDA, Held on Tuesday, July 7, 1981: Argentina—Oil and Gas Credit, and Refinery Conversion, WBGA, http://documents.worldbank.org/curated/en/572181510572473308.

119. Ibid.

120. Ibid.

121. Ibid.

122. Transcript of Meeting of the Executive Directors of the IBRD and IDA, Held on Tuesday, December 1, 1981: Argentina—Second Industrial Credit Project, WBGA, http://documents.worldbank.org/curated/en/455891510572901708.

123. Ibid.

124. Office Memorandum, Nissembaum (Loan Officer), "Argentina-Change in Government," January 18, 1982, File 1592458, Argentina—General 1981–1983, Correspondence, Vol. 1, WBGA.

125. Kraske et al., *Bankers with a Mission,* p. 221.

126. Confidential Office Memorandum, Philippe Bourcier to Yves Rovani, "Argentina and Colombia—Petroleum Projects," February 3, 1983, File 1774556, Argentina—General 1981–1986, Correspondence 03, Records of the Office of the President, WBGA.

127. "Brazil Fights for the Right to Stay in Kindergarten," *Latin American Weekly Report,* October 9, 1981, https://www.latinnews.com/search.html?id=80&archive=41782&search=Argentina%20AND%20World%20Bank&content_match=negative.

128. "Brazil," *Latin American Weekly Report,* February 12, 1982, https://www.latinnews.com/search.html?id=80&archive=43361&search=Argentina%20AND%20World%20Bank&content_match=negative.

129. Embassy in Buenos Aires to Secretary of State, "Politics Not as Usual," March 22, 1982, Unclassified U.S. Department of State Case O-2016-16244, Doc. C06295233, https://www.archives.gov/files/argentina/data/docid-33069106.pdf.

130. "Reagan Sees Argentina Paying Debts," *The New York Times,* May 5, 1982.

131. "Foreign Debt: Tense Talks with the Bankers," *Brazil and Southern Cone,* July 30, 1982, https://www.latinnews.com/search.html?id=80&archive=45616&search=Argentina%20AND%20World%20Bank&content_match=negative.

132. "Dagnino Pastore da un Giro de 180 Grados a la Política Económica Argentina," *El País,* July 7, 1982.

133. Embassy in Buenos Aires to Secretary of State, "Where to on Argentine Debt Issue," August 25, 1982, Unclassified U.S. Department of State Case O-2016-16244, Doc. C06210493, https://www.archives.gov/files/argentina/data/docid-33069106.pdf.

134. "Wehbe Confident of Gaining Breathing Space," *Latin American Weekly Report,* September 10, 1982, https://www.latinnews.com/search.html?id=80&archive=46039&search=Argentina%20AND%20World%20Bank&content_match=negative.

135. Memorandum for the Record, "Meeting Between Clausen and Minister Wehbe," September 5, 1982, File 1774556, Argentina—General 1981–1986, Correspondence 03, Records of the Office of the President, WBGA.

136. "La Renegociación de la Deuda Externa Argentina, a Punto de Alcanzar un Resultado Definitivo," *El País*, October 24, 1982; "Argentina Agrees on Spending Cuts to Get IMF Loan," *The New York Times*, October 28, 1982.

137. Convenio de Financiamniento Compensatorio por Caída de Exportaciones de 1983, January 11, 1983, BCRA, http://www.bcra.gov.ar/Pdfs/Institucional/13-CFF-83.pdf

138. Carta del 07/01/1983 del Ministro de Economía Argentino, Jorge Wehbe, y del Presidente del BCRA, Julio González del Solar, al Director General del FMI, Jacques de Larosiere, January 27, 1983, BCRA, http://www.bcra.gov.ar/Pdfs/Institucional/14-SB-83.pdf.

139. "Talks on Loans to Argentina," *The New York Times*, December 31, 1982.

140. Office Memorandum, "Meeting of Clausen with the Argentine Delegation," Scherer for the Record, February 15, 1983, File 1774556, Argentina—General 1981–1986, Correspondence 03, Records of the Office of the President, WBGA.

141. Ibid.

142. Ibid.

143. Letter, Wehbe to Clausen, February 14, 1983, File 1774556, Argentina—General 1981–1986, Correspondence 03, Records of the Office of the President, WBGA.

144. Letter, Clausen to Wehbe, March 7, 1983, File 1774556, Argentina—General 1981–1986, Correspondence 03, Records of the Office of the President, WBGA.

145. "Argentina: A Troubled Transition," CIA Document, May 20, 1983, Unclassified U.S. Department of State, Case No. O-2016-16244 Doc. No. C06272699.

146. Transcript of Meeting of the Executive Directors of the IBRD and IDA, Held on Tuesday, May 31, 1983, WBGA, http://documents.worldbank.org/curated/en/883971510574765554.

147. Ibid.

148. Ibid.

149. "Washington Is Pleased," *The New York Times*, May 22, 1969.

150. John Gaddis, "On Starting All Over Again: A Naïve Approach to Studying the Cold War," in *Reviewing the Cold War: Approaches, Interpretations, Theory*, ed. Odd Arne Westad (London: Frank Cass, 2000), 30–32.

151. Ibid.; William D. James, "Influencing the United States: Is the Game Worth the Candle for Junior Allies?," *International Politics* 59, no. 2 (2022):1029–44, https://doi.org/10.1057/s41311-021-00331-2; Robert O. Keohane, "The Big Influence of Small Allies," *Foreign Policy*, no. 2 (1971): 161–82, https://doi.org/10.2307/1147864.

Chapter Six

1. Fritz Bartel, *The Triumph of Broken Promises: The End of the Cold War and the Rise of Neoliberalism* (Cambridge, MA: Harvard University Press, 2022), 6.

2. Among the most recent publications on the end of the Cold War, see Fritz Bartel, *The Triumph of Broken Promises: The End of the Cold War and the Rise of Neoliberalism* (Cambridge, MA: Harvard University Press, 2022); Archie Brown, *The Human Factor: Gorbachev, Reagan, and Thatcher, and the End of the Cold War* (New York: Oxford University Press, 2020); Simon Miles, *Engaging the Evil Empire: Washington, Moscow, and the Beginning of the End of the Cold War* (Ithaca: Cornell University Press, 2020); and Robert Service, *The End of the Cold War, 1985–1991* (New York, PublicAffairs, 2015).

3. Office Memorandum, Kutaly Ebiri to Mario Artaza-Rouxel, "Argentina-Social Sector: The Political Implications," December 11, 1986, File 1592501, Argentina—General 1984–1986, Correspondence 01, WBGA.

4. John Williamson, "What Washington Means by Policy Reform," in *Latin American Adjustment: How Much Has Happened?*, ed. John Williamson (Washington, DC: Institute for International Economics, 1990).

5. Among the seminal and recent studies on the origins of neoliberalism, see Johanna Bockman, *Markets in the Name of Socialism: The Left-Wing Origins of Neoliberalism* (Stanford: Stanford University Press, 2011); Ben Clift, *The IMF and the Politics of Austerity in the Wake of the Global Financial Crisis* (Oxford: Oxford University Press, 2018); Quinn Slobodian, *Globalists: The End of Empire and the Birth of Neoliberalism* (Cambridge, MA: Harvard University Press, 2018).

6. Sarah Babb, "The Washington Consensus as Transnational Policy Paradigm: Its Origins, Trajectory and Likely Successor," *Review of International Political Economy*, 20, no. 2 (2012): 268–97, https://doi.org/10.1080/09692290.2011.640435.

7. Svetlana Savranskaya, "Gorvachev and the Third World," in *The End of the Cold War and the Third World: New Perspectives on Regional Conflict*, eds. Artemy Kalinovsky and Sergey Radchenko (London: Routledge, 2011), 21–46.

8. Jorge Schvarzer, "Orígenes Poco Mencionados de la Deuda Externa de América Latina," *Caravelle* 50 (1988): 11–33, https://www.jstor.org/stable/i40038148.

9. Ibid., 16–17.

10. Mario Rapoport, "La Deuda Externa Argentina y la Soberanía Jurídica: Sus Razones Históricas," *Ciclos en la Historia, la Economía y la Sociedad* 22, no. 43 (2014), http://www.scielo.org.ar/scielo.php?script=sci_arttext&pid=S1851-37352014000100001&lng=es&tlng=es.

11. Ibid., 9–10.

12. Savranskaya, "Gorvachev and the Third World," 21–46.

13. María Cecilia Míguez, *Los Partidos Políticos y la Política Exterior Argentina* (Buenos Aires: Ariel, 2013), 35–37.

14. "Robledo: No Entusiasma Este Apoyo al Presidente," *Clarín,* December 12, 1985; "El Plan Baker Rumbo a Quito y Buenos Aires," *Clarín,* December 13, 1985.

15. "U.S. Shift on Latin Debt Seen as a Turning Point in Crisis," *The New York Times,* October 3, 1985.

16. Working Paper, "The Baker Plan. Progress, Shortcomings, and Future," August 1989, International Economics Department, WBGA, https://documents1.worldbank.org/curated/en/512631468764360794/pdf/multiopage.pdf.

17. Ibid.

18. "Voluntad de Conciliar," *Clarín,* December 16, 1985.

19. Manuel Monteagudo, "The Debt Problem: The Baker Plan and the Brady Initiative: A Latin American Perspective," *The International Lawyer* 28, no. 1 (1994): 59–81, https://www.jstor.org/stable/40707125; Neil Shenai and Marijn A. Bolhuis, "How the Brady Plan Delivered on Debt Relief: Lessons and Implications," *IMF Working Paper* 23, no. 258 (2023), https://www.elibrary.imf.org/view/journals/001/2023/258/article-A001-en.xml#:~:text=In%20March%201989%2C%20U.S.%20Treasury,for%20greater%20assurances%20about%20debtors'.

20. Alfonsín sought to establish civilian control over the military and hold them accountable for human rights abuses. He strove to cut the military budget and downsize the armed forces to a level commensurate with an underdeveloped and democratic nation at peace. Between 1983 and 1986, defense expenditures dropped by 40 percent, legal actions against human rights violators within the officer ranks were initiated, and a new defense law was ratified. See David Pion-Berlin, "Between Confrontation and Accommodation: Military and Government Policy in Democratic Argentina," *Journal of Latin American Studies* 23, no. 3 (1991): 543–71, https://doi.org/10.1017/S0022216X00015844.

21. Military uprisings took place between 1987 and 1990. While these rebellions did not result in the overthrow of democratic governance, the passing of the "Full Stop Law" (*Ley de Punto Final*) in December 1986, and the "Law of Due Obedience" (*Ley de Obediencia Debida*) in June 1987, exempted part of the military personnel from responsibility for the crimes committed during the dictatorship. See, among others, Wendy Hunter, "Negotiating Civil-Military Relations in Post-Authoritarian Argentina and Chile," *International Studies Quarterly* 42, no. 2 (1998): 295–317, https://www.jstor.org/stable/2600782; and Deborah Norden, "The Rise of the Lieutenant Colonels: Rebellion in Argentina and Venezuela," *Latin American Perspectives* 23, no. 3 (1996): 74–86, https://www.jstor.org/stable/2634108.

22. William Smith, *Authoritarianism and the Crisis of the Argentine Political Economy* (Stanford: Stanford University Press, 1989), 270; Julieta Pesce, "La Gestión del Ministro Grinspun en un Contexto de Transición Democrática. Errores de Diagnóstico y Subestimación del Poder Económico Local e Internacional," *Ciclos en la Historia, la Economía y la Sociedad* 14, no. 28 (2004): 65–88, http://bibliotecadigital.econ.uba.ar/download/ciclos/ciclos_v14_n28_03.pdf.

23. "A Seis Meses de Asumir, el Gobierno de Raúl Alfonsín Hizo el Lanzamiento de las Cajas PAN, el Gran Antecedente," *La Nación*, June 15, 2003; Jennifer Adair, *In Search of the Lost Decade: Everyday Rights in Post-Dictatorship Argentina* (Berkeley: University of California Press, 2019), 46–47.

24. Kurt Weyland, "Neopopulism and Neoliberalism in Latin America: How Much Affinity?," *Third World Quarterly* 24, no. 6 (2003): 1095–1115, https://www.jstor.org/stable/1555484.

25. Embassy in Buenos Aires to Secretary of State, "Views of Alfonsín," May 13, 1983, Unclassified US Department of State, Case O-2016-16244, Doc. C06295060.

26. Stephen Kaplan, *Globalization and Austerity Politics in Latin America* (Cambridge: Cambridge University Press, 2013), 227; Klaus Friedrich Veigel, *Dictatorship, Democracy, and Globalization: Argentina and the Cost of Paralysis, 1973–2001* (University Park, Pennsylvania: Pennsylvania State University Press, 2009), 130.

27. Argentina—Cancellation of Stand-By Arrangement, January 31, 1984, EBS/84/23, IMF Archives.

28. Letter of Intent, September 18, 1984, EBS/84/203, IMF Archives.

29. "Kohl Asks Argentine Austerity," *The New York Times*, July 9, 1984.

30. A heterodox plan involves a reasonable balance between prices and income policy, on the one hand, and a direct attack against the underlying causes of inflation, on the other. Heterodox plans are based on a temporary price freeze designed to thwart widespread inflationary expectations, as well as on state intervention.

31. James M. Boughton, *Silent Revolution: The International Monetary Fund 1979–1989* (Washington D.C.: The International Monetary Fund, 2001), 399.

32. Kurt Weyland, *The Politics of Market Reform in Fragile Democracies: Argentina, Brazil, Peru, and Venezuela* (New Jersey: Princeton University Press, 2002), 82–83; José Luis Machinea, "Stabilisation Under Alfonsín," in *Argentina in the Crisis Years (1983–1990): From Alfonsín to Menem*, eds. Colin M. Lewis and Nissa Torrents (London: The Institute of Latin American Studies, 1993), 124–43.

33. Kaplan, *Globalization and Austerity Politics*, 228.

34. María Dolores Rocca Rivarola, "Protagonista Opositor, Peronista Desplazado: La Confederación General del Trabajo Durante el Gobierno de Raúl Alfonsín," *Revista Mexicana de Ciencias Políticas y Sociales* 51, no. 207 (2009): 137–54, http://www.scielo.org.mx/scielo.php?script=sci_arttext&pid=S0185-19182009000300008&lng=es&nrm=iso.

35. "The Chairman's Summing-Up at the Conclusion of the 1985 Article IV Consultation with Argentina," EBM/86/43 (March 10, 1986), SUR/86/26, IMF Archives.

36. Rock, *Argentina, 1516–1987,* 400–403.

37. Adair, *In Search of the Lost Decade,* 107–108.

38. Patrick Sharma, *Robert McNamara's Other War: The World Bank and International Development* (Philadelphia: University of Pennsylvania Press, 2017), 140.

39. Federico Pachetti, "A Merger of Equals: The Political Economy of the World Bank's Early Contacts with China," *Journal of Global History* 19, no. 1 (2023): 98–117, https://doi.org/10.1017/S1740022823000281.

40. Office Memorandum, Geoffrey Lamb to Files, "In Confidence: McNamara and Gorvachev," January 21, 1991, Records of the Office of the Vice President, Development Economics and Chief Economist and Later Senior Vice President, Development Economics and Chief Economist (DECVP), Soviet—General—January 1991, Folder ID 30382299, WBGA.

41. Board Paper. Geoff Lamb. "World Bank Group Technical Assistance in the Soviet Union," January 22, 1991, Records of the Office of the Vice President, Development Economics and Chief Economist and later Senior Vice President, Development Economics and Chief Economist (DECVP), Soviet—General—January 1991, Folder ID 30382299, WBGA.

42. Kraske et al., *Bankers with a Mission,* 228–29.

43. Babb, *Behind the Development Banks,* 81–83.

44. "Can He Turn the World Bank Around?," *Washington Post,* June 11, 1986.

45. Kraske et al., *Bankers with a Mission,* 261–62.

46. Patrick Sharma, "Bureaucratic Imperatives and Policy Outcomes: The Origins of World Bank Structural Adjustment Lending," *Review of International Political Economy* 20, no. 4 (2013): 667 –86, https://doi.org/10.1080/09692290.2012.689618.

47. Kraske et al., *Bankers with a Mission,* 230–33.

48. Sarah Babb and Bruce Garruthers, "Conditionality: Forms, Functions, and History," *Annual Review of Law and Social Science* 4 (2008): 13–29, https://doi.org/10.1146/annurev.lawsocsci.4.110707.172254.

49. Babb, *Behind the Development Banks,* 83–91.

50. Transcript of Oral History Interview with A. W. Clausen Held on June 8, 1992, World Bank Oral History Project, https://oralhistory.worldbank.org/en/archive/oralhistory/transcriptdetail/transcript-oral-history-interview-w-clausen-held-june-8-1992.

51. Peter Scherer to Nicolas Ardito Barletta, "Argentina: Elections Results," November 11, 1983, File 1592458, Argentina—General 1981–1983, Correspondence, Vol. 1, WBGA.

52. Ibid.

53. "Mensaje del Señor Presidente de la Nación, Doctor Raúl Alfonsín Dirigido a Todo el País, Delineando la Política Económica y Social del Gobierno,"

December 16, 1983, Recopilación de Discursos, Mensajes y Conferencias de Prensa Efectuados por el Señor Presidente de la Nación, Doctor Raúl Alfonsín, Desde el 10 de Diciembre, 1983, Hasta el 23 de Marzo, 1984 (Buenos Aires: Secretaría de la Nación, 1985), 63–68; "Discurso Pronunciado por el Sr. Presidente de la Nación, Dr. Raúl Alfonsín en el Día del Petróleo," December 13, 1984, Recopilación de Discursos, Mensajes y Conferencias de Prensa Efectuados por el Señor Presidente de la Nación, Doctor Raúl Alfonsín, Desde el 18 de Diciembre, 1984, Hasta el 21 de Marzo, 1985 (Buenos Aires: Secretaría de la Nación, 1985), 17–20.

54. "Argentine-US Relations: First Assessment," Oct. 12, 1984, Unclassified U.S. Department of State Case O-2016-16244 Doc. C06295162.

55. Peter Scherer to Nicolas Ardito Barletta, "Argentina: Elections Results," November 11, 1983.

56. "Mensaje del Señor Presidente de la Nación, Doctor Raúl Alfonsín Haciendo Referencia al Primer Año de Gobierno," December 17, 1984, Recopilación de Discursos, Mensajes y Conferencias de Prensa Efectuados por el Señor Presidente de la Nación, Doctor Raúl Alfonsín, Desde el 13 de Diciembre, 1984, Hasta el 21 de Marzo, 1985 (Buenos Aires: Secretaría de la Nación, 1985), 23–32; "Mensaje del Señor Presidente de la Nación, Doctor Raúl Alfonsín Dirigido a Todo el País, Delineando la Política Económica y Social del Gobierno," December 16, 1983, 64.

57. Peter Scherer to Nicolas Ardito Barletta, "Argentina: Elections Results," November 11, 1983, File 1592458, Argentina—General 1981–1983, Correspondence, Vol. 1, WBGA.

58. Ibid.

59. Office Memorandum, Scherer to Records, "Meeting of the Argentine Delegation with Mr. Clausen," January 16, 1984, File 1774555, Argentina—Clausen Country Files-Correspondence-Vol. 2, Records of President A. W. Clausen, WBGA.

60. Office Memorandum, Peter Scherer to Records, "Meeting of the Argentine Delegation with Clausen on September 22, 1984," October 2, 1984, File 1592503, Argentina-LEAP, Correspondence 84/86-01, WBGA.

61. Office Memorandum, Roberto Chadwick to Files, "Argentina-1984 Annual Meeting," October 9, 1984, File 1592503, Argentina-LEAP, Correspondence 84/86-01, WBGA.

62. Letter, Oscar Oszlak to Peter Scherer, February 23, 1984, File 1592501, Argentina—General 1984–1986, Correspondence 01, WBGA.

63. "Cereals: Big Expansion Planned," *Latin American Economy & Business,* February 24, 1984, https://www.latinnews.com/search.html?id=80&archive=51844&search=Argentina%20AND%20World%20Bank&content_match=negative.

64. "Catching Up with Other Debt News," Latin American Weekly Report, June 8, 1984, https://www.latinnews.com/search.html?id=80&archive=33716&search=Argentina%20AND%20World%20Bank&content_match=negative.

65. "Discurso Pronunciado por el Sr. President de la Nación, Doctor Raúl Alfonsín, Haciendo Referencia a las Gestiones Sobre la Renegociación de la Deuda Externa," April 1, 1984, Recopilación de Discursos, Mensajes y Conferencias de Prensa Efectuados por el Señor Presidente de la Nación, Doctor Raúl Alfonsín, Desde el 1 de Abril, 1984, Hasta el 31 de Mayo, 1984 (Buenos Aires: Secretaría de la Nación, 1985), 5–8.

66. "Argentina Says Accord on Loans is a Triumph," *The New York Times*, April 2, 1984.

67. Claudia Kedar, *The International Monetary Fund and Latin America: The Argentine Puzzle in Context* (Philadelphia: Temple University Press, 2013), 157–58.

68. Confidential Office Memorandum, Scherer to Files, "Meeting with Bankers on Argentina," December 4, 1984, Argentina-Clausen Country Files-Correspondence-Vol. 1, File 1774554, Records of President A. W. Clausen, WBGA.

69. Convenio de Financiamiento Compensatorio for Caída de Exportaciones de 1984, Dec. 4, 1984, BCRA, http://www.bcra.gov.ar/Pdfs/Institucional/15-CFF-84.pdf.

70. "Grinspun Anunció el Acuerdo con el FMI," *Tiempo Argentino*, September 19, 1984; "Argentine Accord on Austerity Plan Accepted at IMF," *The New York Times*, September 26, 1984.

71. Office Memorandum, Scherer to Files, "Argentina: Meeting with President Alfonsín," December 20, 1984, File 1592503, Argentina-LEAP, Correspondence 84/86-01, WBGA.

72. Amnon Mates to Andre Gue, "Argentina-Changes in the Economic Team," March 12, 1985, File 1592503, Argentina-LEAP, Correspondence 84/86-01, WBGA.

73. Office Memorandum Scherer to Knox, "Argentina-Change in Cabinet," February 27, 1985, File 1592501, Argentina—General 1984–1986, Correspondence 01, WBGA.

74. Peter Scherer to Juan Sourrouille, February 28, 1985, File 1592503, Argentina-LEAP, Correspondence 84/86-01, WBGA.

75. Peter Scherer to Records, "Meeting of Clausen with the President of Argentina," March 29, 1985, Argentina-LEAP, Correspondence 84/86-01, WBGA.

76. "Argentine Leader Will Mute Criticism in Requesting Aid from U.S. This Week," *Wall Street Journal*, March 18, 1985.

77. "Reagan Welcomes Argentine Leader," *The New York Times*, March 20, 1985.

78. Secretary of State to Embassy in Buenos Aires, "U.S. Policy, Goals and Objectives in Argentina," June 12, 1985, Unclassified U.S. Department of State Case O-2016-16244 Doc. C06295123.

79. AV-2794, Cadena Nacional: Alfonsín y Sourrouille Presentan el Plan Austral, Parte 1, June 14, 1985, https://www.youtube.com/watch?v=oZ4HAJJu_5g; "Hoy Alfonsín y Sourrouille Anuncian al País Una Audaz Reforma Económica," *Ámbito Financiero*, June 14, 1985.

80. "FMI: Todo Listo para la Firma," *Ámbito Financiero*, June 7, 1985; "Preparan el Pacto con el FMI," *Clarín*, June 9, 1985.

81. Letter Scherer to Machinea, May 9, 1985, Argentina-LEAP, Correspondence 84/86-01, WBGA.

82. Argentina—Gas Utilization and Technical Assistance Project. Memorandum & Recommendation of the President, June 30, 1985, WBGA.

83. Ibid.

84. Transcript of Meeting of the Executive Directors of the IBRD and IDA, Held on Tuesday, June 25, 1985, WBGA, http://documents.worldbank.org/curated/en/662501510577153360.

85. Sokol to Guy Pfefferman, "Argentina—Aide Memoire—Public Sector Investment Review Mission," June 25, 1985, Argentina-LEAP, Correspondence 84/86-01, WBGA.

86. "Argentina-Country Program Paper," June 10, 1985, File 1774555, Argentina-Clausen Country Files-Correspondence-Vol. 2, Records of President A. W. Clausen, WBGA.

87. Office Memorandum, Spiros Voyadzis to Files, "Meeting with Mr. Clausen, Mr. Juan Sourrouille. Friday October 4, 1985," November 27, 1985, Argentina-LEAP, File 166369B General 84/86-02, WBGA

88. "El FMI y el BIRF Apuran a los Bancos," *Clarín*, December 3, 1985.

89. "El Banco Mundial no Duda del Plan Austral," *Clarín*, December 12, 1985.

90. "Habrá Créditos por Sectores," *Clarín*, December 8, 1985; "Balance del Titular del Banco Mundial. Crisis y Perspectivas," *Clarín*, December 10, 1985.

91. Letter, Clausen to Rodolfo Otero, December 30, 1985, Argentina-Clausen Country Files-Correspondence-Vol. 1, File 1774554, Records of President A. W. Clausen, WBGA.

92. Transcript of Meeting of the Executive Directors of the IBRD and IDA, Held on Thursday, December 19, 1985, WBGA, http://documents.worldbank.org/curated/en/625121510573600439.

93. Argentina—Water Supply Project. Memorandum & Recommendation of the President, November 30, 1985, WBGA.

94. Transcript of Meeting of the Executive Directors of the IBRD and IDA, Held on Tuesday, December 10, 1985: Argentina—Water Supply Project, WBGA, http://documents.worldbank.org/curated/en/111081510658611857.

95. David Knox, "Argentina-Agricultural Sector Loan Opening Statement," April 3, 1986, File 1774555, Argentina-Clausen Country Files-Correspondence-Vol. 2, Records of President A. W. Clausen, WBGA.

96. Bank News Release No.86/68, "Argentina Embarks on Reform of Its Agricultural Sector," April 3, 1986, File 1774555, Argentina-Clausen Country Files-Correspondence-Vol. 2, Records of President A. W. Clausen, WBGA; Argentina—Agricultural Sector Loan Project, Report and Recommendations of the President, March 14, 1986, WBGA, https://documents.worldbank.org/pt/publication/documents-reports/documentdetail/481701468212679479/argentina-agricultural-sector-loan-project.

97. Transcript of Joint Meeting of the Executive Directors of the IBRD and IDA, Held on Thursday, April 3, 1986, WBGA, http://documents.worldbank.org/curated/en/601441510575133150.

98. Ibid.

99. "Créditos del Banco Mundial Gestiona Canitrot en EE.UU.," *La Nación,* May 5, 1986.

100. "El Banco Mundial Se Constituye en Una Importante Fuente de Recursos," *La Nación,* May 17, 1986.

101. "Sustancial Mejora en las Relaciones de Argentina con el Banco Mundial," *La Nación,* June 5, 1986.

102. "Aguda Retracción del Crédito para Deudores," *Clarín,* April 2, 1987.

103. "James Baker También Presiona," *Clarín,* April 11, 1987; "EE.UU. Frente al 'Negocio de la Deuda,'" *Clarín,* April 12, 1987.

104. "Sourrouille y Brodersohn Viajan Hoy a Washington," *Clarín,* April 4, 1987; "Anunciaron la Refinanciación de $34.000 Millones," *Clarín,* April 16, 1987.

105. "Contundente Respaldo Brindaron Rhodes y Conable al Plan Austral," *Ámbito Financiero,* May 13, 1987.

106. "Argentina Refinanció 200 Millones de Dólares con el Club de París," *Ámbito Financiero,* May 21, 1987.

107. Confidential Office Memorandum, Peter Eigen to Shahid Husain, "Argentina—Recent Economic Developments," August 20, 1987, Argentina-LEAP, File 134837B General January–August 1987–01, WBGA.

108. Office Memorandum, Desmond McCarthy to Files, "Argentina—Key Measures of the New Economic Reform Package," July 22, 1987, Argentina-LEAP, File 134837B General January–August 1987–01, WBGA.

109. Office Memorandum, Charlotte Jones-Carroll to Pieter Bottelier, "Argentina—IMF Board Meeting—CFC," July 13, 1987, Argentina-LEAP, File 134837B General January–August 1987–01, WBGA.

110. "Argentina's Government Is Shaken by Setbacks," *The New York Times,* November 29, 1987.

111. "Ecos Poco Favorables Ante la Propuesta de Alfonsín por la Deuda," *La Nación,* June 4, 1988; "Álfonsín Pidió Pagar Menor Tasa de Interés," *La Nación,* June 6, 1988.

112. "Fuertes Críticas de Dos Entidades a la Actual Política Económica," *La Nación,* June 30, 1988

113. "Áspero Debate en el Banco Mundial por un Crédito a la Argentina," *La Nación,* June 3, 1988.

114. "La Argentina Frente a Una Nueva Negociación Externa," *La Nación,* July 16, 1988.

115. Attachment I, Annex A, "Main Policy Measures to Strengthen Macroeconomic Environment," August 6, 1988, Argentina-LEAP, File 134837B General 87/89-02, WBGA.

116. "Argentina Stability Plan Holds Firm After Two Months," *United Press International,* October 2, 1988.

117. "Un Signo de Éxito," *La Nación,* September 16, 1988; "Apoyo Crediticio del Banco Mundial," *La Nación,* September 17, 1988.

118. "Argentina Stability Plan Holds Firm after Two Months."

119. "Desolación y Muchos Objetos Destrozados, Tras los Disturbios," *La Nación,* September 10, 1988; "CGT: A Medianoche Comenzó el Paro," *La Nación,* September 12, 1988.

120. "La CGT Critica las Negociaciones con el Banco Mundial," *La Nación,* September 19, 1988.

121. "Argentina Negocia con Bancos," *Ámbito Financiero,* October 4, 1988.

122. "Argentina Se Reunió Sólo con Cuatro de los Bancos Acreedores," *Ámbito Financiero,* October 13, 1988.

123. "Trascendió el Plan para Bajar el Gasto Público Presentado en el Banco Mundial," *Ámbito Financiero,* October 24, 1988.

124. "Argentina Loan Proposal," *The New York Times,* June 2, 1988.

125. "World Bank Directors Approved Four Loans Totaling $1.252 Billion For Argentina," *Notisur,* November 3, 1988, https://digitalrepository.unm.edu/cgi/viewcontent.cgi?article=3420&context=notisur.

126. "Se Fortalece el Plan: El Banco Mundial Aprobó Créditos por u$s 1200 Millones," *Ámbito Financiero,* October 28, 1988.

127. "Banco Mundial Reafirma Su Apoyo a Argentina Pese a los Cuestionamientos de Inglaterra," *Ámbito Financiero,* October 31, 1988.

128. "House Backs Rise in World Bank Funds," *The New York Times,* September 30, 1988.

129. "Gestiones en EE.UU. por la Crisis Energética," *La Nación,* January 8, 1989.

130. "Terragno: Sin Soluciones Rápidas para la Crisis," *La Nación,* January 10, 1989.

131. "Créditos Atrasados por la Burocracia en la Argentina," *La Nación,* January 14, 1989.

132. Argentina—Tax Administration Technical Assistance Project, Memorandum & Recommendation of the President, December 21, 1988, WBGA.

133. Transcript of Meeting of the Executive Directors of the IBRD and IDA, Held on Tuesday, January 24, 1989: Argentina—Tax Administration Technical Assistance Project, WBGA, http://documents.worldbank.org/curated/en/843041510653364843.

134. Office Memorandum, Richard Newfarmer to Pieter Bottelier, "Argentina: Macroeconomic Package," May 2, 1989, Argentina-LEAP, File 134837B General 1987–1989-04, WBGA.

135. Confidential Office Memorandum, Pieter Bottelier to Shahid Husain, "Argentina: Report on My Visit of April 24–25-1989," April 28, 1989, Argentina-LEAP, File 134837B General 1987–1989-04, WBGA.

136. Ibid.

137. Office Memorandum, Ping-Cheung Leh to Moeen Qureshi, "Argentina: Macroeconomic Update," June 1, 1989, Argentina-LEAP, File 134837B General 1987–1989-04, WBGA.

138. "En la Memoria, los Hechos de 1989," *La Nación,* December 6, 2001.

139. Office Memorandum, Lucien Moreau to Distribution, "Argentina: Early Action Needed from New Authorities," June 13, 1989, Argentina-LEAP, File 134837B General 1987–1989-04, WBGA.

140. Garfunkel, "Economic Policy and Economic Performance,"153–54.

141. Kurt Weyland, "Neopopulism and Neoliberalism in Latin America: Unexpected Affinities," *Studies in Comparative International Development* 31 (1996): 3–31, https://doi.org/10.1007/BF02738987. See also Vicente Palermo and John Collins, "Moderate Populism: A Political Approach to Argentina's 1991 Convertibility Plan," *Latin American Perspectives* 25, no. 4 (1998): 36–62, https://www.jstor.org/stable/2633998; and Celia Szusterman, "Carlos Saúl Menem: Variations in the Theme of Populism," *Bulletin of Latin American Research* 19, no. 2 (2000): 193–206, https://doi.org/10.1111/j.1470-9856.2000.tb00099.x.

142. Guillermo Miguel Figari, *De Alfonsín a Menem: Política Exterior y Globalización* (Buenos Aires: Memphis, 1997), chap. 3; Roberto Russell and Laura Zuvanic, "Argentina: Deepening Alignment with the West," *Journal of Interamerican Studies and World Affairs* 33, no. 3 (1991): 113–34, http://dx.doi.org/10.2307/165935.

143. "Un País en Estado de Choque. Menem Somete el País a Una Cirugía Sin Anestecia," *El País,* August 10, 1989.

144. Naomi Klein, *The Shock Doctrine: The Rise of Disaster Capitalism* (New York: Picador, 2008).

145. On the question of whether Menem (and Fujimori) changed their economic plans once in office or not, see Susan C. Stokes, *Mandates and Democracy:*

Neoliberalism by Surprise in Latin America (New York: Cambridge University Press, 2001), chap. 3.

146. Carlos Saúl Menem and Roberto Dromi, *Reforma del Estado y Transformación Nacional* (Buenos Aires: Editorial Ciencias de la Administración, 1990), 19–20.

147. Ibid., 76–80.

148. Veigel, *Dictatorship, Democracy, and Globalization*, 173–74. For the official and full text of Law 23696 of August 17, 1989: http://mepriv.mecon.gov.ar/Normas/23696.htm.

149. Delia Ferreira Rubio and Matteo Goretti, "Cuando el Presidente Gobierna Solo. Menem y los Decretos de Necesidad y Urgencia Hasta la Reforma Constitucional (Julio 1989–Agosto 1994), *Desarrollo Económico* 36, no. 141 (1996): 443–74, http://dx.doi.org/10.2307/3467401.

150. Pablo Gerchunoff and Juan Carlos Torre, "La Política de Liberación Económica en la Administración de Menem," *Desarrollo Económico* 36, no. 143 (1996): 733–68, https://doi.org/10.2307/3467293.

151. Sebastián Pedro Salvia, "The Boom and the Crisis of the Convertibility Plan in Argentina," *Brazilian Journal of Political Economy* 35, no. 2 (2015): 325–42, https://ideas.repec.org/a/ekm/repojs/v35y2015i2p325-342id227.html .

152. Transcript of Meeting of the Executive Directors of the IBRD and IDA, Held on Thursday, August 9, 1990: Argentina—Second Trade Policy Loan Project. WBGA, http://documents.worldbank.org/curated/en/957841510653978057.

153. Haeduck Lee, "Poverty and Income Distribution in Argentina, Patterns and Changes," in Report No. 19992-AR, *Argentina Poverty Assessment: Argentina. Poor People in a Rich Country*, January 2000, WBGA; "El Legado de Menem al Próximo Gobierno," *Página 12*, April 30, 1999.

154. "Más Pobres en la Cuenta de Menem," *Página 12*, June 10, 1999.

155. See "Historial de Acuerdos con el FMI," Banco Central de la República Argentina, https://www.bcra.gob.ar/Institucional/Historial_Acuerdos_FMI.asp.

Conclusions

1. Transcript of Oral History Interview with Robert S. McNamara Held on April 1, May 10, and October 3, 1991, 45–46, https://oralhistory.worldbank.org/en/archive/oralhistory/transcriptdetail/transcript-oral-history-interview-robert-s-mcnamara-held-april-1-may-10-and-october-3.

2. See, among others, Johanna Bockman, *Markets in the Name of Socialism: The Left-Wing Origins of Neoliberalism* (Stanford: Stanford University Press, 2011); and Quinn Slobodian, *Globalists: The End of Empire and the Birth of Neoliberalism* (Cambridge, MA: Harvard University Press, 2018).

Bibliography

Archives and Archival Sources

Argentina

Biblioteca Nacional Mariano Moreno, Hemeroteca

Banco Central de la República Argentina, Archivo Institucional

Banco Central de la República Argentina, Biblioteca Prebisch

Instituto de Investigaciones Gino Germani, Facultad de Ciencias Sociales, Universidad de Buenos Aires (Oral History Project)

Ministerio de Economía, Biblioteca

Ministerio de Relaciones Exteriores, Comercio Exterior y Culto, Archivo Histórico de la Cancillería

IMF

Argentina Subseries, Country File Series, Central Files Boxes 5, 6, 7, 19

Bretton Woods Conference Files

Executive Board Meetings (EBM)

Executive Board Specials (EBS)

United States

National Archives and Records Administration, College Park, Maryland

RG56 General Records of the Department of the Treasury, Records of the Office of the Assistant Secretary for International Affairs, NAC Actions

RG 59 General Records of the State Department, Assistant Secretary of State for Latin American Affairs (Edward J. Miller)

RG 59 General Records of the State Department, Assistant Secretary of State for Inter-American Affairs (Henry F. Holland)

RG59 General Records of the State Department, Central Foreign Policy Files, 1967–1969

World Bank

Central Files, Argentina—General Negotiations, 1947–1956; 1957–1961; 1961–1964; 1966; 1967–1968; 1969–1971; 1972–1974; 1975–1977; 1978–1980; 1981–1983; 1984–1986

Central Files, Argentina—Lending, Economy and Program (LEAP), Correspondence 84/86–01; 84/86–02; 1987–01; 87/89–02; 87/89–04

Central Files, Argentina—Technical Assistance, National Development Council, Vol. 1. (1964–1965)

Central Files, Bank Administration and Policy—Expropriation and Compensation—1969–1971.

Transcripts of Meetings of the Executive Directors of the IBRD and IDA

Online Documents

Argentina Declassification Projects, US Embassy in Argentina. https://ar.usembassy.gov/argentina-declassification-projects/

Avalon Project at the Yale Law School. Documents in Law, History and Diplomacy. https://avalon.law.yale.edu/

Biblioteca de la Academia Nacional de la Historia. https://biblioteca.anh.org.ar/

Boletín Oficial de la República Argentina. https://www.boletinoficial.gob.ar/

Centro de Documentación e Información, Ministerio de Economía. https://www.argentina.gob.ar/centro-de-documentacion-e-informacion

Department of State Bulletin. https://catalog.hathitrust.org/Record/000598610

Foreign Relations of the United States, 1946, The American Republics, Volume 11. https://history.state.gov/historicaldocuments/frus1946v11

Foreign Relations of the United States, 1952–1954, American Republics, Volume 4. https://history.state.gov/historicaldocuments/frus1952-54v04

Foreign Relations of the United States, 1955–1957, American Republics: Central and South America, Volume 7. https://history.state.gov/historicaldocuments/frus1955-57v07

Foreign Relations of the United States, 1958–1960, American Republics, Volume 5. https://history.state.gov/historicaldocuments/frus1958-60v05

Foreign Relations of the United States, 1961–1963, Volume 12, American Republics. https://history.state.gov/historicaldocuments/frus1961-63v12

Foreign Relations of the United States, 1964–1968, Volume 31, South and Central America; Mexico. https://history.state.gov/historicaldocuments/frus1964-68v31

Foreign Relations of the United States, 1969–1976, Volume E-10, Documents on American Republics, 1969–1972. https://history.state.gov/historicaldocuments/frus1969-76ve10
Foreign Relations of the United States, 1969–1976, Volume E-11, Part 2, Documents on South America, 1973–1976. https://history.state.gov/historicaldocuments/frus1969-76ve11p2
IMF eLibrary. https://www.elibrary.imf.org/
John F. Kennedy Presidential Library and Museum. https://www.jfklibrary.org/asset-viewer/archives/jfknsf
Observatorio de la Deuda en la Globalización. https://odg.cat/es/
Oral History Program, World Bank Group Archives. https://oralhistory.worldbank.org/en/archive/oralhistory/home
Records of the Office of the Vice President, Development Economics and Chief Economist and later Senior Vice President, Development Economics and Chief Economist (DECVP), Soviet—General—January 1991. https://thedocs.worldbank.org/en/doc/654491632221253018-0560011991/original/WorldBankGroupArchivesFolder30382299.pdf
Records of the Office of World Bank President A. W. Clausen. https://archivesholdings.worldbank.org/records-of-president-w-clausen
Records of the Office of World Bank President Eugene R. Black. https://archivesholdings.worldbank.org/records-of-president-eugene-r-black
Records of the Office of World Bank President Robert S. McNamara. https://archivesholdings.worldbank.org/records-of-president-robert-s-mcnamara
Richard Nixon Presidential Library and Museum. https://www.nixonlibrary.gov
World Bank Projects by Country/Area—Argentina. https://projects.worldbank.org/en/projects-operations/projects-summary?countrycode_exact=AR&title=Argentina

Newspapers
Ámbito Financiero
Buenos Aires Económico
Clarín
Crónica
El Día (La Plata)
El Economista
El País (Spain)
Foreign Affairs
La Nación
La Opinión
La Prensa

La Razón
Mercado
The New York Times
Página 12
Primera Plana
Tiempo Argentino
Wall Street Journal
Washington Post

Published Sources and Scholarly Publications

Abouharb, M. Rodwan and David L. Cingranelli. "The Human Rights Effects of World Bank Structural Adjustment, 1981–2000." *International Studies Quarterly* 50, no. 2 (2006): 233–62. https://doi.org/10.1111/j.1468-2478.2006.00401.x.

Adair, Jennifer. *In Search of the Lost Decade: Everyday Rights in Post-Dictatorship Argentina.* University of California Press, 2019.

Alacevich, Michele. "Paul Rosenstein-Rodan and the Birth of Development Economics." 2020. Working Paper No. 2020–04, Duke University, Center for the History of Political Economy (CHOPE), Durham, NC. https://www.econstor.eu/bitstream/10419/215545/1/169344366X.pdf.

Alacevich, Michele. *The Political Economy of the World Bank: The Early Years.* Stanford University Press, an imprint of Stanford University Press and The World Bank, 2009.

Altamura, Carlo Edoardo, and Claudia Kedar. "Friends or Foes? Brazil, the IMF, and the World Bank, 1961–1967." *Financial History Review* 28, no. 2 (2021): 205–36. https://doi.org/10.1017/S096856502100007X.

Amicci, Daniel. "La Trayectoria Hacia la Cumbre de Uruguayana: Máxima Expresión de la Aproximación Entre Argentina y Brasil Durante el Desarrollismo." CONfines de Relaciones Internacionales y Ciencia Política 8, no. 15 (2012): 133–56. https://www.scielo.org.mx/scielo.php?script=sci_arttext&pid=S1870-35692012000100006.

Andersen, Thomas Barnebeck, Henrik Hansen, and Thomas Markussen. "US Politics and World Bank IDA-Lending." *The Journal of Development Studies* 42, no. 5 (2006): 772–94. https://doi.org/10.1080/00220380600741946.

Assetto, Valerie. *The Soviet Bloc in the IMF and the IBRD.* Westview Press, 1988.

Aurora, Tearoti Silvia. "El Plan de Desarrollo 1965–1969, un Intento de Planificación en la Argentina." In *XIV Jornadas Interescuelas/Departamentos de Historia. Departamento de Historia de la Facultad de Filosofía y Letras.* Universidad Nacional de Cuyo, Mendoza, 2013. https://www.aacademica.org/000-010/164.

Avenburg, Alejandro. "Entre la Presión y el Apoyo: La Política de Derechos Humanos de los Estados Unidos y el Gobierno Militar Argentino (1976–1978)."

Desarrollo Económico 55, no. 215 (2015): 117–18. http://bibliotecadigital.econ.uba.ar/download/toc/2016/Sep/2890-2015_55_215.pdf.

Ayres, Robert L., ed. *Banking on the Poor: The World Bank and World Poverty.* MIT Press, 1983.

Babb, Sarah. *Behind the Development Banks: Washington Politics, World Poverty, and the Wealth of Nations.* University of Chicago Press, 2009.

Babb, Sarah, and Bruce Carruthers. "Conditionality: Forms, Function, and History." *Annual Review of Law and Social Science* 4 (2008): 13–29. https://doi.org/10.1146/annurev.lawsocsci.4.110707.172254.

Babb, Sarah. "The Washington Consensus as Transnational Policy Paradigm: Its Origins, Trajectory and Likely Successor." *Review of International Political Economy* 20, no. 2 (2012): 268–97. https://doi.org/10.1080/09692290.2011.640435.

Bacha, Edmar L., and Richard E. Feinberg. "The World Bank and Structural Adjustment in Latin America." *World Development* 14, no. 3 (1986): 333–46. https://doi.org/10.1016/0305-750X(86)90073-2.

Bange, Oliver, and Poul Villaume, eds. *The Long Détente: Changing Concepts of Security and Cooperation in Europe, 1950s–1980s.* Central European University Press, 2017.

Barnett, Michael, and Martha Finnemore. *Rules for the World: International Organizations in Global Politics.* Cornell University Press, 2004.

Bartel, Fritz. *The Triumph of Broken Promises: The End of the Cold War and the Rise of Neoliberalism.* Harvard University Press, 2022.

Basha i Novosejt, Aurélie. "Breaking Ranks: Robert McNamara, Adam Yarmolinsky, and the Montreal Speech." *Diplomatic History* 43, no. 3 (2019): 493–516. https://doi.org/10.1093/dh/dhy091.

Basha i Novosejt, Aurélie. *"I Made Mistakes." Robert McNamara's Vietnam War Policy, 1960–1968.* Cambridge University Press, 2019.

Bass, Gary J. *The Blood Telegram: Nixon, Kissinger, and a Forgotten Genocide.* Alfred A. Knopf, 2013.

Baudino, Verónica. "Burguesía Nacional y Estado: La Acción Política de la Unión Industrial Argentina Durante la Revolución Argentina (1966–1969)." *Polis Revista Latinoamericana* 32 (2012). https://journals.openedition.org/polis/6470.

Belini, Claudio. "D.I.N.I.E. y los Límites de la Política Industrial Peronista, 1947–1955." *Desarrollo Económico* 41, no. 161 (2001): 97–119. http://dx.doi.org/10.2307/3455966.

Black, Eugene. *The Diplomacy of Economic Development.* Harvard University Press, 1960.

Black, Eugene. "The World Bank at Work." *Foreign Affairs* 30, no. 3 (1952): 402–11. https://www.jstor.org/stable/20030909.

Bockman, Johanna. *Markets in the Name of Socialism: The Left-Wing Origins of Neoliberalism.* Stanford University Press, 2011.

Boughton, James M. *Silent Revolution: The International Monetary Fund 1979–1989*. The International Monetary Fund, 2001.

Bovard, James. "The World Bank and the Impoverishment of Nations." In *Perpetuating Poverty: The World Bank, the IMF, and the Developing World*, edited by Doug Bandow and Ian Vásquez. Cato Institute, 1994.

Bradlow, Daniel. "The World Bank, the IMF, and Human Rights." *Transnational Law & Contemporary Problems* 6, no. 47 (1996): 47–90. https://digitalcommons.wcl.american.edu/cgi/viewcontent.cgi?article=1942&context=facsch_lawrev.

Brands, Hal. *Latin America's Cold War*. Harvard University Press, 2010.

Brands, Hal. "Richard Nixon and Economic Nationalism in Latin America: The Problem of Expropriations, 1969–1974." *Diplomacy & Statecraft* 18, no. 1 (2007): 215–35. https://doi.org/10.1080/09592290601163126.

Brands, Hal. "Third World Politics in an Age of Global Turmoil: The Latin American Challenge to U.S. and Western Hegemony, 1965–1975." *Diplomatic History* 32, no. 1 (2008): 105–38. https://www.jstor.org/stable/24916057.

Brands, Hal. "The United States and the Peruvian Challenge, 1968–1975." *Diplomacy & Statecraft* 21, no. 3 (2010): 471–90. https://doi.org/10.1080/09592296.2010.508418.

Brennan, James. "Industrialistas y Bolicheros: Business and the Peronist Populist Alliance, 1943–1976." In *Peronism and Argentina*, edited by James Brennan. Rowman & Littlefield, 1998.

Brennan, James. "Prolegomenon to Neoliberalism: The Political Economy of Populist Argentina, 1943–1976." *Latin American Perspectives* 34, no. 3 (2007): 49–66. https://www.jstor.org/stable/27648022.

Brennan, James P., and Mónica B. Gordillo. "Working Class Protest, Popular Revolt, and Urban Insurrection in Argentina: The 1969 'Cordobazo.'" *Journal of Social History* 27, no. 3 (1994): 477–98. https://www.jstor.org/stable/3788983.

Bresser Pereira, Luiz, & Fernando Dall'Acqua. "Economic Populism Versus Keynes: Reinterpreting Budget Deficit in Latin America." *Journal of Post Keynesian Economics* 14, no. 1 (2015): 29–38l. https://doi.org/10.1080/01603477.1991.11489875.

Bresser Pereira, Luiz Carlos. "Modelos de Estado Desarrollista." *Revista de la CEPAL* 2019, no. 128 (2019): 39–52. http://dx.doi.org/10.18356/5e8f70e1-es.

Brown, Archie. *The Human Factor: Gorbachev, Reagan, and Thatcher, and the End of the Cold War*. Oxford University Press, 2020.

Canelo, Paula. "La Política Contra la Economía: Los Elencos Militares Frente al Plan Económico de Martínez de Hoz Durante el Proceso de Reorganización Nacional (1976–1981)." In *Empresarios, Tecnócratas y Militares. La Trama Corporativa de la Última Dictadura*, edited by Alfredo Pucciarelli. Siglo XXI, 2004.

Canitrot, Adolfo. “La Disciplina Como Objetivo de la Política Económica. Un Ensayo Sobre el Programa Económico del Gobierno Argentino Desde 1976.” *Desarrollo Económico* 19, no. 76 (1980): 453–75. https://doi.org/10.2307/3466561.

Cardoso, Fernando Henrique, and Enzo Faletto. *Dependencia y Desarrollo en América Latina*. Siglo XXI, 1977.

Carpenter, Daniel. *The Forging of Bureaucratic Autonomy: Reputations, Networks, and Policy Innovation in Executive Agencies, 1862–1928*. Princeton University Press, 2001.

Cavarozzi, Marcelo. “El ‘Desarrollismo’” y las Relaciones Entre Democracia y Capitalismo Dependiente en Dependencia y Desarrollo en América Latina.” *Latin American Research Review* 17, no. 1 (1982):152–65. https://doi.org/10.1017/S0023879100028569.

Chwieroth, Jeffrey. “Organizational Change ‘From Within’: Exploring the World Bank’s Early Lending Practices.” *Review of International Political Economy* 15, no. 4 (2008): 481–505. https://doi.org/10.1080/09692290802260498.

Chwieroth, Jeffrey M. “‘The Silent Revolution’: How the Staff Exercise Informal Governance Over IMF Lending.” *The Review of International Organizations* 8, no. 3 (2013): 265–90. https://doi.org/10.1007/s11558-012-9154-9.

Ciorciari, John. “The Lawful Scope of Human Rights Criteria in World Bank Credit Decisions: An Interpretive Analysis of the IBRD and IDA Articles of Agreement.” *Cornell International Law Journal* 33, no. 2 (2000): 330–71. https://www.researchgate.net/publication/290288286_The_Lawful_Scope_of_Human_Rights_Criteria_in_World_Bank_Credit_Decisions_An_Interpretive_Analysis_of_the_IBRD_and_IDA_Articles_of_Agreement.

Cisneros, Andrés, and Carlos Escudé. *Historia General de las Relaciones Exteriores de la República Argentina, Vol. XIII*. Nuevohacer, 1998.

Clark, Richard, and Lindsay R. Dolan. “Pleasing the Principal: U.S. Influence in World Bank Policymaking.” *American Journal of Political Science* 65, no. 1 (2021): 36–51. https://www.jstor.org/stable/45415611.

Clark, William. *The McNamara Years at the World Bank: Major Policy Addresses of Robert S. McNamara 1968–1981*. Johns Hopkins University Press, 1981.

Clark, William. “Robert McNamara at the World Bank.” *Foreign Affairs* 60, no. 1 (1981): 167–84. http://www.foreignaffairs.com/articles/35520/william-clark/reconsiderations-robert-mcnamara-at-the-world-bank.

Clift, Ben. *The IMF and the Politics of Austerity in the Wake of the Global Financial Crisis*. Oxford University Press, 2018.

Coll Cárdenas, Marcelo. “El Plan Larkin Visto Desde los Editoriales y Notas de los Diarios La Nación y El Argentino de La Plata.” *Actas de Periodismo y Comunicación Social* 4, no. 3 (2018). https://sedici.unlp.edu.ar/bitstream/handle/10915/93639/Documento_completo.pdf-PDFA.pdf?sequence=1&isAllowed=y.

Connelly, Matthew. *Fatal Misconception: The Struggle to Control World Population*. Belknap Press of Harvard University, 2008.

Cortell, Andrew, and Susan Peterson. "Autonomy and International Organisations." *Journal of International Relations and Development* 25 (2022): 399–424. https://doi.org/10.1057/s41268-021-00243-x.

Cortés Conde, Roberto. "Raúl Prebisch: His Years in Government." *CEPAL Review* 75 (2001): 81–85. https://repositorio.cepal.org/server/api/core/bitstreams/a0b1bd7c-2d38-40fb-a107-e40ccda3f5af/content.

Cox, Robert. "Ideologies and the New International Economic Order: Reflections on Some Recent Literature." *International Organization* 33, no. 2 (1979): 257–302. https://www.jstor.org/stable/2706612.

Dañino, Roberto. "The Legal Aspects of the World Bank's Work on Human Rights." *The International Lawyer* 41, no. 1 (2007): 21–25. https://www.jstor.org/stable/40708088.

Darnton, Christopher. *Rivalry and Alliance Politics in Cold War Latin America*. Johns Hopkins University Press, 2014.

Dawyd, Darío. "El Sindicalismo Peronista Durante el Onganiato. De la CGT de los Argentinos a la Reorganización Sindical (1968–1970)." *Sociohistórica* 33 (2014): 56–76. https://www.sociohistorica.fahce.unlp.edu.ar/article/view/SH2014n33a04.

de la Torre, Carlos. "Populism and the Politics of the Extraordinary in Latin America." *Journal of Political Ideologies* 21, no. 2 (2016): 121–39. https://doi.org/10.1080/13569317.2016.1150137.

de Looper, Johan H. C. "Recent Latin American Experience with Bilateral Trade and Payments Agreements." *IMF Staff Papers* 4, no. 1 (1954–1955): 85–112. https://ideas.repec.org/a/pal/imfstp/v4y1954i1p85-112.html.

de Riz, Liliana. *Historia Argentina: La Política en Suspenso, 1966–1976*. Paidós, 2000.

Delpino, María Florencia. "El Petróleo Argentino Durante los Años de Onganía: Hacia Una Nueva Ley de Hidrocarburos. Repercusiones Internas y Externas." *Ciclos en la Historia, la Economía y la Sociedad* 29, no. 51 (2018): 107–34. http://scienceopen.com/document?vid=c14fafc0-1bed-4afd-b1ef-34789a8ba1b2.

Deudney, Daniel, and John Ikenberry. "The Nature and Sources of Liberal International Order." *Review of International Studies* 25, no. 2 (1999): 179–96. https://doi.org/10.1017/S0260210599001795.

Dorn, Charles, and Kristen Ghodsee. "The Cold War Politicization of Literacy: Communism, UNESCO, and the World Bank." *Diplomatic History* 36, no. 2 (2012): 373–98. https://www.jstor.org/stable/44376156.

Dorn, Glenn. *Peronistas and New Dealers: U.S.-Argentine Rivalry and the Western Hemisphere (1946–1950)*. University Press of the South, 2005.

Dornbusch, Rudiger, and Sebastian Edwards, eds. *The Macroeconomics of Populism in Latin America*. University of Chicago Press, 1991.

Dosman, Edgar J. *The Life and Times of Raúl Prebisch, 1901–1986*. McGill-Queen's University Press, 2008.

Dreher, Axel, Jan-Egbert Sturm, and James Raymond Vreeland. "Development Aid and International Politics: Does Membership on the UN Security Council Influence World Bank Decisions?" *Journal of Development Economics* 88, no. 1 (2009): 1–18. https://doi.org/10.1016/j.jdeveco.2008.02.003.

Edwards, Sebastian. *Left Behind: Latin America and the False Promise of Populism*. University of Chicago Press, 2010.

Elena, Eduardo. "Peronist Consumer Politics and the Problem of Domesticating Markets in Argentina, 1943–1955." *Hispanic American Historical Review* 87, no. 1 (2007): 111–49. https://doi.org/10.1215/00182168-2006-089.

Engerman, David C., and Corinna R. Unger. "Introduction: Towards a Global History of Modernization." *Diplomatic History* 33, no. 3 (2009): 375–85. http://www.jstor.org/stable/44214017.

Engerman, David C., ed. *Staging Growth: Modernization, Development, and the Global Cold War*. University of Massachusetts Press, 2003.

Escobar, Arturo. *Encountering Development*: The Making and Unmaking of the Third World. Princeton University Press, 1995.

Escudé, Carlos. "US Political Destabilisation and Economic Boycott of Argentina During the 1940s." In *Argentina Between the Great Powers, 1939–46*, edited by Guido di Tella and D. Cameron Watt. Macmillan, 1989.

Eshag, Eprime, and R. Thorp. "Las Políticas Económicas Ortodoxas de Perón a Guido (1953–1963): Consecuencias Económicas y Sociales." In *Los Planes de Estabilización en la Argentina*, edited by Aldo Ferrer, Mario S. Brodersohn, Eprime Eshag, et al. Paidós, 1974.

Fajardo, Margarita. *The World That Latin America Created: The United Nations Economic Commission for Latin America in the Development Era*. Harvard University Press, 2022.

Fanese, Griselda, and Emilse Kejner. "La Aneida: Una Epopeya de Mujeres en una Huelga de Obreros. Representaciones de las Mujeres que Participaron en el Choconazo (1969–1970)." *La Aljaba* 11 (2007): 229–47. https://www.scielo.org.ar/scielo.php?script=sci_arttext&pid=S1669-57042007000100011.

Fermandois, Joaquín. "Entusiasmo y Desconfianza. Populismo y Relaciones Internacionales en el Caso Perón-Ibáñez, 1953–1955." *Ayer* 98, no. 2 (2015): 187–211. https://www.jstor.org/stable/24759518.

Ferraro, Agustin E., and Miguel A. Centeno, eds. *State and Nation Making in Latin America and Spain: The Rise and Fall of the Developmental State*. Cambridge University Press, 2019.

Ferreira Rubio, Delia, and Matteo Goretti. "Cuando el Presidente Gobierna Solo. Menem y los Decretos de Necesidad y Urgencia Hasta la Reforma Constitucional (Julio 1989–Agosto 1994), *Desarrollo Económico* 36, no. 141 (1996): 443–74. http://dx.doi.org/10.2307/3467401.

Field Jr., Thomas, Stella Krepp, and Vanni Pettinà, eds. *Latin America and the Global Cold War*. University of North Carolina Press, 2020.

Figari, Guillermo Miguel. *De Alfonsín a Menem: Política Exterior y Globalización*. Memphis, 1997.

Filippini, Mariano, and María Olcese. "Transitional Economic Policies, 1971–3." In *The Political Economy of Argentina, 1946–83*, edited by Guido DiTella and R. Dornbusch. Macmillan Press, 1989.

Finnemore, Martha. *National Interests in International Society*. Cornell University Press, 1996.

Florencia-Osuna, María, and Esteban Pontoriero. "El Impacto de la Doctrina 'de la Seguridad Nacional' en la Argentina Durante la Guerra Fría (1955–1983)." *Izquierdas* 49 (2020): 352–64. https://dx.doi.org/10.4067/S0718-50492020000100221.

Foot, Rosemary. "The Cold War and Human Rights." In *The Cambridge History of the Cold War. Vol. III*, edited by Melvyn P. Leffler and Odd Arne Westad. Cambridge University Press, 2010.

Forsythe, David. *Human Rights and U.S. Foreign Policy: Congress Reconsidered*. University of Florida Press, 1988.

Foss, Sarah. *On Our Own Terms: Development and Indigeneity in Cold War Guatemala*. University of North Carolina Press, 2022.

Franczak, Michael. *Global Inequality and American Foreign Policy in the 1970s*. Cornell University Press, 2022.

Franczak, Michael. "Human Rights and Basic Needs: Jimmy Carter's North-South Dialogue, 1977–81." *Cold War History* 18, no. 4 (2018): 447–64. https://www.doi.org/10.1080/14682745.2018.1468437.

Frank, André Gunder. *Capitalismo y Subdesarrollo en América Latina*. Siglo XXI, 1967.

Frank, André Gunder. *Dependent Accumulation and Underdevelopment*. Macmillan, 1978.

Frenkel, Roberto, and José María Fanelli. "La Argentina y el Fondo en la Década Pasada." *El Trimestre Económico* 54, no. 231 (1987): 75–131. https://www.jstor.org/stable/i23395685.

Frigerio, Rogelio. *Desarrollo y Subdesarrollo Económicos*. Paidós, 1984.

Frigerio, Rogelio. *Estatuto del Subdesarrollo: Las Corrientes del Pensamiento Económico Argentino*. Ediciones Librería del Jurista, 1983.

Frigerio, Rogelio. *Las Condiciones de la Victoria*. A. Monteverde y Cia, 1963.

Frondizi, Arturo. Letter to Alberto Lleras Camargo, January 2, 1962. In *La Política Exterior Argentina*, Arturo Frondizi, 178–213. Transición, 1963.

Frondizi, Arturo. "Mensaje Inaugural." In *Mensajes Presidenciales 1958–1962*, vol. 1, Arturo Frondizi, 9–57. Centro de Estudios Nacionales, 1978.

Frondizi, Arturo. "Mensaje Radiofónico del Señor Presidente de la Nación Doctor Arturo Frondizi, Transmitido el 19 de Febrero de 1959." *Trabajadores y Empresarios Frente al Programa de Estabilización*, 3–16. Servicio de Prensa de la Presidencia de la Nación.

Gaddis, John. "On Starting All Over Again: A Naïve Approach to the Study of the Cold War." In *Reviewing the Cold War: Approaches, Interpretations, Theory*, edited by Odd Arne Westad. Frank Cass, 2000.

Galambos, Louis, and David Milobsky. "Organizing and Reorganizing the World Bank, 1946–1972: A Comparative Perspective." *The Business History Review* 69, no. 2 (1995): 156–90. https://doi.org/10.2307/3117098.

Galasso, Norberto. *De la Banca Baring al FMI: Historia de la Deuda Externa Argentina*. Colihue, 2002.

Gambini, Hugo. *Frondizi. El Estadista Acorralado*. Vergara, 2006.

García Heras, Raúl. *Deuda Externa, Crisis y Política. Banqueros, Fondo Monetario y Banco Mundial en la Argentina, 1973–1986*. Editorial Biblos, 2022.

García Heras, Raúl. *El Fondo Monetario Internacional y el Banco Mundial en la Argentina: Liberalismo, Populismo y Finanzas Internacionales*. Lumiere, 2008.

García Heras, Raúl. *Presiones Externas y Política Económica: El Fondo Monetario Internacional y el Banco Mundial en Argentina, 1955–1966*. Universidad de los Andes, Cátedra Corona, 2003.

García Heras, Raúl. "The Return of International Finance and the Martínez de Hoz Plan in Argentina, 1976–1978." *Latin American Research Review* 53, no. 4 (2018): 799–814. https://www.jstor.org/stable/e26744344.

Garritsen deVries, Margaret. *The IMF in a Changing World, 1945–85*. International Monetary Fund, 1986.

Garritsen deVries, Margaret. "The Retreat of Bilateralism." In *The International Monetary Fund: 1945–1965: Twenty Years of International Monetary Cooperation. Volume II: Analysis*, edited by J. Keith Horsefield. International Monetary Fund, 1969.

Garthoff, Raymond. *Détente and Confrontation: American-Soviet Relations from Nixon to Reagan*. Brookings Institute, 1985.

Genens, Doug. "Fighting Poverty in the Fields: Legal Services and the War on Poverty in Rural California." *Agricultural History* 94, no. 2 (2020): 251–78. https://doi.org/10.3098/ah.2020.094.2.251.

Gerchunoff, Pablo, and Juan Llach. "Capitalismo Industrial, Desarrollo Asociado y Distribución del Ingreso Entre los Dos Gobiernos Peronistas: 1950–1972." *Desarrollo Económico* 15, no. 57 (1975): 3–54. https://doi.org/10.2307/3466209.

Gerchunoff, Pablo, and Lucas Llach. *El Ciclo de la Ilusión y el Desencanto: Un Siglo de Políticas Económicas Argentinas*. Ariel Sociedad Económica, 1998.

Gerchunoff, Pablo, and Juan Carlos Torre. "La Política de Liberación Económica en la Administración de Menem." *Desarrollo Económico* 36, no. 143 (1996): 733–68. https://doi.org/10.2307/3467293.

Gillette, Michael L. *Launching the War on Poverty: An Oral History*. Oxford University Press, 2010.

Gilman, Nils. *Mandarins of the Future: Modernization Theory in Cold War America*. Johns Hopkins University Press, 2003.

Gilman, Nils. "The New International Economic Order: A Reintroduction." *Humanity: An International Journal of Human Rights, Humanitarianism, and Development* 6, no. 1 (2015): 1–16. https://www.researchgate.net/publication/276938153_The_New_International_Economic_Order_A_Reintroduction.

Gilpin, Robert. *The Political Economy of International Relations*. Princeton University Press, 1987.

Gordillo, Mónica B. "Los Prolegómenos del Cordobazo: Los Sindicatos Líderes de Córdoba Dentro de la Estructura de Poder Sindical." *Desarrollo Económico* 31, no. 122 (1991): 163–87. https://www.jstor.org/stable/3466830.

Griffith-Jones, Stephany. "The Alliance for Progress: An Attempt at Interpretation." *Development and Change* 10, no. 3 (1979): 423–43. https://doi.org/10.1111/j.1467-7660.1979.tb00005.x.

Guadagni, Alieto. *Braden o Perón: La Verdad Documental Norteamericana, Setenta Años Después*. Sudamericana, 2008.

Guido, Pablo. "Coordenadas Intelectuales de Álvaro Alsogaray." *Procesos de Mercado: Revista Europea de Economía Política* 8, no. 1 (2011): 209–52. https://www.procesosdemercado.com/index.php/inicio/article/view/265/337.

Haftel, Yoram, and Alexander Thompson. "The Independence of International Organizations: Concept and Applications." *Journal of Conflict Resolution* 50, no. 2 (2006): 253–75. https://doi.org/10.1177/0022002705285288.

Haidar, Victoria. "La Polémica Liberal con los Desarrollismos: Un Análisis del Pensamiento de Álvaro Alsogarary y de Federico Pinedo Entre 1958 y 1973." *Nuevo Mundo, Mundos Nuevos* (2015). http://hdl.handle.net/11336/69441.

Hanhimäki, Jussi M. "Détente in Europe, 1962–1975." In *The Cambridge History of the Cold War. Volume 2: Crises and Détente*, edited by Melvyn P. Leffler and Odd Arne Westad. Cambridge University Press, 2010.

Hanhimäki, Jussi M. "Ironies and Turning Points: Détente in Perspective." In *Reviewing the Cold War: Approaches, Interpretations, Theory*, edited by Odd Arne Westad. Frank Cass, 2000.

Harmer, Tanya. *Allende's Chile & the Inter-American Cold War*. University of North Carolina Press, 2011.

Harvey, Hugo. "Revisitando el Punto de Inflexión Interamericano en la Guerra Fría: La Crisis Dominicana de 1965, la Intervención de Estados Unidos y la

Fuerza Interamericana de la Paz." *Humanidades* 7 (2020): 25–63. https://doi.org/10.25185/7.2.

Hawkins, Darren G., David A. Lake, Daniel L. Nielson, and Michael J. Tierney. "Delegation Under Anarchy: States, International Organizations, and Principal-Agent Theory." In *Delegation and Agency in International Organizations*, edited by Darren G. Hawkins, David A. Lake, Daniel L. Nielson, and Michael J. Tierney. Cambridge University Press, 2006.

Helleiner, Eric. "The Diversity of Economic Nationalism." *New Political Economy* 26, no. 2 (2021): 229–38. https://doi.org/10.1080/13563467.2020.1841137.

Helleiner, Eric. *Forgotten Foundations of Bretton Woods: International Development and the Making of the Postwar Order.* Cornell University Press, 2014.

Helleiner, Eric. "The Life and Times of Embedded Liberalism: Legacies and Innovations Since Bretton Woods." *Review of International Political Economy* 26, no. 6 (2019): 1112–35. https://doi.org/10.1080/09692290.2019.1607767.

Helleiner, Eric, and Hongying Wang. "The Richness of Financial Nationalism: The Case of China." *Pacific Affairs* 92, no. 2 (2019): 211–34. https://www.jstor.org/stable/48541654.

Hennessy, John. "Testimony of Hon. John Hennessy, Assistant Secretary of Treasury for International Affairs," March 28, 1973. In *Multinational Corporations and the US Foreign Policy*, 321–42. US Government Printing Office, 197.

Heredia, Mariana. "El Proceso Como Bisagra. Emergencia y Consolidación del Liberalismo Tecnocrático: FIEL, FM y CEMA." In *Empresarios, Tecnócratas y Militares: La Trama Corporativa de la Última Dictadura*, edited by Alfredo Pucciarelli. Siglo XXI, 2004.

Horsefield, J. Keith. *The International Monetary Fund, 1945–1965: Twenty Years of International Monetary Cooperation, Vol. 1: Chronicle*. IMF, 1969.

Horsefield, J. Keith. *The International Monetary Fund, 1945–1965: Twenty Years of International Monetary Cooperation, Vol. 2: Analysis*. IMF, 1969.

Hošman, Mirek Tobiáš. "Internal Dynamics as Drivers of Change in International Organizations: The Economists' Takeover at the World Bank." *Swiss Journal of Sociology* 49, no. 1 (2023): 41–60. https://doi.org/10.2478/sjs-2023-0004.

Hu, Weixing. "China as a Listian Trading State: Interest, Power, and Economic Ideology." In *America, China, and the Struggle for World Order: Ideas, Traditions, Historical Legacies, and Global Visions*, edited by G. John Ikenberry, Zhu Feng, and Wang Jisi. Palgrave Macmillan, 2015.

Hunter, Wendy. "Negotiating Civil-Military Relations in Post-Authoritarian Argentina and Chile." *International Studies Quarterly* 42, no. 2 (1998): 295–317. https://www.jstor.org/stable/2600782.

Huret, Romain D. *The Experts' War on Poverty: Social Research and the Welfare Agenda in Postwar America.* Cornell University Press, 2018.

Ikenberry, G. John. *After Victory: Institutions, Strategic Restraint, and the Rebuilding of Order After Major Wars*. Princeton University Press, 2001.

Illia, Arturo. *La Política Económica del Gobierno Constitucional*. Unidentified publisher, December 1966 [Biblioteca Ministerio de Economía, Argentina].

Iramain, Lucas, and Verónica Pérez. "Rieles y Política Económica Durante la Última Dictadura Cívico-Militar Argentina (1976–1983)." *Sociohistorica* 39 (2017). https://doi.org/10.24215/18521606e021.

James, William D. "Influencing the United States: Is the Game Worth the Candle for Junior Allies?" *International Politics* 59, no. 2 (2022): 1029–44. https://doi.org/10.1057/s41311-021-00331-2.

Joseph, Gilbert M., and Daniela Spencer. *In From the Cold: Latin America's New Encounter with the Cold War.* Duke University Press, 2008.

Kaja, Ashwin, and Eric Werker. "Corporate Governance at the World Bank and the Dilemma of Global Governance." *The World Bank Economic Review* 24, no. 2 (2010): 171–98. https://www.jstor.org/stable/40891365.

Kalinovsky, Artemy. *Laboratory of Socialist Development: Cold War Politics and Decolonization in Soviet Tajikistan.* Cornell University Press, 2018.

Kaplan, Stephen. *Globalization and Austerity Politics in Latin America.* Cambridge University Press, 2013.

Kapur, Devesh, John P. Lewis, and Richard C. Webb, eds. *The World Bank: Its First Half Century. Vol. 1.* Brookings Institute Press, 1997.

Karl, Robert A. "Reading the Cuban Revolution from Bogotá, 1957–62." *Cold War History* 16, no. 4 (2016): 337–58. https://doi.org/10.1080/14682745.2016.1218848.

Kedar, Claudia. "The Beginning of a Controversial Relationship: The IMF, the World Bank, and Argentina, 1943–46." *Canadian Journal of Latin American and Caribbean Studies* 35, no. 69 (2010): 201–30. https://doi.org/10.1080/08263663.2010.10816993.

Kedar, Claudia. "Economic Neutrality During the Cold War: The World Bank, the United States, and Pinochet's Chile, 1973–1977." *Cold War History* 18, no. 2 (2018): 149–67. https://doi.org/10.1080/14682745.2017.1420056.

Kedar, Claudia. *The International Monetary Fund and Latin America: The Argentine Puzzle in Context.* Temple University Press, 2013.

Kedar, Claudia. "The World Bank Lending and Non-Lending to Latin America: The Case of Argentina, 1971–1976." *Revista de Historia Económica: Journal of Iberian and Latin American Economic History* 37, no. 1 (2018): 111–38. https://doi.org/10.1017/S0212610918000149.

Kedar, Claudia. "The World Bank-United States-Latin American Triangle: The Negotiations with Socialist Chile, 1970–1973." *The International History Review* 39, no. 4 (2017): 667–90. https://doi.org/10.1080/07075332.2016.1239587.

Keller, Renata. "The Latin American Missile Crisis." *Diplomatic History* 39, no. 2 (2015): 195–22. https://doi.org/10.1093/dh/dht134.

Keohane, Robert O. "The Big Influence of Small Allies." *Foreign Policy*, no. 2 (1971): 161–82. https://doi.org/10.2307/1147864.

Kersting, Erasmus K., and Christopher Kilby. "With a Little Help from My Friends: Global Electioneering and World Bank Lending." *Journal of Development Economics* 121, no. 3 (2016):153–65. https://doi.org/10.1016/j.jdeveco.2016.03.010.

Keys, Barbara, and Roland Burke. "Human Rights." In *The Oxford Handbook of the Cold War*, edited by Richard H. Immerman and Petra Goedde. Oxford University Press, 2013. https://doi.org/10.1093/oxfordhb/9780199236961.013.0028.

Kiguel, Miguel A. *Las Crisis Económicas Argentinas: Una Historia de Ajustes y Desajustes*. Sudamericana, 2015.

Kilby, Christopher. "The Political Economy of Conditionality: An Empirical Analysis of World Bank Loan Disbursements." *Journal of Development Economics* 89, no. 1 (2009): 51–61. https://doi.org/10.1016/j.jdeveco.2008.06.014.

Kirkendall, Andrew J. *Hemispheric Alliances: Liberal Democrats and Cold War Latin America*. University of North Carolina Press, 2022.

Klein, Herbert S., and Francisco Vidal Luna. *Brazil 1964–1985: The Military Regimes of Latin America in the Cold War*. Yale University Press, 2017.

Klein, Naomi. *The Shock Doctrine: The Rise of Disaster Capitalism*. Picador, 2008.

Kofas, Jon V. "Stabilization and Class Conflict: The State Department, the IMF, and the IBRD in Chile, 1952–1958." *The International History Review* 21, no. 2 (1999): 352–85. https://doi.org/10.1080/07075332.1999.9640863.

Kofas, Jon V. *The Sword of Damocles: U.S. Financial Hegemony in Colombia and Chile, 1950–1970*. Praeger, 2002.

Konkel, Rob. "The Monetization of Global Poverty: The Concept of Poverty in World Bank History, 1944–90." *Journal of Global History* 9, no. 2 (2014): 276–300. https://doi.org/10.1017/S1740022814000072.

Kraske, Jochen, William H. Becker, William Diamond, and Louis Galambos. *Bankers with a Mission: The Presidents of the World Bank, 1946–91*. Oxford University Press, 1996.

Kressel, Daniel. "The 'Argentine Franco'? The Regime of Juan Carlos Onganía and Its Ideological Dialogue with Francoist Spain (1966–1970)." *The Americas* 78, no. 1 (2021): 89–117. http://dx.doi.org/10.17169/refubium-30531.

Kyun Kim, Yong, and Daniel C. O'Neill. "Transparent Motives: Democratic Advantage in International Credit Markets." *Journal of International Relations and Development* 20, no. 1 (2017): 108–32. https://doi.org/10.1057/jird.2015.1.

Laguado Duca, Arturo Claudio. "Onganía y el Nacionalismo Militar en Argentina." *Universitas Humanística* 62 (2006): 239–59. https://www.redalyc.org/pdf/791/79106210.pdf.

Lanciotti, Norma Silvana. "Inversiones Privadas y Políticas Públicas en el Sector Eléctrico. Argentina, 1920–1958." *XI Jornadas Interescuelas/Departamentos de Historia*. Universidad de Tucumán, San Miguel de Tucumán, 2007. https://cdsa.aacademica.org/000-108/964.pdf.

Lanús, Juan Archibaldo. *De Chapultepec al Beagle: Política Exterior Argentina, 1945–1980*. Emecé, 1984.

Lebovic, James, and Erik Voeten. "The Cost of Shame: International Organisations and Foreign Aid in the Punishing of Human Rights Violators." *Journal of Peace Research* 46, no. 1 (2009): 79–97. https://www.jstor.org/stable/27640800.

Lillich, Richard B. "The Protection of Foreign Investment and the Hickenlooper Amendment." *University of Pennsylvania Law Review* 112, no. 8 (1964): 1116–31. https://doi.org/10.2307/3310530.

Lipson, Charles H. "Corporate Preferences and Public Policies: Foreign Aid Sanctions and Investment Protection." *World Politics* 28, no. 3 (1976): 396–421. https://www.jstor.org/stable/i308696.

Long, Tom. "Latin America and the Liberal International Order: An Agenda for Research." *International Affairs* 94, no. 6 (2018): 1371–90, https://doi.org/10.1093/ia/iiy188.

Long, Tom, and Carsten-Andreas Schulz. "Republican Internationalism: The Nineteenth-Century Roots of Latin American Contributions to International Order." *Cambridge Review of International Affairs* 35, no. 5 (2022): 639–61. https://doi.org/10.1080/09557571.2021.1944983.

López, Mario Justo, Jorge Eduardo Waddell, and Martínez, Juan Pablo. *Historia del Ferrocarril en Argentina: La Política Ferroviaria Entre 1857 y 2015*. Lenguaje Claro Editora, 2016.

Lorenzini, Sara. *Global Development: A Cold War History*. Princeton University Press, 2019.

Lozoya, Jorge, and Jaime Estevez, eds. *Latin American and the New International Economic Order*. Pergamum Press, 1980.

MacDonald, C. A. "The Politics of Intervention: The United States and Argentina, 1941–1946." *Journal of Latin American Studies* 12, no. 2 (1980): 365–96. https://doi.org/10.1017/S0022216X00022719.

MacDonald, Callum A. "The US, the Cold War and Perón." In *Latin America, Economic Imperialism and the State: The Political Economy of the External Connection from Independence to the Present*, edited by Christopher Abel and Colin M. Lewis. Bloomsbury, 1985.

Machinea, José Luis. "Stabilisation Under Alfonsín." In *Argentina in the Crisis Years (1983–1990): From Alfonsín to Menem*, edited by Colin M. Lewis and Nissa Torrents. The Institute of Latin American Studies, 1993.

Manzetti, Luigi. *The International Monetary Fund and Economic Stabilization: The Argentine Case*. Praeger, 1991.

Marchesi, Aldo. *Latin America's Radical Left: Rebellion and Cold War in the Global 1960s*. Cambridge University Press, 2017.

Marongiu, Federico. "Políticas de Shock en la Agonía del Estado Peronista: El Rodrigazo y el Mondelliazo." (2006) MPRA Paper 6338. http://mpra.ub.uni-muenchen.de/6338.

Marshall, Jorge, José L. Mardones, and Isabel Marshall. "IMF Conditionality: The Experiences of Argentina, Brazil and Chile." In *IMF Conditionality*, edited by John Williamson. Institute for International Economics, 1983.

Marshall, Katherine. *The World Bank: From Reconstruction to Development to Equity*. Routledge, 2008.

Martínez de Hoz, José. *Bases para una Argentina Moderna, 1976*–1980. Compañía Impresora Argentina S.A., 1981.

Martínez de Hoz, José. *Quince Años Después*. Emecé, 1991.

Marx, Ruben, and Ana Turdo. "Desarrollismo en Argentina y en Brasil: Un Modelo y Dos Efectos." *I Jornadas de Economía Política* (December 2007). https://www.ungs.edu.ar/wp-content/uploads/2009/02/Turdo_Marx.pdf.

Mason, Edward S., and Robert E. Asher. *The World Bank Since Bretton Woods*. The Brookings Institute, 1973.

Mateo, Graciela. "El Gobierno de Domingo Mercante: Expresión Singular del Peronismo Clásico." In *El Primer Peronismo: De Regreso a los Comienzos*, edited by Raanan Rein and Rosalie Sitman. Lumiere, 2005.

Mazarr, Michael J. "The Real History of the Liberal Order: Neither Myth nor Accident." *Foreign Affairs*. August 7, 2018. https://www.foreignaffairs.com/united-states/real-history-liberal-order.

McNamara, Robert S. *The Essence of Security*. Harper and Row, 1968.

McPherson, Alan L. *Intimate Ties, Bitter Struggles: The United States and Latin America Since 1945*. Potomac Books, 2006.

Menem, Carlos Saúl, and Roberto Dromi. *Reforma del Estado y Transformación Nacional*. Editorial Ciencias de la Administración, 1990.

Míguez, María Cecilia. "¿Anticomunistas, Antiestatistas, Antiperonistas? La "Nacionalización" de la Doctrina de Seguridad Nacional en la Argentina y la Legitimación del Golpe de Estado de 1966." *Revista SAAP* 7, no. 1 (2013): 65–95. https://dialnet.unirioja.es/servlet/articulo?codigo=5119934.

Míguez, María Cecilia. "Illia y Santo Domingo: De las Columnas de *Primera Plana* al Golpe de Estado." *Ciclos en la Historia, la Economía y la Sociedad* 20, nos. 39–40 (2011–2012): 65–192. https://www.scielo.org.ar/img/revistas/ciclos/v20n40/html/v20n40a02.htm.

Míguez, María Cecilia. *Los Partidos Políticos y la Política Exterior Argentina*. Ariel, 2013.

Míguez, María Cecilia. "La Unión Industrial Argentina y el Gobierno de Illia. Los Sectores Civiles y el Golpe de Estado de 1966." *H-Industria* 9, no. 17 (2015): 64–91.

https://scispace.com/papers/la-union-industrial-argentina-y-el-gobierno-de-illia-los-2ij2b2vwqo.

Miles, Simon. *Engaging the Evil Empire: Washington, Moscow, and the Beginning of the End of the Cold War*. Cornell University Press, 2020.

Mochkofsky, Graciela. *Timerman: El Periodista que Quiso Ser Parte del Poder (1923–1999)*. Editorial Sudamericana, 2003.

Mody, Ashoka, and Diego Saravia. "Catalyzing Capital Flows: Do IMF-Supported Programs Work as Commitment Devices?" IMF Working Paper no. 2003/100. https://www.imf.org/en/Publications/WP/Issues/2016/12/30/Catalyzing-Capital-Flows-Do-IMF-Supported-Programs-Work-As-Commitment-Devices-16443.

Moloney, Kim. *Who Matters at the World Bank? Bureaucrats, Policy Change, and Public Sector Governance*. Oxford University Press, 2022.

Monteagudo, Manuel. "The Debt Problem: The Baker Plan and the Brady Initiative: A Latin American Perspective." *The International Lawyer* 28, no. 1 (1994): 59–81. https://www.jstor.org/stable/40707125.

Morgenfeld, Leandro. "Argentina y Estados Unidos, Golpe a Golpe (1966–1976), *Revista SAAP* 8, no. 2 (2014): 521–54. https://www.redalyc.org/pdf/3871/387139302006.pdf.

Morgenfeld, Leandro Ariel, and María Cecilia Míguez. "La Cuestión Petrolera Durante el Gobierno de Illia: Repercusiones en los Estados Unidos y en las Clases Dirigentes Locales." *Realidad Económica* 271 (2012): 51–75. https://ri.conicet.gov.ar/handle/11336/16173.

Morgenfeld, Leandro A. "Desarrollismo, Alianza para el Progreso y Revolución Cubana. Frondizi, Kennedy y el Che en Punta del Este (1961–1962)." *Ciclos en la Historia, la Economía y la Sociedad* 20, nos. 39–40 (2011–2012): 133–63. https://dialnet.unirioja.es/servlet/articulo?codigo=4053876.

Morgenfeld, Leandro Ariel. "El Inicio de la Guerra Fría y el Sistema Interamericano: Argentina Frente a Estados Unidos en la Conferencia de Caracas (1954)." Revista Contemporánea 1, no. 1 (2010): 75–98. https://ojs.fhce.edu.uy/index.php/cont/article/view/1059.

Moris, Halim. "The World Bank and Human Rights: Indispensable Partnership or Mismatched Alliance?" *ILSA Journal of International & Comparative Law* 4 (1997): 173–200. https://nsuworks.nova.edu/cgi/viewcontent.cgi?article=1117&context=ilsajournal.

Moyn, Samuel. "The Return of the Prodigal: The 1970s as a Turning Point in Human Rights History." In *The Breakthrough: Human Rights in the 1970s*, edited by Jan Eckel and Samuel Moyn. University of Pennsylvania Press, 2014.

Muchnik, Daniel. *Argentina Modelo: De la Furia a la Resignación: Economía y Política Entre 1973 y 1998*. Manantial, 1998.

Muchnik, Daniel. *La Patria Financiera: El Juego de la Especulación*. Grupo Editorial Norma, 2005.

Murphy, Craig. *The Emergence of the NIEO Ideology*. Routledge, 1984.

Nápoli, Bruno, M. Celeste Perosino, and Walter Bosisio. *La Dictadura del Capital Financiero: El Golpe Militar Corporativo y la Trama Bursátil*. Ediciones Continente, 2014.

Norden, Deborah L. "The Rise of the Lieutenant Colonels: Rebellion in Argentina and Venezuela." *Latin American Perspectives* 23, no. 3 (1996): 74–86. https://www.jstor.org/stable/2634108.

Northrup, Cynthia, and Elaine C. Prange Turney, eds. *Encyclopedia of Tariffs and Trade in U.S. History*. Greenwood Press, 2003.

Nosiglia, Julio E. *El Desarrollismo*. Centro Editor de América Latina, 1983.

Ocampo, José. "New Economic Thinking in Latin America." *Journal of Latin American Studies* 22, no. 1 (1990): 169–81. http://dx.doi.org/10.1017/s0022216x00015157.

Odisio, Juan, and Marcelo Rougier. "Swimming Against the (Developmentalist) Mainstream: The Liberal Economists in Argentina Between 1955 and 1976." *PSL Quarterly Review* 72, no. 289 (2019): 91–115.

O'Donnell, Guillermo. "Bureaucratic Authoritarianism. Argentina 1966–1973." In *Comparative Perspective*. University of California Press, 1988.

O'Donnell, Guillermo. "Modernización y Golpes Militares: Teoría, Comparación y el Caso Argentino." *Desarrollo Económico* 12, no. 47 (1972): 519–66, http://repositorio.cedes.org/handle/123456789/2923.

O'Donnell, Guillermo. "Reflecciones Sobre las Tendencias de Cambio del Estado Burocrático-Autoritario." *Revista Mexicana de Sociología* 39, no. 1 (1977): 9–59. https://www.jstor.org/stable/i282391.

O'Donnell, María. *Aramburu: El Crimen Político que Dividió al País. El Origen de Montoneros*. Editorial Planeta, 2020.

Oestreich, Joel E. "The Human Rights Responsibilities of the World Bank: A Business Paradigm." *Global Social Policy* 4, no. 1 (2004): 55–76. https://doi.org/10.1177/1468018104040985.

Offner, Amy C. *Sorting Out the Mixed Economy: The Rise and Fall of Welfare and Developmental States in the Americas*. Princeton University Press, 2019.

Onganía, Juan Carlos. Directiva para el Planeamiento y Desarrollo de la Acción del Gobierno. Presidencia de la Nación Argentina, Enunciada por el Señor Presidente de la Nación en la Conferencia de Prensa Realizada en el Salón de Gobernadores, el 4 de Agosto de 1966. Presidencia de la Nación.

Orleck, Annelise, and Lisa Gayle Hazirjian, eds. *The War on Poverty: A New Grassroots History, 1964–1980*. University of Georgia Press, 2011.

Ortega, Fernando Ariel. "De la Modernización a la Racionalización. Políticas Adoptadas por Frondizi Ante la Crisis Ferroviaria (1958–1962). *Revista de*

Historia de la Industria y el Desarrollo en América Latina 4, no. 7 (2010): 1–20. https://dialnet.unirioja.es/servlet/articulo?codigo=5009892.

Ortega, Fernando Ariel. "El Funcionamiento de la Empresa de Ferrocarriles del Estado Argentino (EFEA) Durante el Gobierno de Arturo Frondizi (1958–1962)." *Ponencia Terceras Jornadas de la Asociación Mexicana de Historia Económica* (2015). https://old-site.amhe.mx/jornadas/ponencias2015/ARIEL%20ORTEGA%20FERNANDO%20-%20El%20funcionamiento%20de%20la%20Empresa%20de%20Ferrocarriles%20del%20Estado%20Argentino%20(EFEA)%20durante%20el%20gobierno%20de%20Arturo%20Frondizi%20(1958-1962).pdf.

Pachetti, Federico. "A Merger of Equals: The Political Economy of the World Bank's Early Contacts with China." *Journal of Global History* 19, no. 1 (2023): 98–117. https://doi.org/10.1017/S1740022823000281.

Palacio Deheza, Carlos. *El Plan Martínez de Hoz y la Economía Argentina*. Corregidor, 1981.

Palermo, Vicente, and John Collins. "Moderate Populism: A Political Approach to Argentina's 1991 Convertibility Plan." *Latin American Perspectives* 25, no. 4 (1998): 36–62. https://www.jstor.org/stable/2633998.

Peralta-Ramos, Mónica. *The Political Economy of Argentina: Power and Class Since 1930*. Westview Press, 1992.

Pereira Loureiro, Felipe. "The Alliance for Progress and President João Goulart's Three Year Plan: The Deterioration of U.S.-Brazilian Relations in Cold War Brazil (1962)." *Cold War History* 17, no.1 (2017): 61–79. http://dx.doi.org/10.1080/14682745.2016.1254620.

Pereira Loureiro, Felipe, Hamilton de Carvalho Gomes Jr., and Rebeca Guerreiro Antunes Braga. "A Pericentric Punta del Este: Cuba's Failed Attempt to Join the Latin American Free Trade Area (LAFTA) and the Limits of Brazil's Independent Foreign Policy." *Revista Brasileira de Política Internacional* 61, no. 2 (2018): e003. http://dx.doi.org/10.1590/0034-7329201800203.

Perina, Rubén M. *Onganía, Levingston, Lanusse: Los Militares en la Política Argentina*. Editorial de Belgrano, 1983.

Perón, Juan D. *La Hora de los Pueblos*. CS Ediciones, 1968 (reprinted in 2005).

Pesce, Julieta. "La Gestión del Ministro Grinspun en un Contexto de Transición Democrática. Errores de Diagnóstico y Subestimación del Poder Económico Local e Internacional." *Ciclos en la Historia, la Economía y la Sociedad* 14, no. 28 (2004): 65–88. http://bibliotecadigital.econ.uba.ar/download/ciclos/ciclos_v14_n28_03.pdf.

Pettinà, Vanni. *La Guerra Fría en América Latina*. Colegio de México, 2018.

Pettinà, Vanni. "The Shadows of Cold War Over Latin America: The US Reaction to Fidel Castro's Nationalism, 1956–59." *Cold War History* 11, no. 3 (2011): 317–39. https://www.scribd.com/document/582943763/pettina2010.

Pickel, Andreas. "False Oppositions: Recontextualizing Economic Nationalism in a Globalizing World." In *Economic Nationalism in a Globalizing World*, edited by Eric Helleiner and Andreas Pickel. Cornell University Press, 2004.

Pion-Berlin, David. "Between Confrontation and Accommodation: Military and Government Policy in Democratic Argentina." *Journal of Latin American Studies* 23, no. 3 (1991): 543–71. http://doi.org/10.1017/S0022216X00015844.

Pion-Berlin, David. "The National Security Doctrine, Military Threat Perception, and the 'Dirty War' in Argentina." *Comparative Political Studies* 21, no. 3 (1988): 382–407. http://doi.org/10.1177/0010414088021003004.

Potash, Robert A. *The Army & Politics in Argentina, 1945–1962*. Stanford University Press, 1980.

Prebisch, Raúl. "Five Stages in My Thinking on Development." In *Pioneers in Development*, edited by Gerald M. Meier and Dudley Seers. Oxford University Press, 1984.

Przeworski, Adam. *Democracy and the Market: Political and Economic Reforms in Eastern Europe and Latin America*. Cambridge University Press, 1991.

Quintar, Juan Claudio. *El Choconazo:1969–1970*. Universidad Nacional del Comahue, 1998.

Rabe, Stephen G. "The Johnson Doctrine." *Presidential Studies Quarterly* 36, no. 1 (2006): 48–58. https://doi.org/10.1111/j.1741-5705.2006.00286.x.

Rabe, Stephen G. *The Killing Zone: The United States Cold War in Latin America*. Oxford University Press, 2016.

Rabe, Stephen G. *The Killing Zone: The United States Wages Cold War in Latin America*. Oxford University Press, 2012.

Rabe, Stephen G. *Kissinger and Latin America: Intervention, Human Rights, and Diplomacy*. Cornell University Press, 2021.Rapoport, Mario. "La Argentina y la Guerra Fría. Opciones Económicas y Estratégicas de la Apertura Hacia el Este, 1955–1973." *Ciclos en la Historia, la Economía y la Sociedad* 5, no. 8 (1995): 91–122. http://bibliotecadigital.econ.uba.ar/download/ciclos/ciclos_v5_n8_05.pdf.

Rapoport, Mario, and Claudio Spiguel. "La Argentina y el Plan Marshall: Promesas y Realidades." *Revista Brasileira de Política Internacional* 52, no. 1 (2009): 5–28. https://doi.org/10.1590/S0034-73292009000100001.

Rapoport, Mario. "La Deuda Externa Argentina y la Soberanía Jurídica: Sus Razones Históricas." *Ciclos en la Historia, la Economía y la Sociedad* 22, no. 43 (2014). http://www.scielo.org.ar/scielo.php?script=sci_arttext&pid=S1851-37352014000100001&lng=es&tlng=es.

Rapoport, Mario, and Claudio Spiguel. *Estados Unidos y el Peronismo: La Política Norteamericana en la Argentina, 1949–1955*. Grupo Editor Latinoamericano, 1994.

Rapoport, Mario, Eduardo Madrid, Andrés Musacchio, and Ricardo Vicente. *Historia Económica, Política y Social de la Argentina (1880–2000)*. Ediciones Macchi, 2000.

Rapoport, Mario. "La Saga de los Martínez de Hoz y el Banquero Arrepentido." *Buenos Aires Económico*, May 5, 2010.

Rein, Raanan. *In the Shadow of Perón: Juan Atilio Bramuglia and the Second Line of Argentina's Populist Movement*. Stanford University Press, 2008.

Rivas, Darlene. "United States-Latin American Relations, 1942–1960." In *A Companion to American Foreign Relations*, edited by Robert D. Schulzinger. Wiley, 2003.

Rivero Polo, Felipe. "¡Ni Capitalistas ni Comunistas! Una Revolución en Libertad en la Guerra Fría." In *Eduardo Frei Montalva: Fe, Política y Cambio Social*, edited by David Vásquez and Felipe Rivero. Andros Impresores, 2013.

Rocca Rivarola, María Dolores. "Protagonista Opositor, Peronista Desplazado: La Confederación General del Trabajo Durante el Gobierno de Raúl Alfonsín." *Revista Mexicana de Ciencias Políticas y Sociales* 51, no. 207 (2009): 137–54. http://www.scielo.org.mx/scielo.php?script=sci_arttext&pid=S0185-19182009000300008&lng=es&nrm=iso.

Rojas, Cristina. "The Place of the Social at the World Bank (1949–1981): Mingling Race, Nation, and Knowledge." *Global Social Policy* 15, no. 1 (2014): 23–39. https://doi.org/10.1177/1468018114527471.

Rossi, Hugo A. "La Política Económica de Krieger Vasena y su Participación en el Ingreso de las Empresas Tabacaleras Extranjeras en la Economía Argentina (1967–1969)." *América Latina en la Historia Económica* 29, no. 3 (2022). https://doi.org/10.18232/20073496.1286.

Rot, Gabriel. *Los Orígenes Perdidos de la Guerrilla en la Argentina: La Historia de Jorge Ricardo Massetti y el Ejército Guerrillero del Pueblo*. Ediciones El Cielo por Asalto, 2000.

Rothstein, Robert L. *Global Bargaining: UNCTAD and the Quest for a New International Economic Order*. Princeton University Press, 1979.

Rougier, Marcelo, and Martín Fiszbein. *La Frustración de un Proyecto Económico: El Gobierno Peronista de 1973–76*. Manantial, 2006.

Rougier, Marcelo. *El Pensamiento Económico de Aldo* Ferrer. Manuel Belgrano Ediciones, 2021.

Rougier Voilláz, Marcelo N., and Juan Carlos Odisio. "Del Dicho al Hecho. El 'Modelo Integrado y Abierto' de Aldo Ferrer y la Política Económica en la Argentina de la Segunda Posguerra." *América Latina en la Historia Económica* 19, no. 1 (2012): 99–130. https://www.scielo.org.mx/scielo.php?script=sci_arttext&pid=S1405-22532012000100005.

Rouquié, Alain. *Poder Militar y Sociedad Política en Argentina. Vol. 1*. Emecé, 1981.

Rovira Kaltwasser, Cristóbal. "Populismo y Economía: Una Relación Ambivalente." *Perspectivas* 3 (2019): 1–20. https://library.fes.de/pdf-files/bueros/chile/15478.pdf.

Rovira Kaltwasser, Cristóbal. "The Responses of Populism to Dahl's Democratic Dilemmas." *Political Studies* 62, no. 3 (2013): 470–87. http://doi.org/10.1111/1467-9248.12038.

Russell, Roberto, and Laura Zuvanic. "Argentina: Deepening Alignment with the West." *Journal of Interamerican Studies and World Affairs* 33, no. 3 (1991): 113–34. http://dx.doi.org/10.2307/165935.

Sachs, Jeffrey. "Social Conflict and Populist Policies in Latin America." In *Labor Relations and Economic Performance. Proceedings of a Conference Held by the International Economic Association in Venice, Italy,* edited by Renato Brunetta and Carlo Dell'Aringa. Macmillan, 1989.

Sachs, Jeffrey. "Social Conflict and Populist Policies in Latin America." NBER Working Paper Series, Working paper no. 2897. March 1989. https://www.nber.org/system/files/working_papers/w2897/w2897.pdf.

Saiegh, Sebastian M. "Do Countries Have A 'Democratic Advantage'? Political Institutions, Multilateral Agencies, and Sovereign Borrowing." *Comparative Political Studies* 38, no. 4 (2005): 366–87. https://doi.org/10.1177/0010414004273204.

Salvia, Sebastián Pedro. "The Boom and the Crisis of the Convertibility Plan in Argentina." *Brazilian Journal of Political Economy* 35, no. 2 (2015): 325–42. https://ideas.repec.org/a/ekm/repojs/v35y2015i2p325-342id227.html.

San Román, Pablo de. "Conflicto Político y Reforma Estructural: La Experiencia del Desarrollismo en Argentina Durante la Presidencia de Arturo Frondizi (1958–1962)." Instituto de Estudios Latinoamericanos, *Documentos de Trabajo. IELAT-Instituto de Estudios Latinoamericanos, Universidad de Alcalá,* no. 6 (Sept. 2009). https://ebuah.uah.es/dspace/bitstream/handle/10017/6376/Conflicto%20pol%C3%ADtico%20y%20reforma%20estructural.pdf?sequence=1.

Sarfaty, Galit A. "Why Culture Matters in International Institutions: The Marginality of Human Rights at the World Bank." *American Society of International Law* 102 (2008): 71–74. https://www.jstor.org/stable/25660269.

Savranskaya, Svetlana. "Gorvachev and the Third World." In *The End of the Cold War and the Third World: New Perspectives on Regional Conflict,* edited by Artemy Kalinovsky and Sergey Radchenko. Routledge, 2011.

Scarfi, Juan Pablo. "The Latin American Politics of International Law: Latin American Countries' Engagements with International Law and Their Contradictory Impact on the Liberal International Order." *Cambridge Review of International Affairs* 35, no. 5 (2022): 662–79. http://dx.doi.org/10.1080/09557571.2021.1920887.

Schmidli, William Michael. *The Fate of Freedom Elsewhere: Human Rights and the U.S. Cold War Policy Toward Argentina*. Cornell University Press, 2013.

Schmidli, William Michael. "Institutionalizing Human Rights in U.S. Foreign Policy: U.S.-Argentine Relations, 1976–1980." *Diplomatic History* 35, no. 2 (2011): 351–77. https://www.jstor.org/stable/24916482.

Schmitz, David F. *The United States and Right-Wing Dictatorships, 1965–1989*. Cambridge University Press, 2006.

Schoultz, Lars. *In Their Own Best Interest: A History of the U.S. Effort to Improve Latin Americans*. Harvard University Press, 2018.

Schultz, Kenneth A., and Barry R. Weingast. "The Democratic Advantage: Institutional Foundations of Financial Power in International Competition." *International Organization* 57, no. 1 (2003): 3–42. https://www.jstor.org/stable/3594824.

Schvarzer, Jorge. "Orígenes Poco Mencionados de la Deuda Externa de América Latina." *Caravelle* 50 (1988): 11–33. https://www.jstor.org/stable/i40038148.

Scodeller, Gabriela. "La Huelga Ferroviaria de 1961 en la Provincia de Mendoza." In *I Jornadas Nacionales de Historia Social (La Falda, Córdoba, 30 de mayo al 1 de junio de 2007). Memoria Académica*, 2007. http://www.memoria.fahce.unlp.edu.ar/trab_eventos/ev.9658/ev.9658.pdf.

Seoane, María. *El Burgués Maldito*. Editorial Sudamericana, 1998.

Service, Robert. *The End of the Cold War: 1985–1991*. PublicAffairs, 2015.

Settanni, Sebastián, and Lucrecia Gringauz. "Un Modesto Galeno Pueblerino. La Construcción de la Figura de Arturo Illia en Clarín y La Nación." *Questión* 1, no. 18 (2008). https://perio.unlp.edu.ar/ojs/index.php/question/article/view/604.

Shapley, Deborah. *Promise and Power: The Life and Times of Robert McNamara*. Little Brown & Co., 1993.

Sharma, Patrick. "Between North and South: The World Bank and the New International Economic Order." *Humanity: An International Journal of Human Rights, Humanitarianism, and Development* 6, no. 1 (2015): 189–200. http://dx.doi.org/10.1353/hum.2015.0006.

Sharma, Patrick. "Bureaucratic Imperatives and Policy Outcomes: The Origins of World Bank Structural Adjustment Lending." *Review of International Political Economy* 20, no. 4 (2013): 667–86. http://dx.doi.org/10.1080/09692290.2012.689618.

Sharma, Patrick. "The United States, the World Bank, and the Challenges of International Development in the 1970s." *Diplomatic History* 37, no. 3 (2013): 572–603. https://www.jstor.org/stable/44254308.

Sharma, Patrick Allan. *Robert McNamara's Other War: The World Bank and International Development*. University of Pennsylvania Press, 2017.

Shenai, Neil, and Marijn A. Bolhuis. “How the Brady Plan Delivered on Debt Relief: Lessons and Implications.” *IMF Working Paper* 23, no. 258 (2023). https://www.elibrary.imf.org/view/journals/001/2023/258/article-A001-en.xml#:~:text=In%20March%201989%2C%20U.S.%20Treasury,for%20greater%20assurances%20about%20debtors’.

Sidicaro, Ricardo. *Los Tres Peronismos. Estado y Poder Económico*. Siglo XXI Editores, 2011.

Sikkink, Kathryn. “The Influence of Raúl Prebisch on Economic Policy-Making in Argentina, 1950–1962.” *Latin American Research Review* 23, no. 2 (1988): 91–114. https://www.jstor.org/stable/i322695.

Sikkink, Kathryn. *Mixed Signals: U.S. Human Rights Policy and Latin America*. Cornell University Press, 2004.

Sikkink, Kathryn. *El Proyecto Desarrollista en la Argentina y Brasil: Frondizi y Kubistchek*. Siglo XXI, 2009.

Simmons, Beth A. *Who Adjusts? Domestic Sources of Foreign Economic Policy During the Interwar Years*. Princeton University Press, 1997.

Simonoff, Alejandro. *Los Dilemas de la Autonomía: La Política Exterior de Arturo Illia (1963–1966)*. Nuevohacer, 2007.

Slobodian, Quinn. *Globalists: The End of Empire and the Birth of Neoliberalism*. Harvard University Press, 2018.

Smith, William C. *Authoritarianism and the Crisis of the Argentine Political Economy*. Stanford University Press, 1989.

Smulovitz, Catalina. “La Eficacia Como Crítica y Utopía: Notas Sobre la Caída de Illia.” *Desarrollo Económico* 33, no. 131 (1993): 403–23. http://doi.org/10.2307/3467088.

Snyder, Sarah B. “Human Rights and the Cold War.” In *The Routledge Handbook of the Cold War*, edited by Artemy M. Kalinovsky and Craig Daigle. Routledge, 2014.

Staples, Amy L. S. *The Birth of Development: How the World Bank, Food and Agriculture Organization, and World Health Organization Have Changed the World, 1945–1965*. Kent State University Press, 2006.

Stokes, Susan C. *Mandates and Democracy: Neoliberalism by Surprise in Latin America*. Cambridge University Press, 2001.

Suesse, Marvin. *The Nationalist Dilemma: A Global History of Economic Nationalism, 1776–Present*. Cambridge University Press, 2023.

Suri, Jeremi. *Power and Protest: Global Revolution and the Rise of Détente*. Harvard University Press, 2003.

Szusterman, Celia. “Carlos Saúl Menem: Variations in the Theme of Populism.” *Bulletin of Latin American Research* 19, no. 2 (2000): 193–206. http://doi.org/10.1111/j.1470-9856.2000.tb00099.x.

Szusterman, Celia. *Frondizi and the Politics of Developmentalism in Argentina, 1955–62*. Macmillan, 1993.

Szusterman, Celia. "The 'Revolución Libertadora,' 1955–8." In *The Political Economy of Argentina, 1946–1983*, edited by Guido Di Tella and Rudiger Dornbusch. University of Pittsburgh Press, 1989.

Taffet, Jeffrey. *Foreign Aid as Foreign Policy: The Alliance for Progress in Latin America*. Routledge, 2007.

Tanzi, Vito. *Argentina: An Economic Chronicle. How One of the Richest Countries in the World Lost Its Wealth*. Jorge Pinto Books, 2007.

Tcach, César, and Celso Rodríguez. *Arturo Illia: Un Sueño Breve. El Rol del Peronismo y de los Estados Unidos en el Golpe Militar de 1966*. Edhasa, 2006.

Tcach, César. "Radicalismo y Fuerzas Armadas (1962–1963): Observaciones Desde Córdoba." *Desarrollo Económico* 40, no. 157 (2000): 73–95. https://www.jstor.org/stable/i277205.

Tendler, Judith. "*New Lessons from Old Projects: The Workings of Rural Development in Northeast Brazil*." In *Banking on the Poor: The World Bank and World Poverty*, edited by Robert L. Ayres. MIT Press, 1983.

Thornton, Christy. "Establishing the Limits of the Liberal International Order: Latin America and the Demand for Development." *Cambridge Review of International Affairs* 35, no. 5 (2022): 680–97. https://doi.org/10.1080/09557571.2021.1937059.

Thornton, Christy. *Revolution in Development: Mexico and the Governance of the Global Economy*. University of California Press, 2021.

Timerman, Jacobo. *Prisoner Without a Name, Cell Without a Number*. University of Wisconsin Press, 2002.

Tunstall Allcock, Thomas. *Thomas C. Mann: President Johnson, the Cold War, and the Restructuring of Latin American Foreign Policy*. University of Kentucky Press, 2018.

Veigel, Klaus Friedrich. *Dictatorship, Democracy, and Globalization: Argentina and the Cost of Paralysis, 1973–2001*. Pennsylvania State University Press, 2009.

Verbitsky, Horacio, and Juan Pablo Bohoslavsky, eds. *The Economic Accomplices to the Argentine Dictatorship: Outstanding Debts*. Cambridge University Press, 2016.

Walcher, Dustin. "Petroleum Pitfalls: The United States, Argentine Nationalism, and the 1963 Oil Crisis." *Diplomatic History* 37, no. 1 (2013): 24–57. https://www.jstor.org/stable/i40178305.

Walcher, Dustin. "Structuring the Economy in the Periphery: The United States, the 1958 Argentine Stabilization Agreement, and the Evolution of Global Capitalism." In *Foreign Policy at the Periphery: The Shifting Margins of US International Relations Since World War II*, edited by Bevan Sewell and María Ryan. University of Kentucky Press, 2017.

Walker, Vanessa. *Principles in Power: Latin America and the Politics of U.S. Human Rights Diplomacy*. Cornell University Press, 2020.

Weaver, Catherine. *Hypocrisy Trap: The World Bank and the Poverty of Reform*. Princeton University Press, 2008.

Westad, Odd Arne. *The Cold War: A World History*. Basic Books, 2017.

Westad, Odd Arne. *The Global Cold War: Third World Interventions and the Making of Our Times*. Cambridge University Press, 2007.

Weyland, Kurt. "Clarifying a Contested Concept: Populism in the Study of Latin American Politics." *Comparative Politics* 34, no. 1 (2001): 1–22. https://www.jstor.org/stable/422412.

Weyland, Kurt. "Neopopulism and Neoliberalism in Latin America: How Much Affinity?" *Third World Quarterly* 24, no. 6 (2003): 1095–1115. https://www.jstor.org/stable/i383109.

Weyland, Kurt. "Neopopulism and Neoliberalism in Latin America: Unexpected Affinities." *Studies in Comparative International Development* 31 (1996): 3–31. https://doi.org/10.1007/BF02738987.

Weyland, Kurt. *The Politics of Market Reform in Fragile Democracies: Argentina, Brazil, Peru, and Venezuela*. Princeton University Press, 2002.

Williamson, John. "What Washington Means by Policy Reform." In *Latin American Adjustment: How Much Has Happened?* edited by John Williamson. Institute for International Economics, 1990.

Woods, Ngaire. *The Globalizers: The IMF, the World Bank, and Their Borrowers*. Cornell University Press, 2006.

Zanatta, Loris. *La Internacional Justicialista: Auge y Ocaso de los Sueños Imperiales de Perón*. Sudamericana, 2013.

Zanatta, Loris. "The Rise and Fall of the Third Position. Bolivia, Perón and the Cold War, 1943–1954." *Desarrollo Económico* 45, no. 177 (2006): 1–27. http://socialsciences.scielo.org/scielo.php?script=sci_arttext&pid=S0046-001X2006000100004.

Zapata, Victoria. "La Revolución Argentina (1966–1973)." In *La Argentina y el Mundo Frente al Bicentenario de la Revolución de Mayo: Las Relaciones Exteriores Argentinas Desde la Secesión de España Hasta la Actualidad*, edited by Alejandro César Simonoff. EDULP, 2010.

Index

FSC
www.fsc.org
MIX
Papier | Fördert
gute Waldnutzung
FSC® C083411

Kolibri 360 GmbH
Ferdinand-Jühlke-Straße 7
99095 Erfurt, Deutschland
produktsicherheit@kolibri360.de